T0271186

Systemic Financial Crises

Faced with a systemic financial sector crisis, policy makers need to make difficult choices under pressure. Based on the experience of many countries in recent years, few have been able to achieve a speedy, lasting, and low-cost resolution. This volume considers the strengths and weaknesses of the various policy options, covering both microeconomic (including recapitalization of banks, bank closures, subsidies for distressed borrowers, capital adequacy rules, and corporate governance and bankruptcy law requirements) and macroeconomic (including monetary and fiscal policy) dimensions. The contributors explore the important but little understood trade-offs that are involved, such as among policies that take effect quickly, those that minimize long-term fiscal and economic costs, and those that create favorable incentives for future stability. Successfully implementing crisis management and crisis resolution policy required attention to detail and a good flow of information. The differing underlying institutional requirements for the success of policy tools such as depositor guarantees, government-sponsored asset management companies, and the liberalization of foreign bank entry are discussed.

Patrick Honohan is Senior Financial Policy Advisor at the World Bank. Previously he was Economic Advisor to the Taoiseach (Irish Prime Minister) and spent several years as Professor at the Economic and Social Research Institute, Dublin, and at the Central Bank of Ireland. Dr. Honohan has published widely on macroeconomics and monetary and financial sector issues ranging from exchange rate regimes and purchasing-power parity to migration, cost-benefit analysis, and statistical methodology. Based in Dublin, he is a Member of the Royal Irish Academy and a Research Fellow of the Center for Economic Policy Research, London. He coedited *Financial Liberalization: How Far, How Fast?* (Cambridge University Press, 2001) with Gerard Caprio and Nobel Laureate Joseph Stiglitz.

Luc Laeven is a Senior Financial Economist at the World Bank. He has participated in several financial and private sector operations of the World Bank, focusing on the development of banking systems and corporate sectors. His research focuses on international banking and corporate finance issues and has been published in numerous books and academic journals, including the *Journal of Finance*, the *Journal of Money, Credit, and Banking,* the *Journal of Financial Intermediation*, and the *Journal of Banking and Finance*. He is an Extramural Fellow at Tilburg University and a Research Affiliate in the Financial Economics Programme of the Centre for Economic Policy Research in London.

Systemic Financial Crises

Containment and Resolution

Edited by

PATRICK HONOHAN

The World Bank

LUC LAEVEN

The World Bank

CAMBRIDGE
UNIVERSITY PRESS

CAMBRIDGE
UNIVERSITY PRESS

32 Avenue of the Americas, New York NY 10013-2473, USA

Cambridge University Press is part of the University of Cambridge.

It furthers the University's mission by disseminating knowledge in the pursuit of education, learning and research at the highest international levels of excellence.

www.cambridge.org
Information on this title: www.cambridge.org/9780521851855

First published 2005
First paperback edition 2012

A catalogue record for this publication is available from the British Library

Library of Congress Cataloguing in Publication data
Systemic financial crises : containment and resolution /
edited by Patrick Honohan, Luc Laeven.
p. cm.
ISBN 0-521-85185-8 (casebound)
1. Financial crises. I. Honohan, Patrick. II. Laeven, Luc. III. Title.
HB3722.S97   2005
338.5′ 42 – dc22   2004023979

ISBN 978-0-521-85185-5 Hardback
ISBN 978-1-107-40720-6 Paperback

Contents

Contributors

Charles W. Calomiris
Columbia University

Gerard Caprio
The World Bank

Stijn Claessens
University of Amsterdam and CEPR

Patrick Honohan
The World Bank and CEPR

Daniela Klingebiel
The World Bank

Luc Laeven
The World Bank and CEPR

Carl-Johan Lindgren
Independent private consultant

Joe Peek
University of Kentucky

Rafael Repullo
CEMFI and CEPR

Eric Rosengren
Federal Reserve Bank of Boston

David Smith
Federal Reserve Board

Per Strömberg
University of Chicago, NBER, and CEPR

Adrian Tschoegl
The Wharton School, University of Pennsylvania

Foreword

Gerard Caprio
The World Bank

Citizens around the world need and demand the opportunity for economic advancement. Many possess entrepreneurial skills that would be the envy of those in high-income countries, as witnessed by their ability to survive in wretched conditions. Recent research, a part of which was contributed by the World Bank, has clearly demonstrated that finance is critical to economic development. One factor that keeps poverty elevated and growth depressed is the absence of *reliable* financial services. Many developing countries' financial systems are fragile and periodically are beset by crises – events that set back development, leave banks reluctant to lend, and leave citizens wary of entrusting their savings to the official banking sector. This diversion of savings into inefficient forms is likely one of the great and unmeasured costs of banking crises. Banking crises capture headlines when they are overt, leading to runs on individual banks or even on the entire banking system in the form of capital flight, often a sharp reduction in credit (a "credit crunch"), and a concomitant significant reduction in the standard of living. But episodes of systemic bank insolvency often occur without an overt crisis, yet the effects on economic development are just as damaging.

Although the World Bank's role in finance focuses on developing the infrastructure needed to support a robust financial sector, the Bank also is involved in member countries in times of hidden or overt financial crises. Although the role of providing short-term liquidity support clearly is the domain of the International Monetary Fund, the Bank's expertise is brought to bear in helping authorities to build a sound financial system. Quite often, an overt crisis can marshal support for fundamental policy changes in the financial sector, hence the Bank's involvement.

Financial crises have occurred periodically for as long as banks have existed. Charles Kindleberger, in his classic volume *Manias, Panics, and Crashes*, argued that each generation had to have its own financial crisis; recent events suggest that he may have been conservative in his estimates. Crises recur in part because people forget the lessons from the last one, just as in every stock market boom claims are heard that "this time is different." Although much can be done to make financial systems more robust – in effect, to reduce the magnitude of crises, as well as their frequency – it is critical that authorities be prepared for crises when they occur.

The purpose of this book is to draw on the combination of research and first-hand crisis experience to catalog lessons on a variety of issues that regularly arise in crises: containment, resolution, and broader structural reform. Policy makers would be advised to read this volume now, as it reveals areas for reform that, if enacted in time, will make handling the next crisis easier. But more than most, the present study needs to remain on their bookshelf for the next crisis, as it contains valuable lessons fresh from a wave of crises in the last decade.

This volume is part of the World Bank's ongoing effort to disseminate best practices in various aspects of financial sector reform, and it is hoped that it will be of value to policy makers and to those who study developing countries. In keeping with the usual practice, the views expressed here should be regarded as personal, and they do not necessarily reflect those of the Bank, its shareholders, or member country authorities.

Acknowledgments

This volume is the fruit of a research project sponsored by the World Bank's Financial Sector Department. Drafts of the chapters were discussed at a conference at the World Bank's headquarters in Washington, DC. We are grateful to participants in that conference and especially to the discussants: Giovanni dell'Ariccia, Charles Calomiris, Asli Demirguc-Kunt, Simeon Djankov, Douglas Gale, Thomas Glaessner, Linda Goldberg, Morris Goldstein, Charles Goodhart, Richard Herring, David Hoelscher, Edward Kane, Randall Kroszner, Maria Soledad Martinez Peria, Ashoka Mody, Andrew Powell, Raghuram Rajan, David Skeel, Philip Strahan, and Augusto de la Torre, for valuable comments. Other readers who provided valuable comments, in addition to those noted in individual chapters, include Carole Brookins, Gerard Caprio, James Hanson, Danny Leipziger, Fernando Montes-Negret, and Ruth Neyens, as well as Scott Parris and two anonymous referees for Cambridge University Press. Thanks also to Rose Vo, whose secretarial and organizational assistance was invaluable, and to Guillermo Noguera for excellent research assistance.

PART ONE

INTRODUCTION

ONE

Introduction and Overview

Patrick Honohan and Luc Laeven

INTRODUCTION

Financial sector crises present exceptionally difficult challenges for the policy maker. They often emerge unexpectedly, evolve with breakneck speed, and threaten to strangle a large part of national economic activity unless promptly and decisively addressed. Whether this action is to involve closures of banks, or the introduction of government guarantees to substitute for a loss of confidence, or a realignment of exchange rates, future economic prosperity depends on the relevant decisions being made with a sure sense of what is feasible and credible.

Whatever action is taken to contain the crisis in the initial days and with whatever success in restoring confidence, much work remains. Banks and other firms will be insolvent, leaving broken contracts and a lack of credit to allow business to move forward. If the ground has been well prepared, clearly defined bankruptcy procedures will facilitate a restructuring of ownership. But government intervention may be called for to ensure resolution of these problems and place the system on a sound basis.

Crises can recur, and the probability of this happening likely depends on the actions taken in the past. The threat of moral hazard behavior based on market participants' expectations of bailout, though not necessarily decisive, has to be factored in to the judgment on how to deal with crises.

The chapters of this volume throw light on all of these aspects. Drawing on their findings, this introductory chapter traces the decision points of the typical banking crisis – recognizing that no two crises are the same. We start by offering a brief review of the scale and severity of recent crises, highlighting the difficulty of assessing just how bad things are going to get – indeed there have been some cases from which the bounceback has been so strong that some have argued that the crisis provided a necessary clearing of the air.

Although each of the chapters of Part II has something to say about both containment and resolution phases of the crisis, it is useful to distinguish between these two phases of a crisis. It is the containment stage that attracts the most attention. Here we see bank runs, weekend crisis meetings, emergency liquidity loans, interest rate spikes, and exchange rate pressure.

In the containment stage, speed is of the essence. How can the authorities judge whether forbearance, last resort lending, or official guarantees should be employed, at potentially high fiscal cost, in the hopes of forestalling or minimizing the scale of collapse? If banks are to be closed, how is this to be done without aggravating the loss of depositor confidence? Should banking regulations take explicit advance account of macroeconomic fluctuations so that forbearance is not needed during nonthreatening downturns?

When confidence has been restored and markets are functioning normally, there is usually still a legacy of overindebtedness and undercapitalization: we have moved into the resolution phase. With the crisis contained, policies must be chosen for the resolution of financial and nonfinancial firms in order to minimize overall social costs, restore the corporate system to solvency, and ensure safe and sound banking going forward. The effectiveness of alternatives depends on preexisting legal and governmental infrastructures so that what works well in Sweden (asset management companies, for example) may have disappointing consequences in Senegal. And the lessons of history are not always well learned, as in the recent partial replication in Mexico of selective subsidies to delinquent borrowers of a type employed at considerable cost in Chile in the early 1980s.

The diversity of banking crises means that learning the lessons has been largely based on a case-study approach. But theory and econometrics can also help. Part III of this book provides an insight into the potential contribution of mathematical modeling and of cross-country econometric studies. The complexity of the behavioral interaction between bankers, their customers, and the regulator is such that theory often generates ambiguous predictions. Thus, there is no substitute for looking at available data.

Part IV highlights some of the distinctive structural features and financial reforms that may influence a country's ability to weather a financial shock or prevent future crises. The presence or not of foreign

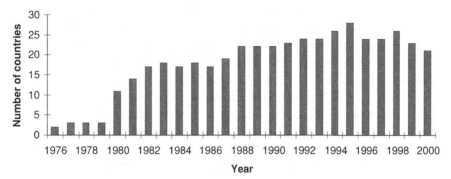

Figure 1.1. Systemic Financial Crises in Progress Worldwide, 1976–2000. *Note:* This figure shows for each year the number of countries in crisis. We exclude transition economies and countries with incomplete data on the timing of the crisis. We only include systemic financial crises. *Source:* Authors' calculations using data from the Caprio, Klingebiel, Laeven, and Noguera (Appendix this volume) database.

banks, their entry in response to crisis, and their preparedness to ride out trouble is one of these dimensions. Another is the nature of bankruptcy law. Finally, the case of Japan, often seen as being stuck in a chronic banking crisis, is examined.

1. REVIEW OF THE SCALE AND SEVERITY OF RECENT CRISES

Even though recurrent crisis has been a feature of banking for centuries, it is clear that banking crises of systemic importance increased in frequency and probably in severity from the 1970s, whether compared with the previous quarter century (which was an exceptional lull period), or with earlier historic periods (Bordo et al. 2001, Caprio and Klingebiel 1996, and Lindgren et al. 1996). Figure 1.1 shows the number of countries in crisis over the past two decades. A concentration of very severe events in 1997–1998 in East Asia and Russia may represent a permanent high water mark, but each subsequent year has brought new cases: Turkey, Argentina, and most recently the Dominican Republic.

There have been several contributory causes to the increase in banking crisis frequency since the early 1970s. It has been a period of change and volatility. The increase in inflation variability and in exchange rate volatility after 1971 increased the vulnerability of the banking system more than other sectors. The great expansion of banking depth in recent decades meant that banking losses, when they occurred, were more likely than before to represent a larger share of GDP. Heightened government involvement in ownership and credit allocation of the banking system in many developing countries during the 1960s and 1970s left a legacy of weak credit culture and a stock of unserviceable loans that became evident from the mid-1980s. Structural change, drastic changes in relative prices, and deep recessions in transition economies added many other cases. Finally, financial and macroeconomic liberalization in weak institutional environments both revealed preexisting insolvencies and exposed many banks to risks for which they were unprepared, having previously functioned in a protected environment of high and stable margins and uncomplicated financial contracts. Botched privatizations were part of this story, as were bank management errors in adapting to and trying to take advantage of the increasingly sophisticated financial engineering of the global market to which they were newly exposed.

The costs of these banking crises have been large, though it is difficult to place a precise value. Some of the losses of the banks themselves have been borne by shareholders and depositors, but most have been assumed by government and thereby socialized, being covered partly through a reduction in government spending and partly through increases in taxes, including the inflation tax. Total estimated fiscal costs of crises in developing countries in the past 25 years exceeds $1 trillion – an amount greater than the cumulative total of international development assistance since World War II.

Fiscal costs may in part be seen as merely a transfer, though the deadweight costs of this transfer are appreciable. But banking collapse also has contributed to economic downturns, partly because of the disruption of financial contracts, including the flow of credit as well as the payments system. Attempts have been made to estimate these economic output losses also, though, as many banking crises – although contributing to recession – have themselves been triggered by economic downturns with other prime causes, it is difficult to isolate that part of the economic downturn that should be attributed to the banking weakness per se. In practice, although estimates of total economic costs differ from fiscal costs in each country, on average across countries they come to about the same magnitude. In some cases, the economic downturn following recognition of the crisis has been short-lived or even absent altogether – as in Ghana. A plausible interpretation of this pattern is that, by clearing the air and re-establishing the banking system on a firmer basis, recognizing and dealing with the crisis can unleash a new dynamism that was absent as long as policymakers were in denial and banks labored under a hidden burden of unacknowledged loan losses.

Predicting systemic banking crises is by no means an easy task. Indeed, the best models that have been developed for this purpose – though they do identify some statistically significant variables, mostly macroeconomic in character – have proved to be unable to predict crises out of sample with any degree of success (Demirgüç-Kunt and Detragiache 1999; Honohan 2000). This is partly because the timing of such crises is often related to an exchange rate or other financial asset price collapse, and these can be inherently unpredictable. It is also partly because the information necessary to infer that a crisis is imminent is closely held, because of the lack of transparency of banks and their assets. Some economies (such as Argentina and Turkey) have experienced multiple crises; for some (such as Korea) the crisis, though profound, has been brief and recovery vigorous; others (such as Japan and the thrift sector of the United States) have remained in a state of barely suppressed crisis for long periods. These experiences confirm the need to be prepared and alert for a crisis, and suggest that good policies and strong institutions can make a big difference.

2. CONTAINMENT STAGE

It is the fast-moving way in which banking crises can often evolve that makes it important to distinguish a containment stage from the policy response. But not all banking crises are the same, and the source, scale, and nature of the rapidly evolving events that need to be dealt with differ, depending in particular on whether the trigger for the crisis is a loss of depositor confidence, regulatory recognition of insolvency, or the knock-on effects of financial asset market disturbances outside the banking system including exchange rate and wider macroeconomic pressures.

The most dangerous form of crisis is that which begins with a depositor run, and it is this form that has been most extensively considered in the theoretical literature. This is both because the short-term and demandable liabilities of banks make them uniquely vulnerable among business entities to a sudden loss of creditor confidence, and also because the payments system for the economy as a whole depends heavily on the smooth functioning of all of the larger banks. Failure of any one of these creates immediate disruption to the payments system and this, as has been observed in recent years, notably in Argentina and Indonesia, is associated with widespread economic distress, at least in the short term and perhaps with lasting consequences.

In other cases, the initial indications of trouble come from a regulatory evaluation of bank capital. A judgment that one or more large banks are insolvent can reflect a reassessment of the viability of their borrowing clients (the reassessment triggered, perhaps, by such extraneous factors as a political event that removes protection from hitherto favored borrowers), or because of the revelation of bank fraud or mismanagement on a large scale (recent events in the Dominican Republic mirroring in some respects the earlier crisis of Venezuela show how large these can be; the 1991 collapse of the Bank of Credit and Commerce International, affecting many countries,[1] also falls into this category). Depositors may not at first react to the regulator's emerging awareness of solvency problems, whether because of lack of information, or because they are confident that the authorities will protect them; instead, it is the potential for looting of the insolvent bank by insiders that generates the urgency for containment action.

The third source of problems, a collapse in financial asset prices, or pressure on the exchange rate, may prompt liquidity demands on the banks that do not reflect a loss of confidence by depositors in the banks themselves. The threat here is of a generalized debt deflation process (modeled as far back as the year 1933 by Irving Fisher), whereby defensive reaction by the banks could result in forced asset sales and a severe credit squeeze both of which in turn threaten the solvency of bank borrowers and others, contributing to a general economic slump.[2]

Containment strategies need to be attuned to the source of the trouble and the behavior that requires containment. The range of possible containment tools is fairly well defined: each has its limitations in terms of direct effectiveness, cost, and likely contribution to moral hazard whether during the current crisis or in subsequent years.

Deposit withdrawals can be addressed by liquidity loans, usually from the central bank when market sources are insufficient (which is all that is meant by the term "lender of last resort"), by an extension of government guarantees of depositors[3] and other bank creditors, or by a temporary suspension of depositor rights in what is often called a "bank holiday."

---

[1] Founded in 1972, by 1990 Bank of Credit and Commerce International had offices in 69 countries.

[2] An interesting, albeit relatively mild, recent example of this process comes from the interaction of a tightening of solvency regulations for U.K. insurance companies and pension funds with a downturn in global equity markets in 2000–2002. Compliance with the regulations, until amended, triggered extensive equity sales by the institutions, and these sales are themselves thought to have accelerated the equity market decline.

[3] With a handful of exceptions, formal deposit insurance schemes have ceilings on the size of covered deposits sufficiently low that their capacity to prevent a fatal bank-run is very

Each of these techniques is designed to buy time, presumably because the authorities believe or hope that the underlying financial condition of the bank is sound and, in the case of the first two, that depositor confidence can soon be restored. None of these techniques is guaranteed success, especially if the credibility and creditworthiness of the government is insufficient. Each is prone to abuse – even the bank holiday, during which corrupt insiders may loot a bank by engineering backdated deposit withdrawals.[4]

Depositor runs often do reflect hidden but suspected solvency problems in some or all of the banks. In such cases, even if effective in stopping the panic, liquidity loans and blanket guarantees have the effect of socializing most of any such insolvency. The scale of losses in recent banking crises means that the decision to adopt either of these policies, usually taken in haste, often proves to have been the single most costly budgetary decision in a country's history. Ideally, armed with adequate information, the authorities could intervene with the insolvent bank in good time and offer guarantees or loans only for the rest if needed.

Preventing looting of an insolvent or near insolvent bank, whether through fraud[5] or desperate, reckless gambling for resurrection (to use the colorful term of Kane, 1989) requires a different set of containment tools, which may include administrative intervention including the temporary assumption of management powers by a regulatory official, or closure, which may, for example, include the subsidized compulsory sale of a bank's good assets to a sound bank, together with the assumption by that bank of all or most of the failed entity's banking liabilities; or more simply an assisted merger. Here the prior availability of the necessary legal powers is critical, given the incentive for bank insiders to hang on, as well as the customary cognitive gaps causing insiders to deny the failure of their bank.

Most complex of all are the cases in which disruption of banking is part of a wider financial and macroeconomic turbulence.[6] In this case, the

limited. In practice, it is interbank lines and wholesale deposits that are withdrawn first and in the largest amounts.
[4] Liquidity loans have often simply been used to fund international transfers out of the system as a whole by large and well-informed depositors until official foreign exchange reserves were close to being exhausted.
[5] Several recent large bank failures have involved the fraudulent concealment of a sizable fraction of the bank's liabilities from supervisors.
[6] It is important for the authorities to recognize their own limitations in this kind of environment. The credibility of government guarantees may be questionable (especially to the extent that fiscal difficulties are at the root of the problem) and liquidity loans may be

bankers may be innocent victims of external circumstances, and it is now that special care is needed to ensure that regulations do not become part of the problem. Forbearance on capital and liquid reserve requirements may prove to be appropriate in these conditions, even though on average banking crises in which forbearance has been exercised have proved to be more costly than those in which it was avoided.[7]

Adopting the correct approach to an emerging financial crisis calls, then, for a clear understanding of what the underlying cause of the crisis is, as well as a quick judgment as to the likely effectiveness of the alternative tools that are available. The actions taken at this time will have a possibly irreversible impact on the ultimate allocation of losses in the system. In addition, the longer term implications in the form of moral hazard for the future also need to be taken into account, as has long been appreciated.[8] To make advance preparation, therefore, adequate sources of information must be put in place through the supervisory process, as well as sufficient legal powers to prevent socially necessary actions being blocked by unwarranted judicial delays. Although, as the crisis matures, it will likely become necessary to establish a special purpose crisis management team, it is important that there should already be a definite assignment of responsibilities between different official agencies including the deposit insurer, the central bank, and the bank regulator in order to ensure that the crucial early stages of containment are dealt with appropriately.

All too often, central banks privilege stability over cost in the heat of the containment phase: if so, they may too liberally extend loans to an illiquid bank that is almost certain to prove insolvent anyway.

In this, or other ways, closure of a nonviable bank is often delayed for too long, even when there are clear signs of insolvency. Furthermore, the process of closure is subject to many pitfalls. This is the refrain of Carl Lindgren's discussion in Chapter 3, which draws on extensive

---

insufficient (especially where dollarization is high, or a fixed exchange rate peg is being adhered to). There may be no good way to protect the real value of bank deposits in such cases, whose ultimate resolution has often involved currency devaluation or forced de-dollarization.

[7] And it may well be that other instances of forbearance had the effect of containing emerging disturbance so well that they are not recorded among the systemic crises – a point that Charles Goodhart has stressed. To that extent, studies of the cost of forbearance may be subject to a sample selection bias – though one that is difficult to correct for with available data.

[8] Kindleberger (1978) cites Lord Liverpool's principled opposition to banking bailouts in the 1820s as an early example.

cross-country experience in containment, especially of the second type of crisis discussed earlier, where the trigger is regulatory recognition of insolvency. He points out that, rather than being a negative or terminal step, closure is better seen as a way of bringing the business of a failed bank back into the market under new ownership. The interval between the initial administrative intervention and a clear resolution of the bank's problems should, he argues, be short for fear of the process triggering contagion throughout the system. But, although some banks may be too big to be closed (because of the implications for the functioning of payments and the rest of the system), no bank is too big for intervention. Lindgren reviews the key requirements for successful intervention policy and how difficult it is to meet them. They include the need from the outset for good information on the financial condition of the bank and clear triggers for action. The reliability of asset valuations, however, deteriorates in the course of a widespread crisis.

Closure of banks with losses distributed to creditors and depositors is, Lindgren observes, a high-wire act in an environment of weak financial institutions and poor macroeconomic prospects. Because few regulators are would-be circus artists, there is a tendency to rely instead on blanket government guarantees, which, if the government's fiscal and political position makes them credible, can work, albeit at the cost of placing the burden on the budget, typically squeezing future provision of needed public services.

More generally, as is clear from Charles Calomiris, Daniela Klingebiel, and Luc Laeven's discussion in Chapter 2, poorly chosen containment policies undermine the potential for successful long-term resolution. Whether containment policies should be strict or accommodating is a matter on which both theory and empirical evidence has been brought to bear as discussed in Section 4. Above all, to ensure a good outcome in the containment phase, the authorities need to have clear objectives.

3. RESOLUTION STAGE

Even when containment has been successful, the panic abated, and corrupt or incompetent bank management removed, much work usually remains before the crisis can be said to be resolved. At this point, the crisis has left banks and nonfinancial firms insolvent and many are in government ownership or under court or regulatory administration. Economic growth is unlikely to resume on a secure basis until productive assets and banking franchises are back in the hands of solvent private entities.

The financial and organizational restructuring of financial and nonfinancial firms during the crisis resolution phase is thus a large task, typically entailing much detailed implementation work in the bankruptcy courts, as well as the use of informal or ad hoc workout procedures. But even in advanced economies, the classic solution of court-mediated liquidation are likely to be too slow, and – in part because of the problems of coordination[9] – too fraught with the risk of a debt-deflation spiral, to yield a good outcome when a sizable fraction of the banking system and the corporate sector generally is insolvent. The disruption of liquidation may also involve much loss of information capital. Even where more sophisticated market-driven approaches to bankruptcy (see Section 5) are available in law and supported by adequate institutional capacity there will typically be a need for *ad hoc* policy intervention. Just what the nature and design of that policy intervention should be: macro or micro, discretionary or uniform, managerial or market-driven, remains disputed territory. Disappointing experiences have been more numerous than success stories. The effectiveness of alternative policy packages clearly depends on the state of development of the national governance arrangements, and on the underlying source of the solvency problems. There are also important trade-offs such as that between speed and durability of the subsequent economic recovery, on the one hand, and the fiscal costs, on the other.

The most recurrent question arising at this time is: should an overindebted corporate entity be somehow subsidized or forgiven some of its debt, or should its assets be transferred to a new corporate structure and new management? This question applies to undercapitalized banks and to overindebted nonbank corporations alike. The feasibility of making such decisions on a case-by-case basis becomes problematic during a systemic crisis resulting in thousands of insolvencies and it becomes necessary to establish a systematic approach. General principles have proved elusive and, as well as depending on the scale of the crisis and the quality of existing legal and other governance institutions, to an extent the best answer is likely to depend, once again, on the source of the crisis.

---

[9] One reason why the market cannot do the job on its own lies in the complexity of the coordination problems that arise between corporations, between the corporate and financial sectors, between the government and the rest of the economy, and with respect to domestic and foreign investors. In a systemic crisis, the fate of an individual corporation and the best course of action for its owners and managers will depend on the actions of many other corporations and financial institutions as well as the general economic outlook. And investors, domestic and foreign, will hesitate to act until they see the actions of owners, the government, workers, and others – resulting in a shortage of new capital just when it is most needed.

Where the problem results from an economy-wide crash, the best prospect for future performance of banks and their borrowing customers may be with their existing owners and managers, given the information and other intangible forms of firm or relationship-specific capital they possess. By contrast, where bank insolvency has been the result of incompetent, reckless, or corrupt banking, or the use of government-controlled banks as quasi-fiscal vehicles or for political purposes, the relevant stock of information and relationship capital is unlikely to be of much social value. Therefore, separating the good assets from their current managers and owners offers better prospects in such circumstances as well as establishing a better precedent for avoiding moral hazard. Information capital is also likely to be relatively unimportant for real estate ventures, which have been central to many recent banking crises.

Some of the policy approaches employed in the resolution phase are more relationship-friendly than others, in the sense that they help to preserve existing banking and control relationships. Several examples (notably from Mexico and different episodes of U.S. banking history) are discussed and evaluated by Calomiris, Klingebiel, and Laeven in Chapter 2.[10]

In an attempt to let the market determine which firms are capable of surviving given some modest assistance, some official schemes have offered loan subsidies to distressed borrowers conditional on the borrower's shareholders injecting some new capital. Likewise, there have been schemes offering injection of government capital funds for insolvent banks whose shareholders were willing to provide matching funds.

To the extent that they are discretionary, schemes of debt relief for bank borrowers carry particular microeconomic risks, not only of corruption but also heightened moral hazard as debtors stop trying to repay in the hope of being added to the list of scheme beneficiaries. A long-lasting deterioration of credit culture can be the result, as appears to have occurred in Mexico.

Generalized forms of debt relief, such as is effectively provided by inflation and currency depreciation, can be regarded as relationship-friendly in the sense introduced earlier. Inflation is also a solution that reduces the budgetary burden. After all, if the crisis is big enough, the government's

---

[10] Earlier studies of the policy approaches adopted during the resolution stage of crises and their impact on economic recovery include Sheng (1996), Klingebiel, Kroszner, and Laeven (2001), and Claessens, Klingebiel, and Laeven (2002).

choices may be limited by what it can afford. Its capacity to subsidize borrowers or inject capital into banks is constrained by its ability over time to raise taxes or cut expenditure. It is for these reasons that inflationary solutions or currency devaluation have been a feature of the resolution of many crises in the past. This amounts to generalized debt relief and a transfer of the costs of the crisis to money holders and other nominal creditors.[11] In this case, the banks as well as the non-bank debtors receive relief, without a climate of debtor delinquency being created. Of course, these are questions of monetary and macroeconomic policy as much as banking policy and need to be considered in the light of the need to preserve an environment of macroeconomic stability into the future.

In contrast, the carving-out of an insolvent bank's bad loan portfolio, and its organizational restructuring under new management and ownership, represents the alternative pole, appropriate when large parts of the bank's information capital was dysfunctional. The bad loan portfolio may be sold back into the market, or disposed of by a government-owned asset management company (AMCs). The effectiveness of government-run AMCs has been quite mixed: better when the assets to be disposed have been primarily real estate, less good when loans to large politically connected firms dominated (Klingebiel, 2000, see also Chapter 2).

Government itself often retains control and ownership of troubled banks for much of the duration of the resolution phase. Whether or not control of the bank passes into public hands, it should eventually emerge, and at this point (though not necessarily before) it must be adequately capitalized. Depending on how earlier loss allocation decisions have been taken, the sums of money that are involved in the recapitalization of the bank so that it can safely be sold into private hands may be huge. Many governments have felt constrained by fiscal and monetary policy considerations from doing the financial restructuring properly. In Chapter 4, Honohan points out that putting the bank on a sound financial footing, which implies avoiding the use of such devices as unmarketable, zero-coupon bonds, can and should be the priority. Without this, banks will

[11] In Chapter 2, Calomiris, Klingebiel, and Laeven review some classic instances here, such as the recourse to greenbacks during the U.S. Civil War, and the U.S. departure from gold during the Great Depression. The latter was accompanied by the legislation preventing the enforcement of gold-guarantees in debt contracts. There were echoes of this in the compulsory pesification of the Argentine banking system in 2001, but in that case the asymmetric nature of the pesification (assets and liabilities of the banks were converted at widely different rates) created bank insolvency rather than relieving it.

feel undercapitalized, whatever the accounts state, and will have an incentive to resume reckless behavior. Fiscal and monetary instruments can be adapted to what is needed on the banking side to rebalance macroeconomic policy.

The review of case studies by Calomiris, Klingebiel, and Laeven in Chapter 2 shows that countries typically apply a combination of resolution strategies, including both government-managed and market-based mechanisms. Both prove to depend for their success on efficient and effective legal, regulatory, supervisory, and political institutions. Furthermore, a lack of attention to incentive problems when designing specific rules governing financial assistance can aggravate moral hazard problems, especially in environments where these institutions are weak, unnecessarily raising the costs of resolution. Policy makers in economies with weak institutions should not expect to achieve the same level of success in financial restructuring as in more developed countries, and they should design resolution mechanisms accordingly. Despite the theoretical attraction of some complex market-based mechanisms, simpler resolution mechanisms that afford quick resolution of outstanding debts, that improve financial system competitiveness, and that offer little discretion to government officials appear to be most effective.

A great deal hinges on the political economy factors that make governments choose certain policies. Policies enacted during crises importantly shape the financial sector and have important long-term impact on financial sector development. Political issues are at the heart of crisis resolution not only because allocation of costs between different groups in society is at issue. Hitherto powerful financiers and industrialists are struggling to retain their influence and their ownership of firms. Extensive subsidies are being made available, forming lucrative rent-seeking opportunities for some. If the crisis occurs at a time of political change, inherited power structures may be weaker, perhaps clearing the way for a solution closer to the public good.[12] All too often, though, crises offer yet another opportunity for the powerful elite to extract rents from the weak and the public at large.

Whenever government steps in to provide subsidy or relief to a banking crisis, it will be difficult for it to credibly commit that government support will not be renewed at the first sign of another panic. Both in the immediate future, and for the long run, the costs of accommodating policies can prove higher than at first appears.

---

[12] Though it can also result in politically based scapegoating.

4. MODELS AND ECONOMETRIC EVIDENCE

Bank behavior both before and during a crisis is sure to take account of extant and expected government policies. The behavior of the bank regulator, the deposit insurer, and the central bank as lender of last resort is likely to interact with the risk-taking strategy of the banks in a complex manner. For example, the theoretical model explored by Repullo in Chapter 5 shows how, even if certain policies might act to reduce bank risk-taking, they can result in higher expected fiscal costs. Repullo's model has each bank choosing the level of default risk of its illiquid loans, bearing in mind the interest rate it will have to pay to attract depositors.[13] These choices will be influenced by the bank's anticipation of the likely terms and availability of a last resort loan from the central bank or the possible extension of blanket deposit insurance in the event of large-scale depositor withdrawals in response to evolving information. Even if, by lowering the cost of deposits, such a relaxed stance could lead to banks choosing less risky portfolios,[14] these policies increase the fiscal exposure to banking losses that do occur. The increased exposure can outweigh any lowered risk-profile; indeed, for the parameter values simulated by Repullo, such policies do actually increase expected fiscal losses relative to a strict, nonaccommodating policy.

In addition, moral hazard can also emerge in other ways. In a closely related model, Repullo (2004) allows fully insured banks to hold also a stock of liquid assets. In that case, although banks will still adapt to the expectation of an accommodating lender of last resort by reducing the riskiness of the loan portfolio, they also will reduce the liquidity buffer, thereby increasing overall risk.

The ambiguous theoretical results reinforce the need for an empirical basis for policy design. Looking at the fiscal cost of banking crises, it appears that these have been systematically higher in countries that have

[13] As Repullo points out, the results of his model are particularly sensitive to the way in which depositor information is modeled. As a result, although he chooses to emphasize them, this particular model's predictions about the likely impact of deposit insurance on risk-taking and on intermediation in low-income countries must be seen as controversial and needing to be balanced not only against alternative theoretical models but especially against the weight of empirical evidence (cf. Demirgüç-Kunt and Kane, 2002). Fuller discussion of policy issues surrounding deposit insurance would take us too far afield.

[14] Though this result is somewhat dependent on the way in which the bank's risk opportunities are modeled. As in Hellman, Murdock, and Stiglitz (2000), the bank always chooses too much risk, but if deposit interest rates are lower, then the degree of excess risk is reduced. This feature of Repullo's model curiously implies that contrary to Bagehot, a penalty rate should not be imposed on liquidity loans.

adopted an accommodating approach (Honohan and Klingebiel, 2003).[15] In Chapter 6, Claessens, Klingebiel, and Laeven, using a cross-country regression approach, look behind this finding to assess whether costs also depend on the quality of a country's underlying legal and political institutions. They find that it is the speed of economic recovery, more than the fiscal costs, that depends on these institutions, and that they also influence the probability of a crisis occurring and the depth of a crisis.

5. STRUCTURAL REFORMS

Given that institutional weaknesses contribute both to the frequency and depth of banking crises as well as influencing the speed of recovery, reforms on these fronts are clearly desirable even when no crisis is in prospect.

There are specific reforms of importance to building an environment that can resist crisis or at least ease its resolution. Bankruptcy and restructuring frameworks are often deficient. Disclosure and accounting rules may be weak for financial institutions and corporations. Equity and creditor rights may be poorly defined. And the judiciary is often inefficient. There also is usually a shortage of qualified managers in the corporate and financial sectors, as well as a lack of qualified domestic restructuring and insolvency specialists – partly because there may be no recent history of corporate and financial sector restructuring.

It is often argued that a financial crisis can be used to advance institutional reforms. It is during the height of the crisis when the pain is felt most that there is an opportunity to break established malpractices and governance structures, to implement new laws and regulations, and to find support for economic and financial reforms.

5.1 Bankruptcy Laws

The importance of structural reform of bankruptcy laws and procedures can hardly be overestimated in this context. Strong but flexible procedures are needed in the resolution phase in order to support the efficient reorganization or exit of distressed firms.[16] When existing bankruptcy laws have

---

[15] Although it could be that having such an approach may have served to prevent some episodes from becoming full-fledged crises.

[16] For recent overviews of bankruptcy laws and procedures, see Hart, La Porta, Lopez-de Silanes, and Moore (1997), and the papers in Claessens, Djankov, and Mody (2001), particularly Stiglitz (2001).

not been tested on their ability to deal with situations of large-scale financial distress, hidden weaknesses in the framework calling for reform are revealed during such periods. Ideally, these deficiencies will be identified and corrected in advance. Although, in some countries, this requires the introduction of a completely new bankruptcy law to support an efficient and orderly exit of firms, in many it will be sufficient to fine-tune existing laws and regulations.

Although most existing bankruptcy regimes around the world can be traced back to a small number of legal origins (Djankov et al. 2003), bankruptcy systems vary considerably from country to country, not only in their design but also in their implementation and effectiveness. The jury is still out as to which system is to be preferred. For example, whether the U.S. system that focuses on reorganization of firms via Chapter 11 is to be preferred over the U.K. system that focuses on exit of distressed firms. A bankruptcy regime affects not only distressed firms, but also sets incentives going forward for surviving firms. A better understanding of the ex ante and ex post considerations of designing appropriate bankruptcy laws is therefore important not only for an efficient, speedy, and orderly workout of distressed firms during the resolution stage of a financial crisis but also to set appropriate incentives.

In Chapter 8, Smith and Strömberg review the role of bankruptcy law in the resolution of financial distress. Existing regimes differ, though less than is often supposed. In particular, the sharp differentiation that is often made between regimes that are debtor-friendly or reorganization-based (as in the United States) and those that are creditor-friendly or liquidation-based (as in the United Kingdom, Germany, Japan, and Sweden) is no longer justified in practice. For one thing, the codes have been converging. In addition, few firms entering reorganization emerge as going concerns. The goal of an effective and economically efficient bankruptcy system is to ensure a smooth transfer of productive assets of distressed firms to their highest-value use. Smith and Strömberg draw an analogy with the venture capital market, suggesting that this market provides lessons for how bankruptcy should function efficiently, as venture capitalists as prime financiers of their firms internalize much of the risk of reorganization, and therefore have devised appropriate contracts, often including the use of preferred equities giving the venture capitalist control when firm performance deteriorates. Because the venture capitalists control the process of reorganization, they may renegotiate existing contracts, and depart from absolute creditor priority in the interest of restoring managerial incentives if retaining the existing managers seems value maximizing. Lessons for national bankruptcy codes include both elements that can seem debtor-friendly (such as stays on collecting collateral) and those that are creditor-friendly (such as ensuring that outside investors have a chance to bid for the assets of the firm).

5.2 Foreign Bank Entry

Allowing the entry of foreign banks is increasingly recognized as a potentially valuable structural reform. Foreign banks can improve the performance of the domestic banking system by placing competitive pressure on local banks. However, because of lobbying by domestic banks for entry barriers to keep economic rents and of other vested interests, governments are often reluctant to allow free entry of foreign banks. A crisis period, when local capital is scarce, is often a time where the balance of power shifts in favor of those who support the entry of foreign banks. The capital and know-how that these banks bring along can help in rebuilding the health of the domestic banking system (cf. the discussion of Mexico in Chapter 2).

In Chapter 7, Tschoegl reviews the motives for countries to allow foreign banks and the reasons for foreign banks to establish operations abroad. He shows that many foreign banks arrive following periods of reform or distress. Foreign banks have often helped the recovery of a financial crisis by acting as rehabilitators of weak banks, although many foreign banks are too small in their host countries to play such a direct role. Most important, foreign banks can provide an indirect, catalytic role to restructuring of domestic banks by offering competitive pressure and raising the level playing field. Also, if foreign banks are better regulated and subject to parent bank oversight, foreign banks operating in developing countries may be better able to resist local suasion, especially during periods of distress.[17] By contrast, not all foreign banks have had a positive impact on the development of local banking markets. Foreign banks could be a channel for contagion if these foreign banks are present in many countries. Another often heard argument against foreign bank presence is that foreign banks might pull out at the time of a crisis, when their presence is most needed. Although it is true that some foreign banks have withdrawn during crisis times, their departure has often followed arbitrary treatment by host country governments. This was certainly the

---

[17] We thank Linda Goldberg for raising this point.

case in the 2001–2 experience of Argentina. On balance, the presence of foreign banks seems to have a positive effect helping to make a financial system less vulnerable to a financial crisis, although foreign banks come in many varieties and some will have a greater impact than others.

5.3 Failing to Seize the Opportunities

Not all countries grasp the opportunity and use a financial crisis to advance institutional reforms. Failure to do so often reflects vested interests and shortsightedness of politicians. Japan, stuck in a chronic banking crisis since the early 1990s, is an exemplary case. Because of a lack of political will, the crisis was not fully addressed when it was revealed. Initial bank restructuring and recapitalization plans and write-offs of nonperforming loans were not far-reaching enough to resolve the underlying problems of Japan's weak banks. Several years down the road, some banks are still struggling and continuous forbearance and support has resulted in massive fiscal outlays. Japan's case shows that an analysis of political economy factors is critical to an understanding of why some countries make more progress and achieve better results in crisis resolution than others. The failure to adequately and speedily address a financial crisis is not specific to Japan – many countries have faced similar problems. Japan does stand out, however, as being an industrial country that has both the capacity and the ability to address a crisis situation, but because of lack of political will has failed to do so. Not only do many other countries face similar problems in the political arena, but policy makers in these countries also need to operate in an environment of budgetary constraints, weak legal institutions, and corruption.

In Chapter 9, Peek and Rosengren analyze the banking reform process in Japan during the 1990s. They show that bank restructuring in Japan has been painfully slow, and that these banking problems contributed to the extended malaise of the Japanese economy during this period. They show that, although the government failed to set adequate incentives for better banking practices going forward and to oblige banks to restructure, the banks themselves also aggravated the situation by continuing their financial support to related, troubled companies. As a result of this support, troubled and noncompetitive firms were able to continue to operate without an incentive to restructure, whereas viable enterprises with growth opportunities faced an increased cost of financing and a lack of available funds. Peek and Rosengren argue that this misallocation of capital by Japanese banks has contributed to stifling Japanese economic growth during the 1990s.

6. CONCLUDING REMARKS

Weak institutions and an inadequate policy framework heighten the risk of banking crisis and reduce an economy's ability to recover speedily from crises that do occur. All too often, it is entrenched interests and perceived political costs that slow the adoption of institutional and policy reform. Yet banking crises have been associated with prolonged economic downturns and a worsening of poverty, devastating governments' ability to finance needed public services and derailing economic development strategies.

The analysis presented in the chapters of this book serve to emphasize the difficulties of implementing an effective containment and resolution strategy. Because the best policy actions depend on the nature of the crisis as well as the state of national institutions, and because many irreversible decisions are necessarily taken at speed under pressure of events, it is important to have maximum information (especially about the condition of banks), a good contingency plan (in terms of institutional lines of authority) and a clear picture of the fiscal trade-offs that may be expected.

Policy errors in managing banking crises have tended to be on the side of excessive socialization of the losses especially in being too quick to provide liquidity loans and generalized guarantees in the containment phase – though these may have been necessary and appropriate in some instances. Fiscal costs also have ballooned as a result of undue lenience in enforcing prudential regulations and in providing excessive borrower subsidies. The moral hazard created by such action can be long lasting, as governments' commitments to avoid repeated bailouts in the future are not easily made credible. Yet, too rigid an approach could also have resulted in undue loss of information capital, and unneeded disruption because of coordination failures in corporate workouts.

The lessons of experience here are complex and not yet fully distilled. We have suggested that the choice should depend in part on the source of the crisis – whether it was caused externally or attributable to poor banking practices – and in part on the quality of domestic institutions. For example, a policy of forbearance or accommodation is more easily defended for well-run banks, possessing valuable information and relationship capital, which have been hit by an exogenous downturn; and the use of government-run AMCs is more likely to be effective when legal and governmental institutions are strong.

Enhancing legal and institutional arrangements for bankruptcy and opening the system to foreign-owned banks are two key long-term reforms that can be implemented in advance and that, together with decisive and coherent policy action in the containment and resolution phases, can help avoid the worst consequences of widespread bank insolvency.

PART TWO

CONTAINMENT AND RESOLUTION

TWO

Financial Crisis Policies and Resolution Mechanisms

A Taxonomy from Cross-Country Experience

Charles W. Calomiris, Daniela Klingebiel, and Luc Laeven

INTRODUCTION

As observed in recent years, systemic financial crises, especially those associated with a currency collapse, can be fast-moving events resulting in wealth destruction, crippling the financial system and magnifying economic decline. The channels of collapse are numerous. What starts as a moderate recession can become a steep decline in economic activity as financial losses generate large exchange rate movements and bank collapses. Exchange rate depreciation damages the net worth of those who have borrowed in foreign currency. Furthermore, a trend of depreciation raises nominal interest rates on loans, and also adversely affects the relative price movements for producers of nontradables. As borrowers' ability to repay declines, bank net worth is destroyed. Additional bank losses may result from banks' direct exposure to interest rate and exchange rate risk.

In the frictionless world of neoclassical economics, the distribution of wealth has no effect on the allocation of investment capital. But in the real world, the wealth of borrowers and banks plays an important allocative role in financial markets. Destruction of the net worth of borrowers, especially a fall in the value of real estate and other assets relied on for bank collateral, and of banks can cause a collapse of the loan market (Keynes 1931, Fisher 1933, and Bernanke 1983).

Declines in banks' net worth, which can result in bank failures, reduce or eliminate banks' abilities to supply loans. This can disproportionately restrict the access to borrowed funds of small and medium-sized enterprises (SMEs) and the producers of nontradables in emerging markets because they have less access to funding sources outside their countries. At a minimum, declines in banks' net worth will trigger increases in their funding costs, to the extent that banks rely on the willingness of market participants to fund their lending activities. Declines in net worth also may hamper banks' ability to restructure assets and work out nonperforming loans as this may require banks to recognize further losses, which could trigger adverse regulatory or market reactions.

Institutional weaknesses are a further complicating factor in crises; many of these likely contributed to the emergence of the crisis in the first place. Institutional weaknesses contribute to the inefficient allocation of capital and the poor management of risk within the financial sector prior to the crisis. After the crisis, weak legal and regulatory institutions hamper the restructuring process by making it more difficult to address and resolve insolvency problems. Disclosure and accounting rules for financial institutions and corporations may be weak. Equity and creditor rights may be poorly defined or weakly enforced. The judicial system is often inefficient or corrupt. Under these circumstances, it is difficult for creditors and debtors to reach agreement on workouts, for balance sheets to be rebuilt, for desirable transfers of ownership of firms or banks to take place, or for new suppliers of credit to be willing to enter the market.

In principle, the goals of financial restructuring are to reestablish the creditor-debtor relationships on which the economy depends for an efficient allocation of capital, and to accomplish that objective at minimal cost. To limit the economic costs of a protracted financial crisis, governments have employed various crisis restructuring mechanisms that are aimed at restoring banks' financial health or at restructuring the balance sheets of the financial institutions' borrowers.

This chapter proposes a taxonomy of the mechanisms that governments have used to help restore the banking system to health and examines the benefits and costs of various alternatives, as well as the prerequisites necessary for success in applying various policy measures, including the institutional quality of the country.

Central to identifying the best policy approaches is the recognition that policy responses that reallocate wealth toward banks and corporate debtors and away from taxpayers face a key trade-off. Such reallocations of wealth can help to restart productive investment, but they have both direct and indirect costs. Direct costs include the taxpayers' wealth that is spent on financial assistance. Indirect costs from financial assistance include misallocations of capital and distortions to incentives that may result from encouraging banks and firms to abuse government protection.

Those distortions may worsen capital allocation and risk management after the resolution of the crisis. For example, some approaches to assistance (e.g., repeated debt forgiveness) may have a crippling effect on the future development of credit markets, and thus can be counterproductive. Countries with strong institutional environments will be better able to limit moral hazard related to specific policy measures.

In this chapter, we rely on a case study approach to measure the extent to which various policy tools have in practice met their objectives, the direct costs of restructuring programs, and the extent to which they were "incentive compatible." We find that countries typically apply a combination of tools to restructure their financial and corporate sectors, including decentralized, market-based mechanisms and government-managed programs. Market-based strategies seek to strengthen the capital base of financial institutions or borrowers to enable them to renegotiate debt and resume new credit supply. Government-led restructuring strategies often include the establishment of an entity to which nonperforming loans are transferred or the government's sale of financial institutions, sometimes to foreign entrants.

Market-based mechanisms can, in principle, resolve coordination problems countries face in the wake of massive debtor and creditor insolvency, with acceptably low direct and indirect costs, particularly when those mechanisms are effective in achieving the desirable objective of selectivity (i.e., focusing taxpayer resources on borrowers and banks that are worth assisting). But these mechanisms depend for their success on an efficient judicial system, a credible supervisory authority with sufficient enforcement capacity, and a lack of corruption in implementation.

Government-managed programs also depend on effective legal, regulatory, and political institutions for their success, though this is not as immediately obvious. For example, a transfer of assets to government-owned asset management companies may not achieve its objectives of resolving the overhang of corporate debt at reasonable cost when legal and political institutions are weak.

The cost of resolution is likely to be higher when insufficient attention to the incentives built into the design of specific rules governing financial assistance has aggravated moral hazard. Policy makers in emerging market economies with weak institutions should, accordingly, not expect to achieve the same level of success in financial restructuring as achieved in some rich countries, and they should design resolution mechanisms accordingly. Despite the theoretical attraction of some complex market-based mechanisms, simpler resolution mechanisms that afford quick resolution of outstanding debts, and that offer little discretion to government officials, are likely to be most effective.

This chapter proceeds as follows. Section 1 briefly reviews the policy setting in which emergency and long-run crisis resolution policies are formed, and reviews the literature on the pitfalls of crisis management and resolution mechanisms for the corporate and banking sector. Section 2 presents a taxonomy of alternative mechanisms, and examines case studies in which countries have employed different tools. The case studies review the specific country circumstances and assess to what extent the resolution was successful in reaching its objectives at reasonable direct and indirect costs, including the costs resulting from a worsening of incentive problems. At the end of each case study, we derive lessons for policy, comparing the objectives of the restructuring measure used with the outcomes, and analyzing the determinants of failure or success. Section 3 concludes by summarizing the main general lessons of the various cases.

1. THE POLICY SETTING

It is useful to recognize the context in which policy responses to financial crises occur. Policy responses to crises naturally divide into immediate reactions in the heat of a crisis, and long-term responses after the end of the crisis, although immediate responses often remain part of the long-run policy response.

Initially, the government's policy options are limited to those policies that do not rely on the formation of new institutions or complex new mechanisms. Immediate policy responses include debt moratoria, which prevent creditors or bank depositors from seeking repayment from debtors or banks. Debt moratoria of one kind or another have a long history; in the United States, their use dates back to the early 19th century. Central bank or government lending to financial institutions or borrowers is an alternative emergency measure with a long history (Bagehot 1873).

Another common immediate response to crisis is to relax the enforcement of financial sector regulations (so-called regulatory forbearance) to permit banks to avoid the costs of regulatory compliance. For example, regulators often cease enforcing banks' capital requirements in order to allow banks and their loan customers to avoid the costs of contractions in loan supply. Supervisors and regulators accomplish this by permitting banks to understate their problem loans or other losses, and thus overstate their equity capital. The use of forbearance is a more recent policy tool than debt moratoria or government lending, because forbearance is only effective in the presence of credible government protection of bank depositors, which is a relatively recent feature of financial systems. Without an explicit or implicit government safety net, depositors would have an incentive to concern themselves about bank solvency irrespective of government regulatory policy; decisions by the government to relax capital standards would have little effect on banks as private market discipline and market-determined minimum capital requirements would be the real constraints on bank behavior.

Forbearance, debt moratoria in the form of suspension of convertibility of deposits, and emergency government lending are motivated by adverse changes in the condition of banks. Banks suffering severe losses tend not only to see rising costs but also to experience liability rationing, either because they must have contract deposits to satisfy their regulatory equity capital requirement, or because depositors at risk of loss prefer to place funds in more stable intermediaries (Calomiris and Kahn 1991 and Calomiris and Gorton 1991 and Calomiris and Mason 1997). Banks, in turn, will transmit those difficulties to their borrowers in the form of a contraction of credit supply. Credit will become more costly and financial distress of borrowers and banks more likely.

In theory, emergency action of any of these three types (suspension of convertibility of deposits, government loans, and forbearance) may alleviate the distress of banks and the contraction of credit supply. Debt moratoria that limit bank collections from their debtors may alleviate the distress of borrowers, which also can be beneficial to banks (if the moratoria limit fire-sale losses that result from asset liquidation) (Diamond and Rajan 2001).

But debt moratoria that help borrowers may hurt banks, and can poison future loan supply, as has been the case in Mexico after 1995. Unless a debt collection moratorium for borrowers is combined with measures that assist banks (loans, forbearance, or deposit suspension), debt forgiveness will put additional adverse pressure on banks and limit the supply of new credit. Assistance to banks in the form of deposit suspension, a reduction in the real value of deposits, government loans to banks, or capital regulation forbearance may permit distressed banks to continue accessing funding sources that underlie the supply of bank credit.

Thus, the long-term consequences of debt forgiveness for credit supply depend on the way it is done: it can either help both banks and borrowers, or hurt banks and future borrowers while helping some of today's borrowers. The effects on depositors also depend on the way debt forgiveness is financed. If losses from debt forgiveness are financed in part by the government, then it is important to recognize that depositors are taxpayers too. We discuss the costs and benefits of debt forgiveness later, using the Civil War and the Great Depression in the United States as examples.

Empirical research has, however, shown that providing assistance to banks and their borrowers can be counterproductive, resulting in increased losses to banks, which often abuse forbearance to take unproductive risks at government expense. The typical result of forbearance is a deeper hole in the net worth of banks, crippling tax burdens to finance bank bailouts, and even more severe credit supply contraction and economic decline than would have occurred in the absence of forbearance (Demirgüç-Kunt and Detragiache 2002, Honohan and Klingebiel 2003, Claessens, Klingebiel, and Laeven 2003).

If systemic financial collapse results in a weakening of legal enforcement of creditors' rights, this can undermine the long-term willingness of healthy banks to lend to healthy borrowers. In extreme circumstances, when most borrowers and banks are insolvent as the result of changes that have occurred in their net worth, the legal rules governing banks and borrowers, or the enforcement of those rules, often change suddenly. Emerging markets' legal systems tend to have weaker enforcement of creditors' rights even during good times (La Porta, Lopez-de-Silanes, Shleifer, and Vishny 1998). But, when crises strike, and debtor insolvency becomes the rule rather than the exception, enforcement of creditors' rights becomes even weaker as the result of actions by government and the courts.

For example, after the Mexican crisis of 1995, Mexico evolved what came to be called a "culture of no payment," in which few debtors paid their creditors and the courts were not inclined to come to the assistance of creditors in forcing payment. In this environment, banks were not repaid and borrowers continued operating for years with little certainty about what they would ultimately have to pay on their outstanding debt. The breakdown of the legal system has plagued many other crisis countries. Asian crisis countries similarly saw a lack of will on the part of courts to enforce bankruptcy laws that protected creditors' interests.

Once emergency measures have been put in place to contain the crisis, the government faces the long-run challenge of rebuilding the financial system, which entails the resumption of a normally functioning credit system and legal system, and the rebuilding of banks' and borrowers' balance sheets. Section 2 considers the long-run options available to the government from the standpoint of country experiences managing long-run crisis resolution.

2. A TAXONOMY OF POLICY APPROACHES TO RESTORING SOLVENCY

Governments have adopted a variety of approaches to helping restore banks to financial health. In this section we present seven strategic options that have been employed. Although other resolution mechanisms have been employed by countries in the past, most of these can be considered as variants of one of the seven discussed here.[1] Between them, these seven options can be said to encapsulate essentially all of the available options. Each is analyzed through case studies in which these policies were applied. We examine the extent to which policies met their respective objectives and draw more general lessons from the country cases. In particular, as financial crises are typically characterized by distress of both financial institutions and corporations, ideally, a resolution mechanism should not only result in a restructuring of bank balance sheets but also achieve corporate restructuring and vice versa.

The seven policies considered are: (1) regulatory forbearance, allowing banks to operate with less than the normal minimum capital; (2) general across-the-board incentives for loan-loss write-offs by banks; (3) more sophisticated conditional government-subsidized, but decentralized, workouts of distressed loans; (4) across-the-board debt forgiveness through numeraire change; (5) the establishment of a government-owned asset management company to buy and resolve distressed loans; (6) government-assisted sales of financial institutions to new owners, typically foreign; and (7) government-assisted recapitalization through injection of funds. These measures can be used in combination, but each represents a distinct approach, with strengths and weaknesses that will now be discussed.

2.1 Forbearance

Forbearance from prudential regulations, as we have already discussed, essentially allows for the delay in the recognition of loan-losses (or capital shortfall) and is aimed at providing financial institutions with time to recapitalize on a flow basis from current earnings. It is usually a policy adopted during the heat of the crisis, and may be continued as part of the long-run resolution strategy, often because of the difficulty of bringing an end to forbearance policy once banks have become massively insolvent.

---

[1] For example, an outright nationalization of banks can be considered an extreme case of a government-assisted recapitalization of financial institutions.

Governments do not generally pursue forbearance as a preferred long-run resolution tool for financial crises, rather they stumble into it as the result of exigencies and a lack of attractive alternatives. Forbearance can be characterized as providing government protection to banks without the discipline of prudential regulation – an approach to long-run financial policy that few governments would consciously choose, and none would admit to choosing (it might be better described as the absence of a policy). As an example of long-run forbearance policy, we consider the U.S. Savings and Loan (S&L) crisis of the 1980s.

The Savings and Loan Crisis in the United States

Federally chartered thrift institutions operating in the United States in the 1970s complied with different regulations than banks, and were supervised by the Federal Home Loan Bank Board. Their activities and range of permissible investments were circumscribed by strict regulations, which effectively required them to engage in a colossal maturity mismatch, holding 30-year fixed rate mortgages as their primary asset and financing themselves with savings accounts that could be withdrawn at any time. The rising inflation of the 1970s, and the monetary policy reaction to that inflation post-1979 by the Federal Reserve Bank, produced a surge in interest rates that resulted in enormous losses of net worth (on a market value basis) for thrifts over the years 1979–1982. Many thrifts were insolvent on a tangible capital basis by 1982 (Barth and Bartholomew 1992).

The initial reaction to the thrift debacle was to broaden thrift powers (to permit them to engage in a broader range of activities, including the purchase of junk bonds, and involvement with derivatives contracts) and to change thrift accounting practices so that insolvent thrifts would be treated as though they were still solvent. The new breed of insolvent, deregulated thrift would now be able to invest in risky assets such as junk bonds, raise (insured) funds on the brokered certificates of deposit (CD) market to finance rapid growth, and be able to engage in derivatives contracts, without any concern that its true (insolvent) circumstances would limit its ability to grow and prosper.

Underlying this initial policy response were two important incentive problems in the government. First, the thrift industry – which had been losing market share to new forms of financial intermediation for the previous quarter of a century – had "captured" its government regulator, the Federal Home Loan Bank Board. Thrifts and their regulator alike were fighting for the survival of "their" industry and jobs, and phony accounting gimmicks and new opportunities to make money quickly seemed to be the only way out. Second, Congress and the Administration had little incentive to force thrifts and the Federal Home Loan Bank Board to recognize thrift losses, because doing so would force the recognition of enormous losses, and lead to the taxpayer financed recapitalization of the Federal Savings and Loan Insurance Corporation (FSLIC). That was a step few politicians in Washington were in a hurry to take in the early and mid 1980s.

Forbearance via phony accounting, combined with deregulation of thrift powers, gave insolvent thrifts the time and flexibility they needed to attempt "resurrection" via a combination of fast growth and higher asset risk. Deposit insurance acts like a put option for insured institutions (Merton 1977), and the value of that option rises with asset risk in a way that is dependent on the solvency of the thrift. For solvent thrifts, the option value of increasing risk is low, and is probably offset by the disutility of increasing the riskiness of the payoff to the equity holder. For insolvent thrifts, the option value of increasing risk is much higher, and since there is little chance of surviving without earning very high profits, little is lost by betting on resurrection. The incentive to increase risk when deposits are insured is often referred to as the moral hazard problem of deposit insurance. Brewer (1995) tests the Merton model of moral hazard for thrifts in the 1980s and finds strong evidence for the view that the combination of forbearance and deposit insurance encouraged thrifts to increase their risk, and ultimately their average losses, substantially.[2]

As estimated losses among thrifts continued to rise – reaching some $200 billion in prospective losses as of 1988 – so did the threat of a political backlash against thrifts, their regulators, and political supporters. With the passing of the electoral and budgetary cycles of 1988, the political incentives shifted toward recognition of loss and institutional reform. Forbearance was out; regulatory discipline was in. The Federal Home Loan Bank Board was abolished and replaced with the Office of Thrift Supervision (OTS), which soon became the most aggressive enforcer of loan-loss recognition in U.S. history. The OTS, FSLIC, and Resolution Trust Corporation moved speedily in combination to force thrifts to recognize losses, shut down if insolvent, and have their assets liquidated in the market. What ensued was one of the fastest processes of en masse real estate asset liquidation that has ever occurred.

---

[2] This experience must be kept in mind in considering the empirical relevance of some of the theoretical predictions relating to deposit insurance derived in Chapter 5.

Lessons from the Case Study

As the earlier analysis shows, forbearance did not result in an improvement of S&L's balance sheets, but rather, encouraged weakly capitalized financial institutions to gamble for resurrection and increase loan-losses. In addition, the restructuring of bank balance sheets did not take place during the forbearance period, as weakly capitalized banks did not have the incentive or the ability to raise enough capital to engage in any meaningful restructuring. Thrifts were encouraged by forbearance to pretend that they were healthy as they desperately tried to grow and bet their way out of their illness.

The U.S. thrift case, along with numerous empirical studies that generalize its lessons (Calomiris 1989 and Hovakimian, Kane, and Laeven 2003) show that forbearance by itself cannot effectively deal with system-wide bank problems and therefore cannot act as an effective resolution mechanism.

Because forbearance combined with deposit insurance is exploited disproportionately by deeply insolvent institutions (which presumably are also the ones that are least worth saving), and because that exploitation can be extremely costly for taxpayers, forbearance is a very wasteful means of channeling taxpayer wealth toward rebuilding the financial system. A mechanism that would subsidize the rebuilding of bank capital *selectively within the best banks* could be far less costly and would accomplish much more in the way of efficient credit allocation in the future than forbearance policy. We discuss this point more fully later when considering the U.S. experience with preferred stock assistance during the 1930s.

2.2 Tax Incentives for Loan-Loss Write-Offs

There are some attractions in relying on tax incentives for loan-loss write-offs as a way of helping the banks to restructure their balance sheets. Because this approach leaves actual restructuring to banks and corporations, it is a market-based and decentralized approach to corporate and bank restructuring. As an example of incentives for loan-loss write-offs, we consider the case of Japan in 1992.

Loan-Loss Write-Offs in Japan

The Japanese banking crisis of the 1990s is unlike the other financial crises studied in this chapter in the sense that there was no sudden crisis but rather a prolonged, steady deterioration in the health of Japan's financial system. This prolonged crisis resulted from a combination of inadequate disclosure of information on the true financial condition of financial institutions, and the slow response to the crisis by the government.

In 1992, when it became clear that Japanese banks had a large amount of nonperforming loans, mainly in the construction and real estate sectors, the Credit Cooperative Purchasing Company (CCPC) was set up to transfer bad real estate loans of member banks. The main advantage for banks of utilizing the CCPC to write off loans was that the claimed losses on loans sold was deductible from taxable income. Until 1992, banks had not been allowed to write off bad debts against taxable income, at least not until an actual bankruptcy procedure against the borrower began. However, because of the mounting problems in some of the major financial institutions in Japan, such deduction from taxable income was approved by the tax authorities.

In the years that followed, further tax policy changes were announced to make it even easier and more attractive for banks to deduct loan-losses for tax purposes. Hence, rather than directly recapitalizing banks and addressing the bad loan problem using public funds, initially the Japanese government relied on tax incentives for recognition of loan-losses to solve the bad loan problem.

Almost all banks took advantage of these tax incentives and liberally deducted losses on loans to assist related, troubled borrowers and on loans transferred to the CCPC (Packer 2000). Despite the "success" of the CCPC program in transferring large amounts of bad loans, the main problem was not attacked, and bad loans continued to rise, as new nonperforming loans replaced those that were previously written down, and the condition of financial institutions continued to deteriorate. Although the government continued to allow banks to write off bad debts against taxable income, loan-losses were not recognized in the amount necessary, as a lax accounting regime did not force financial institutions to recognize losses.

Despite the tax incentives offered, banks remained reluctant to recognize the full extent of loan-losses. One reason is that asset deflation combined with explicit deposit insurance made loan-loss write-offs unattractive. Furthermore, the historical absence of liquidation procedures and limited capacity of the bankruptcy court system made orderly liquidation even more challenging (Packer and Ryser 1992). The continuing growth in nonperforming loans reflected further deterioration in asset values as well as previously unrecognized earlier losses.

The initial strategy of Japan's authorities of relying on tax breaks to assist banks failed to restore the health of the banking system. Financial institutions seriously lacked incentives to engage in effective corporate restructuring as they were allowed to continue to hide their losses and operate with a weak capital base. This resulted in moral hazard behavior by banks and bank borrowers, which was exacerbated by a government guarantee on all bank deposits. Additionally, the Japanese Keiretsu model, in which Japanese banks have close relationships with affiliated firms and Japanese banks own substantial equity positions in those firms, further reduced market discipline and incentives to attack the mounting bad debt problem, and encouraged banks to use government subsidization of losses largely as a means to assist related enterprises (Sheard 1989, Peek and Rosengren 2002, and Chapter 9, this volume).

Lessons from the Case Study
The potential advantage of loan-loss write-offs is that loan-losses are recognized quickly. Speedy recognition is desirable because it encourages the strengthening of the equity capital positions of financial institutions, and because it reinforces the credibility of accounting rules and capital regulation, and thus disciplines risk taking by discouraging banks from undertaking high-risk resurrection strategies. Credible regulation and accounting rules also facilitate the rebuilding of equity by making the financial statements of banks more reliable to potential outside investors. Loan-loss write-offs do not directly address the problem of improving debtor capacity, as corporate restructuring is left to the market. Often, a cleanup of banks' balance sheets is, however, a first step in the direction of restarting corporate lending on a sound market basis.

Among the costs of subsidizing loan-loss write-offs, however, is the incentive cost from channeling taxpayer support to banks and their borrowers, and thereby relieving them of some of the cost of having engaged in unprofitable lending and borrowing. By not imposing losses on corporate borrowers, banks' shareholders, and depositors loan-loss write-off subsidies worsen incentives for prudent behavior. Also, as in the case of forbearance, an across the board subsidy for all bank loans may create an adverse selection problem, because the amount of subsidy is likely to be inversely related to the soundness of the financial institution or borrower receiving the subsidy. This results in both poor incentives and a waste of scarce taxpayer resources, which might be better channeled to support the selective rebuilding of the balance sheets of the best banks and bank customers (see the discussion later of the Reconstruction Finance Corporation's experience in the 1930s). In Japan, the adverse selection problem was even worse, because banks faced little incentive to undertake across-the-board write-offs, but did see value in using subsidized write-offs to assist distressed related firm borrowers.

The Japanese experience of the mid-1990s is representative of how forbearance fails to give incentives to restructure bad loan portfolios and of how principal-agent problems in asset resolution are exacerbated in a system in which banks and their borrowers have ownership links, and in which the government issues a blanket guarantee on all deposits. Finally, the Japanese case illustrates that loan-loss write-offs are unlikely to be an effective resolution mechanism in systemic financial crises because the subsidy may not be sufficient to cover the capital shortfall experienced by the banks, and because banks may lack incentive to take full advantage of the program being offered. As in the case of forbearance, for loan-loss write-offs to be an effective resolution mechanism, they must be combined with other tools, which ensure that banks will make proper use of the assistance they are being given from the government. These include (1) a credible supervisory authority with sufficient enforcement capacity to encourage financial institutions to recognize losses and engage in corporate restructuring, (2) an efficient bankruptcy system to solve coordination problems between debtors and creditors, and allow corporate restructuring to occur, and (3) a high-quality accounting framework that makes it hard for banks to mask nonperforming loans. In Japan, all of these elements were lacking and banks had little incentive under these circumstances to take advantage of government subsidies for loan-loss recognition; they believed they were better off delaying recognition of losses, taking advantage of Japanese regulators' forbearance policy and hoping for a reversal of their losses.

2.3 Conditional Taxpayer Sharing of Loan-losses

Rather than simply offering tax deductibility or some similar general subsidy for loan-losses, a more complex and conditional subsidized workout program for nonperforming loans can be devised, while still retaining a decentralized market-based approach. Of special interest are those in which the borrower too contributes to loan resolution. As an example of such a scheme for government sharing of loan-losses, we consider the Punto Final Program in Mexico.

The Punto Final Program in Mexico
For three years, the Fund for the Protection of Bank Savings (FOBAPROA) program initiated in 1995 had failed to reduce the amount

of past due loans and to provide debtor relief (see case study in Section 2.5). In a final attempt to offer debt relief, the government initiated in December 1998 the Punto Final program, which was a government-led debt-relief program targeted to mortgage holders, agribusinesses, and small and medium-sized enterprises (SMEs). The program offered large subsidies (up to 60 percent of the book value of the loan) to bank debtors to pay back their loans.

The Punto Final program consisted of three debtor-relief programs that were directed toward mortgage holders, the rural and fishing sectors, and enterprises. The discounts depended on the program, the amount of the loan, and on whether the bank restarted lending to the sector. Large loans only received discounts up to a certain amount. The government would increase its share of the discount offered according to the following rule: for every three pesos of new loans extended by the bank, the government would assume an additional one peso of discount. Only new loans to individuals and small and medium-sized enterprises would qualify for counting toward receiving this additional government subsidy. The program thus combined loss sharing between the government and the banking sector with an incentive to restart lending (World Bank 2003).

Although both the Punto Final program and the FOBAPROA program combined an element of loss sharing between the government and the financial institutions, there were four key improvements of the Punto Final program vis-à-vis its predecessor. First, loss sharing was geared toward small loans, as the discount offered was higher for smaller loans. Small borrowers are a desirable group to target, since assisting them improves competition in the economy, and since assistance channeled to these borrowers is less likely to result from their political or economic power over governments or financial institutions. Second, the loss sharing arrangement offered an incentive for banks to restart lending to SMEs and individuals because it linked the size of government assistance to the amount of new lending by the participating bank. Third, the program may have made more effective use of taxpayers' resources, because it relied on borrowers' willingness to participate, and it required borrowers to pay part of their outstanding loans. Borrower self-selection, in principle, can reduce the number of participating borrowers, and reduce taxpayers' cost of resolution per borrower by requiring borrowers to repay part of their loans. Just as important, self-selection may ensure that participants are more likely to be those that were "worth helping." The borrowers willing to repay part of their loans should be those that value access to credit in the future, which also tend to be more value-creating borrowers.

The FOBAPROA program, in contrast, had not been selective, and had greatly benefited large borrowers at high cost to taxpayers, irrespective of the desirability of assisting them, and even if those borrowers were not in default. Fourth, unlike its predecessor, the Punto Final program offered to quickly resolve ongoing disputes between creditors and debtors, and thus made it easier to analyze the balance sheets of participating borrowers and banks going forward. Resolving the uncertainty about how much of their preexisting debts would be repaid is a key requirement for analyzing the balance sheets of borrowers when making new loans. Debt resolution, in theory, should help to make credit available to creditworthy firms.

Despite these potentially attractive features, it would be premature to declare the Punto Final program a model of successful restructuring. One criticism is that it was restricted to too limited a class of borrowers. Despite the advantages of selectivity, it might have been desirable to extend the program to more firms and individuals. Furthermore, the effectiveness of the program in corporate restructuring was plagued by many of the same institutional weaknesses as those that hampered its predecessors. Those included the lack of a credible supervisory authority with sufficient enforcement capacity to incentivize financial institutions to recognize losses and engage in corporate restructuring, the lack of an efficient bankruptcy system (which provides a threat that banks can use to encourage borrowers to participate in voluntary loan workouts), and the presence of politically connected lending in an environment in which politicians, business groups, and banks are intertwined, and seek mutual advantage at the expense of taxpayers.

It is difficult to assess the effectiveness of the Punto Final program, not least because it was preceded by, and coincided with, numerous other financial support and debtor relief programs. After all, the Punto Final program, as its name indicates, was intended to finalize the bailout of the banking sector and the debtor relief program in Mexico. There also were other positive developments – growth, increased banking sector income, and foreign entry into banking – which improved the condition of banks and the supply of credit during this period.

Nevertheless, despite the difficulties of attribution, we note that the banking system did show some improvements in indicators of asset quality, profitability, and capital adequacy during the years 1997–2000, and that Punto Final may have played a role in those improvements. At the end of 2000, almost all banks complied with the minimum requirement of 8 percent of risk-weighted assets, with an average capital adequacy ratio (excluding intervened banks) of about 14 percent. Return on average assets has increased from close to zero in 1995 to 0.9 percent in 2000, but is still low and there is substantial variance in profitability across banks. Indicators of asset quality have improved as well over recent years. For example, past due loans to total loans excluding FOBAPROA decreased from 17.6 percent in 1997 to 8.5 percent in 2000. The improvements in asset quality largely reflect the conclusion of debtor relief programs through the Punto Final program (IMF 2001).

However, even with additional debt relief offered under the Punto Final program, bank lending did not restart as expected. Bank credit to the private sector has contracted from about 19 percent of GDP at end-1998 to 10 percent of GDP at end-2000. The lending environment during this period continued to be negatively affected by the difficulty banks face in repossessing collateral or receiving fair treatment in bankruptcy. The ratio of repossessed collateral to total loans excluding FOBAPROA has remained fairly stable during the period 1997–2000 increasing only slightly from 1.5 percent in 1997 to 1.7 percent in 2000 (IMF 2001). However, Mexico has since made significant progress in improving its bankruptcy framework and asset resolution process, and repossession of collateral has become easier.

Lessons from the Case Study
The conditional sharing of loan-losses can help achieve the recognition of loan-losses by banks, can clean up borrowers' and banks' balance sheets, and indirectly can improve the capital base of financial institutions by encouraging loan repayment. Also, as banks share in the loan-losses, it offers incentives for banks to engage in corporate restructuring and therefore may indirectly improve debtor capacity. The selectivity that comes from conditional programs like Punto Final can result in better targeting of taxpayer resources toward borrowers that were worth saving, because of the type of borrowers that will self-select into the program. In the case of Punto Final, resource savings and effectiveness probably were enhanced by the fact that the program focused primarily on SMEs and other small borrowers, which are less likely to be entwined in the all-too-often corrupt iron triangle of banks, conglomerates, and government officials. Furthermore, by linking assistance to new credit supplied by banks, the Punto Final program helped to further its goal of restarting the credit supply process more than an across-the-board subsidization of write-downs would. Finally, because conditional subsidization requires borrowers to share somewhat in the costs of financial sector subsidies, the adverse incentive effects of these subsidies for future borrowing and

lending behavior will be less than for unconditional subsidies of write downs. For all of these reasons, conditional subsidization of loan-losses through a program like Punto Final seems superior to across the board subsidization of loan write-downs by banks, as in the Japanese case.

By contrast, there are three major limitations to applying the Punto Final model as a resolution strategy. First, the successful implementation of selectivity still depends on the efficiency of the legal system to encourage participation. The incentive of borrowers to participate depends both on the stick of the enforcement of creditors' rights and the carrot of future credit supply (which in turn depends on the existence of creditors' rights). Mexico's implementation of Punto Final coincided with a complete reform of the bankruptcy process and the laws for perfecting collateral interests. Although those initiatives were still ongoing at the time, both borrowers and lenders had reason to believe that creditors' rights were being boosted in the future, and that both the carrot and the stick available to creditors were getting bigger.

Second, to the extent that selectivity creates potential for corruption in allocating subsidies, selectivity is less desirable. We were unable to undertake a microeconomic analysis of the Punto Final program to determine the extent to which the allocation of assistance was executed fairly and efficiently, owing to a lack of available data. That lack of data, in part, seems to reflect the political climate of Mexico and the political controversies that surround debt relief programs. Ironically, without proper disclosure and the opportunity to analyze the use of government funds, it will continue to be difficult for the Mexican public or academic researchers to have confidence in the appropriateness of the disposition of taxpayer resources.

Third, if the goal is a large-scale restructuring of the financial system, the microeconomic advantages of selectivity must be traded off against the macroeconomic advantages of large-scale improvements in corporate debt capacity and bank net worth. For that reason, to be effective, the Punto Final model would have to be applied to a significant share of the population of borrowers (not just SMEs). The strengths of Punto Final, however, are mainly confined to assistance to SMEs, where concerns about corruption in the implementation of selectivity, and concerns about inefficient use of resources to prop up powerful conglomerates may not be as great.

Finally, we note that conditional subsidies and across-the-board write-down subsidies share some of the same limitations. Neither approach distinguishes among banks with respect to the allocation of assistance.

Indeed, banks that made the worst lending decisions prior to the crisis will receive the most assistance after the crisis. Thus neither approach does much to address the adverse-selection and moral-hazard problems of providing assistance to insolvent banks.

Another common feature, and weakness, is that both subsidization approaches depend for their success on the legal and regulatory context in which the subsidies are offered, and especially on (1) a credible supervisory authority with sufficient enforcement capacity to provide incentives for financial institutions to recognize losses and engage in corporate restructuring and (2) an efficient legal system for enforcing collateralization and other lending laws, including a bankruptcy system to encourage corporate restructuring to occur. Without the first element, banks may prefer not to pursue restructuring, and without the second, neither banks nor borrowers may see the same incentives to resolving their debts and entering the market for new credit.

2.4 Debt Forgiveness

This approach uses some combination of legal innovations, the government's power to determine the numeraire and medium of exchange, or taxpayer resources to change the value of corporate or bank debts or to forgive part or all of borrowers' or banks' debts. The objective of debt forgiveness is to reduce the debt overhang problem, and improve the repayment capacity of bank borrowers and banks. Debt forgiveness results in an across the board corporate and banking system restructuring.

As examples of debt forgiveness programs, we consider the suspension of gold convertibility in the United States from December 1861 until January 1879, and the abrogation of the gold standard and gold payment clauses in debt contracts in the United States in the 1930s, both of which involved substantial changes in laws and monetary arrangements to achieve their desired results with no fiscal cost to the government.

The Legal Tender Bailout of Debtors and Banks
during the U.S. Civil War
The U.S. Civil War, which began in March 1861, had created an unexpected surge in the financing needs of the Union. An initially unsuccessful campaign to raise funds at low cost was rescued by the actions of a consortium of banks from the major Eastern cities in the fall of 1861, which intended to distribute the securities to other investors over the course of the ensuing months. Unfortunately, for those bankers, the December 1861 Report of

the Secretary of the Treasury shocked financial markets with its (realistic) view of war expenditure needs and with the Secretary's decision not to seek large additional tax increases. Government debt markets also were depressed by the growing risk of a war with Great Britain. Government debt prices fell and the money center banks, which were still holding a massive amount of the government debt that they had just purchased, were suddenly exposed to the risk of insolvency and bank runs.

The immediate solution was a suspension of convertibility of private bank notes and deposits into gold (the standard of value at the time). The longer-term solution (adopted in February 1862 and envisioned to last as long as wartime finance depressed the value of government debts) was to change the numeraire of the economy from gold to a new form of fiat government currency issue, known variously as U.S. notes, treasury notes, legal tender notes, or greenbacks. The legal tender act also created a new financing option for the government, which would rely on currency issues to fund a large fraction of its wartime expenditures. Thus did the United States embark on its first experiment with legal tender fiat currency, despite the fact that many observers doubted the constitutional power of the government to issue such currency or to make it a legal tender for the settlement of private dollar-denominated debts. By redenominating bank debts into the same depreciated numeraire as bank assets (i.e., government securities), banks' solvency was restored and the financial crisis was resolved. The use of legal tender currency to end the crisis within the banking system was a conscious goal of the legislation (Mitchell 1903 and Hammond 1970).

Creditors and depositors suffered from the depreciation of their claims that resulted from the depreciation of the dollar, but the dollar's depreciation was temporary; by the end of 1866, the dollar had returned to roughly 80 percent of its prewar value. In the meantime, depositors and creditors had gained from the avoidance of massive borrower insolvency and bank failures, which surely would have produced significant adverse macroeconomic consequences. In the event, the early 1860s were a time of prosperity for the U.S. economy (Burns and Mitchell 1946).

Did the legal tender acts undermine the credibility of the U.S. financial and legal system? The long-term costs of the bailout seem to have been negligible. Although inflation risk continued to be a problem in the United States because of the risk of a further change in the monetary standard until the Gold Standard Act of 1900 (Calomiris 1993b), the effects on interest rates were mild, and the late nineteenth century was a time of growth.

The legal tender acts were not reversed immediately after the war, although the government continued to promise an eventual return to gold convertibility at the prewar parity. The constitutionality of legal tender laws was upheld by the courts. President Grant packed the Supreme Court with legal tender advocates to ensure that the Court would not declare the law unconstitutional. Government currency thus became a permanent component of the money supply. Over time, it became increasingly evident that the use of the legal tender acts had been an exceptional act to deal with exceptional circumstances, which may explain why the long-run consequences of the devaluation were so small. The resumption of gold convertibility was achieved on January 1, 1879, requiring that greenbacks be convertible into gold at the prewar parity.

The Suspension of the Gold Standard and Abrogation
of Gold Clauses in the United States
Over the past decade, it has become a matter of widespread agreement that worldwide deflation under the gold standard propelled the world into a depression in the 1930s (Temin 1989 and Eichengreen 1992). An important channel through which deflation promoted depression was the rising real value of debts (Keynes 1931, Fisher 1933, Bernanke 1983, and Calomiris 1993a). As real debt values rose, borrowers became insolvent and were unable to meet fixed debt service from shrinking cash flows. Defaults on bank loans produced bank distress, further worsening the ability of the financial system to allocate funds properly. Wicker (1996) and Calomiris and Mason (2003b, 2003c) find that bank distress in the United States in the early 1930s was largely a consequence of loan-loss problems, rather than liquidity crises per se, and that bank distress was important in deepening the Depression.

President Roosevelt's interest in gold devaluation did not originate from a belief that debt deflation and its effects on credit supply had exacerbated the Depression. Rather, his interest in the gold value of the dollar was primarily linked to his view that raising commodity prices, per se, was crucial to economic recovery. Presidents Hoover and Roosevelt both subscribed to the (now discredited) view that policies that kept wages and prices higher would lead to higher incomes. Despite Roosevelt's initial assurances to the markets that he would not devalue the dollar, by May 1933 he had reversed course, and had received authority from Congress to devalue the dollar with respect to gold. The retreat from unqualified support for the gold standard produced gold outflows and a decline in the value of the dollar.

There was, however, a hitch in the Administration's plan to devalue the dollar to reflate incomes. Unlike the situation in 1861 (indeed, *because* of the policies that had been implemented in 1861) the structure of debt contracts had changed toward the use of gold clauses – contractual protections against devaluation of the dollar that preserved the gold value of nominal debt. The change in the numeraire of private debts and bank deposits during the Civil War had been achieved by establishing a new Constitutional right of the government to redefine the meaning of the dollar. The courts ultimately upheld the government's view that the Constitution granted the federal government both the right to define the value of the dollar and to issue legal tender notes.

One of the long-term consequences of this new breadth of government power over the definition and supply of dollars was the use of gold clauses in both private and public debt offerings. Gold clauses eschewed the use of the dollar as a unit of value, and in so doing, intended to preserve the value of debt obligations no matter what monetary standards the government might adopt for the dollar. Issuers employed gold clauses to eliminate an inflation risk premium from the cost of debt service, and the courts consistently ruled that private parties could use gold clauses to avoid the risk of legal tender changes in the value of the dollar (Kroszner 1999). Virtually all long-term corporate debt contracts and many mortgages in existence by the 1930s contained gold clauses (Macaulay 1938 and Friedman and Schwartz 1963).

The problem for Roosevelt's devaluation strategy was that devaluation would reduce the gold value of income relative to the gold value of debt service (preserved by gold clauses) and risk massive insolvencies for debtors as the result of devaluation. The Administration's response to this conundrum was to try, once again, to establish new constitutional rights – this time, the federal government's right to forbid transacting in gold and its right to abrogate existing gold clauses in private debt contracts. On June 5, 1933, Congress passed a joint resolution declaring gold clauses unenforceable and "against public policy" (Kroszner 1999), and allowing gold-denominated debt obligations to be paid at face value in dollars. During the ensuing months, Roosevelt also acted to devalue the dollar by even more than he had been authorized to do in May 1933.

The abrogation of gold clauses, which amounted to a 69 percent reduction in the value of firms' outstanding debts, was greeted with revulsion by many defenders of the sanctity of contracts, who decried the unconstitutional and unprecedented nature of the intrusion into private contracting.

Legal battles raged, culminating on February 18, 1935, in the dramatic 5–4 decision by the Supreme Court, which found in favor of the constitutionality of gold clause abrogation.

Kroszner (1999) analyzes the responses of various types of securities to the Supreme Court decision and finds that stock and bond prices went up when the decision was announced, and that bonds of firms facing the highest probability of bankruptcy gained the most. Kroszner interprets the increase in the market value of debts with gold clauses as an indication that the abrogation of the clauses raised the probability of repayment such that the value improvement from a higher repayment probability more than offset the depreciation in value from the change in the numeraire. From the standpoint of the debtholders, Kroszner argues, it was "better to forgive than to receive."

These results provide powerful evidence in favor of the usefulness of debt forgiveness as a means of solving coordination problems in renegotiating debt. Few individual creditors would have been willing voluntarily to remove gold clauses from the debts they held, but when all of them were forced to do so collectively, the improvement in aggregate economic circumstances made creditors and debtors better off. Similarly, the losses borne by depositors from depreciation in the value of deposits as the result of abandoning the gold standard were offset to some extent by the reduction in banking distress produced by currency depreciation.

Did the Supreme Court decision undermine investor confidence in the rule of law and in the stability of monetary policy and the value of the currency? Apparently not. Market participants seem to have understood that the Court's decision reflected the practical difficulties under the extreme circumstances of the Depression, and the threat posed by massive corporate bankruptcy, from doing otherwise. Growth continued at a fast pace from 1933 through the fall of 1937, waves of bank failures ceased, and the exchange rate and price level remained stable.

Lessons from the Case Studies

By employing legal powers to bailout debtors, the 1861 and 1933 policy actions avoided any direct fiscal costs from the bailout. Of course, all bailouts are financed by someone. In the case of legally mandated reductions in the real value of debt, debtholders and bank depositors are the source of financing for debt reduction. But, as Kroszner (1999) shows, they also may be net beneficiaries of the policy if the favorable macroeconomic consequences of the bailout increase the probability that the obligations they are holding will be repaid. Furthermore, to the extent that creditors and depositors are taxpayers, one must consider the counterfactual costs depositors would have borne from alternative approaches to financing the bailout, which would have been substantial. In the cases we examined, the costs borne by creditors and depositors were mild, and perhaps on net, creditors and depositors benefited from the policies.

More generally, the advantages of debt forgiveness illustrated by these two cases are three: The first two advantages are effectiveness and speed of action in resolving corporate and banking sector problems. Debt forgiveness recognizes loan-losses and deals with them, thus providing immediate relief to borrowers. It also can be a source of, and an encouragement of, the speedy rebuilding of bank balance sheets. Whether financial institutions' capital is strengthened depends on the extent to which: (1) debt relief substantially improves the probability of loan repayment, (2) depositor debts are also depreciated alongside bank loans (or subsidized directly by the government), and (3) the government or financial institutions provide additional capital after losses are recognized. The third advantage of debt forgiveness is its simplicity, which makes it far less dependent on the quality of legal, regulatory, and political institutions than more complicated alternatives like government-owned asset management companies (AMCs) or the Punto Final program.

A disadvantage of debt forgiveness is that it does not impose losses on corporate borrowers and bank shareholders. Therefore, it may create incentives for poor risk management by borrowers and banks. To the extent that debt forgiveness is only used in extreme circumstances (like the Civil War or the Great Depression), the moral hazard consequences from its use will be low; but if borrowers and bankers see governments as willing to employ this as a form of repeated countercyclical policy, borrower risk-taking will increase. Another disadvantage is the undermining of monetary institutions and the rule of law that comes from repeal of monetary standards and interference in private contracting. Here, too, the costs will depend on the frequency of use and the extent to which the market believes that the government reserves such drastic measures for truly exceptional circumstances.

Moral hazard by bankers and borrowers and reputational costs to the government may be reduced by limiting the amount of forgiveness and linking it to the performance of the borrower or bank debtor receiving forgiveness. But this approach is not practical if debt forgiveness is achieved via an across-the-board change in the real value of debt. But the across-the-board reduction in the real value of debt via a change in the numeraire of debt may still be preferable, given that it does not impose a fiscal burden (which selective bailouts necessarily entail), and given the advantages of speed and simplicity from across-the-board forgiveness noted earlier.

However, for debt forgiveness to be fully successful in restarting the credit supply process on a sound footing, additional conditions are necessary, including an efficient legal and bankruptcy system in credit markets to incentivize borrowers to continue to service the remainder of outstanding debt, and a supervisory framework that forces banks to take advantage of their improved circumstances by rebuilding their capital positions as need be.

2.5 Government-Owned Asset Management Company (AMC)

The establishment of a government-owned and government-managed AMC involves the transfer of nonperforming assets to a government-owned asset management company. The objective of an AMC is to accelerate corporate restructuring. This mechanism adopts a government-based, centralized approach to corporate restructuring. As examples of government-owned AMCs, we consider the cases of Securum and Retrieva in Sweden, and FOBAPROA in Mexico. For a review of AMCs in a select number of other countries, see Klingebiel (2000).

Securum and Retrieva in Sweden
Liberalization of financial sector regulation in Sweden during the 1980s, without an appropriate strengthening of the regulatory and supervisory system, led to a lending boom that fueled a protracted real estate boom (Berggren 1995). From 1987 to 1990, total credit rose from 90 percent of GDP to 140 percent of GDP. During that period, under a fixed exchange rate regime, firms started to borrow in foreign currency to take advantage of lower foreign interest rates. At end-1990, more than 50 percent of outstanding corporate debt was denominated in foreign currency (Drees and Pazarbasioglu 1998).

Tax reforms in the late 1990s that decreased the tax deductibility of interest expenses on real estate investments, in combination with a tightening of monetary policy and lower inflation, raised real after-tax lending rates considerably and contributed to a sharp drop in property and share prices. As a result, Sweden entered a deep recession, which in turn accelerated asset price deflation. In addition, the crisis led to very high interest rates (up to 500 percent) and to a substantial depreciation of the Swedish krona when it started to float in 1992.

Both developments considerably undermined the capability of many borrowers to service their debt and resulted in rising loan-losses in financial institutions, which started to mount during 1991. In the fall of 1991, it became clear that two of the six major banks, Första Sparbanken and Nordbanken, needed to be recapitalized to fulfill their capital requirements. As the state was the major owner of Nordbanken, it injected additional capital into the bank, becoming the owner of 77 percent of the outstanding shares. It also issued a guarantee to the owners of Första Sparbanken for a loan that enabled the bank to fulfill its capital requirement.

In the spring of 1992, it was evident that Nordbanken's problems were considerably more serious than anticipated. Subsequently, the state bought all the remaining outstanding shares. In November 1992, the state injected SEK 10 billion to absorb losses related to provisions for probable loan-losses and split Nordbanken into two entities by transferring most of the nonperforming loans to Securum, an AMC. Securum took over assets with a book value of SEK 67 billion, accounting for 4.4 percent of total banking assets. Assets transferred were mostly real estate–related loans.

In September 1992, it became apparent that Gota Bank would not meet its capital adequacy requirements and the largest owner, Trygg Hansa, refused to provide the bank with additional funds. To calm markets, the government immediately announced a guarantee to Gota's creditors, which was later extended to all other banks (Berggren 1995). In the same month, Gota declared bankruptcy. In December 1992, the government acquired Gota Bank and issued a statement that the bank would be sold immediately. To facilitate the sale, as in the case of Nordbanken, the government split Gota Bank into two entities. Problem loans (most of which were real estate related) totaling SEK 43 billion, or 3 percent of total bank assets, were transferred to a subsidiary, Retrieva, which was to operate as an AMC, leaving the remaining entity to focus on normal banking business.

In December 1992, the government addressed the banking sector weakness more comprehensively and parliament passed the Bank Support Act authorizing the government to provide support flexibly in the form of loan guarantees, capital contributions and other appropriate measures. The Act also formally confirmed the government guarantee on all liabilities. To support the objectives of the Act, parliament set up a separate agency, the Bank Supervisory Authority, which had the authority to decide and manage bank support operations. During 1993, Nordbanken and Gota Bank were merged, retaining the name Nordbanken, and becoming Sweden's fourth largest bank. The bank was operationally restructured and later sold to the private sector. Their respective AMCs – Securum and Retrieva – were merged in December 1995.

The main tasks of the AMCs were to maximize the remaining economic value of the loans transferred. During the first phase of their operations, the AMCs focused their activities on making decisions as to whether to have the debtors file for bankruptcy. In the majority of cases, the AMCs forced the debtors into bankruptcy, taking over the collateral (in most cases real estate property) and leaving the AMCs with the task of disposing of the real estate assets. For example, Securum was the owner of 2500 properties with an estimated market value of SEK 15–20 billion, corresponding to 1–2 percent of all commercial real estate in Sweden (Englund 1999).

Securum sold its real estate assets through public offerings on the Stockholm stock exchange and private sales to companies and individuals. Most of the assets were sold in 1995 and 1996, when the real estate market had started to recover, but nevertheless, prices were still low by historical standards. Securum wrapped up operations much faster than originally envisaged and it was dissolved at the end of 1997.

As the earlier summary illustrates, Securum and Retrieva were not only successful in selling off their assets but also recovered substantial amounts from the disposal of their assets. Several factors contributed to their success. First and most important, the AMCs could rely not only on a strong judicial framework but also on an efficient judicial system, which allowed them to force most of their debtors into bankruptcy when their operations did not prove to be economically viable. The restructuring of the assets also was facilitated by the fact that most of the assets transferred were real estate-related assets. Real estate is easy to restructure from a political standpoint, because restructuring does not tend to involve large layoffs. In addition, the operations of the asset management operations also benefited from a skilled management team, strong governance mechanisms that insured the agency's independence, a limited amount of assets being transferred, and the provision of adequate funding (Klingebiel 2000).

FOBAPROA in Mexico
Starting in December 1994, Mexico suffered a systemic banking crisis, resulting from a banking system characterized by initial low levels of capital at the time of privatization, imprudent lending behavior, poor accounting practices and disclosure, weak regulatory and supervisory environment, and a weak legal and judicial framework in which debtors could default

on their loans with little consequences (Mulas 2001). Connected lending was prevalent, as ownership dispersion requirements and rules separating banks and industrial firms were insufficient to avoid potential conflicts of interest (La Porta, Lopez-de-Silanes, and Zamarripa 2003).

In response to the financial meltdown toward the end of 1994, the government initiated several programs to support the banking system. Most of these programs were implemented through the Fund for the Protection of Bank Savings (FOBAPROA). One of these programs was the Loan Purchase and Recapitalization Program, which exchanged delinquent loans held by banks for government-issued bonds, to recapitalize banks that were undercapitalized.

FOBAPROA was originally created in 1990 as a deposit guarantee agency. FOBAPROA's mandate was broadened as a result of the banking crisis in 1996 beyond deposit insurance responsibilities to make it a bank rescue and intervention agency as well as an asset management company (Mackey 1999). We will focus on FOBAPROA in its function as an asset management company.

The FOBAPROA program failed at asset resolution. In late 1996, the Valuacion y Venta de Activos (VVA) was created as a supporting agent in the sale of FOBAPROA's assets. The VVA's activities were hindered by a number of obstacles. First, initially the government restricted financial institutions including the VVA from foreclosing on assets, because the selling bank remained the loan's legal owner. Second, the sheer size of impaired assets made it difficult to restructure debt and sell assets. At the peak of the program, FOBAPROA held more than 50 percent of the loans in the system. Third, the large scale and the type of assets transferred to FOBAPROA, that is, corporate and politically connected loans, were difficult to resolve for a government agency susceptible to political pressure. The asset transfer was a nontransparent and repeated process that led to perceptions that some banks received more favorable treatment than others. Fourth, VVA's due diligence process was complex and lengthy, as the documentation of loans remained with the banks that administered or held the loans. Fifth, the responsibilities of the VVA and FOBAPROA were poorly defined, complicating the relationship between the two agencies (Mulas 2001).

In June 1997, the resolution activities of the VVA and FOBAPROA were merged into a single agency, the Direccion de Activos Corporativos (DAC), which became the sole agency overseeing corporate asset recovery. In its new function, DAC oversaw and coordinated the corporate debt resolution process of FOBAPROA's loan portfolio.

The sale of impaired assets was mainly through cash collections from auctions. However, DAC experienced problems in selling off assets for some of the same problems as faced by its predecessor. The absence of a secondary market made cash collections from auctions a difficult approach, politically connected loans were difficult to resolve for a government-agency susceptible to political pressure, and substantial deficiencies in the bankruptcy and foreclosure code that limited DAC's ability to bring debtors to the negotiation table. Thus far, only 0.5 percent of the total assets transferred under the FOBAPROA program have been sold, with an average asset recovery rate of only 15 percent (IMF 2003).

The FOBAPROA program also did not have the desired result of reinvigorating the banking sector. Credit to the private sector fell considerably over the period 1995 to 1998. As a share of GDP, private credit dropped from 39 percent at end-1994 to 19 percent at end-1998.

In early 1999, FOBAPROA was disbanded and the assets under its custody were transferred to a new deposit insurance agency, the Bank Savings Protection Institute (IPAB), which was given the authority to manage and dispose of closed banks' assets.

An additional failure of FOBAPROA was that funds were illegally transferred to Mexico's powerful elite. Under the opposition's pressure, the government decided to have an independent audit of the FOBAPROA program, including the loans under FOBAPROA's custody, to be carried out by a Canadian auditor, Michael Mackey. However, the strict bank secrecy laws in Mexico inhibited a thorough examination of the debts transferred to FOBAPROA and allegations of corruption.[3]

The FOBAPROA experience shows that corporate restructuring is hindered if there are inadequate bankruptcy laws and a lack of experienced judges and bankruptcy trustees to effectively manage bankruptcies. Above all, the Mexican experience shows that political-economy factors can profoundly affect the success of government policies through the corruption of the recapitalization process. Recapitalization and asset resolution programs per se do not encourage a restart of lending, especially in a country in which imprudent lending behavior and politically-connected lending are widespread.

---

[3] Mackey (1999) reports that about $7.3 billion of the loans (or more than 10 percent of total loans) transferred to FOBAPROA did not meet the criteria established for inclusion in the Loan Purchase and Recapitalization Program, and that just over $600,000 of those loans was of illegal origin.

Lessons from the Case Studies

In theory, AMCs seem to offer tempting prospects for avoiding many of the shortcomings of market-based solutions. Potential advantages include: (1) economies of scale in administering workouts (as workouts require specialized, and often scarce, skills) and in forming and selling portfolios of assets; (2) benefits from the granting of special powers to the government agency to expedite loan resolution in an environment of weak market incentives and legal institutions; and (3) the interposing of a disinterested third party between bankers and clients, which might break "crony capitalist" connections that otherwise impede efficient transfers of assets from powerful enterprises. The latter may seem particularly beneficial in emerging markets, in which ownership concentration and connections between industrial conglomerates and banks are often very close.

Sweden's AMCs provide examples of some of these potential advantages, but other countries found it difficult to realize those advantages. First, government agents may lack the information and skills of (more highly compensated and incentivized) private market participants. Second, government agencies do not operate in a vacuum; they, too, are creatures of the societies that create them, and government agents must negotiate, rather than dictate, solutions, just as private market participants must do. In negotiations with government agencies and private participants alike, the strength of one's position depends on one's "threat point" (the ability to credibly threaten adverse consequences to one's bargaining opponent, if agreement is not reached).

In an environment where legal, regulatory, and political institutions are weak, the threat point of government officials in restructuring negotiations is substantially curtailed. Uncooperative firms and banks may have little incentive to participate in government initiatives or to settle on reasonable prices if failing to do so has no adverse consequence for them. In an environment in which powerful business leaders do not fear legal or regulatory consequences, and where appeal can be made to corrupt politicians or bureaucrats for protection, even a well-meaning and competent AMC negotiator has little chance of being effective. Thus, the notion that AMCs avoid the dependence on the quality of the legal and regulatory environment that undermines market-based solutions is mistaken because it fails to take into account the effects of weak institutional environments on the ability of AMCs to achieve their objectives (Klingebiel 2000). Third, AMC officials are subject to special incentive problems (corruption and political pressure to favor certain borrowers or to avoid layoffs at large firms), which can make them less willing to push for effective solutions. AMCs tend to be least effective when the transfer of assets amounts to a large share of total system assets, which tends to increase the politicization of the workout process. The problems of poorly structured incentives and large program size tend to magnify each other. Mexico's FOBAPROA was made increasingly unsuccessful as the lack of credible loss sharing on the downside encouraged overparticipation.

Because AMCs can be a means of transferring enormous subsidies to certain banks, firms, and individuals, they often create enormous costs in the form of moral hazard. Whether loan-losses are recognized by banks after the establishment of an AMC depends on the transfer price of assets determined by the managers of the AMC. Bank loan-losses are not recognized if assets are transferred at a price above market value, resulting in a back-door bank recapitalization. An AMC also does not impose losses on corporate borrowers, and therefore, does not set incentives to improve borrower behavior in the future. In fact, it may offer special arrangements to benefit certain borrowers, or avoid pressuring certain debtors to sell, or effectively pass through assistance to cronies through overpriced purchases of loans to connected banks. A related point is that corporate loans, particularly of large conglomerates, are the hardest type of loans to resolve through AMCs, because they are most prone to political influence peddling.

2.6 Government-Assisted Sale of Financial Institutions to Foreign Banks

In some cases, governments have turned to new strategic investors – typically foreign investors – to assume ownership of failing banks. This mechanism is usually a government-assisted sale, with assistance usually taking the form of government sharing of loan-losses to some extent, and also the relaxation of preexisting limits on the activities of foreign banks. The objective of such a sale is to improve the efficiency and the capital base of financial institutions in the country. This resolution mechanism is a government-based and centralized approach to bank restructuring. Because actual corporate restructuring is left to the market, a government-assisted sale of financial institutions is a decentralized approach to corporate restructuring.

To what extent can the sale of distressed domestic banks to foreign entrants substitute for preserving domestic banking franchises? Foreign bank entry is a large potential source of new capital, and one that is less likely to be diverted to value-destroying investments. And foreign entrants into distressed banking systems tend to enjoy a relatively low cost of capital, because they have not suffered capital destroying loan-losses, and because they are better able to raise new capital because the absence of loan-losses also means that markets will impose lower adverse-selection discounts on any new bank capital offerings (Calomiris and Wilson 2004).

Although there is evidence that foreign entry enhances the efficiency and stability of banking systems (Demirgüç-Kunt, Levine, and Min 1998), it can take time for foreign entrants to establish information about borrowers and familiarity with local legal and institutional arrangements. Calomiris and Carey (1994) find that foreign bank entrants into the United States during the U.S. bank "capital crunch" of the 1980s tended to lend disproportionately to lower-risk borrowers, tended to purchase rather than originate loans, and tended to act as syndicate participants rather than lead managers. Furthermore, despite their conservative loan purchases and originations, foreign banks tended to suffer worse loan-losses in the United States than domestic banks in the early 1990s, which further suggests an information cost disadvantage. Although relaxing barriers to foreign entry is clearly a crucial part of resolving a credit crunch and reforming long-term lending practices, foreign bank lending may not be a perfect substitute for domestic bank lending in the short run. At the same time, if foreign entrants can acquire existing franchises and human capital along with their acquisition of assets and real estate, they could make immediate inroads into lending to firms of all kinds.

Another limitation of foreign banking may be its reliability as a source of continuing future credit. Some observers have voiced a concern that foreign banks will be more likely to flee in the future if economic conditions deteriorate (cf. Chapter 7 in this volume). In theory, that could occur because global banks have the option to shift capital among the countries in which they operate, and consequently may reduce their allocation of credit more in reaction to adverse changes in the economy than a domestic bank would.

To gain perspectives into the benefits and potential limitations of foreign bank entry we consider two important recent cases of foreign entry in emerging markets: Argentina and Mexico during the 1990s.

Foreign Entry into Argentine Banking
Argentina, like much of Latin America, had suffered high inflation, economic decline, financial distress, and sovereign default during the 1980s. It

embarked on a major financial and economic liberalization program at the beginning of the 1990s. The program sought to bring an end to hyperinflation (through a credible commitment to dollar convertibility of the peso), privatize state-owned enterprises (including public banks), deregulate the financial system, abolish deposit insurance, and deregulate foreign capital flows. All of these elements were attractive to foreign banks, particularly given the backwardness of the Argentine banking system. The potential for growth of deposits and loans was enormous and the operating inefficiency of the domestic banks was apparent in both large quantities of bad loans and high physical costs of operations.

Foreign banks were permitted to participate fully in the recovery of the financial sector from the beginning, and they became important players from an early date. Total credit to the private sector rose from 10 percent of GDP in 1990 to 19 percent in 1994. As early as 1994, foreign lenders accounted for 25.4 percent of personal loans, 10.3 percent of mortgages, and 19 percent of commercial loans (Dages, Goldberg, and Kinney 2000).

When the spillover effects of the Mexican tequila crisis hit Argentina in 1995, foreign banks played a growing role in credit markets. Foreign banks had lower risk loan portfolios, and hence lower losses during the crisis, and their sources of capital were relatively immune to the local shock. These differences put them in a position to grow their lending and to expand their franchises through the acquisition of weak institutions. Had the tequila crisis been perceived as undermining the long-run desirability of operating in Argentina, the reaction would have been different but, in the event, foreigners viewed the adverse shock as a short-term problem, and therefore, a window of opportunity to build for the future.

By 1999, the foreign-owned bank share in personal lending had grown to 45.8 percent, the share of mortgage lending stood at 31.9 percent, and the commercial lending share was 53.2 percent (Dages, Goldberg, and Kinney 2000). The number and countries of origin of foreign bank entrants were also large and diverse. Major acquisition deals involved new foreign entrants such as Banco Santander, Banco Bilbao Vizcaya, HSBC, Bank of Nova Scotia, Bank Austria, Caisse Nationale de Credit Agricole, Chile's Abinsa and O'Higgins banks, and Brazil's Banco Itau, which joined the already established foreign banks (Citibank, Bank of Boston, ABN AMRO, and Lloyds). Probit analysis of foreign banks' acquisition behavior (Cull 1998) indicates that foreign banks looked for large acquirees as a means to gain market share. The tolerance for weak targets of acquisition, and the desire to build market share quickly made foreign entry particularly valuable.

Foreign bank entry initially was concentrated in the capital city, where foreign banks lent 88.5 percent of their loan portfolio in 1997, compared to only 40.8 percent for private domestic banks, but in provinces that privatized their public banks, foreign bank credit grew rapidly after 1995 (World Bank 1998). Foreign banks also initially supplied credit to sectors that were relatively neglected by domestic banks. In particular, foreign banks were much more focused on financing manufacturing sector growth; 29.8 percent of their loans went to that sector, in contrast to only 13.1 percent for private domestic banks. Foreign banks maintained comparable or slightly better loan portfolio quality than other private banks, indicating a comparable or slightly lower risk loan clientele. For the period 1997–1998, on average, nonperforming loans as a fraction of total loans were 9.7 percent for foreign retail banks and 8.0 percent for foreign wholesale banks. Private domestic retail banks had average nonperforming loan (NPL) ratios comparable to foreign banks (9 percent), but higher median NPL ratios. The average NPL ratio for private domestic wholesale banks was 19.4 percent (Calomiris and Powell 2001). Clearly, foreign bank entry was providing a large, increasingly diverse, and growing supply of credit to the Argentine economy.

The presence of active foreign bank acquirers with available capital also spurred the privatization of many distressed public banks, which otherwise would have been difficult to resolve. From 1995 to 1999, 15 banks were privatized. Privatization also was encouraged by the existence of a special fund, subsidized by the World Bank and other multilateral agencies, to encourage provinces to privatize their public banks (Calomiris and Powell 2001).

The entry of foreign banks contributed to the stability of the economy in the late 1990s, too, both because of their immediate effect in supplying credit in response to the tequila shock, and because of the long-run stabilizing effect of their presence. From the fourth quarter of 1994 to the fourth quarter of 1995 (the window of the tequila crisis) foreign bank lending grew at a 12 percent annual rate, which was higher than the growth rate of private domestic banks. From the end of 1995 through the end of 1999, foreign banks' loan growth was greater than 22 percent per year, which also was higher than domestic private banks' loan growth (Dages, Goldberg, and Kinney 2000).

The long-run stabilizing effect of foreign entry largely operated through the leeway that foreign bank entry and robust loan growth gave regulators to strengthen and enforce the regulation and supervision of the banking sector. Without the robust growth of foreign lending, regulatory discipline would have required the scaling back of lending, which would have been more difficult politically.

Although foreign bank entrants had been patient acquirers of long-term assets and relationships throughout the 1990s, government policy after 2000 has produced a general retreat of foreign investors from Argentina in which the banks have participated. The Argentine fiscal crisis created costs for the banks, first in the form of loan-losses produced by the recession, then in the form of losses because of government pressures on banks to purchase government securities and subsequent sovereign default, and later by "asymmetric pesification" of bank assets and liabilities. Beginning in late 2001, some foreign banks began to retreat from their distressed operations. Scotiabank refused to pump additional capital into its bank and instead abandoned Scotiabank Quilmes, writing off C$540 million. Credit Agricole abandoned its subsidiaries in 2002.

Foreign Entry into Mexican Banking

Mexico's history of foreign bank entry shares some features with Argentina's, but there are important differences. The Mexican government was far more reluctant to admit foreign entrants, and only established unfettered entry rules after 1997, fully two years after the tequila crisis. And because new foreign bank entrants came into the country after the collapse of the domestic financial system, and before a full resolution of the problem of nonpayment of debt, the short-term effects of foreign entry on loan supply understandably have not been as dramatic. Nevertheless, the effects of foreign bank entry on loan supply and on the improvement in the regulatory and supervisory regime have been significant.

The Mexican banking sector was reprivatized in the early 1990s after a decade-long experiment with state-controlled banking. The growth of domestic credit was phenomenal. From the middle of 1989 to the end of 1991, bank credit doubled. From the end of 1991 to the end of 1994, bank credit doubled again.

In a sense, Mexican privatization was doomed from the outset. Many of the privatized banks had massive quantities of low-quality or nonperforming loans at the time of their privatization, and privatization did not entail much in the way of paid in capital contributions by purchasers. Evergreening of bad loans was a firmly established practice even before the tequila crisis, a practice supported by dishonest accounting rules. This practice served the interests of the bank owners, as it helped them to claim to be in compliance with regulatory standards and thus to avoid the costs of recapitalizing the banks. Like the U.S. savings and loan institutions, Mexican banks were betting with someone else's money. Most of that betting took the form of risky peso-denominated lending, but Garber (1998) argues that banks also illegally used offshore derivatives positions to speculate against peso depreciation. And much of the bad lending was to connected enterprises. As is often the case in emerging markets, banks that receive subsidies from the government safety net often channel those to related firms through loans at concessional interest rates. Although Mexican law prohibited industrial firms from owning banks, it did not forbid the owners of industrial firms from owning banks.

So long as the dream of never-ending growth panned out, all would be well. Loans would be repaid and bank capital would accumulate. But that was not to be. Instead, the recession that began at the end of 1993 turned into the fiscal and monetary policy problems, and political chaos, of 1994. The government's policy – which consisted of a lack of fiscal reform, the growth of off-balance sheet fiscal costs, and unsustainable sterilization of reserve outflows – ultimately produced the currency collapse of December 1994, which was followed by massive private sector defaults, which made it unmistakably clear that the banking system was deeply insolvent.

The supply of credit within the banking sector slowed to a trickle after the crisis. Even forbearance was not enough to restart the credit process, for two reasons. First, the legal foundations of creditors' rights were in shambles. With the exception of profitable exporting firms (who had both the means and incentive to pay their debts, and who were less dependent on the Mexican legal system to enforce their contracts) there were few borrowers that could credibly commit to repay any new credit that was granted. Second, forbearance was no longer able to fully protect deeply insolvent banks from the consequences of their insolvency. Deeply insolvent banks had trouble keeping depositors, despite 100 percent deposit insurance. That fact reflected the growing size of the cost of the banking sector losses to taxpayers, which led people to question the government's process to bear all those losses.

Consider the difference between the interest paid on deposits by Bank Serfin (the weakest of the large domestic banks) and by Banamex (the strongest) a year after the tequila crisis. As of 1996, the average total cost of funds for Banamex was 17.37 percent, and for Serfin, 28.93 percent. As is often the case in emerging markets – even in the presence of some form of government insurance – the risk that insurance will not fully cover enormous losses can produce a large default risk premium. Also, some of the cost of funds difference reflected the fact that business depositors (the main holders of sight deposits) preferred to maintain relationships with banks that were likely to be survivors. Sight deposits represented only 12 percent of Serfin's funding sources, whereas they comprised 24 percent of Banamex's deposits. Bancomer, which was less well off than Banamex, but much better off than Serfin, had a 21.89 percent cost of funds and relied on sight deposits for 21 percent of its financing (Calomiris 1998).

In the post-tequila environment, domestic lending was not a growth area (because of the distress of borrowers and the lack of incentive for borrowers to repay debts). Banks that were relatively well off (e.g., Banamex, and to a lesser extent, Bancomer) focused on expanding their brick and mortar franchises to generate cheap deposits, and invested the proceeds in government securities. From 1995 to 1996, Banamex's branches grew from 716 to 912 and Bancomer grew from 885 branches to 1260. Serfin meantime grew slightly from 564 to 578 branches. Asset growth differences were similar: Banamex grew assets by 23 percent during 1996, and Bancomer grew assets 17 percent, while Serfin grew by 12 percent.

Interestingly, despite the limited opportunities for loan growth, the post-1995 period ushered in a new era of expansion in foreign bank presence in Mexico, but that entry did not occur immediately after the tequila crisis. At the time of the crisis, there were only two significant foreign banking franchises operating in Mexico, Citibank and Santander, and of the two, only Citibank (which had been granted an exemption to the ban on foreign control of banks, owing to its long-standing presence in Mexico, dating to the 1920s) was an active lender at the time. Citibank was still a small player, accounting for under 1 percent of banking system loans, and operating only six offices in Mexico City. The initiation of NAFTA in 1994 had begun a gradual and partial process of easing restrictions on foreign entry. Under NAFTA, no U.S. or Canadian bank could exceed 1.5 percent of the total domestic banking market through 1999, and the sum of all foreign banks shares could not exceed 8 percent in 1994 or 15 percent in 1999. In 2000, both the individual and aggregate limits were set to expire, except that foreign acquisitions would still be limited to prohibit any foreign acquirer from gaining more than 4 percent market share per year via acquisition. And for non-NAFTA foreigners, they were not permitted to own more than a 30 percent share in any financial group or commercial bank. These restrictions effectively meant that, as of 1994, no foreign bank could ever hope to acquire one of the largest domestic banks.

The crisis presented enormous growth opportunities for the two foreign banks that were in Mexico. Santander (which was operating seven branches of its Puerto Rican bank in Mexico under a special arrangement) had just begun operations in Mexico and was holding primarily Tesobonos (dollar-indexed assets) at the time of the crisis. It had received permission in advance of the crisis to hedge its exposures in dollars rather than in pesos. When the peso depreciated, its capital position soared and it rapidly became a significant lender to industrial firms. Because of its access to cheap capital and its ability to hedge dollar exposures abroad, it was able to grant three-year dollar-denominated loans to top-tier firms at a time when domestic banks were not offering such attractive terms.

Prior to the crisis, Citicorp had been developing an aggressive strategy for growing its Mexican business. Citicorp had preexisting relationships with many top Mexican firms, the most notable of which was Cemex, the largest company in Mexico and the fourth largest cement producer in the world. Like Santander, Citicorp benefited from the relative weakness of domestic banks after the crisis, particularly to serve the needs of large, high-quality firms for dollar loans and international payments services. Citicorp experienced a 250 percent rise in its Mexican liabilities within six months of the crisis.

The "demonstration effect" of showing clear advantages to the Mexican government and corporations from the presence of Santander and Citibank encouraged rules on foreign entry to be relaxed further. In 1996, after several months of negotiations and due diligence, Santander agreed to take control of Grupo Financiero Invermexico (GFInver) through the purchase of a 75 percent stake. This acquisition marked the first time that an international institution had acquired control of one of the 18 large Mexican banks privatized in the early 1990s. In 1996, Scotiabank (which had purchased an 8.5 percent interest in Inverlat in 1993) was permitted to purchase a controlling interest in that bank. Banco Bilbao Vizcaya Argentario (BBVA) was allowed to acquire Banco Mercantil Probursa in 1995 and Banca Cremi and Banco Oriente in 1996.

In 1997, control over the lower house of government changed hands, partly because political accusations of corruption and favoritism were bolstering the opposition. The FOBAPROA approach to asset resolution was in shambles (see Section 2.5). In 1998, the Mexican Congress approved foreign ownership of up to 100 percent in Mexican banks. In 1998, Citibank became the first U.S. lender to take control of a troubled Mexican bank, buying Banca Confia from the Mexican government for $195 million.

By 1998, foreign banks had come to hold 11.1 percent of consumer loans, 6.4 percent of mortgages, and 19.7 percent of commercial loans (Dages, Goldberg, and Kinney 2000), a remarkable increase from essentially zero in 1995. Dages, Goldberg, and Kinney (2000) find that foreign banks behaved similarly to healthy domestic banks in terms of loan growth. The key to foreign banks' abilities to operate in Mexico, and to help resolve the distress of the banking system, was their access to new capital.

In 2000, a major test of the regulatory authorities came, when the previously announced takeover of Bancomer by BBVA was challenged by a competing offer by Banamex, made on Mexican Independence Day. A combination of Banamex and Bancomer would have produced the best client list in Mexico, and an entity that would likely have benefited from becoming too important to be allowed to fail. From the standpoint of efficiency, competition, the avoidance of moral hazard, increasing access to capital, and putting an end to crony capitalism, the acquisition by BBVA was clearly superior, but Banamex was hoping that nationalism would help it win the day. In the event, the Mexican regulators and politicians did not blink, and BBVA was able to consummate the deal, leaving it with the largest bank franchise in Mexico.

Part of the reason for that landmark decision was that the entry of foreign banking in Mexico had already removed much of the pressure on the government to prop up its domestic banks. In that sense, foreign entry in Mexico was a "virtuous circle," where entry reinforced further entry by undermining the grip that the domestic banks had on the economy and the political and regulatory system. Foreign bank entry gave well-intentioned regulators and politicians an option other than crony capitalism, and they chose it. In addition to the acquisition of Bancomer, in 2000, Santander acquired Serfin, and in 2001, Citibank acquired Banamex, which no longer felt it could compete without the access to capital of a foreign parent institution. In 2002, HSBC bought all the shares of Bital, including those that had been purchased by ING Bank and Banco Santander previously, and added $800 million to Bital's capital.

Despite the rapid transformation and recapitalization of the Mexican banking system brought about by foreign entry, bank lending has been slow to recover, owing to the continuing problem of nonpayment, which has deeper legal roots in the problems of the bankruptcy law and court, and in other creditor rights laws and courts. The Mexican government attempted a total reform of the bankruptcy law and courts, and the law for collateralization, in 1999. Still, the laws have been challenged and legal risks have remained high.

Lessons from the Case Studies

The experiences of Argentina and Mexico cast a very favorable light on the role of foreign banks in resolving domestic bank distress. Government-assisted sales of banks to foreigners can be a cost-effective way to restore bank capital, and proper lending incentives. Foreign banks' access to capital and willingness to invest in long-term relationships allow them to compete very effectively for loans, and provide an important offset to the shrinkage in lending that occurs after the collapse of domestic banks. Unlike the experience of the United States in the 1980s (Calomiris and Carey 1994), in Argentina and Mexico foreign banks were able to enter all niches of the banking market successfully, perhaps because they did so more via acquisition, and because existing domestic banks were in distress. Also, contrary to the fear of foreign entry critics, banks did not flee from either Mexico or Argentina during the major crisis of 1995, but rather redoubled their investments, seeing the crises as windows of opportunity to expand. Several foreign banks, however, did leave Argentina in response to the 2001 crisis and resulting policy-induced losses.

Despite these advantages, which were reaped in both countries, Mexican bank credit has still been slow to grow, because of institutional problems in credit markets that are beyond the banks' control. Bank capital, by itself, does not restore borrowers' financial health, nor bolster creditors' rights enough to make arms-length lending profitable. This case illustrates that the advantages to foreign entry can only be fully reaped (especially in the area of SME lending) if legal institutions permit it. Indeed, some foreign entrants into Mexico have been disappointed by the slow pace of reform in the legal system. If these problems had been foreseen, it is possible that foreign entrants would have been more reluctant to commit capital to Mexico in the 1990s.

One important lesson that comes from both the Argentine and Mexican cases is that the presence of foreign banks helps to improve the regulatory structure of the countries that they enter. Not only do foreign banks directly impose competitive pressure on other banks; they increase competition indirectly by making it more likely that bank supervisors and regulators will decide to end forbearance, enforce bank regulations, and encourage further competition as the means for resolving the system's problems. In other words, the political economy of bank regulation is endogenous to the presence of foreign banks in a desirable way.

2.7 Government-Assisted Recapitalization

Although several of the other measures also implicitly involve government financial support boosting bank capital, this subsection relates to a resolution measure that directly involves the injection of government funds to recapitalize existing financial institutions. Being focused on the strengthening the bank's capital rather than its existing portfolio of assets, such government-assisted recapitalization still allows a decentralized approach to corporate restructuring, which can be left to the market. Whether government-assisted recapitalization is a government-based or market-based approach to bank restructuring depends on how government-assistance is structured.

As examples of government-assisted recapitalization, we consider the RFC-preferred stock program of the United States that began in March 1933, the recapitalization program of Japan beginning in 1998, and the restructuring program of Thailand that began in October 1997.

The Reconstruction Finance Corporation (RFC) in the United States
Measured by bank failure rates, depositor loss rates, or the extent of bank credit contraction, the Great Depression was, and remains, the largest and most persistent shock suffered by the U.S. banking system since (at least) the 1830s. The combination of the high failure rate and high depositor loss rate during the Depression produced a loss rate on total deposits in excess of 2 percent in 1933. Although these losses were large relative to previous U.S. experience, they are quite small relative to the experiences of many countries today.

Despite the "low" failure rates of banks in the 1930s compared to emerging market economies today, the consequences of bank distress for credit supply were large and protracted, as noted by Fisher (1933), Bernanke (1983), and Calomiris and Mason (2003c). Banks with high asset risk and low capital posed a large risk of default to depositors, and depositors withdrew funds as the risk of default rose. The consequence of market discipline was that banks faced strong incentives to contract credit supply before they failed. Market discipline resulted from the fact that the government safety net for banks was quite limited. Assistance during the 1930s included loans from the Fed, loans and (after March 1933) preferred stock purchases from the RFC, and federal deposit insurance on small deposits beginning in 1934. Deposit insurance was limited to small deposits and banks that were insolvent in 1933 were not permitted to qualify for deposit insurance in 1934. And, as we shall see, loans and preferred stock were supplied in a way that limited the potential abuse of such assistance.

Although market discipline was present in the 1930s, and insolvent banks were allowed to fail, the removal of bank assets from bankers' control did not imply the speedy resolution of borrowers' distress. Non-performing loans of insolvent banks were not liquidated quickly during the Depression. As in many crisis countries today, as the stock of failed banks' loans accumulated, the speed of loan resolution slowed. This loan resolution backlog effect is analyzed by Anari, Kolari, and Mason (2002). They find that this measure of financial sector distress is a better forecaster of economic activity, and a better explanatory variable for the persistence of output decline during the Depression, than previously used measures of financial sector distress. The important implication of this research is that system-wide bank failures pose special costs to society, not just because of the loss of lending capacity by banks that have lost capital but additionally because of the effects of bank asset liquidation on consumer liquidity and the accentuated liquidity premium in property markets. It follows that an additional benefit of assistance to banks, and countercyclical macroeconomic policy, during a Depression is their positive effect on the liquidity of bank assets and liabilities. Clearly, the major motivations in the minds of the founders of the RFC for helping some banks remain in existence included both the preservation of suppliers of new credit and the desire to stem the tide of bank asset liquidations and their depressive effect on asset prices.

Initially, the RFC operated under the same conservative lending rules as the Fed. After the ouster of its Chairman in July 1932, RFC collateral standards were relaxed. Lending to banks and other firms grew thereafter. Beginning in March 1933, the RFC's newly created preferred stock purchase program dominated its assistance to banks.

Part of the shift to preferred stock reflected the widespread view that secured loans did not stabilize weak banks (James 1938). Secured loans represented a senior claim on bank assets relative to deposits, and thus effectively worsened the default risk faced by junior depositors. Olson (1977) writes that: "High collateral requirements forced [banks] to isolate their most liquid assets as security for RFC loans. In April 1932, for example, the RFC loaned the Reno National Bank over $1.1 million, but in the process took as collateral over $3 million of the bank's best securities. This in itself left the bank unable to meet any future emergency demands for funds by depositors." In Olson's (1972) view, loans from "... the RFC helped only those basically sound enterprises which needed temporary liquidity." It was not a means of reducing default risk for a capital-impaired bank; thus, it provided little relief to banks from default risk-intolerant market discipline.

Preferred stock, in contrast, was junior to bank deposits, and was not secured by high-quality bank assets. Thus, it offered a means of lowering deposit default risk and thus insulating risky banks from the threat of deposit withdrawal. By March 1934, the RFC had purchased preferred stock in nearly half the commercial banks in the United States. By June 1935, these RFC investments made up more than one third of the outstanding capital of the banking system (Olson 1988).

Mason (1996, 2001) and Calomiris and Mason (2003a) examine the relative effectiveness of loans and preferred stock purchases by the RFC, after controlling for differences in the characteristics of banks receiving both kinds of assistance. According to these results, receiving a loan from the RFC actually raised the probability of bank failure, while receiving preferred stock assistance reduced the probability of failure.

Although this evidence indicates that preferred stock purchases were effective in insulating banks from deposit withdrawal, it is important to emphasize that the RFC preferred stock program was successful because it was neither too conservative nor too liberal with its assistance. The RFC would have made little difference if it had only targeted the lowest risk banks for its subsidies. That was not the case. But, at the same time, the RFC did not provide assistance to deeply insolvent banks, nor would its assistance have been a sufficient subsidy to bail out such banks. Moreover, the conditions attached to RFC preferred stock purchases served to limit bank risk transference to the RFC, which ensured that preferred stock issuers had incentives to limit risk. Thus, capital-impaired (but not deeply insolvent) banks were offered limited protection from market discipline essentially on condition that they did not abuse such protection by transferring too much risk to the government.

How did RFC conditionality ensure this "happy medium" of controlled risk? First, it offered limited subsidies to banks, and avoided trying to save "basket cases." The RFC required banks to submit their regulatory examinations for RFC inspection, and banks that were judged as hopelessly insolvent were rejected. Further evidence of the selective nature of assistance is that dividend rates on RFC preferred stock were typically less than one percent below those earned in the marketplace, and were above market rates on short-term business loans. In part, the limited subsidy offered by the RFC reflected its independent corporate status. Its financial independence led its chief executive, Jesse Jones, to see a need to make the RFC profitable on a cash flow basis, and he proudly proclaimed that it never saw a year of negative profit under his direction. That constraint, obviously, also limited the potential size of the subsidy the RFC could offer. For this very limited subsidy to have made a difference for bank failure risk, recipients could not have been deeply insolvent.

Second, many restrictions on recipients of RFC assistance ensured that banks would not take advantage of RFC aid by increasing their default risk. The RFC was intended to protect banks from a dramatic decline in their capital, but not to encourage capital-impaired banks to imprudently expand their portfolio risk. Indeed, the RFC went to great pains to impose conditions that substituted for depositor discipline on bank risk taking. Those conditions included seniority of RFC dividends to all other stock dividends and voting rights that effectively gave the RFC the ability to direct institutions toward solvency and profitability and limit excessive risk. In many instances, the RFC used its control rights to replace bank officers and significantly alter business practices (Calomiris and Mason 2003a).

The RFC preserved its seniority of claim on bank earnings by limiting common stock dividend payments. Common stock dividends were strictly limited to a specified maximum and remaining earnings were devoted to a preferred stock retirement fund. Some firms avoided applying for RFC-preferred stock purchases out of reluctance to submit themselves to RFC authority.

Finally, although there were numerous attempts by politicians to influence RFC decisions, Mason (1996) suggests that the budgetary structure of the RFC and its decentralized process of decision making insulated the RFC from political manipulation. Field offices were given a large degree of autonomy over valuation of collateral and other judgmental decisions, but were held accountable to the central office for having made errors that reduced RFC earnings (Delaney 1954).

Bank dividends fell dramatically from 1929 to 1934. To what extent was this decline in dividends, and other measures to limit bank default risk, the result of RFC conditionality? Calomiris and Mason (2003a) find that receiving preferred stock assistance significantly increased banks' capital ratios and reduced their dividend payout. Their results confirm that banks that received preferred stock assistance were effectively constrained in the extent to which their stockholders could transfer risk to the RFC.

RFC-preferred stock assistance was a way to help banks smooth the adjustment process toward low default risk. It insulated banks from the threat of sudden deposit withdrawal by reducing deposit default risk, but substituted RFC discipline for market discipline to ensure that banks adopted prudent long-run risk management and capital accumulation policies.

The banking crisis in the United States during the Great Depression provides a useful historical example of how policy makers can balance the opposing needs of protecting banks and maintaining market discipline over banks. The authorities managed to mitigate the loss of capital in the banking system and its effects on credit supply, while retaining market forces that continued to reward relatively prudent banks.

Bank Recapitalization in Japan
When in early 1998 it became apparent that the loan-loss write-off program failed to provide adequate incentives for rational disposal of bad loans (see the case study of this program in Section 2.2), and the financial condition of Japan's financial institutions continued to deteriorate, the government decided to provide direct financial assistance to ailing financial institutions in the form of loans and debt purchases, and subsequently in the form of preferred stock purchases.[4] Two major injections of public funds occurred in March 1998 and March 1999, amounting to ¥1726 billion respectively ¥7459 billion (Calomiris and Mason 2003a).

Although the recapitalization program had the expected effect of increasing the capital of Japanese banks, the program failed to set incentives for prudent behavior in the future because it did not make recapitalizations conditional on the quality of the bank or the risk management and recapitalization behavior of the bank. Unlike the experience with the RFC in the United States in the 1930s, in Japan virtually every bank of any significant size received preferred stock assistance. The government did not try to target assistance selectively or to require banks to find private sources of capital alongside government contributions. And the government was even willing to purchase preferred stock in banks as they continued to pay out large amounts of common stock dividends. Calomiris and Mason (2003a) provide suggestive evidence that the weakest Japanese

---

[4] Up to late 1997, the government had relied on the so-called convoy system in which strong banks were called on to support weaker banks. The stronger banks were given tax incentives to do so.

banks were among the earliest and largest recipients of preferred stock purchases.

It should therefore not be surprising that the effect of the recapitalization program was not lasting. Although the capital adequacy ratio of local banks increased from 6.6 percent in 1998 to 10.0 percent in 2000, by the end of the year 2002 the capital adequacy of this group of banks had again deteriorated to 8.4 percent (Bank of Japan 2003). Japan's recapitalization program also failed to foster corporate restructuring or to restart bank lending. The ratio of private credit to GDP deteriorated from 203 percent in 1996 to 192 percent in 2000, and further to 176 percent in 2002. The lack of credible commitment by the government to end deflationary monetary policy and engage in bank and corporate restructuring set the stage for continuing mismanagement of risk and deterioration of banks' balance sheets as banks continued to postpone asset liquidation in the hope that they could avoid regulatory discipline and receive additional assistance from the government. Although capital injections have been reduced since 1999, the end of this sad story has yet to come.

Bank Recapitalization in Thailand
The Thai case shows a number of similarities with the Japanese case, illustrating that a market-based approach to bank restructuring yields limited results in a weak institutional environment. In Thailand, banks' liabilities were credibly backed by a government guarantee, the government engaged in regulatory forbearance, there was poor supervisory enforcement, the judicial framework for enforcing contracts and bankruptcy laws was weak, and the judiciary was inefficient. These institutional weaknesses undermined the effectiveness of bank recapitalization efforts.

In Thailand, the financial crisis came to light in July 1997, when an ailing financial sector, an export slowdown, and large increases in central bank credit to weak financial institutions triggered a run on the baht. As in the Japanese case, the Thai government was slow to address the financial system distress. It attempted to keep financial institutions afloat by injecting liquidity and engaging in regulatory forbearance and issued an unlimited guarantee on banks' liabilities as a delayed and partial response led to financial turbulence and runs on financial institutions.

On August 14, 1998, the Ministry of Finance and the Bank of Thailand announced a three-pronged plan to enhance the financial sector restructuring program. First, already relatively weak capital adequacy requirements were eased by lowering Tier-1 requirements for banks from 6 percent to 4.25 percent and the Tier-2 requirement was increased from

2.5 percent to 4.25 percent. Second, the government earmarked 300 billion baht for two capital support schemes: the Tier-1 and Tier-2 schemes (World Bank 2000).

Commercial banks were reluctant to take advantage of the government sponsored recapitalization schemes – particularly the Tier-1 scheme. Under the Tier-1 scheme, in return for official money, a bank had to first meet strict loan-loss provisioning rules, requiring a corresponding write down of capital. The scheme would have resulted in a severe dilution of ownership, which could have resulted in a change of management. Instead, large banks used innovative ways to raise new capital to avoid participation in the government scheme and the potential dilution of ownership that came with it. Bangkok Bank, Thai Farmers Bank, Bank of Ayudhya, and Thai Military Bank raised capital in the amount of around 113 billion baht, partly in the form of Capital Augmented Preferred Securities (CAPS) and Stapled Limited Interest Preferred Securities (SLIPS), preventing a dilution effect to existing shareholders.

Yet, this form of capital proved costly, as it increased banks' overall funding costs. Even in the case where a bank booked no earnings in one year and hence paid no dividends for preferred shares-cum-subordinated debentures, investors received about 11 percent from the investment, six percentage points above current deposit rates. This, in combination with the carrying cost for the large amount of NPLs, not only constrained banks' capacity to recapitalize on a flow basis, as was the intention under the government's regulatory forbearance scheme; it also hampered corporate restructuring as capital constrained banks' had little incentive to write down their assets and engage in meaningful corporate restructuring (World Bank 2000). The combination of regulatory policies provided a strong incentive to continue delaying recognition of losses and not participate in the government program, and made matters worse by decreasing the current cash flow of the banks. The result was a lack of progress in recapitalizing banks, recognizing losses, or restructuring corporate debt.

As late as 2002, the nonperforming loan ratio stood at 39 percent of total system loans and Thai banks classified 16 percent of their total assets as nonperforming. In addition, private credit continued to decline. In 2002, private credit to GDP was 103 percent, which was significantly below precrisis levels.

Lessons from the Case Studies
Government-assisted recapitalizations are designed to bolster banks' capital as a means to increase the supply of credit, and to avoid adding to the

supply of liquidated assets, to alleviate downward pressure on the price of risky assets.[5] They do not address the need to recognize loan-losses, nor do they directly tackle the problem of improving debtor capacity. Recapitalizations, however, may make it easier for banks to recognize losses, and therefore, may facilitate corporate restructuring. Recapitalizations also do no affect incentives for borrowers to improve future behavior as losses are not imposed on corporate borrowers. Whether banks' shareholders stand to lose under a recapitalization program depends on how the government assistance is structured. Recapitalizations typically do not involve losses for bank creditors.

The main problem with government-assisted recapitalizations of financial institutions is that they can create moral hazard for banks' shareholders, especially if the extent of government recapitalization is small relative to the negative net worth of recipient banks. When assistance is small relative to losses, banks face little incentive to restate their position honestly, to engage in appropriate risk management or capital accumulation as a condition for receiving assistance, or to subject themselves to regulatory monitoring and discipline. And, even if banks were willing, there may not exist a credible supervisory authority with sufficient enforcement capacity to ensure that recapitalization leads to a recognition of losses, proper rebuilding of capital, and prudent risk management.

Bank recapitalization (RFC-style assistance to banks) worked well in the United States in the 1930s because of appropriate screening and incentives for participants that ensured that the banks worth saving received taxpayer funds, and that they managed their risk and capital structure prudently. Deeply insolvent banks were closed by either the market or by the bank supervisors. Banks receiving aid met specific conditions and were monitored to ensure that they made proper use of their assistance. Preferred stock purchases failed in Japan because of lack of political will to distinguish among banks or to discipline banks when allocating assistance.

Is it possible, in the current protected environment, for government to find a way to provide a credible combination of financial assistance to banks and conditionality that limits the abuse of that assistance?

One approach to doing so would require the adoption of three mutually reinforcing means of limiting such bank abuse: (1) designing programs of assistance that are selective, and thus able to target financial assistance to

---

[5] We have not discussed the nature of the assets that are injected, whether cash or bonds. These matters are taken up by Honohan in Chapter 4.

banks that are worth preserving; (2) specifying clear quantifiable rules that limit access to preferred stock assistance, and tie assistance to effective risk management by recipient banks; and (3) enacting capital regulation that establishes meaningful standards for risk-based capital.

With respect to selectivity, Calomiris (1999) suggests using a common stock issuance matching requirement to encourage the best banks to "self-select" to participate in subsidized preferred stock purchases. That approach would attract capital-impaired but relatively healthy banks with high franchise values, and discourage deeply insolvent banks from applying for government subsidies. Those banks' stockholders would be unable to qualify for subsidized preferred stock purchases because they would be unable to find willing purchasers of new matching common stock offerings.

Despite the theoretical attraction of this approach, not all countries will be capable of implementing it. For selectivity to result in successful bank recapitalization, rules must be enforced rigorously, including bank capital regulations and limitations on dividends. For countries where political influence is strong and regulatory discipline is weak, a preferred stock subsidy based on a common stock matching requirement is unlikely to achieve its desired result.

3. CONCLUSIONS

This chapter has reviewed seven crisis resolution mechanisms, described various cases of their implementation, and compared resolution approaches according to a number of criteria that relate to effectiveness or cost.

The goal of resolution policy is to achieve the necessary rebuilding of banks' and borrowers' balance sheets at the lowest cost, where costs include costs from taxpayers' transfers of wealth and the worsening of incentives in the financial system. Incentives at the margin are crucial to getting the most impact for the least moral hazard distortion. Relatively successful mechanisms share the ability to work with market participants' incentives to achieve their results (e.g., the RFC in the United States in contrast to preferred stock assistance in Japan; the Punto Final program in Mexico in contrast to its predecessor, FOBAPROA; sales of banks to foreigners rather than capital injections to domestic banks). When considering incentives, government should be aware that loss sharing between government and private agents can act as a screening device to minimize current costs and distortions for the future, while saving those financial institutions and corporate borrowers that are worth saving and restoring their balance sheets and incentives. This view meshes well with the approach adopted by Honohan in Chapter 4, in seeking to define best practice for financial side of bank restructuring.

Our second theoretical conclusion is that the strengths and weaknesses of different resolution approaches differ, *assuming that those approaches are executed properly.* Some approaches target the health of borrowers, others the health of banks. Some approaches (e.g., debt forgiveness via a legal redefinition of debt values) entail lower direct costs to taxpayers than others. Some approaches necessarily have worse incentive consequences for banks or borrowers than others. Thus, policy makers that attach differing weights to the various objectives of resolution policy should choose and design combinations of resolution mechanisms accordingly.

Our third conclusion is that when choosing a resolution approach, or a set of approaches, policy makers also should take into account the pitfalls they are likely to experience in executing each resolution approach, and that these pitfalls are a predictable consequence of particular country circumstances, and in particular, the legal, regulatory, and political institutions, and the industrial organization structure of the economy.

In particular, we take an important lesson of our case studies to be that the advantages from allowing foreign bank entry are less dependent on a favorable political environment. In this respect foreign bank entry is exceptional. Indeed, as our case studies illustrate, once foreign banks are permitted to operate, they help to make the financial sector more resistant to political influence peddling (see also Kroszner 1998, and the discussion of foreign banks by Tschoegl in Chapter 7).

Our case studies illustrate that countries operating with different levels of political and legal/regulatory institutional quality might optimally choose different approaches to resolution policy. Also, the magnitude of a crisis and type of crisis affect the appropriate choices of resolution tools. For example, in the United States circa 1988, when the political will to cease forbearing and deal with the S&L debacle finally emerged, the government, thrift regulators and supervisors, and the Resolution Trust Corporation moved swiftly and effectively to close or otherwise resolve insolvent institutions, sell foreclosed assets, and force surviving thrifts to recapitalize. The operation of the Swedish AMCs indicates similar success. Underlying those successes were the institutional foundations of mature capitalist economies, including (1) a commitment to the rule of law and the enforcement of creditors' rights in courts, (2) a longstanding relatively successful tradition in bank supervision and regulation,

74   *Charles W. Calomiris, Daniela Klingebiel, and Luc Laeven*

(3) relatively liquid markets for the sale of assets, (4) a political process that is relatively free of corruption, and (5) the fiscal capacity to finance financial sector resolution costs.

But, as our case studies from emerging markets illustrate, the successful implementation of AMCs in developed economies, like other resolution mechanisms, has not been imitated in emerging market countries, largely because of institutional barriers to success. The problem is that the institutional foundations on which successful AMC liquidation depend – creditors' rights, including the ability to foreclose easily, the absence of favoritism and corruption in the implementation of asset acquisition and resale, and the existence of a bank supervisory and regulatory system that will force banks to honestly recognize losses, manage risk, and recapitalize as necessary – simply do not exist in the vast majority of emerging market economies. (In Chapter 3, Lindgren provides a description of the kinds of practical institutional shortcoming likely to be faced in bank intervention.)

For this reason, emerging market policy makers would benefit from recognizing the inherent limitations of implementing both market-based and government-based resolution policies in emerging markets, and from employing resolution techniques that are less dependent on the favorable preconditions that they do not enjoy. Most obviously, that recognition would lead to less reliance on AMCs, but it would also mitigate the desirability of otherwise highly desirable, but relatively complicated, selective market-based resolution strategies such as the RFC and Punto Final, which rely on significant discretionary and oversight authority to be successful.

We have noted, in particular, that self-selection mechanisms that link government preferred stock purchases to privately raised equity (like the RFC), or that link government-subsidized debt forgiveness to borrower-bank resolution agreements or to new credit supplied by banks (like Punto Final) may be superior mechanisms for rebuilding bank and borrower balance sheets, in principle. By effectively screening for quality through self-selection, these sorts of assistance programs mitigate moral hazard problems and limit the fiscal costs of bailouts. But we also have noted that these mechanisms depend even more than AMCs on favorable institutional preconditions for their success.

We conclude, therefore, that emerging market countries with the weakest institutional conditions may be best served by relying on simple assistance measures that can achieve speedy resolution with less dependence on a high level of political, legal, or economic institutional maturity. The most obvious candidates are across-the-board debt forgiveness via the simultaneous redefinition of the numeraire of debt contracts and bank deposits, or permitting entry by foreign banks. Both approaches have some drawbacks.

Debt forgiveness is less helpful in the long run if the government cannot credibly commit to reserving debt forgiveness as a policy to be used only in the most extreme circumstances, and may not be successful in restarting the credit supply process on a sound footing without an efficient legal and bankruptcy system in credit markets to incentivize borrowers to continue to service the remainder of outstanding debt, and a supervisory framework that forces banks to take advantage of their improved circumstances by rebuilding their capital positions as need be. For governments in most developing countries, it will be difficult to credibly commit to unrepeated debt forgiveness.

The drawback of foreign bank entry is that it can only restart the arms-length credit supply process if legal institutions protecting creditors' rights are sufficiently developed. Again, this is not the case in most developing countries. Nonetheless, in the imperfect world of emerging market finance, foreign bank entry may often be the best policy option available.

ACKNOWLEDGMENTS

We would like to thank Stijn Claessens, Tom Glaessner, Patrick Honohan, Randy Kroszner, and other participants at the World Bank conference on "Systemic Financial Distress: Containment and Resolution" for helpful comments and suggestions, and Guillermo Noguera for excellent research assistance. The views expressed in this chapter are those of the authors and do not necessarily represent those of the World Bank or the American Enterprise Institute.

THREE

Pitfalls in Managing Closures of Financial Institutions

Carl-Johan Lindgren

INTRODUCTION

Closure of a financial institution is essential when it is no longer viable. Unviable financial institutions lead to accrual of losses that eventually will have to be borne by various stakeholders. If allowed to operate, they undermine healthy market competition and create moral hazard by giving owners and managers incentives to gamble for recovery and opportunities for asset looting and criminal "end games." Their continued presence may over time undermine the soundness of an entire financial system. Owners and managers of financial institutions are typically required by law to close an institution once it becomes insolvent and cannot be recapitalized. But numbers can be manipulated and closures or other forms of market exit tend to be delayed and often take place only at supervisors' insistence.

Closures of financial institutions are seldom the routine supervisory actions they should be. Closures are typically preceded by other corrective supervisory actions. Closure should be the ultimate sanction for breaching licensing agreements and prudential rules and be part of supervisors' "toolbox" of corrective measures. Reasons for closures could be lack of financial viability, breaches of prudential requirements, licensing agreements or corrective action plans, or criminal activity, fraud, or gross malfeasance. Clean closures causing little disturbance to the financial system should be viewed as a sign of effective supervision.

Closures often are delayed by supervisors, who are reluctant to take actions that may be seen by the public and politicians as a failure of supervision rather than a failure of an institutions' owners and managers. As a result, closures, and especially closures of banks, often come too late and after problems already have accumulated, and may set in motion contagion dynamics that can affect the entire financial system and the economy at large. As a result, systemic risks are too often invoked as reasons for not closing financial institutions, especially deposit-taking institutions, perhaps with references to well-publicized cases of botched closures elsewhere in the world.

Closure of a financial institution is a process, not an event. Although a closure could be viewed as an event, such as, for example, the moment of termination of an institution's life as a legal entity or even the moment of physical closure of its doors for business, we view closure as a process starting with planning, followed by implementation and ending with the institution's absorption, liquidation, or disappearance. The process may be quick but more often takes months or years to be completed.

Closure is one of the most important ways of keeping a financial system competitive, efficient, and sound. Closures remove unviable institutions and excess capacity from the system. They force owners, managers, and other stakeholders to take responsibility for accumulated losses. In many countries, only closures trigger the legal mechanisms that allow for a distribution of losses to stakeholders other than shareholders. Closures must be executed in a clean and efficient way to maintain a level and competitive playing field and minimize damaging market disturbances. Strategic, administrative, political, and legal complexities of closing financial institutions can be overcome with proper consideration and management of the different steps and constraints involved. That requires careful planning, execution, and downstream follow-up.

This chapter explores the various pitfalls in the process of closing financial institutions and how to deal with them. It covers closure both at the level of individual institutions and on a systemic scale. We focus on banks, which in most countries constitute the core of the financial system, and on government and prudential policy issues rather than corporate policy issues. After a brief discussion in Section 1 of some terms and definitions commonly used in the closure and resolution of financial institutions, Section 2 discusses the various pitfalls that official decision makers will need to be aware of in managing the closure process. The pitfalls have been grouped into 10 different topics. Section 3 concludes with a brief summary and concluding remarks.

Carl-Johan Lindgren

1. TERMS AND DEFINITIONS

A closure typically means the end of a financial institution as a legal entity. A closure is typically accompanied by a withdrawal of an institution's operating license but there are legal frameworks that allow the suspension of operations without revoking a license, which may be withdrawn at some later point. A closure can be an up-front action followed by a resolution and liquidation process, or part of or the end result of an intervention and resolution process.

The closure process seeks to bring assets, liabilities, and any remaining business franchise of an intervened or closed institution back into the market under new ownership. It seeks to do so with minimum market disruption and loss of asset values. All assets and liabilities have to be found final owners and all losses distributed among stakeholders.[1] It can take months or years for this process to be completed.

Intervention means takeover of management and ownership control of an institution by its official supervisor. An intervention gives the authorities an opportunity to review an institution from the inside and time to make more informed decisions about an optimal resolution strategy, which may include closure. In cases in which there is urgency to prevent liquidity support or asset looting but the necessary legal and strategic decisions cannot yet be made, operations may also be temporarily suspended or frozen. Official interventions must be short to prevent the authorities from becoming coresponsible for the problems of the intervened institution.

Resolution implies a reorganization of an intervened or closed institution's assets, liabilities and operations in a variety of forms. Resolution options include mergers, partial sales, purchase and assumption (P&A) operations, establishment of bridge banks, reorganizations and recapitalizations, or legal closure and liquidation. Different resolution options may be combined in a process that constitutes closure. A residual balance sheet may then be liquidated.

Mergers, partial sales, and bridge banks can be part of a closure process. A *merger or sale* of an institution means that all the assets and liabilities

---

[1] The report of a recent Basel Committee Task Force on Dealing with Weak Banks distinguishes between legal and economic closures; it concludes that closure should achieve the former and avoid the latter, that is, the financial intermediary should be closed without closing or destroying the economic transactions that it intermediates; see Basel (2002). The report provides comprehensive guidance on identification of weak banks, on the range of corrective actions that supervisors employ prior to closure, as well as on closures and other options for exit and resolution of individual banks.

of a failing firm are transferred to and absorbed into another institution. In a partial sale or *P&A operation*, only part of the assets of a failing institution are purchased together with part or all of its liabilities. All such resolution options may or may not involve financial support from the government. In a government-assisted operation, a government entity or deposit insurer would pay the purchasing institution, typically in securities, for the difference between the value of the assets and liabilities of the exiting institution. The assets and liabilities of one or more intervened or closed banks may also be transferred to a temporary bridge bank to allow continued operations until a permanent resolution can be found.

Liquidation is the legal process under which the assets of an institution are sold and proceeds used to settle its liabilities in full or in part. Liquidation brings finality to the legal closure of a financial institution. A liquidation can be voluntary or forced, be within or outside general bankruptcy procedures, and may involve courts to varying degrees. Proceeds from the sale of assets are used to pay off the creditors in the order or seniority prescribed by law. Liquidation could apply to all the assets of an institution or only to a residual of bad or complex assets after other resolution options have been used for other assets.

We treat intervention as a precursor to closure, and consider market exit to be closure regardless of whether it has been accomplished through mergers or closures with liquidation. Intervention is often the first step toward closure and market exit of an institution. Table 3.1 shows mergers and closures/liquidations to be the most common forms of exit in 11 major banking crisis cases. Mergers are typically used for larger institutions and closure/liquidation for smaller ones. For example, in Indonesia the 18 banks that were merged had a market share of nearly 45 percent of banking system assets, whereas the 64 banks that were closed had a market share of less than 15 percent. Because of their role in the payments system, the exit of banks is more likely to take place through mergers and P&A transactions, whereas the exit of other financial institutions is more likely to take the form of closure/liquidation.

Systemic problems are common when dealing with closures, especially of banks. We recognize such problems but do not seek to define them very precisely. Systemic problems are often used as excuses for inaction or inappropriate policies, including government guarantees. But reality remains that closure of one or more financial institutions under certain circumstances may threaten the stability of an entire financial system and negatively affect a country's macroeconomic performance. Systemic

Table 3.1 *Changes in Banking Structure During Select Crisis Episodes*

Country	Onset of Crisis Date	Number of Commercial Banks Before the Crisis	Number of Commercial Banks After the Crisis	After Crisis Date	Resolution Techniques				
					Nationalizations	Closures	Mergers and Takeovers	Newly Created	Intervened and Unresolved: Not Open/Open
Argentina	Dec. 1994	205[a]	158[a]	Dec. 1995	0	12	39	4	2[b]/0
Ecuador	Aug. 1998	36	22	Dec. 2001	0	14	0	0	0/0
Finland	Aug. 1991	10	7	Dec. 1995	0	1	2	0	0/0
Indonesia	Aug. 1997	238	145	Oct. 2002	0	64	18	0	11/0
Korea	Nov. 1997	26	17	Jul. 1999	5[c]	5	4	0	0/0
Malaysia	Jul. 1997	35	34	Dec. 2002	0	0	1	0	0/0
Mexico	Dec. 1994	32	27	Dec. 1999	0	0	5	0	0/12[d]
Sweden	Oct. 1991	12	11	Dec. 1993	0	0	1	0	0/0
Thailand	Mar. 1997	15	13	Dec. 2000	1	1	2	1[e]	0/0
Turkey	Dec. 2000	80	64	Dec. 2001	0	7	9	0	0/0
Venezuela	Jan. 1994	47	38	Dec. 1996	0	11	2	4	0/0

Notes: (*a*) Refers to total number of deposit-taking institutions, not only banks. In December 1994, there were 168 commercial banks and 37 nonbank deposit-taking institutions. (*b*) These two institutions were intervened in 1995 and subsequently merged with other financial institutions in 1996. (*c*) Hanvit, Cho Hung, Korea First, and Korea Exchange Bank majority-owned by the government. (*d*) Of which seven in liquidation and five intervened and awaiting resolution. (*e*) Radanasin Bank.

Sources: Claessens et al. (1999), Lindgren et al. (1999), and Hoelscher and Quintyn (2003), and Central Bank websites.

threats need to be analyzed in the context of structural weaknesses in a financial system and the macroeconomic situation at any given time.

2. TEN MAJOR PITFALLS

We discuss 10 topic areas that constitute major pitfalls in the closure of banks and other financial institutions. The number of pitfalls and their delineation is somewhat arbitrary, of course, and they all are closely interrelated. Some pitfalls may be more important than others in any particular case. However, all 10 pitfalls are always present in different form and with different intensity in every intervention or closure of a financial institution regardless of the country and its economic, financial, legal, and institutional structure.

The 10 major pitfalls in the process of managing closures of financial institutions used in this chapter are listed here. The order in which they appear does not reflect their priority or sequence in the process.

1. Perennial measurement problems
2. Identification problems
3. Lack of clear intervention triggers
4. Forbearance and liquidity support
5. Loss sharing
6. Limit contagion
7. Protect asset values
8. Linkages with macroeconomy
9. Legal framework
10. Institutional and political framework

Most of the pitfalls are prevalent early in the process. Measurement and identification are important for the early diagnosis of the nature and scope of a problem. Forbearance and liquidity support, as well as lack of proper intervention triggers, can allow problems to quickly grow out of control early in the process. Proper decisions on loss sharing and how to deal with contagion are also crucial early in the process. Asset management issues tend to become important later in the process but, even in their case, key decisions often have to be made up front, even if implementation comes later. It is always important to form a comprehensive and robust strategy early in the process, as most decisions tend to become irreversible.

The most critical decision, which has to be made early in the process, is loss sharing. Although owners normally can be assumed to lose their stakes without too much controversy, assigning losses to creditors and depositors involves a delicate balance between allowing market discipline to work, on the one hand, and possibly unleashing widespread creditor and depositor runs, on the other hand. A decision to introduce a blanket government guarantee, if financially feasible, may stop contagion but is often extremely costly.

Consistency between closure and macroeconomic policies are important throughout the process. Any closure and resolution strategy must consider the effects it may have on macroeconomic performance and policy, whereas different macroeconomic stress and sustainability scenarios need to be considered as part of any closure/resolution strategy.

Political, institutional, and legal issues are crucial throughout the process of closing financial institutions, which is fraught with constraints and pitfalls that become more complex and critical the more widespread or systemic the problems are. Political will and capacity is the most important ingredient for resolution and closure decisions. Weak or eroding political support often becomes the major pitfall, as costs become more transparent and interest groups mobilize their opposition. Legal, judicial, administrative, and staffing issues are important all along for proper implementation; legal and judicial surprises as well as implementation shortfalls can stop or slow the process at any point.

2.1 Perennial Measurement Problems

Reliable information on weak financial institutions is available the least when needed the most. Information on financial institutions, especially those in trouble, is notoriously insufficient and unreliable. In periods of economic deterioration, accounting losses always lag behind underlying economic losses, especially for loans, which account for the bulk of assets in many institutions. Valuation of problem loans is a largely subjective exercise in which bank managers, external auditors, and supervisors come up with their best estimates using various methodologies. This makes it essential to strictly enforce loan and other asset valuation rules and procedures on a uniform basis. Claims on offshore units and related parties may be opaque and particularly difficult to value.

Valuation of securities and other claims on government also may become highly arbitrary, especially in cases of severe financial stress or debt default in the public sector.[2] In periods of economic turmoil, all

---

[2] The recent situation in Argentina shows how the valuation of government securities becomes highly arbitrary in periods of extreme market volatility and the possibility of "haircuts" of asset values in the context of a public debt restructuring.

asset valuation becomes extremely uncertain, as values shift continuously in response to underlying economic, market, legal, and political circumstances. Needless to say, in the absence of reliable data, intervention or closure becomes difficult to justify.

Capital adequacy ratios (CARs) are often poor measures of the solvency and financial viability of financial institutions. CARs for problem institutions often are inflated, as asset values are overestimated and the institutions' financial losses underestimated. Although economic losses already have occurred, it will take time for them to show up in the CARs. Without adequate and objective accounting and valuation, it will be easy for owners and managers to conceal problems and difficult for supervisors to determine a firm basis for closure. At the same time, firm data and criteria will be needed to legally justify an intervention or closure of an institution and to stand up to possible court challenges.

The data will become less reliable as market conditions deteriorate. Asset valuation may be relatively easy, if the problems affect only an individual institution under relatively normal circumstances in an environment of stable asset values and predictable economic conditions. As more institutions are affected, the valuation problems become more complex, as market conditions and asset values may become adversely affected by the resolution process itself. Far more complexity is added in an environment of systemic banking sector weaknesses, in cases of contagion, dramatic declines in asset values, and major macroeconomic disruptions. Accounting data reported to supervisors will always reflect underlying asset deterioration with a lag, at least until an institution is intervened or closed. At that point, due diligence or liquidation analysis will provide more realistic information.

Intervention or closure often becomes a judgment call when available data indicate problems but give no firm basis for action. Bankers and external auditors may have incentives to obscure and delay the value discovery process. Strict enforcement of loan and other asset valuation rules become essential. Uniformity of rules and criteria will help identify weak and worst institutions. But the valuation process may still be too slow and supervisors may have to intervene or suspend operations of an institution based on partial indicators. They may need to wait with closure decisions until they have prepared a better database and proper valuation from inside the institution. If an intervention were to bring out data to show that an institution is viable after all, it can always be returned to its owners. But such a scenario is rare. Typically, interventions confirm financial problems and produce evidence to support intervention or closure. Given that interventions and closures may be challenged long afterward, all data, assumptions, and criteria should be properly safeguarded to provide evidence later on, if needed.

The liability side of an institution's balance sheet may include surprises. The valuation of the liability side of an institution's balance sheet is normally relatively easy – provided that all liabilities and contingencies are included. It is not uncommon, however, to discover liabilities that have been excluded from an institution's accounts and concealed from auditors and supervisors, possibly for years.[3] Irregular liabilities could include deposits accumulated using all the trappings of legitimate operations and then diverted to the personal use of owners or managers; this could happen domestically or through foreign or offshore affiliates. Like pyramid schemes, clandestine deposit-taking operations can go on as long as they stay liquid. Their size could exceed those on the balance sheet. Once identified, a decision will have to be made on the form and extent to which such liabilities be honored and whether they are to be included in an institution's liquidation. Governments often feel compelled to honor such liabilities in order to maintain confidence in the rest of the system, especially if depositors have dealt in good faith with an officially supervised institution.

External auditors are of little use when better data are needed quickly. The results of regular external audits are typically already available to supervisors but may be unreliable and outdated. Special audits by institutions' regular auditors or outside independent auditors may be useful, if based on detailed additional criteria. But such audits tend to take too much time, so an institution may have to be intervened first and only then subjected to audits and decisions on closure. Independent external audits are suitable to ensure uniformity of criteria and impartiality in cases in which the competence or integrity of the bankers or supervisors are in doubt, or in which insider or government directed lending is prevalent.

If external audits are called for, extreme care needs to be taken so as not to single out any particular institution or group of institutions. An audit can seldom be kept secret. Government-owned or already intervened banks can be subjected to special audits without too many market repercussions. But singling out any private bank or group of banks for audits may well doom them to failure. An audit may have to be done on a system-wide basis even if one or only a few banks or institutions are the

---

[3] The most recent cases of such schemes have been in a bank in Turkey and a bank in the Dominican Republic; in both cases, the size of the illegitimate liabilities have far exceeded the size of the banks' balance sheets.

principal targets. But this may be worthwhile, as case by case diagnosis will be needed if the problems were to become systemic. Special audits must be used as part of a broader strategy to strengthen confidence in a financial system.

Clear guidelines are needed to prevent both over- and undervaluation of bank assets by auditors. Sometimes, auditors may have incentives to obscure and delay value recognition if this means substantially revising a recent audit. In other situations, auditors may wish to protect their reputations and be excessively cautious, and use "liquidation" values rather than higher "going concern" values. Special audits thus need detailed specifications to provide a uniform basis for analysis. To increase their credibility, special audits can be verified through second opinions, other auditors, and ultimately by the supervisory authority – although supervisors at the same time must be careful not to undo the results of the audits.

2.2 Identification Problems

It is essential to assess the distribution of problems and their likely broader systemic impact in parallel with estimates of the magnitude of financial problems. It is important to establish whether problems are confined to a single financial institution or affect several institutions or groups of institutions and whether an institution is part of a financial conglomerate or a broader corporate "group." Their importance in the financial system as a whole and in the payments system also must be established. Dealing with problems in the core banking system or in a single dominant bank rather than in smaller banks or subgroups of near-banks or other financial institutions may require very different closure decisions.

The ownership structure of intervention and closure candidates also needs to be determined in order to fully ascertain the potential impact of different closure strategies. Closure decisions affect potential private and foreign investors, which may be needed in the subsequent resolution process. Closure of government-owned banks needs to be considered in a broader context, especially as they may usefully function as bridge banks when no other resolution vehicles are available. The ownership structure of conglomerates or groups needs to be considered so that a closure does not cause unexpected failures elsewhere in a chain of companies. Finally, linkages between foreign and domestic units need to be considered, as any closure and liquidation decision may involve extremely complex cross-border legal issues.

Closure policy has to be comprehensive for different categories of financial institutions and consistent over time. The sooner the scope and nature of problem institutions and categories can be identified the better. Available data, even if uniformly deficient, must be simulated in different interest, exchange, and economic growth rate scenarios to make sure that a seemingly limited problem does not evolve into a systemic one under plausible assumptions. As far as possible, the intervention and closure strategy that is chosen should be sufficiently robust to cope with a realistic worst case scenario. To the extent problems are considered systemic and of macroeconomic significance, the closure strategy will need to become an integral part of broader macroeconomic policies and considerations. Closure policy must be applied equally to all institutions in the same category (banks, finance companies, etc.).

There are no quantitative ratios or rules of thumb for when a problem is to be considered systemic. It depends on the size and structure of each system and the macroeconomic environment at any given time – a problem may be viewed differently in an economic upturn than in a downturn. The relative size of one or more financial institutions in the financial system as well as the relative size of a system in the economy also matters. The larger the relative size of the system, the more it matters in the economy; a system with assets representing the equivalent of, say, 200 percent of GDP is clearly more important for the economy than one representing, say, 20 percent of GDP. A bank with a market share of 20 percent in the former system will represent 40 percent of GDP, while it would represent only 4 percent in the latter case. So the systemic and macroeconomic effects of closing a bank always have to be considered in a broader context.

It also makes a difference whether the institution(s) subject to potential closure is a large bank at the core of the financial and payments systems or one or more smaller banks or other financial institutions – except, of course, in cases in which smaller institutions' problems directly affect a core institution. Individual institutions and especially core banks may be so important to the financial and payments systems that they are considered "too big to fail." But "too big to be closed" must not mean "too big to be intervened" (owners and managers removed), resolved or reorganized.[4]

In case of a single bank that is unviable, intervention or closure must take place as soon as possible, while making sure that legal and

[4] For a broader discussion of these issues, see Andrews and Josefsson (2003).

institutional requirements and constraints are being met. Closure of a larger rather than smaller number of institutions may increase confidence in remaining institutions. However, every intervention and closure sets a precedent for future similar actions. Therefore, as discussed earlier, if the problems are believed to be widespread, there is a need to have a good understanding of the size and nature of the problem and the required overall strategy before any closures take effect. This is particularly important if the strategy involves loss sharing, as discussed later. In cases of fraud, criminality, or sudden and extreme illiquidity, there may be no choice but to go for immediate suspension or closure, although even in such cases every effort should be made to save asset values through more efficient resolution options.

In case of a systemic problem situation, the closure strategy will be different depending on whether or not a blanket guarantee is used. If a government blanket guarantee for depositors and creditors is used, there is a need to decide up front whether or not it will be applied to all institutions, including those to be closed, or only to those that will remain in operation. Once a credible blanket guarantee is in place, closures can take place in an orderly way without fear of contagion. The impact of burden sharing decisions on closures and the effects of a blanket guarantee are discussed further later.

2.3 Lack of Clear Intervention Triggers

Experience in all countries has shown that it is cheaper to intervene in and resolve problem banks early. The earlier the intervention, the lower the cost for all stakeholders, because losses are likely to be smaller and not yet accumulated. Resolution will be easier because asset prices early on are more stable and more investors (banks and nonbanks) are likely to be interested in buying distressed assets, as fewer such assets are on the market. The more the situation deteriorates, the more asset prices will fall and investor interest dry up – and resolution costs increase. In addition, as losses build up, the likelihood of severe market distortions and broader systemic weakening will increase and may ultimately have huge cost implications that will complicate resolution.

Intervention and closure of a bank or other financial institution must be based on certain legal and regulatory criteria. Such criteria could be insolvency, illiquidity, gross breaches of prudential ratios and regulations, management misconduct, or fraud and criminality. However, such criteria need to be translated into operational definitions and quantitative ratios or limits, which, when reached or breached, will "trigger" the intervention and closure of an institution. Even in countries where the authorities have wide discretionary powers to intervene, defining specific criteria is useful. Intervention "triggers" must be transparent and uniformly applied. There must always be a demonstrable objective and legal basis for any intervention or closure.

CARs are the most common intervention triggers but are often useless for operational purposes, given the asset valuation problems discussed earlier. Since the FDICIA introduced mandatory Prompt Corrective Action (PCA) in the United States in 1991, an increasing number of countries have introduced similar regimes. PCA implies mandatory takeover of a bank when its risk-weighted CAR falls below a certain level, say, 2 percent, which in most cases implies negative net worth once proper valuations have been performed. CARs are excellent intervention triggers in relatively normal times, when they reflect banks' net worth reasonably well. But are less so in a rapidly deteriorating economic environment in which accounting values for financial assets and CARs become inflated and start to lag behind economic realities. This means that reliance on PCA may have severe practical limitations and may even be counterproductive, if a slavish focus on CARs results in delayed interventions and closures.

When solvency triggers do not work, quantitative liquidity triggers often take over. Problem institutions can stay liquid even as their profitability and solvency is eroded. Competitors are often aware of such problems and require risk premiums in the domestic money market and eventually close them out of the interbank market altogether. The central bank/lender of last resort (LOLR) often becomes the only provider of liquidity. Banks with liquidity problems are also likely to have solvency problems. Given that illiquidity can quickly make undercapitalized institutions severely insolvent, the LOLR has to decide how much liquidity support to provide. This relates to the wider issue of forbearance discussed below. LOLR liquidity support expressed on a bank-by-bank basis, say, as a multiple of a bank's capital or net worth, can be used as a trigger. Once the liquidity support reaches the trigger level, the institution is closed or intervened and its operations suspended. Liquidity indicators often show problems long before CARs.

Additional triggers or corroborating evidence are useful. Qualitative conditions like severe incompliance with prudential rules, breach of licensing, or recapitalization agreements, evidence of fraudulent activity, and so on can support liquidity triggers or even be used as intervention triggers on their own. All triggers must be designed to hold up legally, because interventions and closures will destroy and redistribute private property and wealth and therefore have a high likelihood of being challenged in courts. Owners of intervened or closed banks may show documents, certified by their external auditors, to prove that their institution was solvent when it was taken over or closed. Therefore, there is need for supervisors to clearly define the criteria for interventions and closures and be prepared to defend them in court, if challenged.

2.4 Forbearance and Liquidity Support

Forbearance or allowing loss-making institutions to remain in operation despite signs of severe problems or outright breaches of prudential rules will allow losses to accumulate. As discussed earlier, the authorities may not be fully aware of the extent of the deterioration or not have a clear legal basis or operational triggers for intervention or closure decisions. However, there may be breaches of prudential rules and market information that indicate severe problems and a need for immediate corrective actions. In such a situation the supervisory authorities may choose not to pursue such indicators further or simply to ignore them. Allowing financial institutions to continue operations as if everything were normal is referred to as forbearance. It makes the government coresponsible for the accumulation of losses and invariably complicates closure and other resolution options later on.

Supervisors typically employ a string of corrective measures to give a problem institution a chance to improve before being intervened or closed. Only in cases of extremely rapid financial deterioration or discovery of criminal wrongdoing are supervisors likely intervene without giving the institution a chance to survive through corrective measures such as recapitalization or other forms of financial and operational restructuring. However, such corrective measures are often forbearance in disguise as they do little to correct the situation. Recapitalization and restructuring plans may be unrealistic and loosely enforced. Supervisors often accept vague promises of recapitalization from phantom investors.[5] Supervisors also may wishfully expect economic conditions to improve

---

[5] In this context it should be noted that new private investors must not be expected to absorb an existing hidden negative net worth, except perhaps in cases where the losses would have tax carry-over value for another profitable bank. Only when existing losses have been fully recognized can new private investors, domestic and foreign, be expected to have interest in injecting additional capital.

and that the problems of the institutions under their supervision will go away – something that seldom happens. The end result of forbearance is an accumulation of losses and erosion of net worth that may become widespread and lead to severe and costly systemic problems.[6]

It is often the central bank/LOLR that uses liquidity triggers to force a supervisory authority intervene or close an institution. (The LOLR and supervisory authority may, of course, both be the central bank.) Banks and near-banks may have exhausted their capacity to attract deposits or credit at home or abroad and can only rely on the LOLR for liquidity support. They may be highly vulnerable to liquidity shocks and their demand for LOLR support may rapidly increase to levels that jeopardize monetary stability. The LOLR must stop the "bleeding" (of liquidity) but cannot do so without the banks' operations being suspended or closed. This is when liquidity triggers will be essential. When supervisors are forbearing banks and other financial institutions it is typically monetary management constraints that bring about supervisory intervention or closure.

Forbearance facilitated by LOLR liquidity support complicates subsequent interventions and closures. The combination of forbearance and liquidity support makes the monetary and supervisory authorities (often combined in the central bank) accomplices in an arrangement that may be expedient in the short run but will undermine long-term financial stability and complicate future resolution options. By effectively financing a buildup of losses in problem institutions, the LOLR is in effect allowing existing owners and managers to stay in control, loot assets and honor liabilities selectively to related parties, which will make matters worse for other creditors and depositors in the end. In most countries, the LOLR is a privileged creditor, which means that other creditors will be squeezed out as a result of the LOLR's actions, whereas the LOLR itself will carry little risk for its destructive policies. To prevent such abuse by the LOLR, the U.S. FDICIA outlawed LOLR support to institutions believed to be insolvent.

There is a trade-off between denying LOLR support and possibly causing wider systemic problems, on the one hand, and providing such support and preventing systemic problems, on the other hand. LOLR support is supposed to be provided only to solvent institutions facing temporary illiquidity. But temporary illiquidity is hard to establish – permanent illiquidity

---

[6] Honohan and Klingebiel (2003) identified forbearance and open-ended liquidity support as two of the main contributors to the high fiscal cost of banking crises.

starts as being temporary. Most illiquid banks also have solvency problems, albeit not necessarily insurmountable ones. It is extremely difficult to determine whether early liquidity support will help institutions recover and thus reduce eventual losses or just help finance additional losses that never can be recovered. This is where the supervisors' intimate knowledge of financial institutions is crucial. Considerations will change depending where on the timeline toward systemic crisis a financial system is located.[7]

Denying liquidity support may lead to disruptions in the payments system. Interruptions to the payments system are bound to trigger panic and runs on other banks. A decision to cease liquidity support therefore cannot be made independent of intervention or closure decisions. Smaller banks or financial institutions may be closed without affecting the normal operations of the rest of the system. But if the problem lies with a large bank at the core of the payments system, liquidity support can seldom be stopped. Instead, such a bank may be intervened (its owners and managers removed) and kept in operation while its liquidity is stabilized and a resolution strategy implemented.

A common fallacy is to assume that losses or the need for liquidity support will stop once a bank is intervened or closed. Liquidity pressures may subside if depositors and creditors feel that their money is safe but there will be further "flow" losses as costs of financing, managing bank assets (staffing costs, management fees to other institutions), and liquidators add up. Depending on resolution options and loss-sharing decisions, such losses may continue in the institution or may shift elsewhere, for example, to a deposit insurer, liability holders, or the government. These, in turn, may need liquidity support. Only if a closure involves the transfer of all losses to other private stakeholders may claims on LOLR liquidity support stop.

The more government is involved in forbearance and liquidity support, the more it will be held responsible. Market confidence in the government's competence and integrity will erode. The public is likely to consider the government coresponsible and will demand it to assume part or all of the resolution costs. Pressure will mount for a blanket guarantee, even when a case for such a guarantee may not have been there had decisive intervention or closure decisions been taken only a few months or even weeks before. Due diligence valuations following interventions or

---

[7] For an illustrative practitioner's view of this dilemma and other issues surrounding closure and resolution of banks, see De Juan (1999).

closures will gradually reveal the full extent of accumulated losses and the extent of the forbearance. That may further undermine confidence and lead to more interventions and closures.

2.5 Loss Sharing

The most difficult decisions in managing closures relate to loss or burden sharing. It is normally defined in law how losses are to be distributed: owners absorb losses first, holders of subordinated debt next, and so on. As losses often exceed the stakes of owners and subordinated debt holders, losses will have to be covered by other creditors and depositors in accordance with their legally established rankings, which differ from country to country.[8] Liquidators, central bank, tax authorities, and bank personnel often are preferred creditors. Depositors may rank above other creditors and small depositors above large depositors. Classes of claims typically are to be honored from the institution's assets in the preestablished legal order and for remaining claimants on a *pari passu* basis. If there is a deposit insurance scheme, it initially absorbs losses up to its legally stipulated limits and then seeks reimbursement depending on its priority in the creditor queue. In case of a government blanket guarantee of depositors or creditors, all losses after those absorbed by share- and subordinated debt holders and excluded liability categories (like connected parties) will fall on the government.

Loss sharing with existing owners and managers should be pursued as far as possible. Getting shareholders to accept losses may require closure but in many countries this can be done with supervisory identification of the losses and requirement that capital be reduced.[9] Losses of private owners are typically limited to the amount of their shareholdings under company law.[10] Dividends deemed excessive may be reversed. The prospects are slim to impose more losses on existing owners than their share capital, except in cases in which they have acted illegally, for example, borrowed from the institution in violation of connected lending limits

[8] Losses are allocated in accordance with the legal rankings or preferences stipulated in banking, bankruptcy, deposit insurance, and other laws, as may be the case.

[9] In most countries shareholders can be wiped out without closure. Supervisors determine asset values, net worth, and the size of losses to be written off against accumulated reserves and paid up capital. Refusal by a shareholders' assembly to approve a proposed write-down of capital is typically a cause for intervention.

[10] There may also be loss-sharing issues among groups of shareholders, for example, between minority and majority shareholders.

or been involved in fraudulent or criminal activities that may be subject to unlimited liability. To the extent managers can be held similarly culpable they should share in losses to the extent of their financial capabilities.[11]

In some jurisdictions, losses cannot be imposed on creditors or depositors, including holders of subordinated debt, unless an institution is legally closed. Creditors and depositors would then be compensated up to the value of remaining assets in the legally established order of priorities. Compensation is often done in installments based on proceeds from asset recovery. Some countries require the entire liquidation process to be completed before anyone is compensated.

Loss-sharing procedures designed for individual banks in normal times may not be suitable for systemic situations. Allocation of losses to creditors and depositors is an extremely delicate measure, especially in a weak banking system. Loss sharing may be politically unacceptable, as it may run counter to earlier policy assurances, implicit or explicit guarantees, or social contracts, or simply affect too many politically influential interests.[12] But most important, *loss sharing may cause flight to quality*. Creditors and depositors in banks perceived to be weak will run to stronger banks or, if no domestic institutions are deemed to be safe, altogether away from the domestic financial system, that is, capital flight abroad. Given that it is the larger creditors and depositors that run first, limited deposit insurance for small depositors does not change these dynamics.

If there is risk of an indiscriminate systemic run, the government may decide to step in and introduce a blanket guarantee and in effect assume the responsibility for all losses, after shareholders and subordinated debt holders have absorbed theirs. If subordinated debt is used as Tier-2 capital and as an instrument of market discipline, it is essential that the holders of such debt be treated similar to shareholders and lose their stakes in full. A blanket guarantee should be the last option. However, in practice, it is the observed preference of all governments that can afford it. This will be discussed further in the next section.

There is a unique opportunity to impose losses on creditors and depositors of closed institutions before a blanket guarantee is introduced. A government may want to draw a line and inflict losses on creditors and

---

[11] Managers and owners also should be prosecuted to the full extent of the law in cases of fraud and criminality.

[12] For example, although suspensions or closures of banks and other financial institutions were part of the initial measures to stabilize the banking systems in Indonesia, Korea, and Thailand, only Thailand imposed losses on some creditors of the first group of 16 suspended finance companies (near-banks).

depositors of closed institutions, while protecting creditors and depositors in remaining healthier ones. This is politically difficult, however, as such a policy could be seen as arbitrary and biased, especially as the line between institutions to be closed and allowed to remain open may be very hard to establish because of the measurement problems discussed earlier. It may be particularly difficult to apply a different loss-sharing policy to additional institutions that may have to be closed soon after. If such separation is needed, for example, for fiscal reasons, the bias should be in favor of intervening and closing more rather than fewer institutions to give the authorities some respite.

Loss-sharing arrangements are always extremely delicate and must be very carefully considered.[13] They should be designed so that they need not be changed as any tightening of policies later on would be highly inequitable.[14] It is essential for market confidence that all policies and rules with loss-sharing implications be transparent and clearly explained and that they are implemented in as equitable a way as possible across similar types of institutions and over time. If a government decides to assume losses, it must be prepared do so even if the cost turns out to be substantially higher than originally estimates – which typically is the case. An unsustainable government guarantee can often complicate subsequent closure and resolution decisions. The options are discussed further in Chapter 4.

2.6 Limit Contagion

In closing or intervening of individual banks, care must be taken not to cause runs on other banks and undermine confidence in the rest of system. Any major change in old policies and practices, and particularly regarding closures with losses inflicted on creditors and depositors can have devastating systemic effects.[15] Distribution of losses in even a small bank may lead creditors and depositors in other banks to withdraw their funds from other institutions they believe to be weak. Such withdrawals could be slow (a silent run) or reach panic proportions. The withdrawn funds maybe redeposited in banks believed to be stronger, often state- or

---

[13] For a further discussion of loss sharing arrangements, see Sheng (1996).

[14] A tightening of rules would typically mean that stakeholders in the worst institutions would end up receiving the most beneficial treatment.

[15] The most famous case is probably the botched closure of 16 small Indonesian banks in late 1997; see Lindgren et al. (1999). All creditors and depositors of the 16 banks were subsequently compensated in full.

foreign-owned banks, but there also could be an indiscriminate run from all banks in the system regardless of their financial strength. This typically becomes part of capital flight and a run on the currency. Once monetary control is lost, it is not easily regained and the macroeconomic damage can be massive.

Closure of banks with losses distributed to creditors and depositors is a high-wire act in an environment of weak financial institutions and economic prospects. Bank closures must be handled in such a way that they do not lead to expectations of further closures. If initial closures lead to such expectations, there are likely to be runs on banks, often in waves. Any distribution of losses among stakeholders of institutions closed in the early stages must therefore be handled very carefully. If markets and the public can be convinced that initial closures have dealt with all major problems and the rest of the system is sound, the situation might be kept under control, especially if overall economic prospects are positive. In such a situation, closing as many weak or marginal institutions as possibly may help to support claims that remaining institutions are sound and may strengthen confidence in remaining institutions. But if economic and financial conditions are expected to worsen, such policies may not be credible and the situation could deteriorate and cause monetary management to spin out of control.

A government blanket guarantee may be the only way to allow bank closures to proceed in an orderly manner. A blanket guarantee would typically guarantee payment of all bona fide claims of creditors and depositors in domestic currency on their maturity.[16] Such a guarantee is the observed preference of all governments in systemic situations, given that the potential cost (including political costs) of financial contagion and economic dislocations are viewed as being greater than the cost of a blanket guarantee. Once a credible blanket guarantee is in place and the government has assumed responsibility for the claims of depositors and creditors, they have no reason to run, and the pressures on the LOLR typically subside. Closures of banks and other financial institutions can then proceed in an orderly way without fear for contagion on the liability side of financial institutions' balance sheet. (Instead, the contagion risks move to the asset side, as discussed later.)

For a blanket guarantee to work it must be credible. The government must unambiguously back it politically and financially. It typically requires

---

[16] For a description of a proper design of a blanket guarantee and how to reduce moral hazard, see Hoelscher et al. (2003).

special legislation. For a guarantee to be credible, the government also must be seen to have the financial capacity to honor it even in a worst-case scenario. Forcing losses on creditors and depositors in initial closures may increase the credibility of the guarantee by improving the government's capacity to honor it. However, for a blanket guarantee to win credibility it must also be backed up with a comprehensive macroeconomic stabilization package that ensures economic and fiscal sustainability. Transparency of rules as well as efficient and equitable implementation will further improve the credibility of a guarantee.

In cases in which a blanket guarantee is not feasible, closure strategies will need to depend on circumstances. The government may not have the financial capacity to guarantee anything in a credible way. It could still seek to assume losses and share the cost through monetization over time. If contagion and capital flight is acute, some type of standstill or freeze on depositor and creditor claims could be used. Other possible scenarios would include forced conversion of foreign currency obligations into domestic currency or longer maturities, or even debt renegotiations or reductions ("haircuts") of outstanding balances. Regardless of such additional complications, unviable institutions should still be intervened and resolved/closed.

Effective implementation of announced rules for honoring the claims of depositors and creditors will help increase confidence in the authorities' handling of the problems. Market confidence will give decision makers more flexibility. All rules need to be clearly disseminated and equitably and efficiently implemented. The legality of depositor and creditor claims needs to be strictly verified. All *bona fide* deposits, except those of insiders, should be honored. Liabilities of offshore subsidiaries must be carefully ring-fenced. Excessive interest rates may be reduced. Deposits of nonperforming borrowers may be netted against loan balances. To the extent possible, deposits and other liabilities should not be paid in cash but be transferred or sold to other financial institutions (with matching assets).

2.7 Protect Asset Values – Seek Least Cost Resolutions

The intervention or closure of an institution typically reduces the value of its assets.[17] Values of assets decline as the relationships between

---

[17] Exceptions are those rare cases in which the assets of an intervened or closed institution become subject to a different legal framework, which increases the recoverability of the assets (for example, Danaharta in Malaysia).

an institution and its borrowers change. As borrowers sever ongoing banking relationships, they tend to become less able or willing to service their loans. The legal and political framework may facilitate or even encourage nonpayment. If closures result in credits and other financial assets being unattended, values may deteriorate rapidly and losses increase. Loan delinquency is contagious. If allowed to spread, loan values could erode throughout the financial system and could lead to the failure of institutions that initially were sound.

When closing a financial institution, a resolution strategy should already have been decided on. Resolution may start the moment an institution is closed but should have been planned carefully in advance. When a closure is preceded by supervisory intervention, there is typically more time to explore various asset resolution options. A closure strategy should always include adequate arrangements for managing the assets of closed institutions; this could include strengthened legal and institutional infrastructures.

Resolutions should be guided by least cost (or least loss) criteria. This means that asset values be protected and resolutions costs minimized in order to restore maximum value to claim holders. In a resolution with loss sharing, the recovery value is to be maximized for creditors and uninsured depositors. In resolution with a blanket guarantee, recovery value should be maximized (and losses/costs minimized) for the government. Least loss calculations need to be based on estimates of net present asset values under different recovery scenarios, including estimates for operational, recovery and financing costs. That is no easy task, especially in a period of macroeconomic uncertainty, when future prices and interest rates are difficult to predict.

Resolution of closed banks will involve decisions on whether to sell assets in blocks or individually, and whether to hold/rehabilitate or sell/liquidate assets.[18] This involves the traditional dilemma of quick liquidation, possibly at low "fire-sale" prices, on the one hand, and holding on to assets and increasing their value through careful management, on the other hand. Although time should often take priority over price in asset resolutions, this varies depending on circumstances. Quick sales may be more suitable for small-scale problems when markets are still working, whereas "fire sales" (at rock bottom prices) in systemic situations may destroy asset values throughout the financial system and ultimately be far

---

[18] For a broader discussion of asset management issues in a systemic setting, see Lindgren et al. (1999) and Hoelscher et al. (2003).

from a least-cost solution.[19] There are also different ways to structure contingent sales and prices, which, of course, may push any final liquidation far into the future.[20]

Active management of loan relationships and portfolios is essential in order to protect the value of assets. Loans are the main assets of banks and many other financial institutions. If loan files, collateral documentation or client relationships are destroyed or abandoned, asset values can erode sharply. Borrower information must be protected and preserved for performing and nonperforming loans alike. This means protecting the integrity and documentation of loan files and making sure that relationships with borrowers continue to be actively managed. This process may best be managed by new owners of the assets, but until the assets have been sold it will require the involvement of key loan officers in the loan workout and liquidation process even after an institution is intervened or closed.

Given the right conditions, mergers and P&A transactions can be ideal resolution techniques. Over-the-weekend absorption of assets by other banks or financial institutions – government-assisted or unassisted – are textbook examples of how to do efficient least-cost closures. However, such operations typically work only in situations in which problems are not yet widespread, there is a pool of interested buyers/investors, and asset markets are working reasonably well. Such operations seldom work when market conditions have been allowed to deteriorate, asset values are highly questionable, financial weaknesses are believed to be widespread and growing, and the priority of other financial institutions is to preserve their capital and liquidity, that is, simply to stay "alive."

Mergers of two weak institutions or sales of assets at inflated prices to weak institutions are seldom permanent solutions. Such transactions may be orchestrated or under pressure from the government. It often involves state-owned or -controlled banks. Although such transactions may provide a temporary relief for besieged supervisors, they seldom lead to viable solutions and typically only cause larger problems later on.

---

[19] Pricing is always the most difficult issue in asset resolution. Sellers/liquidators want something approximating written-down book values, whereas buyers want bargain prices – the more so the more distressed market conditions are.

[20] There is often a mutual interest in having some type of conditional pricing – the seller wants to share in any possible "upside" and the buyer wants to reduce risk of additional losses. Various types of contingency pricing agreements and debt-to-equity transactions can be structured to bring assets under proper management as soon as possible to prevent further deterioration.

It is essential that only institutions that have the managerial and financial capacity to absorb such assets be allowed to purchase them. Needless to say, owners and managers of acquiring institutions should also meet fit and proper criteria. Prudent mergers and asset transfers will reduce eventual resolution costs to private creditors and the government, as may be the case.

When distressed assets represent an important share in the financial system, special institutional arrangements may have to be relied on. Although decentralized and market-based resolution options may be preferable in principle, they simply may not be available on the scale that is required. A bridge bank may be the preferred vehicle to receive and manage the good assets of one or several intervened or closed institutions. For larger problems, the complexity and volume of the resolution may require specialized government-owned resolution agencies. The least-cost solution is typically a combination of different decentralized and centralized arrangements that rely on available private sector capabilities as much as possible.

Once a financial institution has been intervened or closed, the loss-sharing problems (and moral hazard) move to the asset side of balance sheets. The liquidator or government will assume responsibility for banks or bank assets and must seek to manage them in such a way that asset values are protected and losses minimized. Management arrangements must be put in place to keep pressure on good borrowers to keep serving their loans and match repayment terms for nonperforming loans with delinquent borrowers' capacity to service loans. This may include loan restructuring, with the threat of foreclosure and bankruptcy procedures for recalcitrant borrowers. Loss sharing becomes a negotiating issue between creditors/the government, on the one hand, and bank borrowers, on the other hand.[21] The balance is largely determined by the ability of the political, legal and judicial systems to protect creditor rights. A loss of credit discipline is highly contagious and may lead to destruction of asset values throughout the financial system and the demise of other financial institutions.

---

[21] Borrowers have incentives not to give up control of their collateral or companies. They are often prepared to go to great lengths to defend their property rights, including influencing legislators, judicial, and government officials through legal and illegal means. Financial institutions often end up being forced to give concessions asymmetrically, that is, to share borrowers' losses up front without having a claim on potential future profits. To counter this, they may try to get control of borrowers' businesses and future profits through debt-to-equity swaps and measure to control borrowers' cash flow.

2.8 Linkages with the Macroeconomy

Any closure strategy must take into account how it will affect and how it will be affected by the macroeconomic environment. Closing one or a few small banks or other financial institutions could be expected to have a limited effect. But closure of a significant part of the financial system may affect economic activity, as depositor and creditor balances may be temporarily unavailable or permanently lost, credit relationships broken, and credit discipline eroded. Bank runs may affect monetary stability, lead to capital outflows and pressures on exchange and interest rates that may substantially affect economic activity. The most damaging scenario is one of closures leading to a system-wide freeze of depositor and creditor claims and an interruption in the payments system.

Fiscal costs must be minimized when closures imply government expenditure. There is a need to make sure that any closure strategy involves the least cost to the public sector. This may imply early closures, before losses have been allowed to accumulate because of lax regulations, forbearance, or LOLR liquidity support. Losses absorbed by a funded deposit insurance scheme may reduce government outlays. The government may avoid fiscal costs by not introducing a blanket guarantee – although this may be short lived if the lack of a guarantee causes contagion and leads to much larger costs later on. There may be resistance to closure or resolution because it would involve costs to the government – costs that it "cannot afford," even if its chosen policy obliges it to cover them. That is never a valid argument, because delaying action invariably makes the ultimate fiscal costs even larger.

Once a government has introduced a blanket guarantee and taken responsibility for the liabilities of financial institutions it has to bear all losses that ensue. Losses can be minimized through a well-managed resolution process, which will preserve financial asset values and reduce ultimate losses – that is, a least-cost resolution. With a view to minimizing costs, closure must always be considered as an option. Ultimate fiscal costs also can be kept down by not introducing government subsidies or allowing legal or judicial leniency for borrowers. Governments normally have to issue debt to pay for such losses and may chose to distribute the burden of such debt over time through monetization (inflation). These options are considered more fully in Chapter 4. To the extent the government's capacity to issue new debt is limited, it may not be able to honor its guarantee and the only options available may be a freeze or securitization of depositor's and creditor's claims.

Closures can lead to a credit crunch and affect economic activity. Broken credit relationships of borrowers in certain subsectors or regions can be hard to replace and can lead to unnecessary financial hardships, bankruptcies, and closures of companies. Companies owned by universal banks or part of financial or nonfinancial groups or conglomerates that include closed banks may see their businesses erode as a result of contagion effects and be forced unnecessarily into bankruptcy. As solvency comes under pressure system-wide (perhaps after an initial round of closures) financial institutions become more interested in securing their own solvency and survival than extending new loans. Such a credit crunch often reflects the necessary downsizing of a financial system after a credit bubble. But it still needs to be considered in the overall closure strategy and needs to be explained to politicians and the public alike. If credit discipline is deteriorating, perhaps as a result of dynamics unleashed by the resolution of closed institutions, new credit may dry up altogether.

Any closure of financial institutions that may have a systemic impact must take macroeconomic linkages into consideration. This does not mean that closures decisions be delayed or avoided, only that they take place after a proper analysis of the two-way linkages between different closure and macroeconomic scenarios. The intent should be to strengthen confidence and avoid, as far as possible, any major mid-course changes in the strategy and loss sharing arrangements. Reversal of closure or burden sharing decisions can have devastating effects on market confidence and efforts to normalize the system.

2.9 Legal Framework

A clear and transparent legal framework for intervention or closure of financial institutions is essential.[22] As mentioned earlier, closures (with or without loss sharing) redistribute wealth and are likely to be strongly contested. Close attention, therefore, needs to be paid to the legal backing of every aspect of the closure process, including criteria and triggers for closures, dilution, and write-off of shareholder rights, loss sharing among classes of stakeholders, and so on. Failure to pay attention to procedural issues and what may seem like legal details up front may result in legal hurdles that later may slow down or even bring the entire closure process to a halt.

---

[22] For a broader discussion, see Asser (2002).

There is a need to explore linkages with other legislation, both domestically and abroad. To the extent a financial institution is part of a group that owns other financial or nonfinancial institutions, each part of the group may be subject to different legislation. The intervention or closure of banking, insurance, investment, and securities companies may involve different stakeholder rights, processes, and timetables. In the case of interventions or closures of financial institutions with foreign operations, perhaps in several different jurisdictions, the legal complexities are likely to multiply. It is essential to know the legal implications of different closure or intervention strategies as fully as possible before embarking on them.

There may be a need to clarify existing legislation with new regulations and directives, always with the objective of bringing increased transparency and uniformity to the legal framework. At the same time, there may be political forces working against such transparency, as dealing with institutions on an opaque case-by-case basis gives more opportunities for special favors and financial bailouts in different forms. Transparent laws and regulations will strengthen the willingness of supervisors and other officials to take decisive actions in the public interest. Work on such clarifications must be an integral part of the preparations for interventions or closures.

If problems are systemic, the situation may require a new legal framework, especially if the existing legislation is designed to deal only with individual institutions in normal times. It may be necessary to provide additional intervention powers to the supervisory authority and prescribe new loss sharing arrangements. Normal corporate bankruptcy procedures may be inadequate to deal with financial institutions, especially in a systemic situation and may need to be replaced by new administrative or summary procedures for intervention and closure. If a blanket guarantee is used, it normally must be backed by law to gain necessary force and credibility.

New laws also may be required for the management of asset restructuring and resolution, especially when the volume of assets to be resolved is large. Slow and cumbersome judicial procedures may have to be modernized based on best practices in countries with similar legal traditions. New laws may have to be introduced or existing ones amended to give added flexibility for assets transfers and sales, to remove tax and other hurdles in the resolution process and to guide the establishment of private asset resolution vehicles. Foreclosure and bankruptcy laws and procedures for borrowers may have to be strengthened and streamlined to handle a high volume of cases. Further discussion of alternative approaches to bankruptcy is presented in Chapter 8.

An inefficient or corrupt judiciary may become a major stumbling block for interventions, closures and resolutions. Corruption and inefficiency may affect all levels of the judiciary staff, from judges to administrative clerks. Owners of financial institutions that have been or are about to be intervened or closed may seek to sabotage the judicial process, perhaps by creating endless judicial delays and by using their political clout and financial resources to influence the courts in their favor. Similarly, loan defaulters may fight foreclosures, bankruptcies, and corporate restructuring deals using all means at their disposal – both legal and illegal.

The authorities' intervention and closure strategy must take into account the condition of the judicial system. Unnecessarily slow and cumbersome judicial procedures can derail an intervention or closure strategy. This may be because of a lack of capacity of the judiciary to handle complex cases but also to other influences. Extra-judicial procedures may have to be established that minimize the interference of the courts in the resolution and closure process. Courts may hear appeals but not be allowed to stop interventions or closures. In case of systemic crisis, special courts and additional infrastructure may have to be introduced to facilitate speedy and predictable judicial attention to closure, resolution, and liquidation cases. Increased government budget allocations may be required to strengthen the capacity of overburdened courts.

A key legal issue in interventions, closures, and subsequent resolutions of financial institutions is to make sure that supervisors and other key officials are protected under the law for actions taken in pursuit of their legally mandated tasks. Officials involved in the closure and resolution process are open to intimidation and interference every step of the closure and resolution process. If officials do not feel protected, they will not make decisions in the public interest. The law has to ensure that officials need not fear legal harassment, frivolous lawsuits, and high costs of defending themselves for actions taken in good faith in the conduct of their official duties. The law must seek to give officials the right incentives for making decisions based on what is best for the financial system and the economy.

2.10 Institutional and Political Framework

A common problem in managing closures of financial institutions is a lack of political support. Often politicians are unable to deal with the range of uncertainties that officials face in closures: for example, why data are not firm, why losses cannot be precisely established, why no one told them before, why the extent of possible contagion is not known – just to mention a few. They may lack the will to do anything because of fears of fiscal and macroeconomic consequences or the effect of resolution measures on powerful supporters and constituencies. Ideally, politicians should leave intervention and closure decisions to supervisors, especially in cases of institutions without systemic importance. But there are also key decisions like loss sharing and changes to the legal framework, which are eminently political in nature and where politicians must be fully involved.

Politically well-connected shareholders will try to sabotage closures. They often will try to stop intervention and closure, and delay dilution or loss of their shares. They will fight to preserve control of their institution using all means at their disposal, including intimidation or corruption of government, judiciary, and supervisory officials. They will try to maintain options to buy back their institution or assets at bargain prices after creditors and government have absorbed losses. Closure decisions that are capriciously held up or reversed by a court or government body, or cannot be implemented for lack of police support or other enforcement power may not only expose financial institutions or assets to major losses but also may broadly damage supervisory authority and discipline in the financial system.

After intervention or closure, politically well-connected borrowers will try to avoid servicing their loans. Pressures will mount for lenient application of loan classification and provisioning rules, government imposed debt moratoria, unilateral debt relief, direct subsidies, and so on. Economic hardship and disaster scenarios will be used to scare politicians. Pressures also will be put on the judiciary. Such efforts may be driven by borrowers with the least capacity to honor their contracts or with most political influence, which often may be the same. Even borrowers with capacity to service their loans will join the bandwagon. The end result may be a generalized breakdown of credit discipline that could become extremely expensive to the government, and severely limit the intermediary role of the financial system. Breakdowns in credit discipline are almost always caused by political and judicial decisions.

Coordination among different authorities is essential in managing an effective least-cost closure and resolution process.[23] Official entities often operate at cross-purposes. There is a need to recognize that different authorities have different roles to play in the intervention and closure

---

[23] For a broader discussion, see Nyberg (1997).

process, and that there is a need to share information and coordinate objectives, decisions, and implementation efforts. The more complex and widespread the context of bank closures, the more necessary will be formal institutional arrangements for coordinating decision making. The supervisory authority is formally in charge of interventions and closures (even if decisions de facto may have been made by another government body). It needs to coordinate closely with the monetary authority/LOLR. The government may be involved as owner of state banks, guarantor of depositors or a deposit insurance scheme, and as the ultimate provider of solvency support for the system. Close policy coordination will help in managing interventions and closures, containing systemic problems, and reducing ultimate resolution costs.

An effective intervention, closure, and resolution framework will require support from the highest political authorities. Such support is necessary to give strength to interagency coordination efforts, increase acceptance of technical resolution options, sustain prosecutions in the judicial system and counter lobbying efforts – just to name a few reasons. The more the top political authorities are prepared to limit their involvement to broad objectives and strategies, the more effective and predictable the process is likely to be. Interference by politicians clearly is a major pitfall in managing the intervention, closure, and resolution process.

The existence of a deposit insurance scheme can prove helpful in managing closures. Explicit insurance of small depositors is likely to make closures of individual banks politically easier, even in cases in which large depositors and creditors incur losses. The law of a deposit insurance agency may help clarify intervention and closure procedures, if the agency has been assigned specific responsibilities for closing and resolving banks and other deposit-taking institutions. It also may have specialized staff and other infrastructure ready to deal with closures and resolutions and may be well prepared to draw on the experiences of similar agencies in other countries.

Lack of human resources may be a key constraint for effective interventions and closures. If several financial institutions with large branch networks are intervened and closed at once, hundreds or even thousands of staff and security personnel may need to be involved. This may have to be done in the face of militant resistance from the intervened/closed institutions' personnel or labor unions. Needless to say, this will require careful planning and preparation, including an information campaign. Intervention teams need to be trained in key actions, such as to secure premises, protect assets and files, immobilize correspondent accounts, and so on.[24] At the same time, every effort must be made to keep supervisory attention focused on the soundness of remaining institutions, and especially on the core banking system.

Closures and resolutions will require highly skilled staff, including lawyers, bankers, forensic accountants, loan workout specialists, and so on. Domestically, such expertise may only be found among retirees with relevant past closure experiences. If no domestic expertise is available, it will need to be brought in from abroad. Such expertise is often expensive – but that cannot be allowed to be a constraint, because *not* dealing with losses in a speedy manner is bound to be much more expensive. Local professionals may have to get crash courses in the operational intricacies and pitfalls of interventions, closures and resolutions.

Lack of information and transparency will hamper the closure process and make it more difficult to maintain systemic stability. Too much information at the wrong time, of course, also may hurt the process. As discussed earlier, closures – and especially closures with loss sharing – can easily create panic and contagion. An effective information and communications strategy is a crucial but often neglected aspect of any intervention, resolution, closure, and liquidation. An information strategy must make the public aware of the reasons for closures, the broader context, the treatment of different categories of stakeholders, any loss-sharing requirements, the main features of the restructuring strategy, supportive macroeconomic policies, and the role of the government and its agencies. A well-crafted information campaign can reduce uncertainty and greatly facilitate the closure and resolution process.

Consistency of information is also important. Politicians should seek to avoid making statements and interpretations of the rules, because every exception becomes the new rule, with unpredictable consequences. Clear and consistent information will help prevent rumors and misinformation as well as erosion of private sector confidence. When information is not communicated properly or, worse, when different authorities give conflicting messages, confidence is eroded, possibly to the point where the closure and restructuring process is severely derailed. Regardless of the institutional setup, it is therefore essential to have a single official spokesman for all aspects of an intervention and resolution process, especially regarding details of closures and loss sharing. The strategy must be explained in a transparent manner and in sufficient detail for different audiences, including assurances of equitable treatment of similar types of institutions

---

[24] For a description of such specific actions, see FDIC Closure Manual, FDIC (1998).

and stakeholders over time. Although hard to estimate, the cost of information lapses can be very high and typically end up being borne by the government.

3. CONCLUSIONS

We have discussed pitfalls in managing closures of financial institutions under ten headings. It has considered closure not as a legal event but rather as part of a complex process of institutional exit, which distributes losses and brings bank assets and liabilities back into the market under new ownership with as little loss of value as possible. Intervening and closing financial institutions becomes more complex and critical the more widespread or systemic the problems are, and the more cross-ownership there is among different categories of financial institutions and across legal jurisdictions.

Formidable information and measurement problems often make it difficult to develop a solid strategy and meet legal prerequisites for closures. Values will become firmer only over time as institutions are intervened and due diligence and assets sales get started. It is easier to close one or a few small institutions than a large bank at the core of the payments system. Early intervention is desirable but requires legal basis that may be difficult to establish when solvency measures are unreliable. Forbearance and LOLR liquidity support can seldom be stopped without intervention or closure that may have to be based on liquidity triggers.

The most critical issue in managing closures is loss sharing. Assigning losses to creditors and depositors involves a delicate balance between allowing market discipline to work, on the one hand, and unleashing widespread runs, on the other hand. Contagion may be avoided by introducing a blanket guarantee, which may halt withdrawals and allow closures to proceed in an orderly manner but may also be extremely costly as the government becomes responsible for all losses. A plan for efficient asset management must be ready to be implemented as soon as an institution is intervened or closed.

Any closure strategy must consider the effects on the macroeconomy as well as the effects of different macroeconomic stress scenarios. Closures must scrupulously follow the law to avoid legal hurdles bringing the process to a halt. Weaknesses in the legal and judicial frameworks may have to be dealt with. Political support is crucial albeit often difficult in the face of efforts by influential owners and borrowers to get relief. Having a deposit insurance agency in place may facilitate the closure process.

Coordination between official agencies is essential and may even require a new authority. Lack of skilled staff and expertise may be a major bottleneck. Effective dissemination of information is essential for any resolution and closure strategy to normalize the system.

ACKNOWLEDGMENTS

I am grateful to Jerry Caprio, Augusto de la Torre, David Hoelscher, Patrick Honohan, Luc Laeven, and participants at the World Bank Conference on "Systemic Financial Distress: Containment and Resolution" for helpful comments, and Guillermo Noguera for research assistance.

FOUR

Fiscal, Monetary, and Incentive Implications of Bank Recapitalization

Patrick Honohan

INTRODUCTION

Recapitalizing banking systems is a messy and risky business. Governments come under tremendous pressure to buy all the nonperforming or problematic loans in a distressed banking system, to subsidize the borrowers and to put the banks back on to a profitable basis with a comfortable capital margin. The goal of lobbyists is that there should be "no losers," yet someone has to bear the losses that have been incurred and are reflected in the need for recapitalization. As a result of these pressures, governments often assume obligations greater than they should, given other priorities for the use of public funds. Sometimes they assume more than they can afford leading to subsequent disorderly reliance on the inflation tax.

In the resolution phase, there is time to get things right. For a while, this may be done while keeping the bank under official nationalized control, and while that is the case it is probably too soon to be thinking in terms of recapitalization. Eventually, though, the authorities will generally want to return the bank to normal autonomous functioning under private ownership. This may be done by a financial restructuring of each failed bank, or by merging the continuing business into a healthy bank. In either case, there will have to be an additional transfer of value from official sources. In this way, bank recapitalizations often involve an official injection of resources into failed institutions.

How should this transfer of value, this recapitalization, of failed banks be designed? How can it be done in such a way as to ensure that the new owners and managers have the right incentives to operate the newly recapitalized bank in a prudent manner ensuring its good subsequent performance? How can the government's budget and the interests of the taxpayer be protected? What account needs to be taken of the impact of the recapitalization on aggregate monetary conditions?

Our premise is that practical decisions here have been unduly constrained by fears of the possible side-effects on fiscal and monetary conditions. Properly understood, fiscal and monetary concerns should not prevent financial instrument design from ensuring the best incentives for the correct balance between prudence and risk-taking in the restructured system.

This is not a plea to subordinate fiscal and monetary policy to financial policy, but it does seek to liberate financial sector policy makers from undue peer pressure from their fiscal and monetary counterparts on the grounds that: (1) in the case of monetary policy, sufficient instruments exist to offset potentially damaging effects of bank restructuring; and (2) in the case of fiscal policy, attempts to ease the fiscal pressure of restructuring through instrument design all too often amount to no more that an ineffective attempt to conceal the true extent of the losses by deferring their recognition.

This chapter is organized as follows: Section 1 begins with an overview of the initial budgetary decisions and how the implementation of these budgetary decisions should be logically sequenced. Section 2 examines how an injection of assets in the financial restructuring of failed banks can best be designed to restore bank capital, liquidity, and incentives. Section 3 discusses the capital-type claims that the government may acquire as a counterpart of the asset injection, and to allow it to claw back some of the injection of value in the event of unexpectedly favorable debt recovery. Section 4 examines the consequences for the budget and debt management. Section 5 draws out the implications for monetary policy and macroeconomic stability. Section 6 concludes.

1. DISENTANGLING THE STRANDS

1.1 When to Rescue

Bank restructuring requires much more than getting the financial structures right. When the authorities realize that they have a crisis of bank insolvency on their hands, policy decisions and actions are required in several different dimensions. The authorities will have to intervene in the management of failed banks to stop any further erosion of net asset value. Incompetent or corrupt management will have to be replaced by fit and proper persons supported by adequate operational procedures and information systems, and capable of bringing operating costs under control. The authorities will, we take it, want to put the bank back into private ownership, with suitable new controlling shareholders. Arrangements need to be put in place for recovery of as much as possible of the nonperforming bank assets (see the discussion by Calomiris, Klingebiel, and Laeven in Chapter 2). In what follows, we assume that these prerequisites are being put in place in parallel (Carl Lindgren discussed many of the practical issues in Chapter 3) and more generally that the policy environment is consistent with banks operating both prudently and profitably.[1]

Logically, the first of the required financial decisions relates to the allocation of the net losses as between the various claimants of the bank. If a failed bank is simply to be liquidated, then that process can take its course without further specific official action. But often the government will decide to keep much of the failed bank's activities going, using government funds to honor more of the depositors' claims than can be met from the remaining value of the bank's assets. Such a decision has to take into account the implications for the budget and ultimately for the taxpayer (as the present value of injected government capital must ultimately be supported by increased taxes or decreases in other spending programs).[2]

In making the decision to commit public funds to such a purpose, principles of capital budgeting apply including (1) the often neglected principle of public finance that the marginal social return on public spending needs to be higher than that on private spending (because of the deadweight marginal cost of public funds);[3] and (2) separability of the investment from the financing decision.

The first of these principles sets a high barrier for government bailouts. It implies that the government should not invest public funds except where

---

[1] Useful references for this wider context include Alexander et al. (1997), Dziobek (1998), Enoch et al. (1999), Roulier (1995), and Sheng (1996). Recapitalization of banks with government funds is not recommended when some of these conditions are not present: the likelihood is that unsuitable owners or management will dissipate the newly injected funds as they did their previous capital.

[2] Many of these issues are settled, for good or ill, during the containment phase (cf. Lindgren, Chapter 3). The government's actions in that fast-moving stage will often have locked in such matters as which banks are to continue in operation, and especially what deposits will be honored, irrespective of the banks' internal capacity to do so.

[3] The point is that, in order to raise funds to pay for public projects, the government must impose taxes that, at the margin, impose a costly distortion on private sector behavior (except in the unlikely case that it has at its disposal sufficient lump-sum or corrective taxes). Cf. Squire (1989).

there is a "public good" aspect – a social return that cannot be captured by private entities. As an application of this principle, compensating depositors for losses incurred is not a sufficient reason, to the extent that it is simply a transfer.[4] Avoiding the disruption to the payments system, loss of information capital embodied in the existing banks, and damage to general business confidence that might result from widespread bank liquidations could represent more plausible reasons for employing public funds to rescue a bank, but these costs must be carefully weighed against the alternative uses of the funds on a case-by-case basis for each failing bank.

Therefore, depositors should not always be bailed-out. In practice, even short of leaving them to their share in the liquidation (and to any entitlement they may have from a formal deposit insurance scheme), many alternatives have been tried, including temporary depositor freezes, forced write-downs or conversion of deposits to long-term claims on government. As discussed earlier by Calomiris, Klingebiel, and Laeven (Chapter 2), by deflating the real value of the bank's liabilities, use of the inflation tax through currency depreciation and monetary financing of the banks' deficits represents an alternative resolution, albeit one with its own drawbacks.

1.2 Implications for Fiscal and Monetary Policy

If, nevertheless, there is to be a large injection of public funds, how this is done can have significant consequences for the budget deficit and for the conduct of monetary policy, as well as for the profitability of, and incentive structure for, the recapitalized banks. The principle of separating investment from financing decisions points to how possible conflicts between these can be reconciled.

Injecting marketable instruments into the banking system raises issues of monetary policy. If the banks are thereby made too liquid, the excessive liquidity needs to be mopped-up by other instruments of monetary policy. But the important point is that this can normally be done. Therefore, monetary policy should *respond* to the recapitalization, rather than determining its design.

The fiscal authorities are often keen to defer the fiscal realization of the problem, whether through zero-coupon bonds, nonmarketable

---

[4] Unless it be a redistributional strategy to rescue low-income losers. In practice, depositor bailouts (beyond what has been promised through a formal deposit insurance scheme) tend to go disproportionately to the richest members of society.

instruments, or other mechanisms that appear to reduce the cost but can ultimately increase it. It will not usually be necessary to provide cash, and indeed long-term bonds often seem to be the option that is preferred by governments. But the yield and other characteristics of these bonds do matter. In particular, there is a temptation for the government to issue bonds carrying below-market interest, but this should be avoided especially if it leaves the bank economically insolvent, and thus at risk of looting, despite satisfying simplistic accounting solvency ratios. And other features are also important, including marketability, maturity, and frequency of repricing interest.

Some practitioners argue that the uncertainty surrounding the true recoverable value of the bank's remaining assets means that the authorities should not feel obliged to allocate immediately the maximum amount that could conceivably be required; against this others note that even the new management of an undercapitalized bank could be tempted to adopt too risky a strategy. The proposed resolution here is that the bank must be adequately capitalized, but with the government retaining a claim that enables it to benefit from unexpectedly favorable subsequent performance.

No single approach is likely to meet all possible initial conditions. We attempt to set out the major considerations involved in a way that will allow solutions for specific cases to be developed in a way that is sensitive to country conditions. To some extent the best solution, and indeed the available range of solutions, will depend on the scale of the initial insolvency in the banking system, but other elements of preexisting country conditions, such as the inherited credibility of government policies and the level of development of securities markets, are probably more important in determining the range of instruments and strategies that is available.

Relevant aspects of government credibility include (1) its preexisting indebtedness and its capacity to tax (higher indebtedness relative to taxing capacity imply low credibility for future spending promises); (2) the solidity of contractual commitment (if these are already weak, it is hard for the government to have its promises taken seriously, as its potential contractual partners perceive that reneging in the future will have little cost to it); and (3) the institutional arrangements for monetary and exchange rate policy (where these are weak, the possibility of surprise inflationary finance will always be discounted in any dealings agents may have with the government).

A second key determinant of what is possible is the sophistication, depth, and liquidity of the capital markets. If there is no trading in long-term debt instruments, for example, it is hard to price fixed-interest bonds that might be injected into a bank's balance sheet and, although steps can be taken to develop bond markets, the circumstances surrounding bank failure may not be the very best for doing this.

1.3 The General Solution: Four Distinct Tools to be Applied in a Logical Sequence

The general solution proposed here is that four distinct policy tools need to be used for four distinct goals but in concert. The tools are: injecting assets, adjusting capital claims on the bank, rebalancing the government's own debt management, and managing monetary policy instruments to maintain monetary stability. Once the decision to inject funds has been taken, however, the actual policy instruments that are adopted can be chosen according to the following logical sequence, which simplifies decision making.

First, the government (or its agencies) typically needs to inject assets into the banking system: their effective and actual maturity, their yield and their liquidity should be governed by the goals of restoring the bank to a *capitalization and prospective earnings profile* consistent with safe-and-sound banking. This typically means that the assets should be marketable, bearing floating market-related interest rates and preferably with maturities no longer than those actually traded in the market; in short they should be bankable. The risk-profile of the assets is also a consideration, for example, if their value is still linked to loan recovery, or if the government's own creditworthiness is not high: here financial engineering can help. Throughout, transparency is essential.

Second, the liability side of the bank's balance sheet also may need to be restructured. Government's claims here represent the government's quid-pro-quo for funds injected, and they represent an attempt to secure, in the event of a better-than-expected out-turn for the bank, some return to the taxpayer consistent with an adequate *incentive structure* for the bank's private owners.

Given the policy stance adopted for the first two tools, the remaining two are adjusted to meet the goals of *fiscal and monetary management*. The third step is then rebalancing the government's debt structure. The first two tools will have an impact on the time profile of the government's cash position. Reoptimizing its deficit and debt management policy conditional on this impact will give rise to a need to adjust spending, tax and debt issuance policy.

Finally, monetary policy has sufficient instruments to offset any unto-ward impact of the remaining policies on monetary stability.

This logical ordering allows for a simplified allocation of responsibili-ties between different arms of government: first, financial incentives for the institutions, then fiscal affairs, and finally a monetary response.

2. ENSURING THAT THE BANK HAS ENOUGH CAPITAL, LIQUIDITY, AND INCENTIVES

Probably the most crucial issue in designing the recapitalization of a bank is that of ensuring that the bank truly moves forward with adequate capi-tal.[5] This is not always achieved even by schemes that purport to do so. The most common method, and the one we will concentrate on, involves the government injecting assets into the bank's balance sheet.[6] Typically, this is not cash; instead, nonperforming assets are replaced or supplemented in the bank's portfolio by a government bond or obligation.

Recall that we are starting the analysis from the point at which the government has already (1) decided that a restructured bank will be re-capitalized and taken into majority private ownership; and (2) decided on the issue of loss allocation and on which classes of the old liabilities are to be on the balance sheet. Restating the bank's balance sheet to reflect the best estimate of the expected recoverable value of the old assets, the to-be-recapitalized bank will, before injection of new funds, begin either with negative capital, or with positive but inadequate capital.

The bank's new shareholders will be putting up funds. After all, they will end up with a fully capitalized bank together with some franchise

---

[5] This is not merely common sense. Repeated bank recapitalizations are found to be asso-ciated with higher fiscal costs (Honohan and Klingebiel, 2003). Andrews (2003) provides a complementary presentation of several of the issues discussed in this section.

[6] The two most common alternatives to injecting assets are (1) assumption of some of the liabilities of the bank by the government or by the deposit protection agency (this usually reduces to a bond injection into the system as the authorities mop up the excess liquidity created by the official assumption of liabilities); or (2) subsidization of delinquent borrowers with a view to helping them service their bank borrowings. Subsidization of borrowers can be a costly way of dealing with bank insolvency. Bringing borrowers back to economic health will generally entail larger subventions than those needed simply to make good on their bank borrowings, and the flow of subsidies tends to be long lasting. Besides, the deadweight of unnecessary subsidy that is inevitably involved in government programs is duplicated if both banks and borrowers are being dealt with. Full transparency of such subsidies is rarely achieved. The extraordinary budgetary cost of the early (1982) Chilean crisis is likely at least partly attributable to the decision to bail out borrowers. The more recent experience of Mexico with its Punto Final program is discussed, more sympathetically, by Calomiris, Klingebiel, and Laeven in Chapter 2.

value. Indeed, if the bank's balance sheet contains some positive capital going into the recapitalization, then one may be able to leave it to the new shareholders to inject enough funds to reach the regulatory capital requirement. But if the bank's initial capital is negative, then the government will also be injecting funds.

In this section we ask what the terms and conditions of the injected assets should be. In return for injecting assets, the government may acquire a capital claim on the bank. The terms of such a claim are considered in Section 3.

2.1 Ensuring Credibility of the Instruments Employed

Credibility is the overriding requirement. First, this requires that the operation be entirely transparent, that the resulting fiscal costs can be absorbed, and that the government's prospective debt profile is a sustainable one. It also requires that, even though the government is handing out money now, it is not thereby signaling an open-ended intention to bail out shareholders, managers, or large creditors in the future.

But credibility is also required at the level of the financial instruments used to replace bad debts in the balance sheet of insolvent banks. There is always a temptation for governments to opt for injecting an instrument with low cash outlays. For example, a government might simply offer the bank a non-interest-bearing bullet bond with a long maturity, but the same face value as that of the nonperforming assets. The real value of such a bond falls well short of the value of performing loans of equal face value. A bank that is offered no more than that in return for ceding nonperforming loans is likely to run into difficulties again, as its operations cannot easily be brought back to profitability.

Even if sufficient zero-coupon bonds are injected to bring the *net present value* of the promised payments up to the required level (when calculated at the risk-free discount rate), such an arrangement cannot be regarded as satisfactory from the credibility point of view. A government that acts like that will be suspected of temporizing. Market participants will likely assume that it has no clear idea of how it is going to fund the bullet payment at maturity. Accordingly, holders will discount the value of the bond, attaching only a moderate probability to its being honored in full and on time. Marked-to-market, a bank holding such an asset may still be insolvent, and may feel itself to be insolvent, with all of the incentive problems that creates. If the bond is tradable in a fairly competitive market, these valuation and credibility problems will come out in the open and force the government to face up to them.[7]

2.2 Maturity, Yield, and Negotiability of Injected Assets

In the presence of deep capital markets with a wide range of available maturities, the exact maturity of any marketable government bond injected into the bank will be of little consequence for the incentives facing the bank, as the bank will easily and speedily be able to exchange it for assets of the desired maturity. Even if the injection of funds is large relative to the overall size of the capital markets, the choice of maturity can be left as a matter of overall debt management policy, and not as one of banking policy.

In countries where the capital markets are not so deep, the choice of maturity matters more. Once again there is a temptation for the government to lock the bank in, with the use of long-term bonds not easily (or perhaps at all) marketable. But use of long-term bonds in such circumstances has at least four drawbacks. First, they are difficult to value: if there is no active long-term bond market, the authorities may (and do) argue that the appropriate long-term interest rate is much lower than current short-term interest rates. But unless the bank can convert some of its liabilities into a form that has equally low yield, this will create a long-term profitability gap that will tend to result in decapitalization of the bank over time.

Second, much as with zero-coupon bonds, though to a lesser extent, government reluctance to commit contractually to repaying this indebtedness soon can leave a doubt as to authorities' real commitment to honoring it. If so, this will clearly discourage potential bank owners from investing in the bank.

Third, the strategy may induce too much interest rate risk into the bank's balance sheet. If the long-term bond bears a fixed interest rate, this will expose the bank to the risk that market interest rates will change (this can be avoided by specifying that the bond's interest rate float with the market).

---

[7] These issues arose acutely in the case of the so-called Zunk bonds issued by the Bulgarian government to recapitalize several banks and that were held in the books of the banks at nominal values that, because of the low coupon rates, were much higher than market value (Honohan, 2003).

Fourth, the bank's ability to resume lending to the private sector will be limited for the duration of the bond's maturity, thereby reducing the flexibility of the banking system's response to emerging lending opportunities.

The most straightforward approach then, is to inject a type of asset that is more in line with the sort of asset that a bank would voluntarily hold on its balance sheet: short term, and with the interest rate floating in line with the market. In short, with an asset that can readily be regarded as "bankable."[8] Such an instrument can more easily be made marketable, thereby freeing the bank to move forward with an asset-side strategy that is not dependent on its particular failure history.

2.3 Further Credibility Enhancements

When a government's credibility is in doubt, it may have to go further than just providing a marketable instrument if the banks are to feel secure. A variety of enhancements have been employed to overcome such problems.

Injected recapitalization bonds in West African UEMOA countries were endowed with privileged access to central bank buy-back provisions in the early 1990s – a valuable enhancement, offered as it was by a regional (multicountry) central bank in conditions of some doubt as to the creditworthiness of some of the issuing governments.

In the other CFA zone (CEMAC), Cameroon employed two interesting devices to enhance the credibility of injected bonds when it made them negotiable in 1998–1999. One portion (with medium-long term maturities) was secured by an escrow account at the regional (multicountry) central bank, into which earmarked fiscal receipts were deposited. The remaining portion, with 30-year maturity, were backed ("Brady"-like) by a zero-coupon French government bond of the same maturity (Honohan, 2003).

One innovative approach recently employed in Argentina (see de la Torre, 2000; Honohan, 2003) involved securitization of the bad loan

---

[8] The bonds and loans injected into failed banks by the old Mexican restructuring agency FOBAPROA were not fully certain, nor marketable, and this may have contributed to the much-discussed credit crunch which ensued for several years, though other factors, such as a heightened awareness of the legal difficulties of loan recovery (addressed by legislation enacted in 2000 and 2003) will also have been important as will the lack of capital. At the heart of the subsequent debates surrounding the recapitalization of Mexican banks is the question of exchanging the unfunded promissory notes of FOBAPROA for those of the new agency IPAB, which can borrow on the market and the servicing of whose borrowings are guaranteed on a year-by-year basis by the national central bank.

portfolio (which was assumed by a separate company) into three tranches, with the senior tranche only being left with the restructured bank. On the assumption that recoveries would be sufficient to service the senior tranche in full, this left the bank with a bankable asset (and in any case one which was negotiable). In the event, things did not work out all that smoothly, but the approach had merit.

Less attractive types of enhancement come in the form of guarantees offered bilaterally by the authorities to the restructured bank in respect on the value of their loan portfolio. These can be in the form of yield maintenance agreements, stop-loss guarantees, or put-back options (allowing the bank to sell the asset to the government at a prefixed price). From the point of view of getting the bank on a forward-looking path under financial autonomy, the potential problem is that such bilateral arrangements risk keeping the government too closely involved in the ongoing business of the bank.

Normally, the assets injected will be denominated in local currency. However, when the banking crisis is associated with a currency crisis, or when the banking system is dollarized (De Nicolo, Honohan, and Ize, 2003), local currency assets may not provide an adequate currency match for the bank. Issuance of foreign-currency denominated securities by the government may then be unavoidable; this was done, for example, in Bulgaria.

If the credibility of the government with investors is problematic, then attempts by it to provide enhancement may eventually cost more than they are initially valued in the market. Overcomplex enhancement may prove undesirable for this reason.

3. GOVERNMENT CAPITAL CLAIMS ON THE BANK

As part of the process of recapitalization, the government or its agency also may acquire a claim, often subordinated, on the bank. There are two aspects to this: first is the counterpart of the bond injection. Second is a possible claim on better-than-expected recovery on the failed bank's assets. The purpose of these claims is to ensure that the restructuring is achieved at the least cost (in net present value terms) to the taxpayer.

Recalling the capital budgeting perspective mentioned in Section 1, there is an argument for the government injecting more than the absolute minimum in the restructured bank if, from the private investors' point of view, the risks facing the bank are substantially political in nature. Thus, if investors fear that the government will seek to claw back a

disproportionate recovery in the fortunes of the bank through exceptional explicit or implicit taxation, and if the government does not have
the credibility to convince the market that it has no intention of doing this,
it would be inefficient of the government to sell the bank to a skeptical
market realizing a price discounted by the market's expectation of future
expropriation or disproportionate taxation. That would amount to an
ex post transfer of scarce budgetary funds to the purchasers. So in this
case a financial instrument must be sought that allows the government to
realize some of the upside gain from a recovery of market confidence.

This is not an unrealistic scenario in the middle of a systemic crisis, when
the government's options seem limited and the likelihood of onerous future taxation can seem high. It is in precisely this kind of condition that the
government may wish to consider a risk-and-return sharing investment
in the bank. Thus, the decision as to how much of a stake the government
should take in the newly capitalized bank will be partly dependent on the
outcome of its bargaining strength vis-à-vis new shareholders.

3.1 Impact of Bond Injection on the Liability Side of the Bank's Balance Sheet

As a counterpart of an injection of assets into the bank's balance sheet,
there must obviously be a corresponding increase on the liability side.
If the injection comes without any specific *quid pro quo*, then it will be
the value of the shareholders' funds that increases, as the owners of the
bank's equity normally have the residual claim on the bank's assets, after
other liabilities have been paid.

The bank's capital consists of these shareholders' funds plus other long-
term claims that are subordinated to the claims of depositors.[9] Therefore,
the unrequited injection of an asset into a bank also increases the bank's
capital. (The new asset is clearly not *itself* part of the bank's capital, as the
capital is a residual. The asset may be liquid or illiquid, with a short- or
long-term maturity; none of that affects the degree to which its injection
increases the bank's capital.)

---

[9] The Basel capital accord established some widely accepted rules concerning the calcu-
lation of capital. Given that capital is the residual obtained by subtracting noncapital
liabilities from total assets, we may think of these rules as (1) defining certain measurement principles for the asset side items of the balance sheet (notably related to asset
revaluation reserves and general loan–loan-loss provisions) and (2) specifying which subordinated liabilities can be counted as "capital" and thus need not be subtracted from total
assets.

Note also that the economic value (as distinct from the balance sheet value) of the equity claims may increase by more than the market value of the injected bond to the extent that the injection brings the bank into regulatory compliance, enabling it to move forward and to earn profits from its franchise.

When the government injects an asset, it may therefore also choose to acquire an explicit capital-type claim on the bank, especially if it has injected enough to bring the bank's capital strictly above zero. Otherwise, part of the injection may simply represent a transfer from the taxpayer to the new shareholders.

Comparing the before and after restructuring, therefore, we can imagine the assets side of the bank being increased by (A) an injection by the government and (B) an injection from the (new) owners. The government may (and if there is no injection from the new owners it should) want to acquire (C) some form of capital claim on the liability side.

Note a curious distinction that arises as to the nature of the asset that can be injected. The government is free to inject a claim on itself as an appropriate asset, whereas the private owners must not be allowed to do this. The problem is that, if private shareholders just inject a claim on themselves, they do not truly have much net capital at stake, and they will not therefore have appropriate incentives to minimize the probability of the bank failing (something like this seems to have occurred in the failed Mexican privatizations of the early 1990s).[10]

Simply stated, a natural benchmark solution (though, as noted later, under "scale" it is not the only one) is for the government to inject enough under A to bring the calculated capital up to zero, with the owners injecting the further sums under B required to bring the capital up to the regulatory minimum. In accounting terms, this may appear to be a zero-value transaction for the owners, and as such of limited appeal to private wealth-holders. But in economic terms, and more important in terms of market value, the net present value of the equity that the owners acquire in this scenario will be greater than the cash value of the injected asset. This, as mentioned, is because of the franchise value – the stream of future profits in excess of the risk-free rate of return – of operating the bank.

---

[10] The bank's owners will gain disproportionately from risky management strategies inasmuch as they benefit from the upside risk, but suffer little from the downside. For this and related reasons, most bank regulatory structures place tight limits on lending to persons connected with ownership or management. Because it is neither truly free from the downside risk, nor standing to gain from the upside, the government's injection of its own bonds is not subject to the same moral hazard.

Beyond stating that the restructured bank should obviously have enough capital to meet the standard regulatory requirements, it is unwise to be dogmatic about how the balance between A, B, and C should be struck. The more assets the government injects, the easier it is to attract serious substantial shareholders and give them suitable incentives. (In the failed Mexican privatizations of the early 1990s, the government arguably pressed the new shareholders for too high a cash outlay.) By contrast, public funds are scarce and the government has to bear value-for-money considerations in mind. The experience of the Nordic countries shows that, when the crisis has blown over, divesting the state's ownership shares can be quite remunerative.

In a major crisis, the fiscal authorities may have to envisage injecting funds beyond the point at which the capital of the banking system is back up to zero, as well as to provide some of the required capital for future operation, if the system is not to suffer from a credit crunch resulting from capital starvation (i.e., larger A to make up for smaller B). After all, likely investors in banking will be extremely cautious in the recessionary postcrisis environment. The issue of private versus public ownership looms large here, but a variety of intermediate and dynamic positions can be adopted, useful especially for recapitalizing banks at a time of low private sector confidence, while ensuring a semiautomatic transition to private ownership.

If the authorities do inject funds on this larger scale, they can expect to make a return on the investment, and accordingly they should take a claim C on the bank, the contractual design of which needs to ensure that the claim, on the one hand, does qualify as capital, but, on the other hand, keeps a pressure on the private owners to find enough capital to buy out the government within a relatively short number of years.

3.2 Terms and Conditions of Government's New Capital Claims

Just as the terms and conditions of the bond injection matter, so, too, do the terms and conditions of the new capital claims (item C), which may be acquired by the government as part of the restructuring. In some cases, the terms of these claims have been extremely vague, as in the case of Sri Lanka, where the claim had no particular maturity but was simply repayable "when the bank was in a position to do so." Such a vague conditionality may seem lenient to the new bank, but in fact it can effectively remove all of the bank's financial independence. As they may be unable ever to service fully or repay this debt, the bank's management may be in effect beholden indefinitely to the government and become as it were civil servants, pursuing in practice not the goals of the bank, but those of the relevant government ministry.

Instead, the government's claims on the banks should be expressed in clear and unambiguous terms, and should ideally employ standard financial instruments for which an established jurisprudence exists, allowing any disputes that might arise between the bank's private shareholders and the state agency to be readily resolved at court. This also argues for the legal holder of the government's claims to be a government agency rather than the government itself.

In order not to be excluded from the Basel concept of capital, the government's claims must be sufficiently subordinated to those of depositors. Long-term subordinated debt meets this requirement. If it has five years' initial maturity or longer, it can be counted toward Basel Tier-2 capital (though only for an amount equivalent to 50 percent of core capital), provided it is amortized at 20 percent per annum after its remaining maturity reaches five years. Another alternative is for the government to take perpetual noncumulative preference shares convertible into equity (under specified circumstances, such as renewed deterioration in the bank's capital) and repayable at the option of the bank.

Both of these arrangements have the formal provision from the outset for the government to share in an unexpectedly favorable recovery of the bank's fortunes. Bank shareholders may anyway suspect that, in such an event, they could have to make significant *ex post* payments to government (perhaps in the form of special taxes) designed to claw back part of what will by then appear *ex post* to have been an excessively generous government injection.[11] Better to eliminate the uncertainty by settling this in advance.[12]

Evidently, a range of risk-sharing/profit-sharing alternatives are available. These would differ as to residual control rights (including warrants), profit-sharing rules (including specific sharing rules for earmarked loan recovery) and maturity.

Probably the best way of ensuring that the taxpayer benefits from an unexpectedly favorable debt recovery experience is to establish government claims directly linked to loan recovery. The nonperforming portfolio of loans that has caused the problem is rarely worthless, and may be prove

---

[11] For an account of the 1992 clawback in the case of AIB, see Honohan and Kelly (1997).
[12] Though, as the Mexican case shows, governments may seek to renegotiate even injections of type *A* if circumstances or information should change.

to be worth much more than implied by conservative valuations at the time of the restructuring.[13] To the extent that the bad debt is being removed from the bank, and the recovery managed elsewhere, this issue does not further impinge on the design of the financial restructuring.[14] But if the bad debt remains on the new bank's balance sheet, albeit heavily provisioned or written down, it may be desirable for the government (or its agency) to retain an entitlement to share in the eventual upside of debt recovery. By building in a substantial claw-back of recoveries in this way, the government can safeguard the taxpayer's position even if the initial injection of funds required has been exaggerated by overly conservative accounting. Although this will depress the incentive for the bank to recover, it does provide an improved incentive for the bank not to exaggerate *ex ante* its estimate of the degree to which the loans are unrecoverable.

Such a mechanism has been tried, for example, in Mexico, when as a quid-pro-quo for injecting funds, the government received a claim on the recoveries. This sort of claim need not just be a fixed percentage share.[15] In principle, quite complex contracts with embedded options can be envisaged, but only if there is a shared understanding that the contracts are going to be honored on both sides.[16] Complexity need not be a problem under those circumstances, but clarity is certainly needed. A contract structure that is so vague that it will eventually have to be litigated, or that leaves either side considerable discretion is unlikely to create the correct incentives going forward.[17]

---

[13] It also embodies some informational capital. In the case of the privatized National Bank of Commerce of Tanzania, the new shareholders undertook to recover on the old portfolio for a fee arrangement. The new management found that the recovery process gave them valuable information about the creditworthiness of the bank's old customers.

[14] With good institutional design and contracting for nonperforming asset management and recovery, the government can hope to recover a portion of its initial outlay – perhaps a very high proportion, as was achieved in Sweden (Drees and Pazarbasioglu, 1998). But absent these conditions, devices such as establishing a centralized asset recovery agency may prove to be no more than an additional drain on the budget (Klingebiel, 2000; Calomiris, Klingebiel, and Laeven, Chapter 2; cf. Enoch et al., 1999).

[15] In the Mexican deal, the government was to receive $25 + 0.75r$ percent, where r is the percentage recovery rate. There is further discussion of the Mexican case in Chapter 2.

[16] More popular devices that have been negotiated bilaterally by restructured banks include stop-loss guarantees and yield maintenance arrangements offered by the authorities, or put-back options granted to the bank. Far from giving the government a share in the up side, these particular types of contract generally involve hidden and potentially large future liabilities for the government and often leave the bank with poor incentive to recover.

[17] Few countries have achieved a fully satisfactory solution to the problem of recovery on delinquent loans and seized collateral. In Thailand, most of the loans were still on the

3.3 A Schedular Approach

Bank restructurings can generate expectations regarding the future availability of bailouts. They also present difficulties for transparency, with frequent accusations after the event that particular investors were favored in the restructuring and allowed to acquire a sound bank for too little money.[18]

Some of these difficulties can be avoided by the announcement in a crisis of a special time-bound schedule or menu of capital assistance. Different versions of this have been tried in Thailand and Mexico: the authorities announced that budgetary funds would be available, but only on condition that private shareholders put in a proportionate amount. Similar schedular arrangements have been announced for subsidized loan purchase schemes; in Thailand, shareholders effectively had a menu of alternative options from which to choose (Honohan, 2003).

Of course, any such scheme will have a deadweight cost which advocates of micromanaged intervention may claim to avoid. (Thus, if micromanagement can deliver an exact knowledge of the capital deficiency of the bank, and of its franchise value, this could enable the government to get it going again in an adequately capitalized manner at lower cost.) But by offering a menu, and doing so publicly, the government can draw also on the private sector's strengths in valuing assets and in perceiving business opportunities.[19]

Also, many new investors will be attracted to a semiautomatic recapitalization mechanism, whereas they would be uninterested in entering into a highly contingent and uncertain bilateral negotiation with the government. Thus, provided the menu is generous enough overall, it can help attract a wider group of investors and as such enhance the value of the banking business that the government is trying to rehabilitate.

bank's books three years after the crisis broke; those acquired from nonbank finance companies had been disposed of at a discount of about 75 percent, and even then a new government agency was a residual buyer for many of them. In Mexico, the restructuring agency acquired some of the delinquent loans outright, while in other cases, as mentioned, it acquired a claim on recoveries made by the banks: the projected recovery rate from the acquired loans is only 20 percent. The innovative securitization approach in Argentina, mentioned earlier, was criticized for lacking adequate incentives to promote loan recovery. Cameroon's Société de Recouvrement had recovered less than 3 percent of its portfolio after half a decade.

[18] Credit Lyonnais bank was allowed to negotiate exclusively with the authorities for the purchase of SCB bank in Cameroon in the late 1980s.

[19] But offering a recapitalization menu cannot be a substitute for intervening undercapitalized banks, as is suggested was a problem in Thailand (Claessens and Klingebiel, 1999).

4. IMPLICATIONS FOR DEBT MANAGEMENT

In this section, we look at the implications of the restructuring for the government's budgetary strategy. As before, we begin the analysis at the point at which the government has decided to protect depositors from (some portion of) their prospective losses in a bank which has failed and is being intervened. Some of these costs may be incurred outside of the recapitalization *per se* (as when insured depositors are paid off separately, or when subsidies are paid to delinquent borrowers).

4.1 Need for Ensuring a Feasible Overall Fiscal Plan

All of the discussion of the previous two sections has assumed that the government already has a feasible general plan in terms of absorbing the total costs, whether through increased taxation, reduced spending, the inflation tax, or a new sustainable time-path of overall indebtedness. This is not a foregone conclusion. The market may call into question the government's ability and willingness to meet out of additional tax revenues, or expenditure cutbacks, the liabilities that it has suddenly assumed. The fall-back position of government may be to allow inflation and currency depreciation.[20] Or it may slip into arrears and default. The huge size of some of the failures in recent years has placed a question mark over the viability of governments' budgetary and exchange rate/inflation strategy, and some have argued that this has provided a causal linkage from bank failure to currency collapse.[21] A credible financing plan must be in place to guard against self-fulfilling market expectations driving the economy into a bad equilibrium here. However, these matters are not the focus of this chapter.

4.2 Adjusting Debt Management for the Consequences of Restructuring

As part of the recapitalization, the government will, as discussed, injects some bonds, and may acquire some claims on the newly recapitalized bank. It also may acquire claims over some of the recovery of the failed banks' bad assets. In this way, the government's portfolio of debt and financial assets has altered as a result of the rescue and bank

[20] Whether intended or not (probably not) it was the outcome in Bulgaria in 1996. For a theoretical discussion of this type of problem, see Burnside et al. (1998).
[21] See, for example, Chang and Velasco (2001). Though of course the reverse causality also has been important.

recapitalization. This implies commitment to a stream of cash outflows and receipts – some of them certain, others contingent.

Most budget managers will intuitively look first at the immediate cash costs of any restructuring policy, and then for the implications for cash-flow in the first few years following. This can become an all-determining preoccupation, especially for a government with limited taxing capacity, for one with limited access to the financial markets and for one that is operating under an IMF program that constrains cash outlays. Most options for the recapitalization need not involve substantial immediate cash outlays, but we have stressed that choosing a policy on the basis of its cash-flow implications is unlikely to be the optimal policy, even from a narrow fiscal management perspective.

Instead, as we have proposed, the design of the restructuring should be determined on the basis of banking policy and net present value considerations, and not on cash-flow considerations. Just as investment and financing decisions are normally kept separate, so, too, the government should look at the cash-flow consequences of the restructuring as presenting a task to be resolved by debt management and overall fiscal policy (and not as a reason for reconsidering the design of the restructuring). The decision as to whether this should be financed by taxation, by reduction of public spending, or by additional borrowing is one that is then wholly independent of banking policy considerations. It is a pure question of debt management and overall fiscal policy. In practice, bank failure is sufficiently rare that it will generally be optimal to smooth its impact on taxation and public spending over a number of years. Thus, there will be a need for new borrowing, if available. Some of this borrowing is done, in effect, through the issuance of the bonds that are going to be injected. Unless the maturity of these bonds happens to be just right for debt management purposes, this will give rise to a need for rebalancing the government's remaining debt portfolio.

4.3 Use of Other Government Agencies

A need for additional borrowing by the central government can draw attention to the deterioration in the fiscal position in a way that may can be unwelcome. It is not altogether clear whether accounting treatment really can matter, or whether markets can see through different approaches to accounting for what amounts to the same economic reality. In practice, governments tend to welcome legitimate reasons for keeping expenditures off-budget. That is one motivation for isolating the financing of bank failure through an ancillary government agency such as a deposit insurer.

There are some risks in this approach. If the deposit insurer's borrowings do not carry the full guarantee of the national government, they may have to offer higher yields (a credibility effect). Even though the deposit insurer may benefit from an earmarked tax, such as deposit insurance premia, the revenue may not be sufficient in a crisis. Likewise, if the deposit insurer has a statutorily imposed borrowing ceiling, it may prove unwise to rely on it to make the optimal investment or financing decision.

If it is a government agency that will be assuming the liabilities, then that agency must be in a position to meet cash calls. If it does not itself have cash or liquid reserves, this may be done through its own borrowing, but if it has no statutory authority to borrow, or if it cannot call on a government guarantee, the cost and difficulty of making this borrowing may well induce the agency to seek an alternative approach, which could prove more expensive in the long run. There are examples from the United States in the late 1980s, and from Argentina more recently. These have involved the agency either engineering tax-advantaged arrangements that have passed the cost to the revenue authorities (United States), or substituting assumption of implicit future commitments for explicit borrowing (Argentina), in each case probably increasing the net fiscal cost in the process.

In general, the advantages of leaving the decision to an ancillary agency are chiefly those of achieving focus and perhaps retaining independence from interference from political personalities. Thus, although the use of other agencies in this activity can have some favorable incentive effects for the relevant public officials, and can also improve the accounting presentation of the government's actions, financing is unlikely to be the strong point of ancillary agencies (this includes the central bank).[22]

5. IMPLICATIONS FOR MONETARY POLICY

The final piece of the jigsaw is the response of monetary policy instruments to ensure that the resolution does not destabilize monetary conditions in an unintended way. Basically, our approach is to see the bank restructuring as something to which monetary policy should respond. In other

[22] In the Mexican case, the new agency IPAB was effectively going to the markets in competition with the Federal Government.

words, monetary consequences should not be a central consideration or a constraint for those designing the restructuring.

Nevertheless, the impact of bank resolution policy on monetary conditions can come in either of two forms: a direct effect through central bank cash injections in a failing bank, or indirectly through the consequences of fiscal action to restructure the failed bank.

Ideally, then, the financial restructuring is handled as a directly fiscal matter, in which case the role of monetary policy is to adjust liquidity conditions to ensure that the goals of monetary policy are not accidentally compromised by the financial instruments that have been created by the restructuring. However, in practice, the central bank is often the first official agency in line to provide financial support to a failing bank (the Thai case is a clear example).

5.1 Direct Central Bank Lending

The term "lender of last resort" often proves to be a misnomer in this respect. Although it may be a last resort in the sense that all potential private sector lenders have refused, the central bank is often the only government agency with the resources and the authority to make large liquidity loans promptly in a crisis. Indeed, unless governed by restrictive legislation such as that of a currency board, the central bank always has the wherewithal to cover domestic currency obligations arising out of a bank failure.

Central banking doctrine makes a sharp distinction between liquidity loans and solvency support. The former are made to a bank that is under cash pressure, but is expected to be able ultimately to liquidate its portfolio. According to the doctrine liquidity loans should only be made against adequate collateral. According to the same doctrine, solvency support (i.e., loans to an insolvent institution) should not be made by the monetary authority, as this will fuel inflation. If this doctrine is followed, then we are in the ideal situation in which monetary consequences can be separated from fiscal consequences.

Unfortunately, distinguishing between the solvent and the insolvent among illiquid banks is not easy to accomplish in the limited time available for deciding whether or not to grant a liquidity loan. Even if the central bank suspects that the bank is insolvent, it will come under pressure to meet the short-term needs. And the quality of the collateral available to secure the lending is likely to prove questionable, especially in a generalized crisis. In short, the central bank will often find itself with claims on an insolvent bank, and as such become a primary source of capital injections into the banking system.

And these will be cash injections. Unless the cash injection is sterilized, the consequence will be inflation (or, if there is a fixed exchange rate, an outflow of funds through the current account of balance of payments). The "inflation tax" has often been used to help pay for banking collapses. It is a tax with rather arbitrary incidence (the very poor and the very rich do not hold much cash; also unexpected inflation results in substantial transfers between different segments of society whose incomes depend on contracts fixed in nominal terms). Furthermore, an unexpected surge in inflation can trigger a lengthy process of adjustment during which inflation well overshoots what is strictly needed to pay for the initial deficiency. Getting this under control again can often result in a recession; besides which, cross-country studies establish that, beyond a moderate level, inflation damages growth. Any country choosing this route should recognize what it is doing, and not see the use of central bank funds as an easy option.

If there is a fixed exchange rate regime in effect, or when the failing bank has significant foreign exchange obligations, the central bank may no longer be able to provide cash to meet the claims of depositors and still hold to the exchange rate peg. This has been seen in graphic form in a currency board arrangement (as in Argentina in 2001).[23] Closely related to this are the abrogation of gold pegs and gold clauses in U.S. history described in Chapter 2.

One of the least satisfactory aspects of central bank financing of bank insolvency is that accounting for such support is often opaque. The total cost absorbed, whether by the fiscal authorities or by the inflation tax, is usually hard to determine. Among the difficulties are the off-market interest rates normally applied to many central bank assets and liabilities; support to an insolvent bank will change the amounts subject to these off-market rates. Few if any central banks properly and fully account for the implicit subsidies and taxes that are thereby triggered. For example, because the production of high-powered money appears in accounting terms to be virtually costless, any interest return on a loan made by the central bank may appear to be profitable, but it represents an expansion of the base for inflation tax.[24] Another example comes from exchange rate guarantees, preferential exchange rates provided to failing banks

[23] Bulgaria's legislation places continuing statutory constraints on the currency board's authority to make loans reflecting the absolute priority given to the exchange rate peg.
[24] For a discussion of alternative measures of seigniorage and the inflation tax, see Honohan (1996).

that need to repay foreign debt and similar arrangements undertaken just before or after an exchange rate collapse triggered by the banking problems.

Many a central bank has found itself technically insolvent and unable to pay its administrative expenses because of an accumulation of such implicit forms of assistance. This can damage the operational and policy independence of the central bank, and needs to be corrected through a financial restructuring of the central bank.

5.2 Protecting Monetary Stability

Returning, though, to the preferable case, in which the restructuring of the failed (commercial) bank has been rightly treated in the first instance as a fiscal matter, what remains to be discussed is the needed central bank response to ensure maintenance of monetary stability.

Here the important points are threefold. First, there must be a clear understanding between monetary and fiscal authorities as to whether there is to be a monetary relaxation to absorb some of the cost of the banking crash through the inflation tax. Under many if not most circumstances the answer will be no, but the point being made here is that additional and unnecessary problems will arise if the policy strategy of the fiscal and monetary authorities are inconsistent, as they will be if the government is counting on partial inflation tax financing, while the central bank has not paid out its nominal anchor.

Second (and subject to the first point), as a general proposition, the monetary authorities should not allow the bank financial restructuring *per se* to affect aggregates that predict the evolution of inflation (or of the other target variables of monetary policy). To the extent that they are found to be affected by the restructuring, the central bank will need to take offsetting measures. An important distinction here is that, while the restructuring is focused on the affected banks, the monetary policy response is addressed to the equilibrium of the system as a whole.

For instance, a restructuring that leaves certain banks highly liquid (perhaps because the government has injected treasury bills) may result in a lowering of interbank interest rates, or an expansion of aggregate domestic credit, or in a depreciation of the currency. Any or all of these are likely to be among the most important indicators of monetary policy stance in the economy, and the central bank will need to act to offset these tendencies using the instruments available to it, which will vary depending on the development and sophistication of the money markets, but that could include open market sales, increasing the interest rate on standing facilities, increasing reserve requirements, or sales of foreign exchange into the market.

The point here is that the central bank needs to be vigilant so that it can take the needed offsetting action. A simple policy framework based on a model of demand and supply of base money would clearly point to a need for the central bank to offset any changes in the *supply* of base money that may have resulted from the restructuring, and this is the basic message to keep in mind.[25] But the real world is more complex and the task is not straightforward. In particular, some standard monetary policy indicators will have lost their traditional reliability (cf. Martinez Peria, 2000).

This is especially true of domestic credit. The financial restructuring will have resulted in a write-down of the total stock of performing credit. What is the "correct" rate at which credit should expand from the new low base? On the one hand, the caution of banks "once-bitten" may lead to a continuing credit crunch driven by lack of lender confidence. On the other hand, a rapid recovery of credit aggregates to their former level may result in macroeconomic overheating.

Another example is when deposits that have been frozen because of the bank failure are released through the financial restructuring of the bank. Whether or not this is reflected in a jump in the measured money stock depends on the decision of statisticians at the time; but it may or may not be associated with an actual increase in spending that could threaten monetary policy goals. This situation needs to be assessed as it evolves.

There is no alternative here to a having a very clear and unambiguous definition of the goals of monetary policy. Only then can policy measures be adequately formulated and adapted to ensure that these goals are being met.

If the focus of monetary policy is on inflation, or on maintaining the exchange rate, then the central bank can devote its energies exclusively to achieving that goal by being prepared constantly to reevaluate and update the problematic causal linkages. Nowadays this is, after all, the normal practice of central banks.

A banking crisis is not just a question of accounting adjustments. There can also be strong shifts in depositor confidence. The classic example is Argentina in 1994–1995, where the banking system suffered a deposit

[25] In a currency board system, the central bank's legal capacity to undertake such action will be limited. This places more of the onus on the fiscal authority to ensure that it does not destabilize monetary conditions through the design of the restructuring. In this way the currency board system inhibits the separability of policy for which we have been arguing.

outflow equivalent to about one fifth of the deposit base.[26] Once again a simple model based on demand and supply of base money suggests that the central bank should accommodate any shift in the *demand* for base money. Where the goal of monetary policy is inflation targeting, this will be a useful starting point for the practical implementation of policy. In a fixed exchange rate regime, the capacity of the central bank to deliver on this policy may be limited by its foreign exchange reserves, and in a currency board system the central bank law also will impose restrictions.

6. CONCLUSIONS

Many issues that should remain separate tend to be lumped together in considering how to recapitalize banks. We have attempted to show how the issues concerning banking, the budget, and monetary stability can each be dealt with in a distinct manner.

Before anything else is done, the government must have a coherent medium-term fiscal strategy that determines broadly how the costs of the banking crisis are going to be absorbed. This is a prerequisite. After that, logically the first part to be got right is the banking aspect. The failed bank must be securely reestablished with enough capital and franchise value to move forward as a normal bank. We have shown that this will typically entail new financial instruments involving the government on both asset side and liability side of the bank's balance sheet. The bank should not be left with maturity, currency, or repricing mismatches. Assets that are injected should be bankable and preferably negotiable. The liability structure should give the bank insiders the incentive to manage the bank prudently.

The sophistication and complexity of the financial instruments used can be considerable, but only if the government has the credibility to warrant market confidence that it will deliver on the contracts without attempting to use its law-making powers to renege *de facto*. We have seen that innovative use of segregated sinking funds and "Brady"-type bonds can help when government credibility is weak.

In the event of a systemic crisis, a menu or schedular approach can be more effective in bringing the private sector into play, and reducing the moral hazard and other drawbacks of a discretionary approach. The government will be interested in recovering some of its investment as the bank returns to profitability and the impaired loan portfolio is liquidated,

[26] For a detailed account and analysis, see d'Amato et al. (1997).

but the financing and investment aspects of the transaction should be kept distinct. The restructuring of the bank will alter both the size and the maturity and other characteristics of the government's debt. Optimizing these aspects should be done separately, and with the market as a whole, rather than just with the affected banks.

Although restructuring should be a fiscal matter, the central bank may often become drawn into it through inappropriate use of lender of last resort facilities. Accounting for the central bank's solvency support is rarely transparent, but should be. The restructuring and the governments fiscal response can have marked effects on monetary stability. But these side-effects need not normally be taken into account by the supervisory/prudential or fiscal authorities, because ensuring that monetary conditions remain on target is the task of the monetary authority, and one for which it normally has enough systemic instruments at its disposal (though this may not be the case in a currency board regime). For instance, it needs to offset unintended effects on the aggregate supply of liquidity, while probably accommodating shifts in liquidity demand.

ACKNOWLEDGMENTS

I am grateful to Stijn Claessens, Charles Goodhart, Ed Kane, Luc Laeven, Millard Long, Hana Polackova Brixi, Andre Ryba, and Esen Ulgenerk, and participants at the conference "Systemic Financial Distress: Containment and Resolution" held at the World Bank, October 8–9, 2003, for helpful comments on an earlier draft; and to Guillermo Noguera for assiduous research assistance.

PART THREE

MODELS AND ECONOMETRIC EVIDENCE

FIVE

Policies for Banking Crises

A Theoretical Framework

Rafael Repullo

INTRODUCTION

Recent cross-country studies by Honohan and Klingebiel (2003) and Claessens, Klingebiel, and Laeven (Chapter 6) examine to what extent the fiscal costs incurred in a banking crisis can be attributed to specific measures adopted by the governments during the early stages of the crisis, and conclude that "blanket deposit guarantees, open-ended liquidity support, repeated recapitalizations, debtor bailouts and regulatory forbearance all tend to add significantly and sizably to (fiscal) costs."[1]

The purpose of this chapter is to provide a theoretical framework that can help to understand the different effects of these policies on ex ante risk-shifting incentives and ex post fiscal costs. Specifically, we set up a *model of information-based bank runs* in which there is a profit-maximizing bank that is funded with insured and uninsured deposits that require an expected return that is normalized to zero. There is a *moral hazard* problem in that after raising these funds, the bank privately chooses the risk of its loan portfolio. Subsequently, the uninsured depositors observe a signal that contains information on the future return of this portfolio, and withdraw their funds if the signal is bad. In such case, the bank is liquidated unless the government provides the required emergency liquidity or extends the insurance to all depositors. Assuming that the adoption of any of these measures is correctly anticipated by the depositors and the bank, we characterize the equilibrium interest rate of the uninsured deposits and the equilibrium choice of risk by the bank.

---

[1] See Honohan and Klingebiel (2003, p. 1540).

Our model of information-based bank runs builds on Diamond and Dybvig (1983), Jacklin and Bhattacharya (1988), and Alonso (1996), but although they focus on the characterization of the optimal risk-sharing arrangements between two types of consumers (early and late), our focus is on the analysis of the strategic interaction between the uninsured depositors and the bank. To simplify the presentation, we do not have a short-term safe technology, and to provide a richer model of risk-shifting, we introduce a one-dimensional set of long-term risky technologies that differ in their success probability and their success return. Finally, we also assume that deposit insurance premia are equal to zero.

The equilibrium of this model is given by the solution of two equations that correspond to the first-order condition that characterizes the bank's choice of risk and the uninsured depositors' participation constraint. Two important results are obtained. First, a minimum proportion of insured deposits may be required to guarantee the existence of an equilibrium. Second, this minimum proportion is decreasing in the quality of the uninsured depositors' information, so the deposit insurance subsidy may be particularly important to realize the benefits of intermediated finance in less-developed economies.[2]

To understand these results, it is important to realize that in our model the higher the proportion of insured deposits, the lower the bank's incentives to take risk. The intuition for this can be explained as follows. Consider a setup in which a risk-neutral bank raises a unit of deposits at an interest rate c, and invests these funds in an asset that yields a gross return $R(p)$, with probability p, and zero otherwise. Moreover, suppose that p is privately chosen by the bank at the time of investment, and that $R(p)$ is decreasing in p, so riskier investments yield a higher success return. Under limited liability, the bank chooses p in order to maximize $p[R(p) - (1 + c)]$. Assuming that $R(p)$ is also concave, the bank's choice of p is characterized by the first-order condition $R(p) + pR'(p) = 1 + c$. As the left-hand-side of this condition is decreasing in p, we conclude that the higher the value of c the lower the value of p chosen by the bank. In other words, higher deposit rates lead the bank to invest in a portfolio with a lower success probability and a higher success return.

Applying this result to a situation in which the bank is funded with both insured and uninsured deposits, and assuming that the cost of insured deposits (including any deposit insurance premia) is lower than the cost

---

[2] Cull, Senbet, and Sorge (2000) find that explicit deposit insurance favorably impacts the level of financial activity, but only in countries with strong institutional development.

of uninsured deposits,[3] it trivially follows that the higher the proportion of insured deposits the lower the average interest rate c and hence the higher the success probability p chosen by the bank.[4] Moreover, to the extent that the adoption of crises policies that bail out uninsured depositors (such as unrestricted liquidity support or blanket deposit guarantees) are anticipated, these depositors will require a lower interest rate and so the bank will have an incentive to choose safer investments.

It should be noticed that the positive relationship between the bank's funding costs and its portfolio risk is not really new, as it is a simple implication of the analysis in the classical paper on credit rationing of Stiglitz and Weiss (1981). In particular, they show how "higher interest rates induce firms to undertake projects with lower probabilities of success but higher payoffs when successful."[5] Applying the same argument to banks instead of firms gives the key result.

Our analysis of the policies for banking crises starts with a benchmark in which such accommodative policy measures are not implemented. In this benchmark, there is a supervisor that observes a signal on the future return of the bank's portfolio. A bad supervisory signal is interpreted as the finding that the bank is violating some key prudential regulations. In the benchmark model, the bank is closed when either the signal observed by the uninsured depositors is bad, so they run on the bank, or the signal observed by the supervisor is bad, in which case the bank's license to operate is withdrawn.

Against this benchmark, we proceed to analyze three policies that the supervisor may implement at the outset of a crisis. Under forbearance, we consider a situation in which the uninsured depositors observe a good signal, so they do not run on the bank, and the supervisor observes a bad signal but nevertheless allows the bank to continue to operate. Unlike forbearance, the other two policies are responses to a crisis situation in which the uninsured depositors run on the bank and the supervisor reacts by either extending deposit insurance to all depositors or providing unrestricted liquidity to the bank so it can cover the withdrawals. We show that the qualitative effect of the three policies is the same: if they are correctly anticipated, in equilibrium the uninsured depositors will require a lower

---

[3] Obviously, with actuarially fair deposit insurance premia c would be independent of the proportion of insured deposits. But actuarially fair premia are difficult to implement in a context where the risk chosen by the bank is not observable.

[4] In line with this argument, Demirgüç-Kunt and Huizinga (2004) show that banks' interest expenses are lower in countries with explicit deposit insurance systems.

[5] See Stiglitz and Weiss (1981, p. 393).

interest rate, and the bank will choose a higher success probability. We also show that the fiscal cost associated with any of these policies is higher than the fiscal cost in the benchmark model, except when the proportion of insured deposits is very high, because in this case the early closure of the bank implies a large compensation to the insured deposits that would be saved if the bank were allowed to stay open and eventually succeeded. Finally, we analyze a restricted liquidity support policy in which there is a central bank that acts as a traditional lender of last resort, supporting the bank when there is a run but only if the supervisory signal is good. This policy is associated with smaller incentive effects and smaller (potentially even negative) fiscal costs.

It is important to stress the limitations of our results. We are not providing a normative analysis because we do not derive the optimal policy in terms of deposit insurance and crisis support. This would require specifying a social welfare function in which the benefits of prudent bank behavior would be traded off against the social cost of the public funds required to cover the losses associated with bank failures.[6] Also, our positive analysis is somewhat incomplete because the decision of the supervisor is not endogenized. A possible way to do this would be to follow the political economy approach of Repullo (2000, 2004) and Kahn and Santos (2001), where government agencies have objective functions that are related to their surpluses or deficits. But this is not done here. Our objective is more modest, namely to provide a simple framework that yields some new insights that can guide future work in this field. In addition, it is important to note that our analysis is based on a model of a single bank, and so it cannot address contagion and systemic issues.[7] Incorporating these issues into our framework seems a priority for future research.

The chapter is organized as follows. Section 1 presents the model of information-based runs. Section 2 analyzes the effects of the policies for dealing with banking crises, and Section 3 offers some concluding remarks. Proofs of the results are contained in the Appendix.

1. A MODEL OF INFORMATION-BASED BANK RUNS

Consider a model with three dates ($t = 0$, 1, 2) and three classes of agents: a large number of risk-neutral *depositors*, a risk-neutral *bank*, and a

---

[6] Obviously, the optimal level of protection would be increasing with the efficiency of the tax system, reaching full coverage if lump-sum taxes were feasible.

[7] See Goodhart and Illing (2002, Part III) for various models of bank runs and contagion.

government agency called the *supervisor*. The bank raises one unit of deposits at $t = 0$, and invests these funds in a risky asset that yields a random *gross return* R at $t = 2$. The probability distribution of R is described by

$$R = \begin{cases} R_0, & \text{with probability } 1 - p, \\ R_1, & \text{with probability } p, \end{cases} \tag{1}$$

where $p \in [0, 1]$, is a parameter chosen by the bank at $t = 0$. We assume that $R_0 < 1 < R_1$, so $1 - p$ measures the riskiness of the bank's portfolio. The risky asset is illiquid in that there is no secondary market for it to be traded at $t = 1$. However, the asset can be fully liquidated at $t = 1$, which yields a *liquidation value* $L \in (0, 1)$.

Depositors are interested in consuming at $t = 2$, and have the option of withdrawing their funds at $t = 1$ and invest them in a safe asset with zero net return.[8] A given fraction $D \in (0, 1)$ of the bank's deposits are insured by the supervisor, whereas the rest, $1 - D$, are uninsured. Uninsured deposits are assumed to be junior to the insured deposits. To simplify the presentation, deposit insurance premia will be set equal to zero.

Both insured and uninsured depositors require an expected net return equal to the return of the safe asset. Consequently, the interest rate of the insured deposits will be zero, while the interest rate of the uninsured deposits, denoted by r will be such that their expected net return is equal to zero.

At $t = 1$ uninsured depositors observe a *signal* $s \in \{s_0, s_1\}$ on the return of the bank's risky asset. We assume that the uninsured depositors run on the bank if and only if they observe the (bad) signal s_0.[9] In such case, the bank is liquidated at $t = 1$, and since the uninsured deposits are junior to the insured deposits the uninsured depositors get $\max\{L - D, 0\}$.

We introduce the following assumptions.

Assumption 1. $R_0 = 0$ and $R_1 = R(p)$ *is decreasing and concave, with* $R(1) \geq 1$ *and* $R(1) + R'(1) \leq 0$.

Assumption 2. $\Pr(s_0 \mid R_0) = \Pr(s_1 \mid R_1) = q \in [\frac{1}{2}, 1]$.

Assumption 1 implies that the expected final return of the risky asset, $E(R) = pR(p)$, reaches a maximum at $\hat{p} \in (0, 1]$, which is characterized

[8] The withdrawal option could be justified by introducing preference shocks à la Diamond and Dybvig (1983), so the early consumers would use it. In this case, the bank should invest a fraction of its portfolio in the safe asset. For simplicity, we do not distinguish between early and late consumers.
[9] See Alonso (1996) for a formal analysis of the decision of the uninsured depositors.

by the first-order condition

$$R(\hat{p}) + \hat{p}R'(\hat{p}) = 0. \tag{2}$$

To see this, notice that the first derivative of $pR(p)$ with respect to p equals $R(0) > 0$ for $p = 0$ and $R(1) + R'(1) \leq 0$ for $p = 1$, and the second derivative satisfies $2R'(p) + pR''(p) < 0$. Thus, increases in p below (above) $\hat{p}$ increase (decrease) the expected final return of the risky asset. Moreover, we have $\hat{p}R(\hat{p}) \geq R(1) \geq 1$. Assumption 1 is borrowed from Allen and Gale (2000, Chapter 8), and allows to analyze in a continuous manner the risk-shifting effects of different institutional settings.

Assumption 2 introduces a parameter q that describes the quality of the uninsured depositors' information.[10] This information is only about whether the return R of the bank's risky asset will be low (R_0) or high (R_1), and not about the particular value $R(p)$ taken by the high return. By Bayes's law, it immediately follows that

$$\Pr(R_1 \mid s_0) = \frac{(1-q)p}{q + (1-2q)p}, \tag{3}$$

and

$$\Pr(R_1 \mid s_1) = \frac{qp}{1 - q - (1-2q)p}. \tag{4}$$

Hence, when $q = \frac{1}{2}$ we have $\Pr(R_1 \mid s_0) = \Pr(R_1 \mid s_1) = p$, so the signal is uninformative, while when $q = 1$ we have $\Pr(R_1 \mid s_0) = 0$ and $\Pr(R_1 \mid s_1) = 1$, so the signal completely reveals whether the return R will be R_0 or R_1. As $\Pr(R_1 \mid s_0) < p < \Pr(R_1 \mid s_1)$ for $p < 1$ and $q > \frac{1}{2}$, s_0 and s_1 will be called the bad and the good signal, respectively.

By limited liability, the bank gets a zero payoff if it is liquidated at $t = 1$ or fails at $t = 2$, and gets $R(p) - D - (1 - D)(1 + r)$ if it succeeds at $t = 2$. This event happens when the uninsured depositors observe the good signal s_1 (so they do not run at $t = 1$) and the return of the risky asset is $R_1 = R(p)$. By Assumption 2 we have $\Pr(s_1, R_1) = \Pr(s_1 \mid R_1)\Pr(R_1) = qp$, so the bank's payoff function is

$$V(p; r) = qp[R(p) - D - (1 - D)(1 + r)], \tag{5}$$

The uninsured depositors get $\max\{L - D, 0\}$ when they observe the bad signal s_0 and run on the bank at $t = 1$, they get $(1 - D)(1 + r)$ when the bank succeeds at $t = 2$ (that is, when they observe the good signal s_1

---

[10] More generally, we could have $\Pr(s_0 \mid R_0) \neq \Pr(s_1 \mid R_1)$, but this would not change the results.

and the return of the risky asset is R_1), and they get zero when the bank fails at $t = 2$ (that is, when they observe the good signal s_1 and the return of the risky asset is R_0). By Assumption 2 we have $\Pr(s_0) = q + (1 - 2q)p$ and $\Pr(s_1, R_1) = \Pr(s_1 \mid R_1)\Pr(R_1) = qp$, so the payoff of the uninsured depositors is given by

$$U(r; p) = [q + (1 - 2q)p] \max\{L - D,\ 0\} + qp(1 - D)(1 + r). \qquad (6)$$

An *equilibrium* is a pair $(r^*,\ p^*)$, where r^* is the interest rate of the uninsured deposits and p^* is the success probability chosen by the bank, such that p^* maximizes the bank's payoff function $V(p; r^*)$ and r^* satisfies the uninsured depositors' participation constraint

$$U(r^*; p^*) = 1 - D. \qquad (7)$$

In this definition, it is important to realize that the interest rate r^* is set before the bank's choice of risk, and is such that, taking into account the bank's equilibrium success probability p^*, the expected net return of the uninsured deposits is equal to zero.

The first-order condition that characterizes the equilibrium success probability p^* is

$$R(p^*) + p^* R'(p^*) = D + (1 - D)(1 + r^*). \qquad (8)$$

Since $R(p) + pR'(p)$ is decreasing by Assumption 1, it follows from (2) and (8) that p^* is strictly below the first-best $\hat{p}$, so the bank will be choosing too much risk. This is just the standard risk-shifting effect that follows from debt financing under limited liability.

An equilibrium exists if equations (7) and (8) have a solution. It is easy to check that the interest rate r^* that satisfies the participation constraint (7) is decreasing in the success probability p^*, because the higher the success probability the lower the interest rate required by the uninsured depositors. Also, the success probability p^* that solves the first-order condition (8) is decreasing in the interest rate r^*, because the higher the interest rate the lower the success probability chosen by the bank. As shown in Figure 5.1, the fact that these two derivatives are negative imply that in general we may find multiple equilibria: high (low) rates induce the bank to choose high (low) risk, rationalizing the depositors' expectations.

In cases in which there are multiple equilibria, we focus on the equilibrium which is closest to the first-best $\hat{p}$, that is, the one with the highest value of p^* (and the lowest value of r^*) For this equilibrium, we can prove the following result.

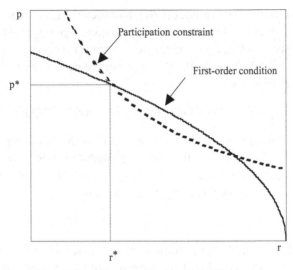

Figure 5.1. Characterization of equilibrium.

Proposition 1. *The success probability p^* is increasing and the interest rate r^* is decreasing in the proportion D of insured deposits (whenever $D \geq L$) and in the quality q of the uninsured depositors' information.*

The intuition for this result is the following. When the proportion D of insured deposits is greater than the liquidation value L, having more insured deposits reduces the overall cost of funding. This reduces the bank's incentives to take risk, which translates into a lower interest rate of uninsured deposits. By contrast, when the proportion D of insured deposits is below L, there is an opposite effect, because as insured deposits are senior, having more insured deposits reduces the payoff of the uninsured depositors when they run on the bank, so they may require a higher compensation. This may increase the bank's overall cost of funding and, consequently, its incentives to take risk. By contrast, a better quality of the uninsured depositors' information increases their expected payoff, and leads to a reduction in the interest rate that they require, which in turn reduces the bank's incentives to take risk.

The supervisor has to pay to the insured depositors $\max\{D - L, 0\}$ when the bank is liquidated at $t = 1$ and D when the bank fails at $t = 2$. By Assumption 2 the first event happens with probability $\Pr(s_0) = q + (1 - 2q)p$ and the second event happens with probability

$\Pr(s_1, R_0) = \Pr(s_1 \mid R_0) \Pr(R_0) = (1 - q)(1 - p),$[11] so the equilibrium expected cost for the supervisor is given by

$$C^* = [q + (1 - 2q)p^*] \max\{D - L, 0\} + (1 - q)(1 - p^*)D. \qquad (9)$$

Because the supervisor is a government agency that does not get any income (recall that we are assuming that deposit insurance premia are zero), this cost has to be funded by general tax revenues, so it may be called the *fiscal cost* of bank failure.

The effect of an increase in the proportion D of insured deposits on the fiscal cost C^* is ambiguous because, although an increase in D directly increases the two terms in the right-hand side of (9), by Proposition 1 it also may increase the equilibrium success probability p^* chosen by the bank, an effect that operates in the opposite direction.[12] In contrast, an increase in the quality q of the uninsured depositors' information reduces the fiscal cost C^*, because in this case both the direct and the indirect effects go in the same direction.[13]

Given that some of the comparative statics results are ambiguous, in what follows we work out a simple example. The focus is on the qualitative effects, so we will not calibrate the model to get plausible numerical results, but instead choose simple functional forms and round parameter values.

Specifically, suppose that $R(p) = 3 - p^2$, and let $L = 0.50$.[14] Figure 5.2 shows the equilibrium success probability p^* and the corresponding fiscal cost C^* as a function of the proportion D of uninsured deposits and for two different values, $q = 0.60$ and $q = 0.65$, of the quality of the uninsured depositors' information.

A number of results are worth noting. First, a minimum proportion of insured deposits is required for the existence of an equilibrium, and this critical share is decreasing in the quality q of the uninsured depositors' information. Second, the success probability p^* is everywhere increasing in the proportion D of insured deposits (even for $D < L$). Third, when the

---

[11] We are implicitly assuming that $D < 1$, because when all deposits are insured $(D = 1)$ the bank is never liquidated at $t = 1$, in which case $C^* = \Pr(R_0) = 1 - p^*$.

[12] However, since $C^* = 0$ for $D = 0$ and $C^* > 0$ for $D > 0$, if there is an equilibrium for all D, the fiscal cost C^* must be increasing for some range of values of D.

[13] The direct effect is negative since $\partial C^*/\partial q = (1 - p^*)[\max\{D - L, 0\} - D] - p^* \max\{D - L, 0\} < 0$, and the indirect effect is also negative since $\partial C^*/\partial p^* = (1 - 2q)\max\{D - L, 0\} - (1 - q)D < 0$ and $\partial p^*/\partial q > 0$ by Proposition 1.

[14] Clearly, $R(p) = 3 - p^2$ is decreasing and concave, with $R(1) = 2 \geq 1$ and $R(1) + R'(1) = 0 \leq 0$, so Assumption 1 is satisfied.

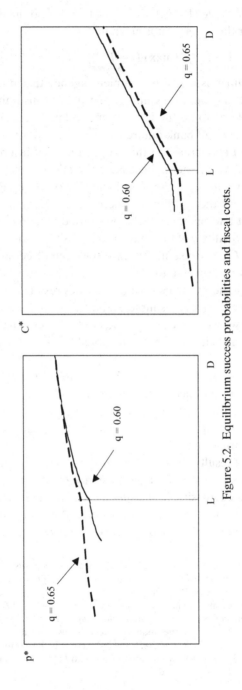

Figure 5.2. Equilibrium success probabilities and fiscal costs.

proportion D of insured deposits converges to 1 (full deposit insurance), the success probability p^* converges to a limit that is independent of the quality q of the uninsured depositors' information.[15] Fourth, the fiscal cost C^* is everywhere increasing in the proportion D of insured deposits.[16] Finally, the success probability p^* is increasing and the fiscal cost C^* is decreasing in the quality q of the uninsured depositors' information. Hence, having better informed uninsured depositors also ameliorates the bank's risk-shifting incentives, so policies designed to increase information disclosure (like those in Pillar 3 of the new regulation of bank capital proposed by the Basel Committee on Banking Supervision (2004)), would be beneficial.

The main implication of these results is that, contrary to the conventional view, the provision of deposit insurance serves to ameliorate the bank's risk-shifting incentives, and hence to reduce the probability of a banking crisis. The flip side is that deposit insurance has a fiscal cost that is increasing in the proportion of insured deposits. To the extent that the social cost of public funds, which derives from tax distortions, is positive, it would be possible to derive an optimal level of insurance, but we will not pursue this here.

A second interesting implication is that for economies with poor information (low q), where the moral hazard problem is particularly severe, having a minimum proportion of insured deposits may be essential to realize the benefits of intermediated finance.

Summing up, we have set up a model of a bank that chooses the riskiness of its portfolio and is funded with exogenously given proportions of insured and uninsured deposits. The uninsured depositors observe a signal on the quality of the bank's portfolio, and run on the bank when the signal is bad, which leads to its early liquidation. The interest rate of the uninsured deposits is determined by a participation constraint that equals their expected return to a given constant. We have characterized the equilibrium of the model and shown how it depends on the proportion of insured deposits and the quality of the uninsured depositors' information. Although the model is designed to study the effects of different policies for banking crises, some interesting results on the beneficial effects of deposit insurance on risk-shifting incentives of deposit insurance and the quality if the uninsured depositors' information have been obtained.

---

[15] To explain this result, notice that when D tends to 1 the first-order condition (8) converges to $R(p^*) + p^* R'(p^*) = 1$, an equation that does not depend on q and whose solution is $p^* = \sqrt{2/3} = 0.82$.

[16] However, as noted in footnote 11, the fiscal cost C^* is not continuous at $D = 1$. In fact, for $L = 0.50$ one can show that C^* jumps down in the limit if and only if $q < p^*$.

2. POLICIES FOR BANKING CRISES

This section uses our model of information-based runs to analyze the effects of three policies that the supervisor may implement at the outset of a crisis. Two of them, namely extending the coverage of deposit insurance to all depositors and providing unrestricted liquidity support to the bank, are responses to a crisis situation in which the uninsured depositors observe the bad signal and run on the bank. The other is different in that there is no bank run, but the supervisor has confidential information showing that the bank is not satisfying some key prudential regulations, and may decide to act on this information or to forbear.

We assume that the supervisor observes at $t = 1$ a signal $s' \in \{s'_0, s'_1\}$ on the return of the bank's risky asset, which is interpreted as the outcome of banking supervision.

We make the following assumption.

Assumption 3. $\Pr(s'_0 \mid R_0) = \Pr(s'_1 \mid R_1) = q' \in [\frac{1}{2}, 1]$ and $\Pr(R \mid s, s') = \Pr(R \mid s')$.

Assumption 3 introduces a new parameter q' that describes the quality of the supervisory information. In addition, it states that adding signal s to signal s' does not change the conditional distribution of the return of the bank's risky asset, so the supervisory signal incorporates the uninsured depositor's information.[17] This implies the following result.

Lemma 1. *The quality q' of the supervisory information is greater than or equal to the quality q of the uninsured depositors' information. Moreover, we have*

$$\delta = \Pr(s_0 \mid s'_0) = \Pr(s_1 \mid s'_1) = 1 - \frac{q' - q}{2q' - 1}. \tag{10}$$

Hence, if the two signals were perfectly correlated, we would have $\delta = 1$ and $q' = q$. Otherwise, $\delta < 1$ and $q' > q$, which is what will be assumed henceforth.[18]

As before, by Bayes's law we have

$$\Pr(R_1 \mid s'_0) = \frac{(1 - q')p}{q' + (1 - 2q')p}, \tag{11}$$

---

[17] This is without loss of generality, because the uninsured depositors' signal, s_0 or s_1, is perfectly correlated with their behavior, run or not run.

[18] Assumption 3 also implies $\Pr(R, s \mid s') = \Pr(R \mid s, s') \Pr(s \mid s') = \Pr(R \mid s') \Pr(s \mid s')$, so conditional on the supervisory signal s', the asset return R and uninsured depositors' signal s are independent.

and

$$\Pr(R_1 \mid s_1') = \frac{q'p}{1 - q' - (1 - 2q')p} \tag{12}$$

which implies $\Pr(R_1 \mid s_0') < p < \Pr(R_1 \mid s_1')$ for $q' > \frac{1}{2}$, so s_0' and s_1' will be called the bad and the good signal, respectively.

In what follows, we examine the effects on risk-shifting incentives and fiscal costs of bank failure of each of the three policies for banking crises mentioned earlier. Importantly, we do not derive the use of any of these policies from the maximization of an objective function for the supervisor, but simply look at their incentive and budgetary implications.

The *benchmark model* for the three policies is one in which the supervisor does not nothing to prevent the failure of the bank following a run. Moreover, the bad supervisory signal s_0' is interpreted as the finding that the bank is not properly accounting for the deterioration of its assets, which leads to the violation of some key prudential regulations. Although these regulations are not spelled out in detail, it is convenient to think about minimum capital requirements. The benchmark model also assumes that the bank shareholders do not have the ability or the incentives to recapitalize the bank, and that the supervisor does not forbear, which leads to the withdrawal of the license and the closure of the bank.

Therefore, in the benchmark model the bank is liquidated at $t = 1$ when either the uninsured depositors observe the bad signal s_0 or the supervisor observes the bad signal s_0', an event that by Assumptions 3 and Lemma 1 happens with probability

$$\Pr(s_0 \text{ or } s_0') = 1 - \Pr(s_1, s_1')$$
$$= 1 - \Pr(s_1 \mid s_1')\Pr(s_1') = 1 - \delta[1 - q' - (1 - 2q')p]. \tag{13}$$

The bank fails at $t = 2$ when the uninsured depositors observe the good signal s_1, the supervisor also observes the good signal s_1', and the return of the risky asset is R_0, an event that by Assumption 3 and Lemma 1 happens with probability

$$\Pr(s_1, s_1', R_0) = \Pr(R_0 \mid s_1, s_1')\Pr(s_1, s_1')$$
$$= \Pr(R_0 \mid s_1')\Pr(s_1 \mid s_1')\Pr(s_1')$$
$$= \Pr(s_1 \mid s_1')\Pr(s_1', R_0)$$
$$= \Pr(s_1 \mid s_1')\Pr(s_1' \mid R_0)\Pr(R_0) = \delta(1 - q')(1 - p). \tag{14}$$

And the bank succeeds at $t = 2$ when the uninsured depositors observe the good signal s_1, the supervisor also observes the good signal s_1', and the return of the risky asset is R_1, an event that by Assumption 3 and Lemma 1 happens with probability

$$
\begin{aligned}
\Pr(s_1, s_1', R_1) &= \Pr(R_1 \mid s_1, s_1')\Pr(s_1, s_1') \\
&= \Pr(R_1 \mid s_1')\Pr(s_1 \mid s_1')\Pr(s_1') \\
&= \Pr(s_1 \mid s_1')\Pr(s_1', R_1) \\
&= \Pr(s_1 \mid s_1')\Pr(s_1' \mid R_1)\Pr(R_1) = \delta q' p.
\end{aligned}
\tag{15}
$$

By limited liability, the bank gets a zero payoff if it is liquidated at $t = 1$ or fails at $t = 2$, and gets $R(p) - D - (1 - D)(1 + r)$ if it succeeds at $t = 2$, so its payoff function is given by

$$
V^0(p; r) = \delta q' p[R(p) - D - (1 - D)(1 + r)].
\tag{16}
$$

The uninsured depositors get $\max\{L - D, 0\}$ when the bank is liquidated at $t = 1$, they get $(1 - D)(1 + r)$ when the bank succeeds at $t = 2$, and they get zero when the bank fails at $t = 2$, so their payoff function is given by

$$
\begin{aligned}
U^0(r; p) &= [1 - \delta(1 - q' - (1 - 2q')p)]\max\{L - D, 0\} \\
&\quad + \delta q' p(1 - D)(1 + r).
\end{aligned}
\tag{17}
$$

An *equilibrium for the benchmark model* is a pair (r^0, p^0) such that p^0 maximizes the bank's payoff function $V^0(p; r^0)$ and r^0 satisfies the uninsured depositors' participation constraint $U^0(r^0; p^0) = 1 - D$.

As in the previous section, there may be multiple equilibria, in which case we focus on the equilibrium with the highest success probability p^0, for which one can prove the same result as in Proposition 1: p^0 is increasing in the proportion D of insured deposits whenever $D \geq L$, the effect being ambiguous otherwise.

The supervisor pays to the insured depositors $\max\{D - L, 0\}$ when the bank is liquidated at $t = 1$ and D when the bank fails at $t = 2$, so the fiscal cost in the benchmark equilibrium is

$$
C^0 = [1 - \delta(1 - q' - (1 - 2q')p^0)]\max\{D - L, 0\} + \delta(1 - q')(1 - p^0)D.
\tag{18}
$$

We are now ready to analyze the effects of three policies that the supervisor may implement at the outset of a crisis. Because some of the effects are ambiguous, we rely on numerical solutions using the functional form $R(p) = 3 - p^2$ and the parameter values $L = 0.50$, $q = 0.65$, and $q' = 0.75$, which by Lemma 1 imply $\delta = \Pr(s_0 \mid s_0') = \Pr(s_1 \mid s_1') = 0.80$.

2.1 Forbearance

Consider a situation in which at $t = 1$ the uninsured depositors observe the good signal s_1, so they do not run on the bank, but the supervisor observes the bad signal s_0'. This is interpreted as the violation of some key prudential regulations, so the supervisor may decide either to close the bank (the benchmark case) or to forbear.

In the forbearance case, the supervisory information is completely irrelevant. Hence we are in the same situation as in the model of Section 2. The bank is only liquidated at $t = 1$ when the uninsured depositors observe the bad signal s_0, it fails at $t = 2$ when they observe the good signal s_1 and the return of the risky asset is R_0, and it succeeds at $t = 2$ when they observe the good signal s_1 and the return of the risky asset is R_1. Therefore, as in (5) and (6), the payoff functions of the bank and the uninsured depositors are given by

$$V^F(p; r) = qp[R(p) - D - (1 - D)(1 + r)],\qquad(19)$$

and

$$U^F(r; p) = [q + (1 - 2q)p]\max\{L - D, 0\} + qp(1 - D)(1 + r).\qquad(20)$$

It is important to stress that in these expressions we are assuming that both the bank and the uninsured depositors correctly anticipate the supervisory forbearance.

An *equilibrium with forbearance* is a pair (r^F, p^F) such that p^F maximizes the bank's payoff function $V^F(p; r^F)$ and r^F satisfies the uninsured depositors' participation constraint $U^F(r^F, p^F) = 1 - D$.

To compare the equilibrium (r^F, p^F) with the benchmark equilibrium (r^0, p^0) we have to examine what happens to the two conditions that characterize these equilibria, namely the bank's first-order condition and the uninsured depositors' participation constraint. Since the only difference between $V^0(p; r)$ and $V^F(p; r)$ in (16) and (19) is that the constant that multiplies the term $p[R(p) - D - (1 - D)(1 + r)]$ is $\delta q'$ instead of q, it follows that the two first-order conditions are identical. Therefore, in order to compare the two equilibria we only have to find out what happens to the relationship between r and p in the participation constraints $U^0(r; p) = 1 - D$ and $U^F(r; p) = 1 - D$, which is done in the following result.

Proposition 2. $p^F > p^0$ *and* $r^F < r^0$, *whenever* $D \geq L$.

Hence, when the proportion of insured deposits is sufficiently large, regulatory forbearance reduces the interest rate required by uninformed depositors and increases the probability of success chosen by the bank.

The intuition for this result is that when $D \geq L$ the uninformed depositors only get a positive payoff if the bank succeeds at $t = 2$, but since $\Pr(s_1, R_1) > \Pr(s_1, s_1', R_1)$ the probability of getting $(1 - D)(1 + r)$ is higher under forbearance, which in equilibrium implies a lower deposit rate and a higher probability of success. In terms of Figure 5.1, the explanation is that the participation constraint curve shifts to the left, so the chosen equilibrium moves up along the first-order condition curve. By contrast, when $D < L$ there is an opposite effect, because as $\Pr(s_0) < \Pr(s_0 \text{ or } s_0')$ or the probability of getting $\max\{L - D, 0\}$ is lower under forbearance.

The fiscal cost in the forbearance case is computed as follows. The supervisor pays the insured depositors $\max\{D - L, 0\}$ when the bank is liquidated at $t = 1$ and D when the bank fails at $t = 2$. Because $\Pr(s_0) = q + (1 - 2q)p^F$ and $\Pr(s_1, R_0) = \Pr(s_1 \mid R_0)\Pr(R_0) = (1 - q)(1 - p^F)$, the fiscal cost with regulatory forbearance is

$$C^F = [q + (1 - 2q)p^F]\max\{D - L, 0\} + (1 - q)(1 - p^F)D \qquad (21)$$

The comparison between the fiscal cost C^F for the forbearance model and the fiscal cost C^0 for the benchmark model is not straightforward. The numerical solution for our parametric specification is depicted in Figure 5.3, which shows the equilibrium success probabilities, p^F and p^0, and the corresponding fiscal costs, C^F and C^0, as a function of the proportion D of insured deposits.

Figure 5.3 shows that the expectation of supervisory forbearance reduces the minimum value of the proportion D of insured deposits that is required for the existence of an equilibrium. Moreover, the success probabilities p^F and p^0 are everywhere increasing in the proportion D of insured deposits, with $p^F > p^0$ except in the limit when $D = 1$ (full deposit insurance) where $p^F = p^0$. The fiscal costs C^F and C^0 are also everywhere increasing in D, with $C^F > C^0$ except for high values of D where $C^F < C^0$. The reason for this result is that when the proportion D of insured deposits is large, the early closure of the bank by the supervisor in the benchmark model (when $s' = s_0'$) implies a large compensation to the insured depositors that would be saved if the bank were allowed to stay open and eventually succeeded.[19]

---

[19] This effect would not obtain for high values of the quality q' of the supervisory information, because in this case early closure would always be cheaper for the supervisor.

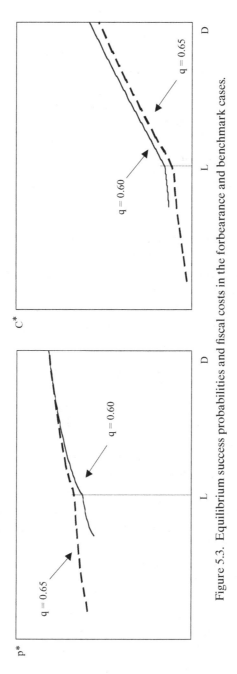

Figure 5.3. Equilibrium success probabilities and fiscal costs in the forbearance and benchmark cases.

153

2.2 Deposit Guarantees

Consider now a situation in which, after the uninsured depositors observe the bad signal s_0 at $t = 1$, the supervisor may decide either to extend the insurance coverage to all depositors or let the bank fail (the benchmark case).

If the supervisor extends the insurance regardless of the signals of the uninsured depositors and the supervisor there will be no liquidation at $t = 1$. Hence, the bank gets $R(p) - D - (1 - D)(1 + r)$ with probability $\Pr(R_1) = p$, so its payoff function is given by

$$V^G(p; r) = p[R(p) - D - (1 - D)(1 + r)]. \tag{22}$$

Assuming that the supervisor only insures the principal (and not the interest initially offered), the uninsured depositors get $(1 - D)(1 + r)$ when the bank succeeds at $t = 2$, they get $1 - D$ when they observe the bad signal s_0 and the bank fails at $t = 2$ (because of the extension of the insurance coverage), and they get zero when they observe the good signal s_1 and the bank fails at $t = 2$ (because in this case they are not insured). Since $\Pr(R_1) = p$ and $\Pr(s_0, R_0) = \Pr(s_0 \mid R_0)\Pr(R_0) = q(1 - p)$, their payoff function is given by

$$U^G(r; p) = q(1 - p)(1 - D) + p(1 - D)(1 + r). \tag{23}$$

As in the forbearance case, it important to stress that in (22) and (23) we are assuming that both the bank and the uninsured depositors correctly anticipate the behavior of the supervisor.

An *equilibrium with extended deposit guarantees* is a pair (r^G, p^G) such that p^G maximizes the bank's payoff function $V^G(p; r^G)$ and r^G satisfies the uninsured depositors' participation constraint $U^G(r^G, p^G) = 1 - D$.

To compare the equilibrium (r^G, p^G) with the benchmark equilibrium (r^0, p^0) we have to examine what happens to the two conditions that characterize these equilibria, namely the bank's first-order condition and the uninsured depositors' participation constraint. Because the only difference between $V^0(p; r)$ and $V^G(p; r)$ in (16) and (22) is that the constant that multiplies the term $p[R(p) - D - (1 - D)(1 + r)]$ is $\delta q'$ instead of 1, it follows that the two first-order conditions are identical. Therefore, in order to compare the two equilibria we only have to find out what happens to the relationship between r and p in the participation constraints $U^0(r; p) = 1 - D$ and $U^G(r; p) = 1 - D$, which is done in the following result.

Proposition 3. $p^G > p^0$ and $r^G < r^0$, whenever $D \geq L$.

The intuition for this result is that when $D \geq L$ the uninsured depositors get a higher payoff when they observe the bad signal s_0 and the bank fails at $t = 2$, because they are covered by the extension of the insurance, and they also get a higher payoff when they observe the good signal s_1, the supervisor observes the bad signal s_0', and the bank succeeds at $t = 2$, because in the benchmark case the bank would have been closed by the supervisor. In equilibrium both effects imply a lower deposit rate and a higher probability of success. In terms of Figure 5.1, the explanation is that the participation constraint curve shifts to the left, so the chosen equilibrium moves up along the first-order condition curve. By contrast, when $D < L$ there is an opposite effect, because when the uninsured depositors observe the good signal s_1, the supervisor observes the bad signal s_0', and the bank fails at $t = 2$, they get $\max\{L - D, 0\}$ in the benchmark case and zero in the extended deposit guarantees case.

The corresponding fiscal cost is computed as follows. The supervisor pays D to the insured depositors when the bank fails at $t = 2$ and it pays $1 - D$ to the uninsured depositors when they observe the bad signal s_0 and the bank fails at $t = 2$. Since $\Pr(R_0) = 1 - p^G$ and $\Pr(s_0, R_0) = \Pr(s_0 \mid R_0)\Pr(R_0) = q(1 - p^G)$, the fiscal cost is

$$C^G = (1 - p^G)D + q(1 - p^G)(1 - D). \tag{24}$$

The comparison between the fiscal cost C^G for the extended deposit guarantees model and the fiscal cost C^0 for the benchmark model is in principle ambiguous. The numerical solution for our parametric specification is depicted in Figure 5.4, which shows the equilibrium success probabilities, p^G and p^0, and the corresponding fiscal costs, C^G and C^0, as a function of the proportion D of insured deposits.

Figure 5.4 shows that the expectation of the extension of deposit guarantees to all depositors reduces (to zero) the minimum value of the proportion D of insured deposits that is required for the existence of an equilibrium. The success probabilities p^G is slightly increasing in the proportion D of insured deposits, with $p^G > p^0$ except in the limit when $D = 1$ (full deposit insurance) where $p^G = p^0$. The fiscal cost C^G is also increasing in D, with $C^G > C^0$ except for high values of D where $C^G < C^0$. The reason for this result is that when the proportion D of insured deposits is large, the early closure of the bank by either the uninsured depositors (when $s = s_0$) or the supervisor (when $s' = s_0'$) in the benchmark model implies a large compensation to the insured depositors,

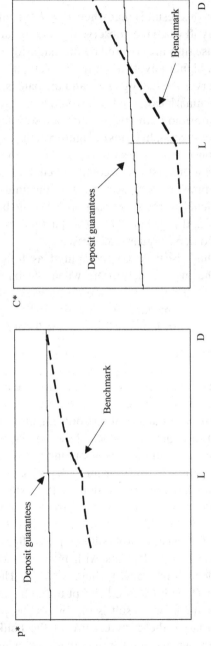

Figure 5.4. Equilibrium success probabilities and fiscal costs in the extended deposit guarantees and benchmark cases.

which would be saved if the bank were allowed to stay open and eventually succeeded.

2.3 Liquidity Support

Consider next a situation in which, after the uninsured depositors observe the bad signal s_0 at $t = 1$, the supervisor, acting as a lender of last resort, may decide either to provide emergency liquidity to cover the withdrawal of uninsured deposits or let the bank fail (the benchmark case). To simplify the presentation, we assume that the lender of last resort charges the bank the same interest rate r initially required by the uninsured depositors.

If the supervisor provides the emergency liquidity regardless of the signals of the uniformed depositors and the supervisor there will be no liquidation at $t = 1$. Hence, the bank will get $R(p) - D - (1 - D)(1 + r)$ with probability $\Pr(R_1) = p$, so its payoff function is the same as in the case of extended deposit guarantees, that is

$$V^L(p; r) = p[R(p) - D - (1 - D)(1 + r)]. \qquad (25)$$

Assuming that the uninsured depositors can only claim at $t = 1$ the principal (and not the interest initially offered), the uninsured depositors get $1 - D$ when they observe the bad signal s_0 and withdraw their funds at $t = 1$, they get $(1 - D)(1 + r)$ when they observe the good signal s_1 and the bank succeeds at $t = 2$, and they get zero when they observe the good signal s_1 and the bank fails at $t = 2$. Because $\Pr(s_0) = q + (1 - 2q)p$ and $\Pr(s_1, R_1) = \Pr(s_1 \mid R_1)\Pr(R_1) = qp$, their payoff function is given by

$$U^L(r; p) = [q + (1 - 2q)p](1 - D) + qp(1 - D)(1 + r) \qquad (26)$$

An *equilibrium with unrestricted liquidity support* is a pair (r^L, p^L) such that p^L maximizes the bank's payoff function $V^L(p; r^L)$ and r^L satisfies the uninsured depositors' participation constraint $U^L(r^L, p^L) = 1 - D$.

To compare the equilibrium (r^L, p^L) with the benchmark equilibrium (r^0, p^0) we note that by our previous arguments the bank's first-order conditions are identical, so we only have to find out what happens to the relationship between r and p in the participation constraints $U^0(r; p) = 1 - D$ and $U^L(r; p) = 1 - D$, which is done in the following result.

Proposition 4. $p^L > p^0$ *and* $r^L < r^0$, *whenever* $D \geq L$.

The intuition for this result is that when $D \geq L$ the uninsured depositors get a higher payoff when they observe the bad signal s_0 and the bank fails at $t = 2$, because they are able to withdraw their funds at $t = 1$, and they also get a higher payoff when they observe the good signal s_1, the supervisor observes the bad signal s_0', and the bank succeeds at $t = 2$, because in the benchmark case the bank would have been closed by the supervisor. In equilibrium both effects imply a lower deposit rate and a higher probability of success. In terms of Figure 5.1, the explanation is that the participation constraint curve shifts to the left, so the chosen equilibrium moves up along the first-order condition curve. By contrast, when $D < L$ there is an opposite effect, because when the uninsured depositors observe the good signal s_1, the supervisor observes the bad signal s_0', and the bank fails at $t = 2$, they get $\max\{L - D, 0\}$ in the benchmark case and zero in the unrestricted liquidity support case.

The corresponding fiscal cost is computed as follows. The supervisor pays the insured depositors D when the bank fails at $t = 2$ and it loses its loan $1 - D$ when the uninsured depositors observe the bad signal s_0 and the bank fails at $t = 2$, and it gains $(1 - D)r^L$ when the uninsured depositors observe the bad signal s_0 and the bank succeeds at $t = 2$. Because $\Pr(R_0) = 1 - p^L$, $\Pr(s_0, R_0) = \Pr(s_0 \mid R_0)\Pr(R_0) = q(1 - p^L)$, and $\Pr(s_0, R_1) = \Pr(s_0 \mid R_1)\Pr(R_1) = (1 - q)p^L$, the fiscal cost is

$$C^L = (1 - p^L)D + q(1 - p^L)(1 - D) - (1 - q)p^L(1 - D)r^L. \quad (27)$$

The comparison between the fiscal cost C^L for the unrestricted liquidity support model and the fiscal cost C^0 for the benchmark model is in principle ambiguous. The numerical solution for our parametric specification gives a result that is very similar to that of the model with extended deposit guarantees depicted in Figure 5.4, except for the fact that p^L and C^L are slightly below p^G and C^G.[20]

The previous analysis assumes that the supervisor directly provides the liquidity support. An alternative setup is one in which there is a *central bank*, different from the deposit insurer, that supervises the bank and is willing to support it when the uninsured depositors observe the bad signal s_0 but only if the supervisory signal is s_1'. The interpretation is that the central bank requires "good banking securities" (using Bagehot's (1873) terminology) for its last resort lending. In addition, we assume that the central bank does not forbear, so it closes the bank when it observes the bad signal s_0'.

[20] The effect on p is easy to explain: From (26) and (23) it follows that $U^L = U^G - p(1 - q)(1 - D)r < U^G$, so in terms of Figure 5.1 the participation constraint in the liquidity support case is shifted out relative to the participation constraint in the deposit guarantees case, which gives $p^L < p^G$. By contrast, the result $C^L < C^G$ is explained by the interest payment in the liquidity support case, which compensates the decrease in p.

In this setup, the bank is liquidated at $t = 1$ when the central bank observes the bad signal s_0', an event that happens with probability $\Pr(s_0') = q' + (1 - 2q')p$. The bank fails at $t = 2$ when the central bank observes the good signal s_1' and the return of the risky asset is R_0, an event that happens with probability $\Pr(s_1', R_0) = \Pr(s_1' \mid R_0)\Pr(R_0) = (1 - q')(1 - p)$. And the bank succeeds at $t = 2$ when the central bank observes the good signal s_1' and the return of the risky asset is R_1, an event that happens with probability $\Pr(s_1', R_1) = \Pr(s_1' \mid R_1)\Pr(R_1) = q'p$. Hence the payoff function of the bank is given by

$$V^{CB}(p; r) = q'p[R(p) - D - (1 - D)(1 + r)]. \tag{28}$$

The uninsured depositors get $\max\{L - D, 0\}$ when the central bank observes the bad signal s_0' (because the bank is liquidated at $t = 1$), they get $1 - D$ when they observe the bad signal s_0 and the central bank observes the good signal s_1' (because they are able to withdraw their funds), they get $(1 - D)(1 + r)$ when they observe the good signal s_1, the supervisor also observes the good signal s_1', and the return of the risky asset is R_1, and they get zero when they observe the good signal s_1, the supervisor also observes the good signal s_1', and the return of the risky asset is R_0. Because $\Pr(s_0') = q' + (1 - 2q')p$, $\Pr(s_0, s_1') = \Pr(s_0 \mid s_1')\Pr(s_1') = (1 - \delta)[1 - q' - (1 - 2q')p]$ and by (15) we have $\Pr(s_1, s_1', R_1) = \delta q'p$, their payoff function is given by

$$U^{CB}(r; p) = [q' + (1 - 2q')p]\max\{L - D, 0\}$$
$$+ (1 - \delta)[1 - q' - (1 - 2q')p](1 - D) + \delta q'p(1 - D)(1 + r). \tag{29}$$

An *equilibrium with restricted (central bank) liquidity support* is a pair (r^{CB}, p^{CB}) such that p^{CB} maximizes the bank's payoff function $V^{CB}(p; r^{CB})$ and r^{CB} satisfies the uninsured depositors' participation constraint $U^{CB}(r^{CB}, p^{CB}) = 1 - D$.

To compare the equilibrium (r^{CB}, p^{CB}) with the benchmark equilibrium (r^0, p^0) we note, once again, that by our previous arguments the bank's first-order conditions are identical, so we only have to find out what happens to the relationship between r and p in the participation constraints $U^0(r; p) = 1 - D$ and $U^{CB}(r; p) = 1 - D$, which is done in the following result.

Proposition 5. $p^{CB} > p^0$ and $r^{CB} < r^0$.

The intuition for this result is that the uninsured depositors get a higher payoff when they observe the bad signal s_0 and the supervisor observes the good signal s'_1, because they are able to withdraw their funds at $t = 1$, getting $1 - D$ instead of $\max\{L - D, 0\}$ as in the benchmark case. In terms of Figure 5.1, the participation constraint curve always shifts to the left, so the chosen equilibrium moves up along the first-order condition curve.

The fiscal cost for the consolidated entity comprising the central bank and the deposit insurer is computed as follows. The deposit insurer pays the insured depositors $\max\{D - L, 0\}$ when the bank is liquidated at $t = 1$ and D when the bank fails at $t = 2$. The central bank loses its loan $1 - D$ when the uninsured depositors observe the bad signal s_0, the central bank observes the good signal s'_1, and the bank fails at $t = 2$, and it gains $(1 - D)r^{CB}$ when the uninsured depositors observe the bad signal s_0, the central bank observes the good signal s'_1, and the bank succeeds at $t = 2$. Because $\Pr(s'_0) = q' + (1 - 2q')p^{CB}$, $\Pr(s'_1, R_0) = \Pr(s'_1 \mid R_0)\Pr(R_0) = (1 - q')(1 - p^{CB})$, and by Assumption 3 and Lemma 1 we have

$$\Pr(s_0, s'_1, R_0) = \Pr(R_0 \mid s_0, s'_1)\Pr(s_0, s'_1)$$

$$= \Pr(R_0 \mid s'_1)\Pr(s_0 \mid s'_1)\Pr(s'_1)$$

$$= \Pr(s_0 \mid s'_1)\Pr(s'_1, R_0)$$

$$= \Pr(s_0 \mid s'_1)\Pr(s'_1 \mid R_0)\Pr(R_0) = (1 - \delta)(1 - q')(1 - p^{CB}),$$

and similarly $\Pr(s_0, s'_1, R_1) = (1 - \delta)q'p^{CB}$, the fiscal cost is

$$C^{CB} = [q' + (1 - 2q')p^{CB}]\max\{D - L, 0\} + (1 - q')(1 - p^{CB})D$$

$$+ (1 - \delta)(1 - q')(1 - p^{CB})(1 - D) - (1 - \delta)q'p^{CB}(1 - D)r^{CB}. \tag{30}$$

The comparison between the fiscal cost C^{CB} for the restricted liquidity support model and the fiscal cost C^0 for the benchmark model is in principle ambiguous. The numerical solution for our parametric specification is depicted in Figure 5.5, which shows the equilibrium success probabilities, p^{CB} and p^0, and the corresponding fiscal costs, C^{CB} and C^0, as a function of the proportion D of insured deposits.

Figure 5.5 shows that the expectation of the provision of liquidity support by the central bank reduces (to zero) the minimum value of the proportion D of insured deposits that is required for the existence of an equilibrium. The success probability p^{CB} is increasing in the proportion D of insured deposits, with $p^{CB} > p^0$ except in the limit when $D = 1$ (full deposit insurance) where $p^{CB} = p^0$. The fiscal cost C^{CB} is also increasing

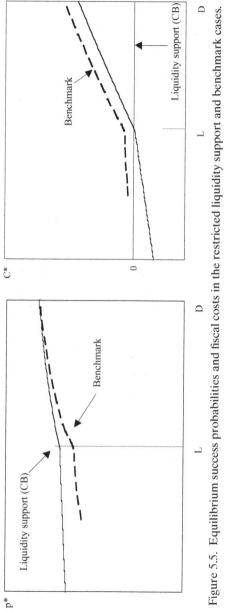

Figure 5.5. Equilibrium success probabilities and fiscal costs in the restricted liquidity support and benchmark cases.

161

in D. Interestingly, we have $C^{CB} < C^0$, with C^{CB} becoming negative (i.e., a positive expected revenue) for low values of D. The reason for this result is that in this case the cost to the deposit insurer is small, whereas the central bank is lending only when it observes the good signal s_1', which implies that interest payment when the bank succeeds more than offsets the losses when the bank fails.

We have assumed until now that the supervisor or the central bank only charge the normal market interest rate for their last resort lending, in contrast with the classical doctrine on the lender of last resort put forward by Bagehot (1873) that required that "these loans should only be made at a very high interest rate." However, the effect of penalty rates on the bank's choice of risk is straightforward: they increase the expected interest payments when the bank succeeds at $t = 2$ and, consequently, the bank reacts to this higher cost by choosing a higher risk and higher return portfolio. Thus, in line with the results in Repullo (2004), penalty rates increase the bank's incentives to take risk.

To close this section, we briefly comment on one feature of banking in the real world that has been absent from our model, namely bank capital. Introducing the possibility of raising equity capital at $t = 0$ would not change our results, because if the cost of capital is greater than or equal to the return required by depositors it is never optimal for the bank owners to provide any capital. Moreover, the effect of a minimum capital requirement k would be the same as in Repullo (2004): the bank's success payoff would become $R(p) - (1 - k)D - (1 - k)(1 - D)(1 + r)$, so the first-order condition that characterizes the bank's choice of risk would be

$$R(p^*) + p^* R'(p^*) = (1 - k)D + (1 - k)(1 - D)(1 + r^*).$$

Because the left-hand side of this expression is decreasing in p^*, it follows that capital requirements reduce the bank's incentives to take risk.

3. CONCLUDING REMARKS

Most of the literature on the design of the financial safety net has repeatedly argued that any form of insurance creates moral hazard and hence leads to greater risk-taking. However, as noted by Demirgüç-Kunt and Kane (2002, p. 176), "this insight has been persistently emphasized by academics, but mostly dismissed or denigrated by policy makers." We show that the intuition of policy makers may not have been wrong after all (cf. Folkerts-Landau and Lindgren, 1998). Our result follows from two arguments: (1) insured depositors require a lower interest rate for their funds, and (2) as in the model of Stiglitz and Weiss (1981) a lower cost of funding reduces the banks' incentives to take risks.

The stark contrast between our result and the extant literature deserves further discussion. It is true that in general any form of insurance has the potential to create a moral hazard problem. However, the point is that in the context of banking the absence of deposit insurance does not eliminate the moral hazard that comes from the fact that the choice of investment is done (or may be changed) after the funds are raised, and this choice is in general not verifiable so deposit rates cannot be made contingent on it. The traditional story is based on the idea that even though deposit rates cannot be made explicitly contingent on risk, monitoring by uninsured depositors can make them contingent ex post, so by reducing the incentives to monitor banks deposit insurance is an important source of moral hazard.

A simple way to formalize this argument would be as follows. Suppose that instead of observing a signal s on the return of the bank's risky asset, the uninsured depositors observe the bank's choice of p. Furthermore, suppose that they can make the deposit rate r contingent on the choice of p (for example, by threatening to withdraw their funds). In this case, the bank would maximize its payoff function

$$p[R(p) - D - (1 - D)(1 + r(p))]$$

subject to the uninsured depositors' participation constraint

$$p(1 - D)(1 + r(p)) = 1 - D.$$

Substituting this constraint into the bank's objective function yields

$$p[R(p) - D] - (1 - D),$$

so the first-order condition that characterizes the success probability $\tilde{p}$ chosen by the bank is

$$R(\tilde{p}) + \tilde{p}R'(\tilde{p}) = D. \tag{31}$$

Because we have assumed that $R(p) + pR'(p)$ is decreasing, it follows from (31) that $\tilde{p}$ is decreasing in the proportion D of insured deposits. Moreover, comparing (31) with (2), it also follows that the success probability $\tilde{p}$ chosen by the bank converges to the first-best $\hat{p}$ when the proportion of insured deposits D tends to zero. Thus, in this setting having no deposit insurance would be optimal.

Two objections can be made to this argument. The standard one is that small depositors do not have the ability or the incentives to monitor banks.[21] The nonstandard one that we are putting forward is that one should distinguish between the *monitoring of actions* and the *monitoring of the consequences of those actions*.[22] As noted earlier, the former eliminates the moral hazard problem in the absence of deposit insurance. The latter, however, does not eliminate this problem. In our model, this monitoring yields signal s which changes the bank's payoff function from

$$p[R(p) - D - (1 - D)(1 + r)]$$

to

$$pq[R(p) - D - (1 - D)(1 + r)],$$

where $q = \Pr(s_1 \mid R_1)$ is the quality of the uninsured depositors' information. Clearly, multiplying the payoff function by a constant does not have any effect on the first-order condition that characterizes the bank's choice of risk. Moreover, the higher the proportion of insured deposits D the lower the bank's average cost of funds, and hence the lower the bank's incentives to take risks.

Because arguably this is the most plausible type of monitoring,[23] we conclude that there is no presumption that deposit insurance worsens the bank's risk-shifting incentives.[24] Similarly, accommodative resolution policies for banking crises need not induce banks to take greater risks. On the contrary, to the extent that they reduce the interest rate required by uninsured depositors, they could in fact ameliorate the bank's risk-shifting incentives, but at the expense of higher fiscal costs. At any rate, this is an important policy area in which further research, both theoretical and empirical, is much needed.

[21] As forcefully argued by Corrigan (1991, pp. 49–50), "I think it is sheer fantasy to assume that individual investors and depositors – and perhaps even large and relatively sophisticated investors and depositors – can make truly informed credit judgments about highly complex financial instruments and institutions."

[22] See Prat (2003) for a detailed discussion of the related distinction between signals on actions and signals on the consequences of actions.

[23] Also, this is the one that has been studied in the literature. For example, Martinez-Peria and Schmukler (2001) show that depositors in Argentina, Chile, and Mexico punish banks when their fundamentals deteriorate (not when they pursue riskier strategies), both by withdrawing their deposits and by requiring higher interest rates.

[24] Interestingly, Gropp and Vesala (2004) find evidence that the introduction of explicit deposit insurance in the European Union may have significantly reduced banks' risk-taking.

ACKNOWLEDGMENTS

I would like to thank Patrick Bolton, Douglas Gale, and Javier Suarez for their comments, and Abel Elizalde for his excellent research assistance. Financial support from the World Bank is gratefully acknowledged.

APPENDIX

Proof of Proposition 1

Differentiating (7) and (8) gives

$$\begin{bmatrix} a_{11} & a_{12} \\ a_{21} & a_{22} \end{bmatrix} \begin{bmatrix} dr^* \\ dp^* \end{bmatrix} = \begin{bmatrix} a_{13} & a_{14} \\ a_{23} & 0 \end{bmatrix} \begin{bmatrix} dD \\ dq \end{bmatrix},$$

where

$$a_{11} = -qp^*(1-D) < 0,$$

$$a_{12} = (2q-1)\max\{L-D, 0\} - q(1-D)(1+r^*)$$
$$< (2q-1)(1-D) - q(1-D) = (q-1)(1-D) < 0,$$

$$a_{13} = 1 - [(1-q)p^* + q(1-p^*)] - qp^*(1+r^*)$$
$$= [(1-q)p^* + q(1-p^*)]\left(\frac{\max\{L-D, 0\}}{1-D} - 1\right) < 0, \quad \text{if } D < L,$$

$$a_{13} = 1 - qp^*(1+r^*) = 0, \quad \text{if } D \geq L,$$

$$a_{14} = (1-2p^*)\max\{L-D, 0\} + p^*(1-D)(1+r^*) > 0, \quad \text{if } p \leq \tfrac{1}{2},$$

$$a_{14} = (1-2p^*)\max\{L-D, 0\} + p^*(1-D)(1+r^*)$$
$$> (1-2p^*)(1-D) + p^*(1-D) = (1-p^*)(1-D) > 0, \quad \text{if } p > \tfrac{1}{2},$$

$$a_{21} = -(1-D) < 0,$$

$$a_{22} = 2R'(p^*) + p^*R''(p^*) < 0,$$

$$a_{23} = -r^* < 0.$$

Because the equilibrium with the highest value of p^* (and the lowest value of r^*) is characterized by the condition $a_{11}a_{22} - a_{12}a_{21} > 0$, we conclude that

$$\frac{\partial r^*}{\partial D} = \frac{a_{13}a_{22} - a_{12}a_{23}}{a_{11}a_{22} - a_{12}a_{21}} \gtrless 0 \quad \text{and} \quad \frac{\partial p^*}{\partial D} = \frac{a_{11}a_{23} - a_{13}a_{21}}{a_{11}a_{22} - a_{12}a_{21}} \gtrless 0, \quad \text{if } D < L,$$

$$\frac{\partial r^*}{\partial D} = \frac{-a_{12}a_{23}}{a_{11}a_{22} - a_{12}a_{21}} < 0 \quad \text{and} \quad \frac{\partial p^*}{\partial D} = \frac{a_{11}a_{23}}{a_{11}a_{22} - a_{12}a_{21}} > 0, \quad \text{if } D \geq L,$$

$$\frac{\partial r^*}{\partial q} = \frac{a_{14}a_{22}}{a_{11}a_{22} - a_{12}a_{21}} < 0 \quad \text{and} \quad \frac{\partial p^*}{\partial q} = \frac{-a_{14}a_{21}}{a_{11}a_{22} - a_{12}a_{21}} > 0.$$

Proof of Lemma 1

By the definition of conditional probabilities and Assumption 3 we have

$$\Pr(s \mid R, s') = \frac{\Pr(R \mid s, s')\Pr(s \mid s')}{\Pr(R \mid s')} = \Pr(s \mid s'),$$

which implies

$$\Pr(s \mid R) = \Pr(s \mid R, s_0')\Pr(s_0' \mid R) + \Pr(s \mid R, s_1')\Pr(s_1' \mid R)$$
$$= \Pr(s \mid s_0')\Pr(s_0' \mid R) + \Pr(s \mid s_1')\Pr(s_1' \mid R).$$

Substituting $s = s_0, s_1$ and $R = R_0, R_1$ in this result, and using the definitions of q and q', we get the following system linear equations:

$$q = \Pr(s_0 \mid s_0')q' + \Pr(s_0 \mid s_1')(1 - q'),$$
$$1 - q = \Pr(s_1 \mid s_0')q' + \Pr(s_1 \mid s_1')(1 - q'),$$
$$q = \Pr(s_1 \mid s_0')(1 - q') + \Pr(s_1 \mid s_1')q',$$
$$1 - q = \Pr(s_0 \mid s_0')(1 - q') + \Pr(s_0 \mid s_1')q',$$

whose solution gives

$$\delta = \Pr(s_0 \mid s_0') = \Pr(s_1 \mid s_1') = 1 - \frac{q' - q}{2q' - 1}.$$

Moreover, because δ is a probability, we have $\delta \le 1$, which implies $q' \ge q$.

Proof of Proposition 2

Using the fact that by Assumptions 2 and 3 and Lemma 1, we have

$$\Pr(s_0 \text{ or } s_0') = \Pr(s_0) + \Pr(s_0') - \Pr(s_0, s_0')$$
$$= \Pr(s_0) + \Pr(s_0') - \Pr(s_0 \mid s_0')\Pr(s_0')$$
$$= q + (1 - 2q)p + (1 - \delta)[q' + (1 - 2q')p],$$

so (17) can also be written as

$$U^0(r; p) = [q + (1 - 2q)p + (1 - \delta)(q' + (1 - 2q')p)]\max\{L - D, 0\}$$
$$+ \delta q'p(1 - D)(1 + r).$$

But then using the definition (20) of $U^F(r; p)$ we have

$$U^0(r; p) = U^F(r; p) + (1 - \delta)[q' + (1 - 2q')p)]\max\{L - D, 0\}$$
$$- (q - \delta q')p(1 - D)(1 + r).)$$

Because $q - \delta q' = (1 - \delta)(1 - q') > 0$ by the proof of Lemma 1, if $\max\{L - D, 0\} = 0$ we have $U^0(r; p) < U^F(r; p)$, so the participation constraint in the forbearance case is shifted to the left, which implies $p^F > p^0$ and $r^F < r^0$. By contrast, if $\max\{L - D, 0\} > 0$ the second term in the previous expression is positive while the third is negative, so we have $U^0(r; p) \gtrless U^F(r; p)$, and the result is ambiguous.

Proof of Proposition 3

Using the expression of $U^0(r; p)$ in the proof of Proposition 2 and the definition (23) of $U^G(r; p)$ we have

$$U^0(r; p) = U^G(r; p) + [(1 - q)p + (1 - \delta)(q' + (1 - 2q')p)]$$
$$\times \max\{L - D, 0\} - q(1 - p)[(1 - D) - \max\{L - D, 0\}]$$
$$- (1 - \delta q')p(1 - D)(1 + r).)$$

Hence, if $\max\{L - D, 0\} = 0$ we have $U^0(r; p) < U^G(r; p)$, so the participation constraint in the unlimited deposit guarantees case is shifted to the left, which implies $p^G > p^0$ and $r^G < r^0$. By contrast, if $\max\{L - D, 0\} > 0$ the second term in the previous expression is positive while the third and the fourth are negative, so we have $U^0(r; p) \gtrless U^G(r; p)$, and the result is ambiguous.

Proof of Proposition 4

Using the expression of $U^0(r; p)$ in the proof of Proposition 2 and the definition (26) of $U^L(r; p)$ we have

$$U^0(r; p) = U^L(r; p) + (1 - \delta)[q' + (1 - 2q')p]\max\{L - D, 0\}$$
$$- [q + (1 - 2q)p][(1 - D) - \max\{L - D, 0\}]$$
$$- (q - \delta q')p(1 - D)(1 + r).)$$

Because $q - \delta q' = (1 - \delta)(1 - q') > 0$ by the proof of Lemma 1, if $\max\{L - D, 0\} = 0$ we have $U^0(r; p) < U^L(r; p)$, so the participation constraint in the unrestricted liquidity support case is shifted to the left, which implies $p^L > p^0$ and $r^L < r^0$. By contrast, if $\max\{L - D, 0\} > 0$ the second term in the previous expression is positive while the third and the fourth are negative, so we have $U^0(r; p) \gtrless U^L(r; p)$, and the result is ambiguous.

Proof of Proposition 5

Using the definitions (17) and (26) of $U^0(r; p)$ and $U^L(r; p)$ we have

$$U^0(r; p) = U^{CB}(r; p) - (1 - \delta)[1 - q' - (1 - 2q')p][(1 - D) \\ - \max\{L - D, 0\}] < U^{CB}(r; p).$$

Hence, the participation constraint in the central bank liquidity support case is shifted to the left, which implies $p^{CB} > p^0$ and $r^{CB} < r^0$.

SIX

Crisis Resolution, Policies, and Institutions

Empirical Evidence

Stijn Claessens, Daniela Klingebiel, and Luc Laeven

INTRODUCTION

The large-scale corporate defaults and sharp increases in nonperforming loans that have characterized the many systemic crises of recent years (as described in Chapter 1 and detailed in the Appendix), have typically been accompanied by a general economic slowdown and large fiscal costs of resolution. As emerges clearly from the discussion of previous chapters in this volume, choosing the best way of resolving a systemic crisis and accelerating economic recovery is far from unproblematic. There has been little agreement on what constitutes best practice or even good practice. Many approaches have been proposed and tried to resolve systemic crises more efficiently. Sometimes, contradictory policy recommendations have been made in the midst of a crisis, as happened notably in case of East Asia, but also elsewhere. Part of these differences may arise because objectives of the policy advice have varied. Some have focused on reducing the fiscal costs of financial crises, others on limiting the economic costs in terms of lost output and on accelerating restructuring, whereas again others have focused on achieving long-term, structural reforms. But trade-offs may arise between these objectives. Governments may, for example, through certain policies consciously incur large fiscal outlays in resolving a banking crisis, with the objective of accelerating recovery. Or structural reforms may only be politically feasible in the context of a severe crisis with large output losses and high fiscal costs.

Theory is also ambiguous in its recommendations. One reason for this is that resolution involves inherently complicated coordination problems. The fate of an individual corporation or financial institution and the best course of action for its owners and managers will depend on the actions of many others and the general economic outlook. Because of these coordination problems, as well as a lack of capital and the importance of the financial system to economic growth, governments often take the lead in systemic restructuring, especially of the banking system. In the process, governments often incur large fiscal costs, presumably with the objective of accelerating the recovery from the crisis. A complicating factor is that a crisis is typically aggravated by institutional weaknesses, many of which likely contributed to the emergence of the crisis in the first place. Bankruptcy and restructuring frameworks are often deficient. Disclosure and accounting rules for financial institutions and corporations may be weak. Equity and creditor rights may be poorly defined or weakly enforced. And the judiciary system is often inefficient. The government itself may face credibility problems as it may be partly to blame for the crisis, and, in general, faces time consistency problems. And corruption may be large.

Against this background, it becomes essential to turn to systemic empirical research. To date, the body of such research supporting particular policy views or clarifying the role of institutional factors remains limited. Most research has focused on individual cases, making it difficult to generalize. Cross-country analysis can help shed light on how fiscal outlays relate to the speed of recovery and how this may vary with the institutional environment of countries. This can help prioritize policies as policies that increase the fiscal outlays of resolving a crisis may or may not accelerate the economic recovery depending on the institutional environment of the country. So far, there has been limited cross-country analysis on how fiscal outlays and recovery relate. The main paper to date is Honohan and Klingebiel (2003). They find that accommodative policy measures, such as substantial liquidity support, explicit government guarantee on financial institutions' liabilities and forbearance from prudential regulations, tend to be fiscally costly and that these particular policies do not accelerate the speed of recovery. However, they focus less on the institutional frameworks within which these policies take place. It might well be that the effectiveness of fiscal outlays depends on the institutional environment, or even that the importance of the institutional environment dominates the effectiveness of any fiscal outlays.

We are interested in examining what combination of fiscal outlays, policy choices and institutional frameworks have proven to be the most effective in terms of resolving a systemic crisis. Specifically, we investigate how fiscal outlays associated with resolving a systemic crisis relate to economic output losses and how this relationship depends on a country's policy choices and institutional characteristics. We try to answer these questions using a country-level database on fiscal outlays and output losses for 29 countries with systemic banking crises.

We confirm that the size of fiscal cost is related to the extent to which countries adopt accommodative policies, in particular explicit government guarantees on financial institutions' liabilities and forbearance from prudential regulations. Furthermore, we find that output losses are not reduced by crisis-related fiscal outlays and that none of the specific policy measures associated with higher fiscal costs positively affects this relationship. Indeed, use of some of these policy measures is associated with a negative impact of fiscal outlays on economic recovery. By contrast, we find that better institutional development – general quality of institutions, less corruption, and a more efficient judicial system – is uniformly positively associated with faster recovery. These measures of institutional development are also important determinants of the fiscal outlays. These results suggest that countries should adopt strict policies to resolve a crisis; furthermore they should use the crisis as an opportunity to implement medium-term structural reforms, which also will help avoid future systemic crises. Our empirical analysis provides a starting point to uncover which elements of the institutional framework are most important for accelerating the recovery. Ranking the returns from institutional reforms in this way can help guide policy makers in setting priorities for reform.

The chapter itself is structured as follows. Section 1 briefly reviews the related literature, describes some of the main debates regarding systemic crisis resolution, and develops the main hypotheses. The section also reviews the key policy measures for resolving a financial crisis that are associated with fiscal outlays. Section 2 provides a description of the data and the empirical methodology used. Section 3 provides the results of the regressions that explain the policy determinants of fiscal outlays and explain the speed of recovery, relative to the fiscal outlays. Section 4 concludes.

1. LITERATURE REVIEW AND KEY POLICY MEASURES

We start with a definition of a systemic crisis. Under our definition, in a systemic crisis, a country's corporate and financial sectors experience a large number of defaults and financial institutions and corporations face great difficulties repaying contracts on time. As a result, nonperforming loans increase sharply and all or most of the aggregate banking system capital is exhausted. This situation may be accompanied by depressed asset prices (such as equity and real estate prices) on the heels of runups before the crisis, sharp increases in real interest rates, and a slowdown or reversal in capital flows. In countries with longer-term structural problems – such as early on in many transition economies – a systemic crisis may not be accompanied by such changes in asset prices and capital flows, partly because runups in prices and capital flows may not have occurred.[1]

In reviewing the literature on systemic crises, especially for emerging markets, it is useful to differentiate between three phases of systemic restructuring (see also Chapter 2). During the first phase, which can be called the containment phase, the financial crisis is still unfolding. During this phase, governments tend to implement policies aimed at restoring public confidence to minimize the repercussions on the real sector of the loss of confidence by depositors and other investors in the financial system. The second phase involves the actual financial, and to a lesser extent operational, restructuring of financial institutions and corporations. The third phase involves structural reforms, including changes in laws and regulations, and other institutional reforms, the privatization of any nationalized financial institutions and corporations, and so on. In this chapter, we discuss mainly the containment phase, and to a certain extent the restructuring phase. We do not include the third phase in our analysis and refer the reader to the more general literature on financial sector development (e.g., World Bank 2001, and Levine 2004).

During the late 1980s and early 1990s, most research on systemic crisis resolution focused on single crises, making it difficult to generalize. In his early comparative study, Sheng (1996) concluded that a comprehensive and credible plan could avoid a small crisis from becoming a systemic crisis, minimize adverse effects if a crisis nevertheless occurred, and limit overall losses. Caprio and Klingebiel (1996) expanded on those lessons studying 26 crises and Dziobek and Pazarbasioglu (1998) analyzed the experiences of 24 countries that faced crises in the 1980s and early 1990s. Also studying a cross-section of crises, Lindgren, Garcia, and Saal (1996) analyzed in particular the linkages between macroeconomic policy and

---

[1] Note that this definition of a systemic crisis excludes situations of systemic stress or heightened risks, such as the 1987 U.S. stock markets crash, the uncertainty surrounding the year 2000 (Y2K) turnover, or the events of September 11, 2001, which paralyzed payments and clearing systems. During these periods, central banks in many countries were involved in large-scale liquidity support as the banking systems were under (expected) stress, but the stress situations were short-lived and largely limited to the financial sectors.

bank soundness, reviewing the causes and consequences of banking sector problems and discussing how the banking system can be strengthened,
nationally and internationally. Honohan (1997) highlighted the contrasts
between crises associated with macroeconomic turbulence and management failures, and those associated with government interference, each
type requiring its own distinctive early warning and corrective policies.

The main lesson from these efforts is that managing a financial crisis is
much different in emerging markets than in industrial countries because
emerging markets have weaker institutions, crises are often larger, and
other initial circumstances differ. As a result, best practices from industrial
countries do not easily transfer to developing countries. Another key
lesson is that there appear to be trade-offs between various policies, both
in terms of individual objectives as well as between objectives (such as
containing fiscal costs, speeding recovery, and preventing a recurrence of
a crisis).

Cross-country research efforts focusing on the speed and shape of general economic recovery from a financial crisis are more plentiful, but most
often do not distinguish or analyze specific (financial sector) policies, beyond the provision of international liquidity support or the presence of a
(structural) adjustment program. They also often do not focus specifically
on banking crises, but also include currency and other crises.[2] Two recent
papers, Eichengreen and Rose (2003) and Lee and Park (2003), find a
V-shaped recovery to be the norm in currency crises and find no discern-
able impact of crises on longer-term growth. Others do find, however,
a more protracted recovery and some long-term costs in terms of output growth, particularly for crises in emerging markets and for the more
recent crises.[3] In terms of adjustment programs, Lee and Park (2003)
find that an IMF program is associated with much sharper V-shaped
recovery from a financial crisis, but not with better postcrisis recovery,
suggesting that liquidity issues are paramount in crises, whereas structural reforms, as presumably encouraged by the IMF, mattered less. Analyzing the impact of IMF and World Bank programs in both crisis and
noncrisis situations, Easterly (2003) finds no effects of the presence of a
structural adjustment program on the average rate of growth of countries. Hutchinson (2003) even finds that, in general, participation in IMF

---

[2] Most banking crises are twin crises, that is, also currency crises, but most currency crises
are not also banking crises.

[3] For a review of the evidence on the causes and effects of currency crises see Goldstein,
Kaminsky, and Reinhart (2000). They also summarize the findings of eight other studies
(in their Table 7.4).

programs is associated with a reduction in GDP growth, which may, however, reflect reverse causality. He finds specifically that participation in IMF programs associated with balance-of-payments crises does not mitigate output losses, concluding that "the cure of an IMF program may be worse than the disease."

From these analyses, one could conclude that crises are typically liquidity crises and that policy (choices), as reflected in the presence of an IMF or World Bank program, matters little in crisis resolution or may even make matters worse. One caveat is that these analyses did not investigate banking crises specifically, and many currency crises are not also banking crises. For banking crises only, the literature on the speed of recovery is more limited. Goldstein, Kaminsky, and Reinhart (2000) document the more protracted nature of the recovery from a banking crisis compared to a currency crisis. For their sample of 76 currency crises and 26 banking crises, output takes on average almost twice as long to recover from a banking crisis than from a currency crisis (18 versus 10 months). Imports recover only after 29 months for a banking crisis compared to after 18 months for a currency crisis. Banking crises appear thus more deleterious than currency crises, and do not seem to fit the V-shaped recovery pattern. Rojas-Suarez and Weisbrod (1996) examine the resolution of several banking crises in Latin America. They highlight the sluggishness of the banking resolution process in many episodes. Still these studies, as most others on currency and other financial crises, do not study the effects of specific policy measures, and as such do not shed light on the question of which policy measures are most successful in accelerating economic recovery in the aftermath of a crisis, and on the importance of the quality of the institutional environment.

In terms of cross-country studies investigating specific financial sector restructuring policies, the main effort to date has been Honohan and Klingebiel (2003). They show that much of the variation in the fiscal cost of 40 crises in industrial and developing economies in 1980–1997 can be explained by government approaches to resolving crises. They find that governments that provided open-ended liquidity support and blanket deposit guarantees and engaged in repeated, incomplete recapitalizations tended to incur much higher costs in resolving financial crises.[4] They also find no obvious trade-off between fiscal costs and subsequent economic

---

[4] This view is challenged by another study, Hoggarth, Reis, and Saporta (2002), which did not find a statistically significant relationship between fiscal costs and lender of last resort use when controlling for a number of other factors, including whether there was also a currency crisis at the same time.

growth (or overall output losses). Countries that used policies such as open-ended liquidity support, blanket guarantees, and forbearance did not recover faster. Rather, liquidity support appeared to make recovery from a crisis longer and output losses larger – a finding confirmed by Bordo et al. (2001). Their findings suggest that the two most important policies during the containment phase are to limit liquidity support and not to extend blanket guarantees.

There are also some cross-country studies investigating specific systemic bank restructuring policies that do not involve fiscal outlays. One study, Baer and Klingebiel (1995), analyzes the exceptions to the model of governments guaranteeing all liabilities in an effort to restore confidence. They show that in some crises – notably the United States (1933), Japan (1946), Argentina (1980–1982), and Estonia (1992) – governments imposed losses on depositors with little or no adverse macroeconomic consequences or flight to cash or foreign currency. Economic recovery was relatively rapid and financial intermediation, including household deposits, was soon restored. Thus, allocating losses to creditors or depositors will not necessarily lead to runs on banks or end in contraction of aggregate money, credit, and output. Baer and Klingebiel also suggest that intermittent regulatory intervention and forbearance make depositors more nervous and undermine regulatory credibility – especially if regulators had previously argued that the institutions involved were solvent. Both findings suggest that more accommodative policies and higher fiscal outlays do not necessarily lead to faster recovery.

Another effort to distinguish the impact of policy on recovery, but using individual firm level data, is Claessens, Klingebiel, and Laeven (2003). They study 687 corporations from eight crisis countries. When analyzing the impact of policies on firms, they find that a package of specific resolution measures can help accelerate recovery from a crisis. These policies, however, did not necessarily lead to more sustainable, longer-run debt situations, suggesting that they induce moral hazard on the part of financial institutions and corporations. Furthermore, they studied a small cross-section of countries, raising the question as to whether these results can be generalized. Klingebiel, Kroszner, and Laeven (2002) investigate how financial crises affect the growth of sectors that depend on external sources of finance to various degrees. They use industry level data on real sectoral growth in value added and external financial dependence from 19 countries over 30 years and find that sectors highly dependent on external finance tend to experience a greater contraction of value added during a crisis in deeper financial systems than in countries with shallower financial systems. Finally, the International Monetary Fund (2003) has recently developed lessons from financial crises, although not in an empirical manner.

The studies on the containment and restructuring phase reviewed have typically analyzed a limited number of specific policies. In particular, three main policies have received much attention in the studies and debates: substantial liquidity support, explicit government guarantees of deposits, and forbearance from prudential regulation. These three policies are in many ways indicative of whether a more accommodative or strict "model" to crisis resolution is being followed. Countries applying substantial liquidity support,[5] explicit government guarantees of deposits[6] and large-scale forbearance from prudential regulations can be said to have an accommodative approach to crisis resolution, whereas those countries with limited liquidity support, no or limited guarantees and no forbearance from prudential regulations have a strict approach. Another advantage of focusing on these policies is that they are easily identifiable for empirical analyses.

These three policies are nevertheless not the only ones countries can adopt. Furthermore, except for explicit government guarantees of deposits,[7] these policies can still vary as to their intensity: countries can provide more or less liquidity support or practice more or less forbearance.

Countries not only vary in their adoption of policies aimed at containing and resolving a systemic crisis, but also in the quality of their institutional framework and in their general level of development. The institutional framework most relevant to systemic bank restructuring includes the laws, regulations, and institutions under which banks and corporations, including their management and owners, operate. The "optimal" framework for crisis resolution is easy to describe: A country's insolvency system should enable financial institutions to enforce their claims on corporations, allow for speedy financial restructuring of viable corporations, and provide for the efficient liquidation of enterprises that

---

[5] Substantial liquidity support is defined as a situation in which the government provides levels of liquidity support that exceed aggregate banking sector capital or also provides support to institutions that are clearly known to be insolvent.

[6] A government is considered to be providing an explicit full guarantee to depositors if it explicitly protects all depositors and creditors. Although it is typically assumed that existence of depositor guarantees can encourage bank risk-taking, the previous chapter shows that theory is not unambiguous on this point. For a review of the economics of deposit guarantees, see Demirgüç-Kunt and Kane (2002).

[7] Even here there can be differences ex ante in the exact coverage of the guarantee and ex post in the degree to which the government effectively honors the guarantee.

have no prospects of economic value–added and cannot be rehabilitated. A proper prudential framework for banks includes accounting, classification, and provisioning rules that force a realistic marking of assets to market. Finally, regulations and laws should ensure that undercapitalized financial institutions are properly disciplined and closed if necessary. Institutions involved in these areas should be properly governed, accountable, and staffed with well-trained people facing the right incentives and having no conflicts of interest.

But, this optimal framework is most often not what countries with a systemic crisis face, especially not developing countries. Here, the country will often be experiencing a systemic crisis exactly because of its institutional deficiencies. Insolvency procedures for corporations and financial institutions may be poorly designed or the judicial system poorly equipped to handle large-scale financial distress. The transparency of decision-making processes may be limited and corruption prevalent. Ownership links between banks and corporations may be extensive, making restructuring more complex, even to the point that the debtor and creditor are the same party. Political economy factors more generally will typically complicate the resolution.[8]

These institutional deficiencies will affect the efficacy of the policy measures in terms of accelerating recovery, can lower the benefits of fiscal outlays, and can increase the overall fiscal costs. How this may happen can be obvious in some cases. It will, for example, not be productive to let the supervisory agency also be the agency that takes the lead in the restructuring of financial institutions when the agency is largely to blame for the crisis, because it did not enforce existing regulations. In those situations, policies such as forbearance may be less productive and can be expected to raise fiscal costs, because financial institutions have few incentives to use the forbearance to recapitalize on a flow basis, that is, with retained earnings. They may instead "gamble for resurrection" because the supervisory authority does not have the credibility that it will enforce the regulation in the future more strictly. By the same token, one cannot expect that ex-ante recapitalizations of banks (financed by the government) will result in corporate restructuring in countries where the bankruptcy system is not functioning or many ownership links exist between banks and corporations and the supervisory authority has little

---

[8] There are some that argue that the various policies chosen are purely the outcome of political economy circumstances that also triggered the crisis, and the whole loss-allocation is therefore a foregone conclusion. See, for example, Dooley and Verma (2003).

credibility in enforcing prudential regulations. Notwithstanding this, in other, intermediate circumstances in which the institutional framework is not optimal but also not poor, the efficacy of fiscal outlays and the effects of various resolution policies on economic recovery are unclear.

It is not immediately obvious how resolution policies can best be adapted to take account of weaknesses in the institutional environment. The risk of government failure in such circumstances would argue against intervention; by contrast, weak institutions also impair the private sector's ability to make an unaided recovery from crisis. In the end, the importance of the institutional framework for the efficacy of resolution policies and its impact on fiscal outlays and economic recovery in the aftermath of a crisis is an empirical question. Some accommodative policies for crisis resolution, although fiscally expensive, may accelerate economic recovery when institutions are weak while others may delay economic recovery. So far, however, no empirical analysis has attempted to shed light on these questions.

2. DATA AND EMPIRICAL METHODOLOGY

We are interested in examining whether the quality of the institutional framework has an impact on the efficacy of policies for financial crisis resolution. Specifically, we want to explain whether a country's (weak) institutional framework can render accommodative policies of crisis resolution ineffective, meaning that the adoption of these policies will eventually result in higher fiscal outlays and higher economic output losses compared to situations where a country is equipped with a better institutional framework. We try to answer these questions using a country-level database. In this section, we first describe the data (for a detailed description of the variables and sources see Appendix Table A.6.1) and then the methodologies we apply.

For data on fiscal outlays, we use Honohan and Klingebiel (2003), and update the data for recent crises using Kane and Klingebiel (2002), Caprio and Klingebiel (2003), and IMF (2003). Data are collected for 36 banking crisis episodes from 1977 to the present. The fiscal outlay figure includes both fiscal and quasi-fiscal outlays for financial system restructuring, including the recapitalization costs for banks, bailout costs related to the government covering obligations because of depositors and creditors, and debt relief schemes for bank borrowers. We scale the fiscal outlay estimates by gross domestic product (GDP). The variable, FISCAL OUTLAY, thus represents the fiscal outlay estimate of financial distress as a percentage of GDP. In what follows, drawing on previous results we use this as a summary measure of the degree of accommodative stand of the government during the containment and initial restructuring process of a crisis.

We also collect data on a number of accommodative policies. Data on these policy responses come from Honohan and Klingebiel (2003), and are updated for recent crises by Kane and Klingebiel (2002), Caprio and Klingebiel (2003), and IMF (2003). As noted, we focus on three policies: substantial LIQUIDITY SUPPORT, EXPLICIT GUARANTEE on deposits, and regulatory FORBEARANCE. We use a dummy variable for each of the three policies. Data on policy responses are collected for 35 banking crisis episodes from 1977 to the present.[9]

In addition to explicit guarantees, deposits can also have an implicit government guarantee on deposits. For example, deposits in government-owned financial institutions are often (assumed to be) implicitly guaranteed by the government. Like explicit guarantees, implicit guarantees may affect the fiscal outlays during a crisis, and we will therefore want to control for the existence of implicit guarantees in our empirical analysis. We consider an implicit guarantee to be in place if the banking system is largely state-owned (75 percent or more) and the government has not issued an explicit guarantee. We refer to this dummy variable as IMPLICIT GUARANTEE.

Many financial crises were preceeded by asset bubbles and credit booms. These may also affect the severity of the crises and the fiscal outlays, because when the boom is larger, the bust also may be larger and the crisis may be more costly to resolve. Because we do not have data on asset prices for most of the precrisis periods in our sample, we can only use (excessive) credit growth as a control measure for the size of the precrisis boom. We measure credit growth as the difference between real growth in bank credit to the private sector and real GDP growth during the three years prior to the start of the crisis. We call this variable CREDIT GROWTH.

For the aggregate economic recovery, we construct proxies for economic output losses suffered because of a crisis. We use two approaches here. One way is comparing, in real terms, the precrisis GDP level of a certain country with the GDP level during the following years until the precrisis level is reached. This approach considers precrisis GDP growth rates to a country's trend or potential growth rate. The precrisis, trend GDP

---

[9] We do not have data on policy responses for Jordan.

growth is calculated as the average of GDP growth rates from year t-3 to t-1, where year t is the start of the crisis. Then, each GDP growth rate from year t onward is compared to the trend until the trend growth is reached. The output loss is defined as the sum of the difference between the actual and the trend growth rate over all the years until trend growth is reached again. This approach follows the methodology used in IMF's World Economic Outlook (1998), although we recalculate and update the data to include some recent crises. We call this variable OUTPUT LOSS (IMF).[10]

The second version of the output loss variable results from using the Barro (1991) growth model to estimate a country's GDP potential growth rates. We refer to this variable as OUTPUT LOSS (BARRO). Instead of using precrisis data to estimate the trend growth rate, we obtain predicted values of per capita GDP growth from equation (2) in Barro (1991, p. 410). The exact equation is: Average GDP per capita growth from 1960 to 1980 = 0.0302 − 0.0111 * GDP per capita in 1960 + 0.00051 * (GDP per capita in 1960)^2 + 0.0323 * Secondary school enrollment rate + 0.0270 * Primary school enrollment rate − 0.122 * Government consumption/ GDP − 0.0200 * Number of revolutions − 0.0309 * Number of assassinations − 0.0148 * Deviation from the PPP in 1960.

For simplicity, the last three regressors are considered to be zero. We collect data for the other variables using the Barro-Lee and Summers-Heston databases. We use GDP per capita and the enrollment rates for primary and secondary school for three years before the start of the crisis. For government consumption scaled by GDP, we take the average ratio for the period between eight years and three years before the start of the crisis. The quadratic form in the model of GDP per capita implies a positive relation between GDP per capita level and growth for values of GDP per capita above $10,800.[11] We therefore restrict the realizations of the GDP per capita level variable to be no larger than $10,800. For each country, we insert the realizations of the variables at three years before the start of the crisis into the Barro equation and adjust for population growth rates to obtain the predicted GDP growth rates. Finally, we compare this

---

[10] We also counted the number of years a country needs to get to the same GDP level as prior to the crisis. We ran the same regression for this variable and found similar results as for the two output loss measures.

[11] The quadratic form can be viewed as an approximation to a functional form that asymptotically approaches a zero relation between growth and level of per capita GDP, with the relation coming close to zero when real GDP is above $10,800 (Barro 1991). For simplicity, we cut off the GDP per capita data at $10,800, thus forcing a flat relationship for higher actual GDP per capita.

predicted rate with the actual growth rates during the crisis and, following the IMF methodology, summarize the differential growth rates into an output loss variable.[12]

For a country's institutional and legal environment, we use three indicators. QUALITY OF INSTITUTIONS is a broad measure of institutional quality developed by Kaufmann, Kraay, and Zoido-Lobaton (KKZ, 1999) and captures the quality of institutions in the country. CORRUPTION is a measure of the level of corruption in the government from La Porta et al. (1998) and JUDICIAL EFFICIENCY is an index of the efficiency of the judicial system, also from La Porta et al. (1998).

Our sample of countries includes those countries that experienced a systemic crisis during the last 30 years, as reported by Caprio and Klingebiel (1999), and where we also have data on FISCAL OUTLAYS and institutional characteristics (QUALITY OF INSTITUTIONS, CORRUPTION, and JUDICIAL EFFICIENCY). Some countries experienced multiple systemic crises during our sample period (for example, Argentina) and in these cases each systemic crisis is included in our sample. Because our sample of systemic crisis cases would be biased if certain country characteristics that can explain why some countries are more prone to systemic crises than others also affect the speed of recovery from a financial crisis, we also include a control group of (a) countries that did not experience a systemic crisis during the sample period, but that did experience a nonsystemic crisis (where we use the classification in Caprio and Klingebiel (1999) to identify whether the crisis is systemic or nonsystemic), and (b) countries that did not experience a crisis at all during the sample period. Our total sample of 40 countries consists of 29 countries with a total of 32 systemic crises, five countries with a nonsystemic crisis,

---

[12] There are also a number of other measures that can be used to estimate the output loss. These differ in terms of the assumptions made about trend growth and the timing of the precrisis and postcrisis period. Generally, we got similar results for the fiscal outlay, policy, and institutional variables. Still, it is worthy to note there are many other factors determining the potential GDP level of a certain country at a certain time. Furthermore, since it is not possible to isolate the effect of the banking crisis on GDP from other shocks, none of these output loss measures correctly captures the effect of the banking crisis on GDP and the full economic costs of a banking crisis. This caveat is the more important as there can be large differences between the measures. In his discussion of the analysis of Hoggarth, Reis, and Saporta (2002), for example, Honohan (2002) shows that their cumulative loss in output has a correlation of only 0.33 with the IMF-loss of growth measure. Hoggarth et al. also show that using a lost cumulative output – instead of the lost cumulative growth measure, output losses during crises in developed countries are as high, or higher, on average than those in emerging economies, a conclusion that contrasts with other research.

and six countries with no crisis. Naturally, for the noncrisis countries we do not have data on fiscal outlays, accommodative policies, and output losses. As data on some variables are also not available for some crisis countries, the sample size varies on the particular regressions used. See Appendix Table A.6.1 for the raw data by (non) crisis episode, and Appendix Table A.6.2 for a list of crises covered and detailed information on each crisis.

3. ESTIMATION RESULTS

We are interested in measuring the effects of accommodative policies and a country's institutional environment on fiscal outlays for crisis resolution and the speed of economic recovery in the aftermath of a banking crisis. We start our empirical analysis by investigating to what extent fiscal outlays vary with the quality of the institutional environment of a country. Specifically, we regress FISCAL OUTLAYS on our three measures of a country's institutional environment (institutional quality, corruption, and judicial efficiency). We also include in these regressions the three specific accommodative policies – explicit guarantees, liquidity support, and forbearance – to investigate whether a country's institutional environment can explain differences in fiscal outlays, after controlling for the effect of these accommodative policies. Finally, we include the credit growth variable to control for the impact of precrisis credit booms on fiscal outlays.

The econometric results of explaining fiscal outlays are presented in Table 6.1. The results are based on a sample of (both systemic and nonsystemic) crisis countries, but exclude countries without information on fiscal outlays or policy variables, which means we end up with a sample of 35 countries. In terms of policy measures, we find that all three accommodative policies considered (substantial liquidity support, explicit guarantees and regulatory forbearance) add to fiscal outlays, consistent with the results in Honohan and Klingebiel (2003), and consistent with the view that government incurs fiscal costs to minimize the impact of the crisis. Government guarantees and forbearance are the policies associated with the highest fiscal outlays. In terms of a country's institutional environment, we find that a better institutional environment tends to lower fiscal outlays related to crisis resolution. Credit growth precrisis and implicit guarantees do not appear to be correlated with fiscal outlays once we control for institutions and the other three policies.

Next, we move to the output loss regressions. We are interested in whether better institutions accelerate recovery, that is, limit output losses.

Table 6.1 Explaining Fiscal Cost/GDP

This table shows country-level regressions estimated through ordinary least squares. Dependent variable is fiscal cost over GDP. The sample of countries is described in the Appendix Table A.6.1. The policy variables explicit guarantee, liquidity support, and forbearance are zero-one dummies where a one is assigned when the country implemented the policy instrument. Implicit guarantee takes value one if deposits of state-owned institutions account for more than 75 percent of total banking deposits, and zero otherwise. Quality of institutions is a measure of the quality of institutions developed by KKZ (1999) and takes higher values when the quality of institutions is higher. Corruption index is a subcomponent of the Political Risk Rating constructed by ICRG and takes higher values when lower levels of corruption are perceived. Efficiency of the judicial system takes higher values for countries with more efficiency and integrity of the legal environment. Credit growth is the difference between real private credit growth and real GDP growth. A constant is included but not reported. Robust standard errors are in brackets. *, **, and *** indicate significance at 10 percent, 5 percent, and 1 percent levels, respectively.

	(1)	(2)	(3)	(4)	(5)	(6)	(7)	(8)	(9)	(10)	(11)
Explicit guarantee	10.495** (4.477)			12.574** (4.672)			12.346** (4.812)			8.057 (6.263)	8.902 (5.379)
Implicit guarantee	6.674 (8.187)			18.181 (20.800)			19.871 (18.195)			19.731 (16.879)	18.134 (16.822)
Liquidity support		7.411 (5.278)			8.640 (6.044)			9.253 (6.085)		5.370 (6.361)	6.715 (6.057)
Forbearance			11.944*** (4.096)			13.336** (4.779)			13.446** (4.835)	11.939** (4.820)	10.101** (4.153)
Quality of institutions	−6.245* (3.134)	−6.535* (3.211)	−4.254 (3.422)								
Corruption				−2.960*** (1.047)	−2.810** (1.189)	−1.782 (1.258)					
Judicial efficiency							−3.132** (0.930)	−3.022** (1.098)	−2.170* (1.118)	−2.150** (0.909)	−2.237** (0.886)
Credit growth											0.383 (0.321)
Observations	35	35	35	26	26	26	26	26	26	26	26
R-squared	0.21	0.17	0.23	0.38	0.26	0.33	0.40	0.29	0.37	0.55	0.58

183

We also want to investigate the effects of fiscal outlays on economic recovery, as in theory these are aimed at limiting output losses and speeding up economic recovery. However, fiscal outlays may not represent policy choices, but rather result from institutional weaknesses. Indeed, the previous regression results showed that fiscal outlays are in part driven by the quality of a country's institutions. We therefore do not include the fiscal outlays variable itself into our output loss regressions but, rather, the residual term of a regression of fiscal outlays on the three institutional variables.[13] This residual term captures "excessive" fiscal outlays in the sense that a positive value indicates that the country incurred greater fiscal outlays to address its crisis than a country with a similar level of institutional development. This "excessive" fiscal outlay variable thus captures those fiscal costs purely associated with accommodative policies, such as the three specific policies documented – substantial liquidity support, explicit guarantees, and regulatory forbearance – as well as other fiscal outlays aimed at crisis recovery, such as debt relief schemes for bank borrowers, not documented.[14]

The output loss regression results are reported in Table 6.2. The results are based on a sample of (both systemic and nonsystemic) crisis countries, but exclude countries without information on fiscal cost or institutional variables. The first part of the table reports the results with OUTPUT LOSS (IMF) as dependent variable and the second part of the table reports the results for OUTPUT LOSS (BARRO) as dependent variable.

We find that accommodative policies do not achieve their intended goal of reducing output losses. For both output loss measures we find that excessive fiscal outlays arising from accommodative policies do not tend to accelerate economic recovery. In fact, the results indicate that accommodative policies even delay economic recovery as the signs are all positive (and generally statistically significant). By contrast, we find that a better institutional framework, as characterized by less corruption

---

[13] The results that follow do not alter qualitatively if we use the fiscal outlay variable itself rather than the fiscal outlay residual variable.

[14] Even after controlling for institutional development, fiscal outlays may differ not only because a country makes more excessive use of accommodative policies or experienced bigger credit booms, but also because of differences in the severity of the crisis. As such, fiscal outlays may be endogenous to the speed of recovery from the crisis. We did use 2SLS regressions to control for this possibility, but did not find qualitatively different results.

Table 6.2. *Explaining Output Loss*

This table shows country-level regressions estimated by ordinary least squares. The dependent variable in columns (1) to (3) is the natural logarithm of 1 plus OUTPUT LOSS (IMF). The dependent variable in columns (4) to (6) is the natural logarithm of 1 plus OUTPUT LOSS (BARRO). QUALITY OF INSTITUTIONS is a measure of the quality of institutions developed by KKZ (1999) and takes higher values when the quality of institutions is higher. CORRUPTION is a measure of corruption developed by ICRG and takes higher values when lower levels of corruption are perceived. JUDICIAL EFFICIENCY is a measure of the efficiency of the judicial system and takes higher values for countries with more efficiency of the judiciary. FISCAL COST RESIDUAL is the residual term in the regression of fiscal cost on quality of institutions, corruption, and judicial efficiency. A constant is included but not reported. Robust standard errors are in brackets. *, **, and *** indicate significance at 10 percent, 5 percent, and 1 percent levels, respectively.

	(1)	(2)	(3)	(4)	(5)	(6)
	Output loss (IMF)			Output loss (Barro)		
Quality of institutions	−0.396 (0.341)			−0.651* (0.341)		
Corruption		−0.223* (0.109)			−0.280*** (0.092)	
Judicial efficiency			−0.041 (0.115)			−0.184** (0.082)
Fiscal outlay residual	0.052*** (0.016)	0.051*** (0.015)	0.052*** (0.016)	0.023* (0.012)	0.021** (0.010)	0.020 (0.012)
Observations	28	28	28	27	27	27
R-squared	0.28	0.36	0.25	0.21	0.32	0.19

and greater judicial efficiency, does reduce output losses, even when controlling for excessive fiscal outlays. This result is robust for the corruption variable under the two output loss measures, whereas the indicators for the quality of institutions and judicial efficiency are only statistically significant for the BARRO output loss measure.

To test the robustness of these results, we run a number of other regressions. It could be that the severity of a crisis is because of other factors, which may be correlated with the institutional and excessive fiscal outlay variables we use. This could lead us to wrongly conclude that the quality of the institutional environment and degree of accommodative policies affect the speed of recovery. Obviously, many aspects, both domestic and international, can affect the speed of recovery and it is difficult to be exhaustive. We nevertheless did consider a large number of other explanatory variables that should address most missing variables concerns.

These additional variables included World GDP real growth at the start of the crisis, the presence of an explicit deposit insurance scheme at the onset of the crisis, the average inflation rate prior to the crisis, the degree of state ownership in banks, the degree of dollarization in the country, and the level of private credit to GDP. We did not find any of these variables to have a significant explanatory power on the speed of recovery nor to affect in a qualitative way the coefficients of the institutional environment and excessive fiscal outlay variables we use in Table 6.2 (we do not report these results).

A second robustness test investigates whether our results are biased because the possibility of a crisis occurring is related to the quality of institutions in the country. Institutionally worse developed countries may more likely have a deep crisis; studying only crisis countries could then lead us to conclude incorrectly that institutional factors determine the speed of recovery. To control for such potential sample selection bias, we estimate a Heckman model where the selection variable CRISIS takes the value of one if the country has experienced a crisis during the period 1977 to the present and the value of zero if the country has not experienced a crisis during this period. In a second-stage regression for the speed of recovery, we then control for the selection bias related to the country's institutional weaknesses. In this second-stage regression, we investigate again the importance of the institutional environment and the residual fiscal outlays on the speed of recovery. The Heckman regression results with CRISIS as dependent variable in the first-stage regression and our two output loss variables as dependent variables in the second-stage regression are reported in Table 6.3.

The first-stage regression results confirm our prior that countries with weak institutions are more prone to crises. Unfortunately, our sample of noncrisis countries is small, only 6 observations, and the sample selection correction is thus not that powerful. The Heckman results should therefore be interpreted with the necessary caution. The second-stage regression results nevertheless confirm our earlier findings based on OLS regressions: better institutions reduce output losses and excessive fiscal outlays retard recovery. Controlling for potential sample selection bias thus does not seem to affect the main result.

Overall, we find that countries with weaker institutions tend to experience banking crises that take longer to recover from. The likely channels are various. At the micro-level, the resolution of a crisis is likely to take longer in countries with weaker institutions, especially more inefficient legal institutions. Good insolvency laws and well-functioning judicial

Table 6.3. *Explaining Output Loss: Heckman Model*

This table shows country-level regressions estimated using Heckman's maximum likelihood estimator. The dependent variable in the second stage regression in columns (1) to (3) is (the natural logarithm of 1 plus the) OUTPUT LOSS (IMF). The dependent variable in the second stage regression in columns (4) to (6) is (the natural logarithm of 1 plus the) OUTPUT LOSS (BARRO). The dependent variable of the first-stage regression is CRISIS, which is a dummy variable that indicates whether the country has experienced a financial crisis in the last 30 years, or not. QUALITY OF INSTITUTIONS is a measure of the quality of institutions developed by KKZ (1999) and takes higher values when the quality of institutions is higher. CORRUPTION is a measure of corruption developed by ICRG and takes higher values when lower levels of corruption are perceived. JUDICIAL EFFICIENCY is a measure of the efficiency of the judicial system and takes higher values for countries with more efficiency of the judiciary. FISCAL OUTLAY RESIDUAL is the residual term in the regression of fiscal outlay on quality of institutions, corruption, and judicial efficiency. A constant is included but not reported. Robust standard errors are in brackets. *, **, and *** indicate significance at 10 percent, 5 percent, and 1 percent levels, respectively.

	(1)	(2)	(3)	(4)	(5)	(6)
	Output loss (IMF)			Output loss (Barro)		
Quality of institutions	−0.089 (0.379)			−0.429 (0.425)		
Corruption		−0.390*** (0.034)			−0.324*** (0.094)	
Judicial efficiency			−0.082*** (0.031)			−0.146 (0.097)
Fiscal outlay residual	0.054*** (0.016)	0.043*** (0.014)	0.061*** (0.000)	0.023** (0.011)	0.021** (0.009)	0.020* (0.012)
First-stage						
Quality of institutions	−1.747*** (0.353)			−1.587*** (0.316)		
Corruption		−0.334*** (0.027)			−0.417*** (0.102)	
Judicial efficiency			−0.236*** (0.020)			−0.257*** (0.062)
Observations	35	34	34	34	33	33
Censored observations	7	6	6	7	6	6
Uncensored observations	28	28	28	27	27	27

systems are necessary to speedily restructure corporations in financial distress. Good legal institutions are also crucial in resolving the debt overhang in the financial system and allowing bank balance sheets to be restored. Efficient legal systems can help resolve the coordination problems between creditors and debtors. At the more aggregate level, in weaker environments supervisory authorities, and policy makers more generally, may have limited ability and credibility to enforce prudential regulations against financial institutions, intervene in financial institutions that do not comply with prudential regulations, and encourage large corporations to restructure speedily. As such, the recovery can be expected to take longer in institutionally weak countries. The specific negative correlation between recovery and corruption, which is the most robust result, may indicate that more corrupt governments tend to provide assistance to banks and corporations not based on their financial soundness and compliance with regulations, but rather based on government ties with dominant shareholders and the business sectors in general and on political objectives. This lack of market-based dealings thereby prolongs the recovery.

Our second main result is that accommodative policy instruments, as reflected in excessive fiscal outlays, are not effective in terms of helping the country's economy to recover faster and to minimize output losses. Excessive fiscal transfers may mean that assistance is provided to institutions that have limited franchise value and fiscal support has then little effect on recovery. Fiscal outlays then represent more the costs of looting, with no economic gains, rather than support to reduce debt overhangs and overcome coordination problems in resolving claims.

Overall, our empirical findings reveal that both poor institutions and accommodating policies can significantly slow the recovery from a financial crisis. To gauge the relative importance of institutions and policies, Table 6.4 shows the effects of a change in excessive fiscal outlays or improvement in institutions on output losses, using both output loss measures. For these simulations, we use the regression results of Table 6.2. We find that a one standard deviation reduction in excessive fiscal outlays lowers the output losses according to the IMF definition by about 4.1 percent of GDP and according to the Barro definition by about 3.1 percent of GDP. In terms of institutional development, a country that improved its institutions by one standard deviation would have its predicted output losses using the IMF definition reduced by between 0.5 percent of GDP (judicial efficiency) and 2.3 percent of GDP (corruption and quality of institutions) and using the Barro definition between 2.4 percent of GDP

Table 6.4. *Estimated Impact of Changes in Fiscal Outlay and Quality of Institutions on Output Losses*

This table shows simulations for changes in output losses. The results for the changes in output loss (IMF) and output loss (Barro) are based on the regression results from Table 6.2. The simulations calculate the effects on the outcome variables if the respective fiscal outlay were to be one standard deviation lower than its mean, or if the institutional index were to be one standard deviation higher than its mean.

	Change in output loss (IMF) (as percentage of GDP)	Change in output loss (BARRO) (as percentage of GDP)
Fiscal outlays		
Excessive fiscal outlays	−4.14	−3.08
Institutional framework		
Quality of institutions	−2.33	−4.79
Corruption	−2.34	−3.42
Judicial efficiency	−0.53	−2.43

(judicial efficiency) and 4.8 percent of GDP (quality of institutions). These effects are sizable. The results suggest that reductions in (excessive) fiscal outlays and improvements in the institutional environment are important economically, as both contribute about equally in terms of accelerating the recovery.

4. CONCLUSIONS

We have examined the impact of accommodative policy instruments on fiscal costs of a crisis and on accelerating economic recovery in the aftermath of a crisis. We then examined the link between the quality of a country's institutional frameworks, the effectiveness of accommodative crisis resolution policies, as measured by the size of excessive fiscal costs associated with the crisis, and economic output losses. We find accommodative policy measures, such as government guarantees on deposits and forbearance, to be fiscally costly, as also documented by Honohan and Klingebiel (2003). Moreover, when examining the question of whether these accommodative policy measures result in faster economic recovery, we find that output losses are not reduced by excessive fiscal outlays. Therefore there does not appear to be a trade-off between the size of the fiscal cost and the speed of economic recovery. Indeed, we find evidence that applying accommodative policies resulting in high fiscal outlays slows down economic recovery. We do find evidence that a better institutional framework not only lowers fiscal outlays of crisis resolution but also reduces the economic costs of a crisis.

Accommodative policy measures are thus not only fiscally costly, they also do not accelerate economic recovery; rather they can even slow down economic recovery. At the same time, the results suggest that sound legal and other institutions are important components for a resolution of the crisis that are not only cost-effective but also speedy. The best approach for a country to resolve a systemic crisis appears to be to implement strict resolution policies and focus on improving its institutional framework. The importance of the quality of the institutional framework may not be surprising, as institutional development has often been found to be important for a country's growth, productivity, and stability. Our analysis, however, provides more motivation to disentangle the elements of the institutional framework that are most important to help reduce the costs of a financial crisis and improve the recovery from a crisis, and the "returns" of such improvements. Such an analysis may in turn help guide policy makers in setting priorities for reform.

ACKNOWLEDGMENTS

We would like to thank Jerry Caprio, Asli Demirgüç-Kunt, Charles Goodhart, Dick Herring, Patrick Honohan, Ed Kane, Augusto de la Torre, and other participants in the conference "Systemic Financial Distress: Containment and Resolution" held at the World Bank, October 8–9, 2003, for very useful comments, and Guillermo Noguera for excellent research assistance. The views expressed in this chapter are those of the authors and do not necessarily represent those of the World Bank.

Table A.6.1. *Description of Variables*

Variable Name	Description	Source
Fiscal outlay	The ex post fiscal outlay estimate of financial distress as a percentage of GDP. It includes both fiscal and quasi-fiscal outlays for financial system restructuring, including the recapitalization costs for banks, bailout costs related to covering depositors and creditors, and debt relief schemes for bank borrowers.	Honohan and Klingebiel (2003), and IMF (2003)
Output loss (IMF)	Output loss, calculated as the sum of the differences between the actual and trend growth rates for the period t until the year in which the trend growth is reached, where trend GDP growth is calculated as the average of GDP growth rates from t-3 to t-1, and t is the starting year of the crisis. The approach follows IMF World Economic Outlook (1998) and the data are updated to include some recent crises.	IMF World Economic Outlook (2002)
Output loss (BARRO)	Same as output loss (IMF), but the trend growth is estimated as the predicted value from equation (2) in Barro (1991). The equation is: Average GDP per capita growth from 1960 to 1980 = $0.0302 - 0.0111 *$ GDP per capita in 1960 $+ 0.00051 *$ (GDP per capita in 1960)$^\wedge 2 + 0.0323 *$ Secondary school enrollment rate $+ 0.0270 *$ Primary school enrollment rate $- 0.122 *$ Government consumption/GDP $- 0.0200 *$ Number of revolutions $- 0.0309 *$ Number of assassinations $- 0.0148 *$ Deviation from the PPP in 1960. The realizations of the last three variables are set to zero. The sources of the other variables are the Barro-Lee and Summers-Heston databases. We use GDP per capita and the school enrollment rates at three years before the start of the crisis. Government consumption is averaged over the period 8 to 3 years before the start of the crisis. Per capita GDP is limited from above to $10800.	Barro (1991), Barro and Lee (1997), Summers and Heston (1991), IMF World Economic Outlook (2002)
Explicit guarantee	This variable takes a value of one when the government issues an explicit guarantee to depositors in private banks, and zero otherwise.	Honohan and Klingebiel (2003). For Ecuador, we update the data with information provided by the World Bank Ecuador country team.

(continued)

Table A.6.1 (*continued*)

Variable Name	Description	Source
Implicit guarantee	This variable takes a value of one when deposits of state-owned institutions account for more than 75 percent of total banking deposits (suggesting that market participants are implicitly protected), and zero otherwise.	Honohan and Klingebiel (2003)
Liquidity support	This variable takes a value of one when the government provides substantial liquidity support to insolvent institutions and zero otherwise. Substantial is defined as liquidity support surpassing total aggregate financial system capital.	Honohan and Klingebiel (2003)
Forbearance	This variable takes a value of one when the government gives forbearance in the sense that regulations (in particular loan classification and loan-loss provisioning) are relaxed or the current regulatory framework is not enforced for at least a twelve months period to allow banks to recapitalize on a flow basis; or competition is restricted.	Honohan and Klingebiel (2003)
Quality of institutions	Index of the quality of institutions. The measure refers to 1998 and captures six dimensions of institutional quality: (1) democracy, (2) political instability, (3) rule of law, (4) bureaucratic regulation, (5) government effectiveness, and (6) corruption. An increase in the index means better institutions.	Kaufman, Kraay, and Zoido-Lobaton (1999)
Corruption	Measure of corruption in government. Average of the months of April and October of the monthly index between 1982 and 1995. Scale from 0 to 10, with lower scores for higher levels of corruption. Original source is the International Country Risk Guide from Political Risk Services.	La Porta, Lopez-de-Silanes, Shleifer, and Vishny (1998).
Judicial efficiency	Assessment of the efficiency of the legal environment as it affects business. Average between 1980 and 1983. Scale from 0 to 10, lower scores represent lower efficiency levels. The original source is Business International Company.	La Porta, Lopez-de-Silanes, Shleifer, and Vishny (1998).
Credit growth	Average real growth in bank credit to the private sector minus average real growth in GDP during the three years prior to the start of the crisis.	Authors' calculations using data from the International Financial Statistics (IFS) database maintained by the International Monetary Fund (IMF).

Table A.6.2. Country-Level Crisis Database

Country	Type of Crisis	Crisis Period	Fiscal Outlay (Percentage of GDP)	Output Loss (IMF) (Percentage of GDP)	Output Loss (BARRO) (Percentage of GDP)	Explicit Guarantee	Implicit Guarantee	Unlimited Liquidity Support	Forbearance	Quality of Institutions	Corruption	Judicial Efficiency
Argentina	systemic	1980–82	55.1	17.0	25.0	no	yes	no	yes	0.33	6.02	6.00
Argentina	systemic	1995	2.0	12.2	7.3	no	no	no	yes	0.33	6.02	6.00
Australia	nonsystemic	1989–92	2.0	0.0	0.0	no	no	no	no	1.41	8.52	10.00
Austria	no crisis									1.37	8.57	9.50
Belgium	no crisis									0.90	8.82	9.50
Brazil	systemic	1994–99	13.2	0.0	0.0	no	no	no	yes	0.00	6.32	5.75
Chile	systemic	1981–83	42.0	46.0	25.1	no	no	yes	yes	0.87	5.30	7.25
Colombia	systemic	1982–87	5.0	7.0	83.6	no	yes	yes	no	-0.41	5.00	7.25
Czech Republic	systemic	1989–91	12.0	0.0		yes	no	no	yes	0.68		
Ecuador	systemic	1998–2001	20.0	12.0	0.0	yes	no	yes	no	-0.32	5.18	6.25
Finland	systemic	1991–94	11.2	21.0	16.7	yes	no	yes	no	1.62	10.00	10.00
France	nonsystemic	1994–95	0.7	0.0	2.7	no	no	no	no	1.02	9.05	8.00
Ghana	systemic	1982–89	6.0	7.0	22.6	no	yes	yes	yes	-0.14		
Hungary	systemic	1991–95	10.0	14.0	36.4	no	yes	yes	yes	0.87		
Indonesia	systemic	1997–2002	55.0	39.0	35.0	yes	no	yes	yes	-0.76	2.15	2.5
Ireland	no crisis									1.40	8.52	8.75
Jamaica	systemic	1996–2000	43.9	7.0	32.3	yes	no	yes	yes	-0.03		
Japan	systemic	1991–	24.0	48.0	4.5	yes	no	yes	yes	0.95	8.52	10.00
Jordan	nonsystemic	1989–90	10.0	16.9	12.9	no	no	yes	yes	0.33	5.48	8.66
Korea, Rep. of	systemic	1997–2002	28.0	17.0	10.0	yes	no	yes	yes	0.48	5.3	6.00
Malaysia	systemic	1997–2001	16.4	33.0	11.9	yes	no	yes	yes	0.51	7.38	9.00

(continued)

Table A.6.2 (continued)

Country	Type of Crisis	Crisis Period	Fiscal Outlay (Percentage of GDP)	Output Loss (IMF) (Percentage of GDP)	Output Loss (BARRO) (Percentage of GDP)	Explicit Guarantee	Implicit Guarantee	Unlimited Liquidity Support	Forbearance	Quality of Institutions	Corruption	Judicial Efficiency
Mexico	systemic	1994–2000	19.3	10.0	14.5	yes	no	yes	yes	−0.07	4.77	6.00
Netherlands	no crisis									1.64	10.00	10.00
New Zealand	nonsystemic	1987–90	1.0	0.0	10.2	no	no	yes	no	1.59	10.00	10.00
Norway	systemic	1990–93	8.0	0.0	0.0	yes	no	yes	no	1.53	10.00	10.00
Paraguay	systemic	1995–2000	13.0	0.0	22.9	yes	no	yes	yes	−0.56		
Philippines	systemic	1983–87	3.0	26.0	38.3	no	no	yes	yes	0.21	2.92	4.75
Philippines	systemic	1998–	13.2	10.1	19.1	no	no	no	no	0.21	2.92	4.75
Poland	systemic	1992–95	3.5	0.0	0.1	no	yes	yes	yes	0.70		
Portugal	no crisis									1.20	7.38	5.50
Senegal	systemic	1988–91	17.0	0.0	4.8	no	yes	yes	yes	−0.30		
Slovenia	systemic	1992–94	14.6	0.0	6.2	yes	no	no	yes	0.85		
Spain	systemic	1977–85	5.6	0.0		no	no	yes	no	1.11	7.38	6.25
Sri Lanka	systemic	1989–93	5.0	1.0	7.8	yes	no	yes	yes	−0.38	5.00	7.00
Sweden	systemic	1991–94	4.0	11.0	2.6	yes	no	no	no	1.53	10.00	10.00
Switzerland	no crisis									1.72	10.00	10.00
Thailand	systemic	1997–2002	34.8	40.0	26.7	yes	no	yes	yes	0.15	5.18	3.25
Turkey	systemic	1982–85	2.5	0.0	3.7	no	no	no	no	−0.33	5.18	4.00
Turkey	systemic	2000–	30.5	0.0	12.9	yes	no	yes	yes	−0.33	5.18	4.00
United States	nonsystemic	1988–91	3.2	0.0	0.0	no	no	no	yes	1.29	8.63	10.00
Uruguay	systemic	1981–84	31.2	41.0	19.8	yes	yes	yes	yes	0.56		
Venezuela	systemic	1994–95	22	14.0	12.5	no	no	yes	yes	−0.37	4.70	6.50

PART FOUR

STRUCTURAL REFORMS

SEVEN

Financial Crises and the Presence of Foreign Banks

Adrian Tschoegl

INTRODUCTION

Foreign banks have entered many transition and emerging economies in recent years, sometimes before economic and banking crises have developed, and often after. Today, in a number of countries foreign banks own as much as 90 percent or more of the banking systems' assets. The question then naturally arises as to what the effect of the foreign presence is on crises, especially on preventing or ameliorating them, in addition to their possible role in the restructuring phase already flagged in Chapter 2.

This chapter first discusses the motives, modes, and regulation of foreign banks. In analyzing foreign entry, it is important to distinguish between classic or traditional foreign banks and the innovators, which in turn one can classify either as "bettors," "prospectors," or "restructurers." Innovators enter in response to the opportunities that crises create, but this chapter argues that their entry and the reforms that accompany it erode the very conditions that drew the banks. In the long run, then, it may well be that the relative and possibly even absolute importance of foreign-owned banks in host-country banking systems may shrink. A further distinction is in the mode of entry, as among affiliate, branch, and subsidiary, a choice that is largely based on the foreigners' motives for entry.

Section 2 observes that foreign banks have in most cases not played an important role in the emergence of crises, primarily because they did not have a significant presence before the crisis began. Finally, however, Section 3 argues that foreign banks can help in the aftermath of a crisis by acting as microeconomic rehabilitators of failed banks and as instruments of system-wide reform.

1. FOREIGN DIRECT INVESTMENT IN BANKING IN DEVELOPING ECONOMIES

To provide some background to the discussion of the role of foreign banks in financial crises, this section deals with motives, modes, and regulation. Motives are the strategies of the foreign banks that bring them to the host countries. Modes deals with the legal form of the banks' presence. Finally, regulation is critical to understanding the scope of activities in which foreign banks may engage.

1.1 Motives

One can broadly classify foreign banks into two categories based on their strategies in the host countries: the traditionals and the innovators. The traditionals consist of those many foreign banks, especially those operating via a branch or a small, wholly owned subsidiary in a national financial center, that are mainly engaging in classic international banking. These banks process trade payments, finance trade, trade foreign exchange, and lend to corporations, both to their home country clients operating in the host country and to host country firms that require an alternative to the services that local banks can offer. The traditionals do not seek to engage in retail banking, with the limited exception of ethnic banks, that is, banks that have come to serve the needs of recent or perhaps even long-established emigrants from the home country resident in the host country.

Deregulation, transition, and crisis have created opportunities for the second group, the innovators. The innovators are innovative in two nonexclusive ways: frequently their responses to the new opportunities represent behaviors that are new to the banks themselves, and their responses are to bring governance, methods, and products that are new (or at least scarce) in the markets that they enter. They also bring capital, but this is in many ways their least important function. The innovators come in three varieties: the bettors, the prospectors, and the restructurers.

The bettors include everything from various quangos (quasi-autonomous, nongovernmental organizations) and development banks to banks, investment or private equity firms, and individuals betting on the postderegulation environment or on the success of transition. Some examples would include the International Finance Corporation, the Deutsche Entwicklungsgesellschaft, and the European Bank for Reconstruction and Development. The bettors' involvement is heavily financial. Through their activities they acquire a portfolio of investments. They hope to create the bulk of the value to themselves through having made good bets on the capabilities of the institutions and the management teams in which they invest. In time, one can expect them to exit due either to the success or to the failure of their investments. In the meantime they may perform a screening and signaling function. Their involvement as major investors (10–40 percent share positions) gives the banks in which they invest some legitimacy in an environment in which there may be numerous new and reorganizing local banks.

What distinguishes the bettors from the prospectors and the restructurers is that the bettors do not actually manage the banks in which they invest. The bettors' governance role is frequently a negative one – they impede malfeasance. Their presence therefore is a signal of probity but because they do not manage their investment, less so one of competence. The bettors invest together with a strategic investor that has the largest and often a majority stake. A strategic investor is a firm, usually operating in the same or a similar field, which takes a controlling equity stake. The strategic investors acquire their targets and manage them. These strategic investors do expect to earn a return on risk capital, but more important they also expect to earn a return on the management skills, systems, and experience that they bring to bear.

The structure of strategic investor supported by bettors is similar in practice if not in legal form to the commandite of the pre–Great Depression world. The strategic investor is analogous to the general partner in a commandite and the bettors are analogous to the limited partners. Strategic investors may be domestic or foreign, and the foreigners in turn may be prospectors or restructurers.

The prospectors are foreign banks that perceive the existence of a possible opportunity in the unsettled situation following opening, crisis, or deregulation. The prospectors typically have no particular experience with the host country or clients there. The prospectors simply are willing, often for idiosyncratic reasons, to engage in exploratory forays. What distinguishes prospectors from restructurers (see later) is that the prospectors' engagement is exploratory rather than part of a broader strategy.

The prospectors establish small subsidiaries or joint ventures, or take large equity positions in local banks that are small relative to the foreign bank. If the foray shows promise they are willing to expand further. If it

Table 7.1a *History of Allied Irish Banks*

Year	Event
Allied Irish Bank in Poland	
Late 1980s	AIB had a surplus of senior managers so it lent them out as consultants working in the transition economies, particularly the Czech Republic, Hungary, and Poland.
1993	At the request of the IBRD and the EBRD, AIB agreed to a twinning arrangement with Wielkopolski Bank Kredytowy (WBK).
1995	AIB took a 16.3 percent stake in WBK.
1996	It acquired a further 20 percent from the Polish government.
1997	AIB acquired shares in WBK from the EBRD, bringing its ownership to 60 percent.
1999	AIB reached an agreement with the Polish State Treasury to acquire an 80 percent shareholding in Bank Zachodni.
2000	AIB merged Wielkopolski Bank Kredytowy and Bank Zachodni to form Bank Zachodni WBK.
Present	AIB currently owns 70.50 percent of BZ WBK and the remaining shares are widely held. Both WBK and Zachodni were regional retail banks rather than banks to the corporate sector.
Allied Irish Bank in Singapore	
1999	AIB entered into a strategic alliance with Keppel Tat Lee Bank (KTL) in Singapore. AIB acquired one percent of the shares of KTL and an option to acquire a further 25 percent.
2001	Overseas Chinese Banking Corporation, also of Singapore, made an offer to acquire KTL. AIB chose to sell out to OCBC, at a notable profit.

Note: Having sold its AllFirst subsidiary in the United States (Tschoegl 2002b), AIB has no retail banking operation outside Ireland and the United Kingdom other than Bank Zachodni WBK.
Source: Harrington and Lawton (2003).

does not, they cut their losses, generally by selling out to local or other foreign banks. The metaphor here is the gold mine model of Moffett et al. (1989). The prospector sinks an exploratory shaft in a promising location. If he does not strike gold-bearing ore, the prospector moves on. If he does strike gold the mine then follows the ore vein, wherever it leads. One illustrative example is Allied Irish Banks (AIB) and its investments in Poland and Singapore (Table 7.1a). A more complex example involving several prospectors is Prager Handelsbank (Table 7.1b).

Many prospectors establish de novo ventures because they have very focused strategies. Examples would include Porsche Bank and Opel Bank

Table 7.1b. *History of Prager Handelsbank*

Year	Event
1989	Four banks established Prager Handelsbank (PH): Ceskoslovenska Obchodni Banka (CSOB; 45 percent), DG Bank (30 percent), Zivnostenska Banka (10 percent), Raiffeisen Zentralbank Oesterreich (Wien) (10 percent) and BHF Bank (5 percent). The plan was that PH would specialize in financing foreign trade transactions, especially between Germany, Czechoslovakia and Austria.
1990	PH opened its head office in Frankfurt.
1991	PH opened a rep office in Prague but for legal reasons could not open a branch.
1992	CSOB (55 percent) and DG Bank (35 percent) acquired the shares of Zivnostenska banka and BHF-Bank. BHF-Bank had acquired a 40 percent stake in Zivnostenska banka at the beginning of the year.
1997	CSOB bought out its partners in PH.
2000	CSOB sold PH to Belgium's KBC Bank. KBC had acquired 66 percent of CSOB in May 1999. At the end of the 1999 it obtained another 16.66 percent during the sale of a stake in CSOB held by the National Bank of Slovakia. KBC integrated PH into KBC Deutschland and the name disappeared.

Source: News reports.

in Hungary, both of which specialize in consumer finance, especially the purchase of their owners' cars. The evidence in Majnoni et al. (2003) for Hungary suggests that greenfield operations achieve higher profitability than restructured ones because of the introduction of new financial products.

The last category is that of the restructurers. These acquire a large bank in a privatization or a rescue and proceed to attempt to fix it. The investment is not a trial foray but rather a large-scale commitment. Frequently, it is part of a program of similar investments. Banks such as Unicredito (Italy), Erste Bank (Austria), KBC (Belgium), Société Générale (France), and others have acquired banks throughout the transition economies. As can be seen from Table 7.2, these restructurers have acquired banks in four or more countries. From the names of the local banks alone one can infer that these are recent acquisitions. (The names differ from country to country and the parent has not yet rebranded the subsidiaries with a common identity.) Also, in the Czech Republic and Slovakia all four compete with each other; in other countries, though only one to three of

Table 7.2. *European Banks' Patterns of Acquisition in Central and Eastern Europe*

Country	Unicredito	Erste Bank	KBC	Société Générale
Poland	Bank Pekao		Kredyt Bank	
Czech Republic	Zivnostenska Banka	Ceska sporitelna	CSOB	Komercni Banka
Slovakia	Unibanka	Slovenska Sporitelna	CSOB	Komercni Banka Bratislava
Slovenia			Nova Ljubljanska Banka[a]	SKB Banka
Croatia	Zagrebacka Banka	Erste & Steiermärkische Bank[b]		
Serbia				Société Générale Yougoslav Bank
Hungary		Erste Bank Hungary[c] Postabank	K&H Bank	
Romania	Unicredit Romania			Banque Roumaine de Développement
Bulgaria	Bulbank			SG Expressbank

Note: (*a*) Associated bank. (*b*) ex-Bjelovarska Banka, Trgovacka Banka, Cakovecka Banka, and Rijecka Banka. (*c*) ex-Mezöbank.
Source: Bank Web sites.

these banks are present, other foreign banks are also present. The presence of several foreign banks from different countries brings a rivalry to the market for bank services.

Although the identities of the restructurers may change, one can find similar patterns in other regions of the world. Nordic banks have been active in the Baltic. Greek banks such as National Bank of Greece, Commercial Bank of Greece, and Alpha Bank have been equally acquisitive in the Balkans–Black Sea region. Somewhat similarly, banks such as Santander and BBVA (Spain) and HSBC (U.K.) have acquired banks throughout Latin America (Guillén and Tschoegl 2000).

Although some prospectors and restructurers may hope to sell out within the medium term (say 3–7 years), most view their engagement as open-ended. At entry, they have no exit plan but instead anticipate retaining ownership into the indefinite future, subject of course to profitability. However, in time one can expect that most will sell their operations to local banks as the evolution of the host markets erodes their comparative advantage vis-à-vis their local competitors.

The basis for the argument for the long-run return of the financial systems to predominantly domestic control is the metaphor of ecological succession (Koford and Tschoegl 2002). Ecological succession is a dynamic model that posits that the first plants to arrive in disturbed or clear soil stabilize the soil and change light conditions, creating opportunities for successor species. This in turn provides opportunities for yet other species. The mix of plant and animal species continues to evolve until the system reaches the final steady state of a climax forest. Of course, when fire, flood, or landslide clears a patch in the forest, the process starts again in that patch. During the process, one must be careful not to assume that the current situation is in equilibrium. One should not mistake a current phase, especially not an early one, for the ultimate steady state.

The foreign banks are the fast growing plants that are the first responders to the new opportunity given by the disturbed, hospitable soil that crises or transition have created. This does not mean that all foreign banks are innovators; some international banks will remain with traditional international banking. It just means that among the foreign banks there are those that will respond quickly and in ways that take them beyond traditional international banking. They can respond quickly because they are well-capitalized, efficient, and have surplus managerial resources (Kindleberger 1969 and Tschoegl 2004).

In all this, it is important to remember that the ecological succession metaphor concerns itself with the evolution of a system after a disturbance. It is not designed to deal with steady states. It is not a model for the role of foreign banks in mature, stable markets, though as Norway shows (Engwall et al. 2001 and Tschoegl 2002a), even in mature markets it has applicability in crises. For a discussion of the role of foreign banks in a large, competitive market such as the United States, see Tschoegl (2001).

We can think of the share of banking system assets in foreign banks relative to total banking system assets as the proportion of the system's biomass accounted for by the fast responding plants. One feature of the ecological succession process is that there is both a numerator and a denominator effect. The behavior of the foreign banks themselves has a large effect on the numerator. Over the long term, the response of the domestically owned banks will have a large effect on the denominator.

As the foreign banks enter, especially when they acquire host country banks in privatizations, rescues, and repairs, the numerator grows more rapidly than the denominator. What draws the foreign banks is the opportunities the situations present, now that the banks are able or even encouraged to enter. Weill (2003) found that in the Czech Republic and Poland, foreign-owned banks were more efficient than domestic-owned banks but that this was not because of scale differences or the structure of activities. Demirgüç-Kunt and Huizinga (1999) and Claessens et al. (2001) found that foreign banks tended to have higher margins and profits than domestic banks in developing countries, but that the opposite held in industrial countries. Similarly, Dopico and Wilcox (2002) found that foreign banks were more pervasive in countries where banking was more profitable and where the banking sector was smaller relative to GDP. Conversely, foreign banks had a smaller presence in mature, competitive markets.

Although markets that are growing, underbanked, or uncompetitive draw foreign banks, by their entry the foreign banks change the environment. The literature on the effect of foreign banks on host country banking systems, especially margins, suggests that the effect is precisely to undermine the conditions associated with the presence of foreign banks. For instance, Lensink and Hermes (2004) found that foreign entry is associated with shrinking margins in developing countries, but not necessarily in developed countries. For the Philippines, Unite and Sullivan (2003) found that foreign competition compelled domestic banks to be more efficient, to focus operations, and to become less dependent on relationship-based banking practices.

This means that over time, measured in decades, the foreign banks will find that the conditions that drew them have eroded, and some will withdraw, selling their subsidiaries to locally owned banks. When one examines histories of particular banks or of banking systems in particular countries, one can rapidly identify a number of mechanisms that operate to reduce the foreign presence. Some foreign banks sell out because they find they are not competitive. Others sell because their parent is in difficulty at home and sells the foreign operation in order to raise funds. Yet others sell out to local investors and banks when host country markets are depressed and the foreign owners see little benefit from staying. Finally, some simply sell out to local banks growing by acquisition.

For instance, in 1999 Sumitomo Bank sold the subsidiary it had established in California in 1952 to Zions Bancorp, which was expanding into California. Of course, sometimes the exiting bank will sell to another foreign bank. Thus, UFJ Holdings (the company created in Japan to merge Sanwa Bank, Tokai Bank and Toyo Trust) announced the sale of United California Bank to BancWest, a subsidiary of Banque Nationale de Paris Paribas, which had entered in 1970. Sanwa had established its subsidiary in 1972 and Tokai in 1974. In both the Sumitomo and Sanwa-Tokai cases the parents sold not because of difficulties with their California operations but, rather, because of difficulties at home. Of the eight subsidiaries that Japanese banks established in California between 1952 and 1978, three remain, the rest having disappeared through merger into the survivors or sale; assets in California subsidiaries of Japanese banks peaked in the early 1990s and have fallen since though the largest subsidiary, Bank of Tokyo-Mitsubishi's Union Bank of California continues to grow (Tschoegl 2003).

Similarly, in 2003 Banco Bilbao Vizcaya Argentaria sold its Brazilian operations to Bradesco. BBVA had bought Banco Excel-Economico in 1998 for one real. BBVA sold because it realized that it would be too expensive to achieve a profitable scale. As part of the sale price, BBVA took a small equity stake in Bradesco, thus converting its strategy for Brazil from that of a restructurer to that of a bettor. In 2003, Lloyds TSB sold its Brazilian operations to HSBC (Hongkong and Shanghai Bank Corporation). HSBC had entered in 1997 and the purchase of Lloyds is its third in Brazil. Lloyds' association with Brazil dated back to ancestors of the Bank of London and South America (BOLSA), which in 1863 and 1864 were the first banks in Brazil. However, Lloyds' management has decided to focus on its operations in the United Kingdom; for example, it agreed in October 2003 to sell National Bank of New Zealand, with which it has been associated since the 1870s, to ANZ Bank.

To this point the discussion has focused on the numerator of the ratio of assets in foreign-owned banks to total assets in the banking system. There is, however, a denominator effect as well. The argument here comes from Huang and Di (2003). They point out that the conditions that constrain foreign firms also may constrain host country firms. If, as we have argued earlier, the conditions constrain host country firms more than they do foreign firms, the foreign firms may increase their ownership of assets in the host country. However, the liberalization and regulatory reform that accompanied the entry of the foreign firms benefits the domestic firms as well. It will take time for them to overcome their administrative heritage from the previous conditions but once they do, one can expect them to grow rapidly. The result will be an increase in the numerator, and a decline in the ratio, even without denominator effects.

Foreign banks have not displayed any long-term *comparative* advantage in retail banking vis-à-vis host country banks, especially in reaching rural areas and the unbanked. This means that local banks will have more scope to continue to dominate retail banking, as long as they can retain or achieve absolute cost and efficiency advantage as well as comparative advantage. As the local banks improve their efficiency, foreign banks will increasingly specialize once more in international activities, even if they do not immediately exit retail banking. Still, it is not unusual to see a foreign bank sell its retail activities to a local bank while it retains a branch in the national financial capital to enable it to continue to offer corporate and wholesale banking services.

Saying that over time one should expect to see foreign banks exiting retail banking abroad does not mean that all foreign banks will do so. Currently, HSBC is striving to become, in the words of its slogan, "the world's local bank" (Tschoegl 2003). Some particularly capable foreign banks may retain a presence for a long time. However, one must keep in mind, too, that over time management changes and HSBC's push in North America is only about 20 years old, whereas that in Latin America is about five.

It can be argued that increasing globalization makes the metaphor of ecological succession suspect. However, Goldsmith (1969, 360–367), referring to the 19th and early 20th centuries, the first era of globalization, noted that outside of Europe and North America the development of financial systems was widely based on foreign banks but that over time the foreign banks had lost their predominance as local banks arose and waxed. Goldsmith does not go into detail; his focus was on macroeconomics. Triner's (1996 and 2002) description of the development of banking in Brazil, especially after the reforms of 1905, shows a pattern consistent with the ecological succession metaphor. Koford and Tschoegl (2002) apply the metaphor to the history of foreign banks in Bulgaria since the late 19th century. Tschoegl's earlier papers on the foreign bank presence in Japan (Tschoegl 1988) and Saudi Arabia (Tschoegl 2002c) and Phylatkis's (1988) paper on the eclipsing of British banks in Cyprus before independence, also offer evidence for the applicability of the metaphor in that era.

1.2 Modes

The three most common forms of legal presence are branches, affiliates, and subsidiaries, though their availability to foreign banks varies by country. That is, some countries permit foreign banks to operate via a branch but not a subsidiary, or vice versa. Legal form is not an arbitrary formality but can be intimately tied to both the banks' strategies and to the regulatory environment. The distinction between the three is not a matter of arcane legal minutiae but rather can be of substantive importance, especially in crises.

A branch is an integral part of the parent. A branch may make loans or take deposits; generally it may provide a full range of banking services. Banks prefer to use foreign branches for wholesale and corporate banking activities in host countries, including foreign exchange and money market trading. The reason is that a branch generally lends, borrows and trades on the basis of its parent's full capital base. Thus the branch can lend more to any one borrower than could a similar-sized subsidiary (see later) and, in borrowing and trading, the branch shares the parent's credit rating. Because it is part of the parent bank, a branch requires careful supervision as mistakes at a branch could bankrupt the parent. However, what facilitates supervision is that branches' activities such as trading and lending to local subsidiaries of home country firms are ones that the bank must necessarily manage centrally.

An affiliate or associate is an independent legal entity (i.e., locally incorporated) in which the foreign bank has less than majority ownership. Generally, foreign banks prefer not to put their name on affiliates as that would suggest full responsibility for an entity over which they do not exercise full control. Furthermore, if through a combination of share ownership and management contract the foreign bank does exercise control, then it will wish eventually to assume full control to capture more of the return from its management without having to dispute transfer pricing decisions with minority shareholders.

A subsidiary, like an affiliate, is a separate legal entity incorporated in the host country, but one in which the foreign parent has majority ownership. A subsidiary may fail even though the parent is solvent. Conversely, a subsidiary may be solvent even though the parent has failed. The subsidiary lends based on its own capitalization rather than that of the parent, something that can prove to be a major constraint. Certainly, a subsidiary can refer to its parent a loan that exceeds its allowable lending limits but, in that case, the bank could lend from its branch in the first place. Thus, many banks conclude that a subsidiary provides a relatively poor platform from which to conduct corporate lending or trading activities (Heinkel and Levi 1992).

Generally, a branch costs less to establish than a subsidiary. There are no costs of incorporation, no need to report annually or quarterly to local registrars of companies, no need for a board of directors, and so forth. However, when a bank has sufficient assets at risk where the risk is location-specific there may come a time when it becomes sensible to incorporate locally.

Du (2003) has pointed out that multinational companies may borrow from local banks to enlist the services of those banks as monitors of the local operation. The local bank, as local creditor with often first rights to any assets in bankruptcy, has an incentive to intervene quickly if it senses problems. Similarly, a foreign bank with a number of branches in a country thousands of miles from home, branches whose profitability depends on a local economy about which the parent knows little, may decide to incorporate locally to enlist the governance services of the local central bank, and local depositors when there is no deposit insurance. These parties are more likely to sense and react to some problems of which headquarters, dependent on reports from its managers, might be unaware. Thus, when the assets at stake are large enough and the local regulatory authorities are capable, the foreign parent may decide that the costs of incorporation are an acceptable cost for assistance with governance.

As the United States deregulated banking, many multibank holding companies merged their subsidiaries, converting their offices into direct branches of the parent (Wheelock and Wilson 2002). The earlier argument suggests one reason they could do so was because all were already subject to oversight by the Federal Reserve and Federal Deposit Insurance Corporation; amalgamating did not imply any loss of a local regulator. By contrast, the little cross-border acquisition activity within the European Union (EU) has led to little or no amalgamation (and has been limited primarily to the Nordic countries).

Interestingly, looking at the United States as a host country, the 10 banks that control the 12 largest subsidiaries of foreign banks (accounting for about 90 percent of the assets in U.S. subsidiaries of foreign banks) continue to choose the subsidiary form rather than branches of the parent (Tschoegl 2002b). The parent banks involved do have branches, but these are in financial centers and engage in wholesale and corporate banking. They are not retail banking operations (Tschoegl 2001). HSBC Canada, the largest foreign bank and the seventh largest bank in Canada, continues to operate via a subsidiary even though it now has the option to adopt the branch form, and even though several foreign banks with only one office in Toronto switched when the option became available in 1999.

It is important to emphasize that this argument for incorporation has nothing to do with taxes. Although tax conditions can be relevant, a subsidiary, especially one that the parent does not own outright, tends to have much less flexibility in its tax management than a branch. When one observes a parent maintaining, say in the United States, both a branch for corporate and wholesale banking and a subsidiary for retail banking, this argues that taxes are not the issue and that the branch's lack of local limited liability is important for trading.

The choice between operating via a branch or via a subsidiary also may have little to do with the value of the option to abandon implicit in limited liability (see later). Incorporation as a device for enlisting the governance assistance of host country regulators is a much more promising explanation.

Regulators in the home and host country frequently try to retain the advantage to them of one form or the other. Thus regulators in the home country may attempt to "ring fence" the parent's assets to insulate them from developments in the bank's branches abroad. At the same time, regulators in the host country may require a branch to allocate a certain amount of capital to the branch to protect local depositors in the event the parent fails. Local regulators also may require a parent bank to issue a "comfort letter" pledging support to a subsidiary. Still, as we discuss in the next section, regulators monitor and regulate branches differently from subsidiaries.

The issue of the choice between branch and subsidiary can have implications for the role of foreign banks in a crisis. In a crisis, local depositors frequently engage in a "flight to quality." That is, they withdraw their funds from domestic banks in which they have lost confidence and redeposit the funds in less risky banks. Often these are government-owned banks, but also often these are foreign banks. Depositors will find the branches of a foreign bank, especially one from a country with good regulatory supervision, particularly attractive. Branches cannot fail unless the parent fails, and the probability of the parent failing generally does not depend highly on conditions in the host economy. Also, most parents of foreign branches are large relative to the size of the branch. Still, although shifting deposits to branches of foreign banks may be a sensible strategy, it is usually of limited use to most citizens because of the paucity of accessible offices. Most foreign banks maintain only one location, which they have placed in the host country's financial center. Obviously, the option is of some use to corporations.

Subsidiaries and affiliates may also benefit from a flight to quality but, if so, this will depend more on the quality of the management of the bank than on the bank's legal status. Both subsidiaries and affiliates are host-country legal persons and their performance is heavily bound up with domestic politics and economics. A subsidiary may benefit from the perception that the parent will stand behind it to protect the parent's name and reputation. Obviously, this perception will be much weaker in the case of an affiliate, especially one that has not advertised its links to the foreign parent. In either case, the expectation of parental support is a bet and not a consequence of legal form as is the case with branches. For the parent, the existence of limited liability is an option to abandon with the strike price being the loss of reputation if it walks away. However, the strike price is stochastic in that it depends on the reason behind the parent invoking limited liability. The cases of Crédit Agricole, Scotiabank, and MBK Mercobank in Argentina are illuminating. In all three cases, the foreign shareholders or parents, unwilling to recapitalize failed subsidiaries, turned them over to the Argentine government for rescue. In the cases of Crédit Agricole and Scotiabank, the reasons for failure were the Argentine government's economic policy decisions. This is a very different matter than if the reason had been corporate mismanagement or malfeasance.

Scotiabank (formerly Bank of Nova Scotia) refused to pump in more capital and instead abandoned Scotiabank Quilmes, writing off C$540 million in the process. The government transferred Quilmes to Banco Comafi and Banco Bansud, which appeared to have roughly split it between them, and which took over all the liabilities, not just the deposits. Scotiabank did make a voluntary payment of 20 cents on the dollar to holders of its subsidiary's medium term notes and other debt. It may have done so to shore up its reputation in the global market for its debt. It also gave severance pay to the 500 employees (out of 1,700) who lost their jobs.

Crédit Agricole exercised the option implicit in limited liability and walked away from its three subsidiaries in 2002. It simply refused to send the around 200 million pesos (US$61.5 million) they would require to stay afloat. The three subsidiaries – Banco Bisel, Banco del Suquia and Banco de Entre Rios – have 353 branches that serve farmers in the provinces. The government-owned Banco de la Nación Argentina, the largest bank in the country, temporarily stepped in to keep the three running.

Regardless of the arguments, the data suggests that the phenomenon of a flight to quality does not provide foreign banks with a long-term advantage. Market share shifts to foreign banks during most crises (absent acquisitions of local banks) appear to amount to only a percentage or two of the banking systems' total assets and may be short-lived.

1.3 Regulation

The Basle Concordat of 1975 (amended in 1983), established that home country supervisory authorities are responsible for solvency supervision of the parent's branches abroad. This is logical as it is the home country authorities that have legal access to the parent's books, and because a branch fails when its parent fails. Host and parent country supervisory authorities are jointly responsible for solvency supervision of subsidiaries, with the host country having primary responsibility. Again, this is logical as the subsidiary is a legal person of the host country and so the local authorities have access to its books. Also, a subsidiary can fail even when the parent is solvent. However, the home country authorities are responsible for supervision on a consolidated basis as subsidiaries affect the parent's solvency and the parent cannot disclaim all responsibility for its subsidiaries. This provision for joint responsibility followed the collapse of Banco Ambrosiano in 1982.

When Banco Ambrosiano collapsed, the Italian authorities protected Italian depositors by transferring the bank's business to a new Italian entity. However, they disclaimed responsibility for the obligations of Ambrosiano's Luxembourg subsidiary and the Latin American subsidiaries.

When BCCI failed in 1991, the local regulators in such countries as Canada and Mauritius dealt with the local operations. The Bank of Canada closed Bank of Credit and Commerce Canada. Bank of Mauritius issued a license to the Somaia group to establish Delphis Bank to take over BCCI's banking business. When Demirbank failed in Turkey in 2000, its subsidiary in Bulgaria continued to function and there was no run on the bank. Instead, the Bulgarian subsidiary was simply an asset that the Turkish authorities sold.

Again, countries differ in terms of whether they permit foreign banks to operate as branches, affiliates, or subsidiaries. When banks use affiliates, frequently this is in response to host countries' laws limiting foreign ownership in the banking sector. The laws force the foreign parent into minority ownership as a condition of entry or continuation of operations. Generally, foreign banks convert affiliates to subsidiaries when they can. Still, in some cases foreign banks continue to maintain affiliates rather than subsidiaries, perhaps in order to limit the parent's responsibility. Belgolaise, a subsidiary of Belgium's Fortis Bank that specializes in banking in Africa, operates almost exclusively through affiliates.

Countries that have wished to open their banking sectors to foreign banks sufficiently to avoid reciprocity concerns while limiting the foreign banks' scope, have opted to permit subsidiaries rather than branches (Tschoegl 1981). Canada would be a case in point, at least before the NAFTA treaty forced change. Countries that have wished to limit foreign banks to the wholesale and corporate markets and to keep them out of the retail market have permitted branches but not subsidiaries. Japan would be a case in point, at least before the need to recapitalize some large, failed banks forced change.

In addition to these basic considerations, countries have also had to decide whether or not to permit foreign banks to buy local banks. Even in cases in which the country permits the foreign bank to establish a subsidiary it commonly still forbids it to acquire local banks. This has the effect of limiting the foreign bank to organic growth, something that can be quite slow. HSBC entered Canada in 1979 but only started to grow rapidly in 1986 when it acquired the failed Bank of British Columbia; HSBC Canada followed this with seven more acquisitions, which between them had acquired six banks, mostly subsidiaries of other foreign banks (Tschoegl 2003). Similarly, the foreign banks that own the largest US subsidiaries or affiliates of foreign banks have all grown by acquisition (Tschoegl 2002b). The same appears generally to be the case in those transition and developing countries where there are large foreign banks. The primary exceptions are those cases where the foreign banks came when a country was a colony or before there were locally-owned banks. In these cases, the foreign banks have had the time to grow into a substantial presence, for example, in Jamaica (Table 7.3), Malaysia (Table 7.4), and the Pacific Islands, though even here the foreign banks have been involved in mergers and acquisitions, especially among themselves.

2. EFFECT OF FOREIGN BANK PRESENCE IN CRISES

In general, foreign banks have had little effect in crises, primarily because they did not have a material presence before the crisis began. Of the following 12 countries (treating the Pacific Islands as one country), in 8 (Bulgaria, Czech Republic, Hungary, Indonesia, Mexico, Norway, Tanzania, and Thailand), the foreign banks' share of banking system assets ranged from nil to well under 20 percent. In four countries (Argentina, Jamaica, Malaysia, and the Pacific Islands), it was in excess of 20 percent.

One could well hypothesize that countries that had the sort of policies that would encourage the entry of foreign banks are not likely to have the

Table 7.3. *Ownership Structure of Jamaica's Banking System before and after the Crisis*

Bank	1998 Assets	1998 Percent	2001 Assets	2001 Percent	Growth 1998–2001 Percent
Bank of Nova Scotia	57087[a]	34	87279[a]	36	53
Citibank	5187[a]	3	9285[a]	4	79
Canadian Imperial	11138[a]	7	16618[a]	7	49
Trafalgar Commercial	858	0.5			
First Global Bank			2,991	1	249
Citizens Bank	12870[b]	8			
Eagle Commercial Bank	3295[b]	2			
Island Victoria Bank	2504[b]	1.5			
Workers Savings & Loan	4836[b]	3			
RBTT			33298[a]	14	42
National Bank of Commerce	72281[b]	43	90349[a]	38	25
TOTAL	170,058	100	239,820	100	41
Percent foreign-owned	43.2		98.8		

Note: (*a*) Foreign-owned banks; (*b*) Banks with Financial Sector Adjustment Company (FINSAC) intervention that were subsequently privatized by the government.
Source: Bank of Jamaica.

sort of policies that lead to crises. Beck et al. (2003) found that crises were less likely in economies with fewer regulatory restrictions on bank competition and national institutions that encourage competition. At the very least, the empirical evidence suggested that developing-country banking systems that had lower entry barriers to foreign-owned banks gained

Table 7.4. *Foreign Bank Presence in Malaysia before and after the 1998 Financial Crisis*

Year	Domestic Assets	Domestic Percent	Foreign Assets	Foreign Percent	Total Assets	Total Percent	Foreign/ Total Percent
1996	279,986		80,141		360,127		22
1997	376,434	34.4	103,815	29.5	480,249	33.4	22
1998	352,765	−6.3	101,748	−2.0	454,513	−5.4	22
1999	373,646	5.9	109,961	8.1	483,607	6.4	23
2000	388,727	4.0	123,988	12.8	512,715	6.0	24
2001	398,156	2.4	131,580	6.1	529,736	3.3	25
2002	425,792	6.9	137,158	4.2	562,950	6.3	24

Note: Assets are reported in RM Millions and percentages are year-on-year changes in total assets.
Source: Bank Negara Malaysia.

directly and indirectly. They were less vulnerable to crises and the domestic banks were more efficient than in countries with greater barriers.
Barth et al. (2004) found that the negative correlation with the likelihood
of a banking crisis is not with foreign bank ownership per se, but rather
with limitations on foreign bank entry and ownership. Independent of actual foreign bank entry, the authors found that the likelihood of a major
banking crisis was positively associated with greater limitations on foreign
bank participation.

Even in those cases in which foreign banks have had a large presence
and there has been a crisis, such as the Pacific islands in the Australian
sphere of influence or Jamaica, the crisis has been limited to the need
to bail out depositors in the government-owned bank. The knock-on effects have been limited. All depositors in the foreign banks have been
unaffected and depositors in the government bank have at most only lost
temporary access to their deposits, if that. There has been no material
credit restriction because the reason for the failure of the government
bank was that its lending went to unproductive purposes. The net effect
of the crisis has been simply to transfer money from taxpayers to the
recipients of the political lending of the failed bank.

The great exception has been Argentina. Here part of the problem has
been the asymmetric pesification that acted as a tax on bank capital and
transfer to depositors, leading some foreign banks to pull out. For more
complete treatments of the Argentine case, see Calomiris, Klingebiel, and
Laeven (Chapter 2).

The foreign banks tend to have a stabilizing effect on the economy
to the degree that they are present. Subsidiaries of foreign banks tend
not to be as affected by crises as the domestic banks, in part because
they have been more conservative in their lending. Dages et al. (2000)
concluded from their study of foreign banks in Argentina and Mexico
over the 1994–1999 period that foreign banks exhibited stronger and less
volatile loan growth than domestic banks. However, it was the asset quality of bank portfolios and not ownership per se that appeared to be the
decisive factor. Branches of foreign banks also benefit from having specialized in lending for trade, especially export trade, and in lending to
foreign and large corporations. Because crises often result from or cause
a depreciation of the host country currency, exporting firms benefit from
the crisis. Thus, though foreign banks do suffer from the general downturn
that occurs in economies in crisis, they often suffer less than do domestic
banks.

In addition, branches certainly, and subsidiaries probably, benefit from the parents' support. This has two linked consequences. First, when the foreign banks benefit from a flight to quality this reduces the demand for foreign exchange for flight capital and the consequent pressure on the exchange rate. Second, this gives the foreign banks the funds to continue to lend to host-country firms, which reduces the credit crunch effect of a crisis.

In Jamaica, as the problems in the banking sector grew, depositors engaged in a flight to quality, withdrawing their savings from what they perceived to be weak institutions, mainly indigenous ones, and depositing them in the branches of foreign banks (Kirkpatrick and Tennant 2002). If one examines the market share of the three banks that were foreign-owned before the crisis, all grew faster than the banks requiring government intervention. Furthermore, all gained at the expense of the formerly government-owned National Bank of Commerce (Table 7.3).

When domestic banks are weak, the subsidiaries of foreign banks may have better access to funding in foreign exchange, especially in times of stress. However, the evidence suggests that strong domestic banks can do as well or even better than the foreign subsidiaries (Reynoso 2002).

Again, the primary constraint on these positive effects is the relatively small presence of foreign banks. A second constraint is that while the country is undergoing a crisis, risk managers at the foreign banks' headquarters may require their banks to curtail lending. The need to match the currency of the assets to those of the liabilities will then have the foreign banks purchasing government bonds. This probably results in a trivial reduction in the governments' funding costs but may crowd out private borrowing.

There is one last point about stabilization that is worth mentioning. The reverse of the coin that foreign banks may be less affected than host country banks by problems in the host country economy is that the foreign banks may be more affected by problems in the home country. Both Peek and Rosengren (2000) and Williams (1996), for instance, have documented how problems at home resulted in Japanese banks curtailing their lending abroad. Here the effect was more pronounced with branches than subsidiaries. Capital adequacy issues at the parent affect the ability of branches to lend but do not affect subsidiaries in the host countries. The Japanese parent banks' problems led them to curtail the lending activities of their branches and agencies in California but did not affect the lending of their subsidiaries (Laderman 1999).

3. ROLES OF FOREIGN BANKS IN RESOLVING CRISES

The experience of the 1990s brought an ever-widening recognition of the advantages of inviting foreign banks in (Buch 1997). Foreign banks can operate in two different roles: in the microeconomic role of rehabilitators of troubled individual banks and in a systemwide role as instruments of reform of the banking system. However, here, too, foreign banks have their limitations.

3.1 Microeconomic Rehabilitators

The restructurers acquire failed or laggard institutions that they then rehabilitate. The transformation process typically begins with the foreign acquirer recapitalizing the acquisition and includes both the closing of unprofitable branches and operations (and the redundancy of staff), and the introduction of systems and processes, especially what is known as "a credit culture."

As mentioned earlier, frequently governments that have permitted some entry have still blocked foreign banks from acquiring control of domestic banks. It is not unusual for the governments to remove this restriction in crises. Foreigners frequently are the only parties able to recapitalize troubled banks as the other domestic banks are themselves not strong and the government wishes to limit its expenditures where it can. Examples of this abound; Mexico and Tanzania are cases in point.

After the 1994 Peso Crisis put Mexico's newly privatized banks back into government hands, in 1998 the Mexican Congress finally permitted foreign ownership of up to 100 percent in Mexican banks. Currently, the top three banks in Mexico – Banamex (Citibank), BBVA Bancomer, and Santander Serfin – the fifth – Bital (HSBC) – and the seventh – Inverlat (Scotiabank) – are all foreign-owned and account for over 80 percent of banking system assets. The degree of foreign ownership is as high as in some Eastern European countries and the ownership is concentrated in far fewer banks.

In 1996, the Tanzanian government began to privatize the largest government-owned banks, which between 1967 and 1991 had been the only banks in the country. In 2000 it privatized the National Bank of Commerce to Amalgamated Banks of South Africa (ABSA). As of mid-2000, foreign-owned banks accounted for over 55 percent of the assets in the Tanzanian banking system. The top six institutions, of which four are foreign owned, accounted for 89 percent of the assets in all banks and nonbank financial institutions.

As Claessens and Lee (2003) have found, foreign banks introduce improved risk-management practices and "imported" bank supervision from parent country regulators. Also, as Lwiza and Nwankwo (2002) point out for Tanzania, and Guillén and Tschoegl (2000) for Argentina, Chile, and Mexico, foreign banks frequently compete by introducing new financial products and services. That is, they introduce to the host country products and services that they have previously developed and deployed elsewhere. In a study of foreign bank ownership in Hungary, Majnoni et al. (2003) found that greenfield banks clearly outpaced other foreign-owned banks in terms of profitability. However, improvements in profitability derived from the introduction of new products and a broader array of financial services rather than from higher intermediation margins.

As worthwhile as these contributions are, they are not a panacea against the risk of crises. Competition between banks will tend to transfer efficiency gains to customers. Somewhat counter-intuitively, even better risk control will probably not affect the likelihood of crises. It may reduce the incidence of failure at individual banks, but will be ineffective for the many cases where the problem is not the banks' lack of ability to manage risk but rather a lack of will.

3.2 Instruments of Systemwide Reform

Foreign banks act as instruments of systemwide reform when governments admit them in order to change the structure of the banking system. There are two situations where allowing foreign banks to acquire domestic banks is likely to reduce the incidence of bank crises: when the foreigners take over formerly government-owned banks or when they take over owner-managed banks. Government ownership often results in subpar average returns; owner-management often results in high variance of returns. Ownership by foreign banks can address both problems. However, in both situations, the increasing role in the banking system of foreign banks is likely to be correlated with an apparent reduction in credit outstanding.

The first situation in which foreign ownership of banks may help reduce the likelihood of a recurrence of crisis occurs when the foreign banks acquire formerly government-owned banks. That is, foreign ownership of the banks impedes a government's exploitation of its banks to keep alive failing, but politically sensitive companies, and the concomitant need periodically to bail out the banks. As Gros (2003) points out, permitting foreign banks to acquire government banks can constitute a commitment and transparency device.

As part of a series of measures aimed at "limiting Leviathan," in June 1997 the Bulgarian government adopted a currency board, which removed the government's control over monetary policy and stabilized the currency (Koford 2000). The government also pushed forward privatization of the banking system to limit its own power to use the banking system to support bankrupt firms. By privatizing the banks, the government removed them from its own direct control. Furthermore, the government reasoned that foreign banks could draw on their parents for liquidity when the currency board system limited the BNB's ability to act as a lender of last resort (Šević 2000). In May 2003 the government completed the privatization process when it sold 100 percent of DSK, the state savings bank, to OTP (Országos Takarékpénztár és Kereskedelmi Bank), itself the former Hungarian state savings bank. DSK accounts for about 14 percent of assets in the Bulgarian banking system so now foreign owners account for about 86 percent of assets in the banking system (Table 7.5).

Limiting the government's discretion was also the motivation for permitting foreign banks to acquire domestic banks via privatizations in the cases of Hungary and the Czech Republic. Hungary liberalized before Bulgaria, and the Czech Republic after.

In 1986–1987, the Hungarian government authorized foreign banks to enter via foreign majority-owned joint ventures with Hungarian banks. However, the great influx of foreign banks began in 1990. The banking crisis of the early 1990s left the government-owned banks and several private Hungarian banks in desperate straits. The government decided not to rescue the banks through an infusion of capital, recognizing that as long as the government owned the banks in whole or in part, borrowers and managers would expect a bailout, which in turn would lead to problems of moral hazard. Also, the government recognized that conflicts of interest could arise when a bank's owners were also its largest customers.

Having decided on privatization, the government generally sought strategic investors rather than dispersed ownership, except in the case of the state savings bank, even though the only possible strategic investors were foreign firms, as Hungarian nonfinancial firms lacked the capital and the skills. The government's decision to permit foreign banks to acquire Hungarian private banks and to privatize the banking system led both to a deepening of entry and further entry (Bonin and Wachtel 1999).

Table 7.5. *Foreign Ownership of Banks in Bulgaria*

Ownership		1991	1992	1993	1994	1995	1996	1997	1998	1999	2000	2001	2002
State	Number	72	69	25	15	12	7	6	5	7	3	3	2
	Savings	1	1	1	1	1	1	1	1				
	Share (%)	98.5	96.8	93.6	84.4	76.9	82.5			51.1	17.6	18.1	14.2
Bulgarian private	Number	6	11	15	23	22	13	13	11	7	9	10	10
	Share (%)	1.5	3.2	6.4	15.6	22.4	15.2			6.9	9.9	10.3	11.2
Foreign	Subsidiaries				0	3	5	9	10	13	15	16	16
	Branches				2	4	4	5	7	7	8	7	6
	Share (%)				0.1	0.6	2.3		25	42	73	72	74
All banks	Number	79	81	41	41	42	30	34	34	34	35	35	34
	Assets (BL Bn)	463	582	810	1,072	1,089	3,301	8,076	7,589	8,223	9,774	11,908	14,558
Herfindahl		0.38	0.33	0.30	0.15	0.11	0.19	0.12	0.11	0.12	0.11	0.09	0.08

Note: Herfindahl is the Hirschman-Herfindahl index, calculated as the sum of the squares of each bank's share of the total assets in the banking system. The Herfindahl index ranges between 0, which represents complete dispersion, and 1, which represents a situation of monopoly.

Source: Bulgarian National Bank; Ignatiev (1997); Miller and Petranov (1996); Miller and Petranov (2001).

Table 7.6. *Foreign Bank Presence in Hungary*

Rank	Bank	Owner	Country of Origin of Owner	Assets (1) (Ft Bn)	(%)	Branches (2) (Number)	(%)
1	OTP[a]			2,393	30	430	42
2	K+H	KBC Bank	Belgium	1,196	15	163	16
3	MKB	Bayerische Landesbank	Germany	964	12	30	3
4	CIB	IntesaBCI	Italy	831	10	45	4
5	HVB	Bank Austria	Austria	579	7	38	4
6	Raiffeisen Bank	Raiffeisen Bank	Austria	554	7	43	4
7	Postabank	Erste Bank	Austria	407	5	114	11
8	Erste Bank	Erste Bank	Austria	393	5	79	8
9	Budapest Bank	GE Capital	USA	332	4	56	6
10	Citibank	Citibank	USA	322	4	19	2
TOTAL				7,971	100	1017	100

Note: a) OTP is about 30–40 percent foreign owned, but the shares are widely held. Data as of end-2003.
Source: Financial Times.

Currently, foreign banks account for about 70 percent of banking system assets (Table 7.6).

Hasan and Marton (2003) examined the Hungarian banking sector during the transition process. They found that flexible approaches to privatization and liberal policies toward foreign banks' involvement with domestic institutions helped to build a relatively stable and increasingly efficient banking system. Furthermore, foreign banks and banks with higher foreign bank ownership involvement were associated with lower inefficiency.

The Czech government was reluctant to permit strategic investors, especially foreign ones. (This is part of a long-seated distrust. In 1920, after the dissolution of the Hapsburg Empire, Czechoslovakia passed a Nostrification Law that required firms with assets in Czechoslovakia to incorporate there.) The government nominally privatized the major banks by selling just under 50 percent of each in voucher privatizations. The remaining shares remained with entities such as the National Pension Fund or the Ministry of Finance. Once the government bowed to necessity in 1998, things moved quickly. By the end of 1999 foreign institutions controlled almost 50 percent of total bank assets (Table 7.7). That percentage may

Table 7.7. *Foreign Ownership of Banks in the Czech Republic*

	Czech-Controlled				Foreign Controlled			Unlicensed Banks[a]
	State Financial Institutions	State-Owned Banks	Czech-Controlled Banks	Under Conservatorship	Banks	Branches	Total	
1990	4	1	0	0	0	0	5	x
1990	4	1	4	0	0	0	9	x
1991	4	1	15	0	4	0	24	x
1992	1	4	21	0	9	2	37	x
1993	1	4	28	1	12	6	52	x
1994	1	4	28	1	13	8	55	2
1995	1	6	25	0	13	10	55	5
1996	1	6	18	5	14	9	53	7
1997	1	6	15	4	15	9	50	11
1998	1	5	14	0	15	10	45	18
1999	1	4	10	0	17	10	42	21
2000	1	4	8	1	16	10	40	23
2001	0	3	8	1	16	10	38	25
2002	0	2	9	0	17	9	37	27

Note: a) Banks in liquidation, bankruptcy, noncommencement of operation, no longer operating because of merger, or transformed into a nonbank entity.

Source: Česká Národní Banka.

have reached more than 90 percent with the privatization of Komercni Banka (Mathieson and Roldos 2001).

More generally, government ownership of banks can bring with it certain problems. La Porta et al. (2002) found that higher government ownership of banks in 1970 was associated with slower subsequent financial development and slower growth in per capita income and productivity. They argued that their evidence supported "political" theories that government ownership of banks politicizes resource allocation and reduces inefficiency. In a wide-ranging study, Dinç (2002) found that government-owned banks increased their lending in election years. Restructured and overdue loans also increased. Despite the claim that government-owned banks fund projects private banks cannot finance, government-owned banks tended to fund the government by holding more government debt than private banks did. Both government-owned and private banks held a similar share of loans to assets on average across the electoral cycle.

As Šević (2001) points out, in small states the relationship between citizens, civil servants, and politicians is often close. There, government-owned banks are thus vulnerable to problems of cronyism, support buying, and corruption. Again, in the cases such as Jamaica, the Pacific Islands, and Tanzania, the solution has been the privatization of the government-owned bank after its restructuring.

The second reform situation involves owner-managed banks. In East Asia, family control of corporations is ubiquitous. The percentage of total market capitalization that the top 10 families control ranges from 2 percent in Japan (which is almost an order of magnitude lower than the 18 percent in Taiwan, the next lowest country) to 58 percent in Indonesia (Claessens et al. 1999). The figure for Singapore is 27 percent, almost identical to that in Korea and not much greater than the 25 percent in Malaysia. In the Philippines, the figure is 53 percent; one family, the Ayalas, alone accounts for 17 percent.

Owner-managed firms have different governance problems from those of publicly owned firms. A key strength of owner-managed firms is the absence of principal-agent problems, and there is some evidence that owner-managed firms have a better performance than publicly owned firms do (Tan et al. 2001). However, owner-managed firms possibly also have a higher variance in their performance because the owner-manager does not have to persuade others, such as a board of directors, of his strategy. No one can say no, either to good ideas or to bad ones. In addition, often the owner-managed bank is part of an economic group. In these cases one can expect that top management will overrule cautious credit

Table 7.8. *Foreign Bank Ownership in Thailand*

	1996	2001
Branches of foreign banks	14	18
Local banks w/majority foreign ownership	0	4
Number of local banks	15	12
Assets in branches or subsidiaries of foreign banks	8.5%	17.5%

Source: Thai Ministry of Finance.

officers should the officers be reluctant to lend to a related company (see Laeven 2001 for evidence of lending to insiders and related parties in Russia).

It is therefore not surprising that Laeven (1999) found that family-owned and company-owned banks were among the most risky banks, whereas foreign-owned banks took little risk relative to other banks in East Asia. Furthermore, the banks requiring restructuring after the 1997 Asian crisis were mostly family-owned or company-owned and tended to have had excessive credit growth. They were rarely foreign-owned.

When these owner-managed banks got into trouble, frequently the only potential rescuers were foreign banks as even the sounder host country banks were still weakened by the crisis. For instance, related and crony lending was clearly a problem in Mexico to the point that one could describe the situation as one of looting (La Porta et al. 2003).

In Thailand, too many of the banks had lent on the basis of crony-ism, rather than credit assessment (Wiwattanakantang et al. 2002). What facilitated the cronyism was that 12 of the 15 commercial banks were family owned. Dealing with the crisis involved the government taking over six banks. Foreign banks acquired three banks from the government. United Overseas Bank acquired Radanasin Bank, which had itself, un-der duress from the regulatory authorities, taken over the defunct Laem Thong Bank. Standard Chartered acquired Nakornthon Bank. In addi-tion, Development Bank of Singapore acquired Thai Danu Bank and ABN AMRO purchased the Bank of Asia, on a buy-now, set-the-price-later plan. The government still owns three banks, which account for about 27 percent of banking system assets and attempts to sell these to foreign banks have fallen through. As a result, although the share of foreign own-ers in banking system assets approximately doubled, relative to the situ-ation in Latin America or Central Europe, it remained small (Table 7.8). Still, even in banks where the owning families managed to retain con-trol, foreign ownership increased when the regulators forced the banks

Adrian Tschoegl

Table 7.9. *Foreign Bank Ownership in Indonesia*

	Year	State-Owned	Private	Regional Development	Foreign and Joint-Venture
Banks	1997	7	160	27	44
	2000	5	83	26	39
Branches	1997	1,748	5,133	776	90
	2000	1,734	3,777	798	71
Assets	1997	152.6	237.9	12.7	44.2
		34%	53%	3%	10%
	2000	458.7	331.9	23.2	113.9
		49%	36%	3%	12%
Deposits	1997	68.6	146	8	6.9
		30%	64%	3%	3%
	2000	237.7	228	17.6	25.2
		47%	45%	3%	5%

Source: Bank Indonesia.

to bring in additional capital. At Bangkok Bank, Bank of Ayudhya, Siam Commercial Bank, Thai Farmer's Bank foreign ownership was 25 percent in 1997; it was 48, 40, 49, and 49 percent respectively at the end of 1999 (Hewison 2001).

Finally, related and crony lending was also a problem in Indonesia. Government-owned banks accounted for 34 percent of banking system assets and 30 percent of deposits. By contrast, foreign JVs and branches accounted for 10 and 3 percent. Since the crisis, the government has permitted foreign banks to convert joint ventures to wholly owned subsidiaries, and has started to move toward permitting foreign banks to acquire domestic banks. However, impediments to foreign ownership meant that the government generally had to acquire the failed banks. Even though assets and deposits in foreign banks have grown, the number of foreign banks and branches has fallen, and the total foreign share remains small (Table 7.9).

In both the government ownership and owner-management situations, transfer of the affected banks to foreign ownership may correlate with a decline in total loans outstanding in the banking system. One reason is an artifact of the rescue itself and the other is a consequence of the change in ownership.

To make a failed bank saleable, whether it is government owned or owner-managed, the regulatory authorities typically strip it of its worst assets, often putting them into an asset recovery unit. This was the pattern, for instance, in the privatizations of Argentine provincial banks in the mid-1990s (Clarke and Cull 2002). Any comparison of the failed bank before and after the advent of foreign ownership will show a decline in the size of the loan book, but the direction of the causality is from reduction to the change in ownership, not vice versa. Also the comparison conceals the fact that the accounts, by not marking the loans to their salvage value, overstated the loans outstanding before transfer. Clarke et al. (2003) found that privatization of Argentine provincial banks was associated with a temporary reduction in credit because of cleaning of the portfolios of the banks that were being privatized. Thereafter, growth in lending by the privatized and other banks restored credit to preprivatization levels within a few years.

Still, foreign ownership will automatically bring a change in lending policy, completely apart from any effect of more stringent standards. The result will be that the new owners will reduce or even stop their lending to many of the acquired bank's traditional customers. Until the bank can develop a new customer base, something that may take time, especially when the host country economy is in recession, the size of the loan book will drop and investments in securities, such as government bonds, will increase.

There is one situation in which foreign bank entry could increase the likelihood of crisis even though the entry generates an expansion of credit. The problem occurs when the entry disrupts a cartel. One technology for protecting depositors is to reduce the probability of banks failing. Governments frequently accomplish this by permitting banks to cartelize. In their insightful paper, Breton and Wintrobe (1978) explain regulation by "moral suasion" as an exchange between the authorities and the commercial banks. The authorities provide information and other services that facilitate collusion, and deter entry. Weak banks survive and strong banks live comfortably. In return, the banks comply with the goals of the authorities, including submitting to implicit taxes such as social policies that build support for the authorities. The entry of foreign banks can undermine the exchange for at least two reasons. First, the increase in the number and variety of participants complicates the task of establishing agreement among the banks vis-à-vis the regulators. For the foreign banks, the operations in say, Trans-Amazonia, are only a small part of their total operations whereas operations there represent almost all of the activities of Trans-Amazonian banks. The foreign banks are also likely to have a different mix of activities than local banks. Foreign banks are, therefore, likely to react in different ways to the authorities' strictures than will Trans-Amazonian banks. Second, the foreign banks, if they do not wish to cooperate, can appeal for support to their home governments, making domestic policy issues matters of international trade and investment policy. The net effect on lending of the entry of the foreign banks depends on the balance between two opposing effects. On the one hand, the disruption of the cartel should lead to higher rates on deposits, lower rates on loans, and increasing lending. Levine (2002) finds that countries that restrict foreign banks from entering, even if they permit domestic entry, suffer from higher net interest margins. On the other hand, narrower margins may put some host country banks at risk. If they fail, this will, at least temporarily, disrupt banking relationships and may reduce lending. Still, Clarke et al. (2001) find some evidence that the net effect on credit is positive.

One last issue has to do with government-owned banks even when these have not failed. As Marichal (1997) points out, dominance of banking by government-owned banks, especially in Argentina, Brazil, Chile, and Mexico, dates from the 19th century. The government favored these banks with its business and with other concessions, but at the same time assigned these banks a development or policy role. Today, this may take a variety of forms, including the maintenance of bank branches in rural areas and small towns where business would not normally justify a bank branch, lending for agriculture or other favored sectors on better-than-market terms, and sometimes, simply the provision of jobs. What has made this possible is an implicit cross-subsidy scheme. These government-owned banks have implicitly taxed the urban and competitive corporate sectors while subsidizing the policy targets. The tax has taken the form of wider than otherwise necessary spreads between deposit and lending rates. In this context, there may not be significant differences in the performance of private and government-owned banks. Sarkar et al. (1998) found that in the absence of well-functioning capital markets, public and private enterprises in India's banking industry performed comparably.

The entry of foreign banks can undermine the cross-subsidy system. The foreign banks offer better deposit rates to urban middle and upper class customers, better lending rates to the same customers on credit cards and mortgages, and better lending rates to profitable corporations. This leaves the government-owned banks with the burden of the policy branches and loans, but with a reduced ability to fund them. The result then is that the government-owned banks appear less profitable and less competent relative to the foreign-owned banks. The government-owned banks may be less well-run, but this is then a mandated inefficiency.

Ultimately, the government faces the problem that if it privatizes these apparently unprofitable banks that it owns, the result will be that the new owners will close uneconomic rural branches, call in unprofitable loans, and initiate mass redundancies among bank employees. These consequences may impede the privatization process by creating opponents. As Clarke and Cull (2002) found in the case of the privatization of Argentinean provincial banks, overstaffing, high levels of provincial unemployment and higher shares of public employment all correlated with a lower likelihood of privatization.

A possible positive outcome of the whole process may be an increased transparency for the costs of the government's policies. The problem is that the benefits of the subsidies may be less quantifiable and some socially worthwhile policies such as the integration of rural areas into the modern economy may suffer. In principle, the government can initiate a system of explicit subsidies to banks, for instance, to maintain rural branches, or programs for them to act as administering agents for schemes for subsidized lending. However, such policies are easier to posit in the abstract than to establish in the face of political and practical difficulties.

3.3 Limitations

Although foreign banks can rescue ailing institutions, remove assets from direct government control, bring competition and transfer technology, they come with handicaps. One is the liability of foreignness and another is a liability of size.

The liability of foreignness simply refers to the fact that the foreign bank is operating at a distance and in an unfamiliar environment (Hymer 1960, 1976). Both of these factors are likely to degrade the quality of the decisions that the foreign bank makes, at least relative to those that host-country firms would make, because of their effect on the quality of information. This is the argument that Hymer and later Kindleberger (1969) made to explain why it is necessary for foreign firms to have an offsetting advantage if they are to survive the competition from domestic firms.

Of course, in acquiring a host country subsidiary the parent bank acquiers local managers who have local knowledge. However, it may be instructive to think about two extreme scenarios. If the parent gives the local managers no discretion, then it makes no use of their knowledge. If the foreign bank is competing with equally capable local banks the foreigner is at a disadvantage. If the parent gives the local managers complete discretion then the parent is conceding that its decisions add no value. The more capable its local managers become, the more authority the foreign parent should devolve. Ultimately, the question will arise as to the point of owning the foreign operation when shareholders could hold it directly. One can make the argument that foreign banks can bypass their need for local knowledge by using credit scoring approaches. Clarke et al. (2003) conjecture that it was foreign banks' increased use of such models that enabled them to increase their lending in provinces outside of Buenos Aires. However, in time capable local banks will come to use such models, too, again leaving the foreign banks with no offsetting edge vis-à-vis the liability of foreignness.

The liability of size refers to the argument that large banks and small banks do different things. Berger et al. (2004) argue, on the basis of theories of incomplete contracting, that small banks may be better than large banks at processing soft information. Bank lending to small firms is one area that relies heavily on soft information in developed economies, and even more so in developing economies where the infrastructure to produce hard information is, at best, nascent. They find that large banks were less willing than small banks to lend to firms that do not keep formal financial records and were more likely to have impersonal, shorter, and less exclusive relationships with borrowers. Similarly, using data from Texas, Brickley et al. (2003) found that small locally owned banks had a comparative advantage over large banks within specific environments.

By necessity, the foreign banks that participate in restructuring tend to be large. Much depends though on how much autonomy the foreign banks allow their subsidiaries to have. If the banks the foreign banks acquire act like even larger banks, it follows then that one can expect that foreign-owned banks will tend to neglect lending to small firms. If they act like autonomous entities, the effect may be muted, but then the parent's ownership is not adding value.

To address this question, Clarke et al. (2001) used bank level data for Argentina, Chile, Colombia, and Peru for the mid-1990s. They had mixed results, perhaps reflecting differing strategies of foreign banks and the varying duration of the foreign parent's presence in the host country, something that may matter if the foreign parent's first order of business is to change the credit policy at its acquisition. Berger et al. (2001), using a data set on Argentine banks, firms, and loans, found evidence suggestive of the possibility that large and foreign banks may have difficulty extending relationship loans to informationally opaque small firms. Of course, even a finding that foreign banks do not have a comparative advantage for small-scale lending does not imply that increased market share of foreign banks would reduce systemwide credit access.

If foreign banks tend to lend to informationally less opaque firms, principally foreign firms and large domestic firms, this can give rise to charges that the foreign banks "cream skim" or "cherry pick," leaving the worst risks to the domestic banks. Barajas et al. (2000) found that foreign entry in Colombia's banking sector improved bank behavior by enhancing operating efficiency and competition but may have resulted in increased risk and a subsequent deterioration in loan quality, particularly among domestic banks.

However, this is precisely the result one would hope would occur. Each class of banks lends where it has a comparative advantage. As long as the domestic banks charge appropriate risk-adjusted interest rates there is no issue.

One might then ask what about the risk to the system through deposit insurance? If foreign and domestic banks pay the same deposit insurance premium, in that case one may conjecture that domestic banks are underpaying for deposit insurance and the foreign banks are overpaying for it. Then the outcome of the combination of "cherry picking" and deposit insurance would be a transfer from foreign banks to domestic banks.

Furthermore, when foreign banks specialize in lending to good risks, they are in the long-run competing with commercial paper and bond markets, and therefore specializing in the least profitable markets, leaving the more profitable markets to the domestic banks. Lastly, the evidence for India for the 1995–1996 to 2000–2001 period is that foreign banks were aggressive in credit markets rather than "cherry picking" (Bhaumik and Piesse 2003).

4. CONCLUSIONS

What foreign banks can bring to banking systems that have undergone a crisis is two services. The most obvious service is that foreign banks can recapitalize and rehabilitate the failed banks that they acquire. In many cases, the new foreign parent also accomplishes a skill transfer, inculcating a credit culture and risk management. The more important service that foreign banks can perform is to be instruments of systemwide reform. By taking over formerly government or owner-managed banks the foreign banks can reduce the likelihood of crises. Government ownership and owner-management are subject to specific weakness that ownership by foreign banks can obviate. Experience has shown that one does not have to induce foreign banks to provide these services.

As Nikolai Bukharin (1917) wrote: "It is finance capital that appears to be the all-pervading form of capital, that form which, like nature, suffers from a *horror vacui*, since it rushes to fill every 'vacuum,' whether in a 'tropical,' 'sub-tropical,' or 'polar' region, if only profits flow in sufficient quantities."

Bukharin correctly identified that some foreign banks will react to opportunities. However, he elided over a precondition and failed to identify a consequence. The precondition is that foreign banks require that conditions be propitious. This means that foreign banks will take over cleaned-up banks, but there are few signs that the foreigners themselves are willing to assume the burdens of writing off loans. It also means that foreign banks are more likely to enter after reforms that facilitate their operations.

The consequence that Bukharin missed is that the foreign banks' initial entry is only a phase in a succession process. Some part of the entry is normal international banking activity that will persist indefinitely, but never be of much quantitative importance. A second part is a betting on the success of the transition or restructuring process. As their bets succeed or fail, the bettors will sell their shares, either for a gain or a loss. The third part, and the one that draws the most concern in many countries around the world, is the majority ownership of large commercial banks by foreign strategic investors, that is, investors that manage the banks and who entered either in an exploratory foray that led them further or who entered to restructure a major host country bank.

However, to the degree that the strategic investors are successful, any predominance in host economies is likely to erode over time. As the banks, foreign- and domestic-owned alike, become more competitive and adept, the foreign owners will no longer have a comparative advantage in general retail and commercial banking, even if they retain an absolute advantage. Thus, in time, we can expect many foreign owners, if not all, to sell their retail banking activities to domestic owners. They may retain a branch in the national financial center to conduct corporate and wholesale banking but will leave retail and general commercial banking to local banks. More important, the reforms that accompanied the entry of the foreign banks will free the domestic banks to compete and grow, increasing their relative importance. This succession process will take decades at best, but it is ongoing.

ACKNOWLEDGMENTS

I would like to thank Gerard Caprio, Patrick Honohan, and Luc Laeven, as well as Charles Calomiris, Linda Goldberg, Maria Soledad Martinez Peria, Eric Rosengren, and other participants at the World Bank conference on "Systemic Financial Distress: Containment and Resolution" for helpful comments on an earlier draft, and Guillermo Noguera for research assistance.

EIGHT

Maximizing the Value of Distressed Assets

Bankruptcy Law and the Efficient Reorganization of Firms

David Smith and Per Strömberg

INTRODUCTION

Earlier chapters have stressed the importance during the resolution of a systemic financial crisis of preserving asset value and helping ensure a quick recovery of economic activity. Key to achieving these goals is the presence of an effective bankruptcy system. But which type of system is likely to be most effective? Many observers have noted the historical differences between U.S. corporate bankruptcy procedures and those in other countries. The U.S. law has been described as "debtor-friendly," oriented toward reorganizing the existing company (i.e., giving the debtor a second chance), and accustomed to deviating from contractual payoff priorities. The traditional bankruptcy procedures in many other developed countries including the United Kingdom, Germany, Japan, and Sweden are described, in contrast, as "creditor-friendly," favoring the liquidation of the debtor's assets to pay off creditors in the order of their priority. A relatively large literature has arisen debating the relative merits of each system.[1]

Perhaps with an eye to the perceived success of the U.S. system, many countries have recently begun to institute more debtor-friendly, U.S.-styled reorganization codes into their bankruptcy laws.[2] Indeed, the World Bank, International Monetary Fund (IMF), and the European Union

---

[1] Early contributions include Roe (1983), Baird (1986), Jackson (1986), Jensen (1989), and Aghion, Hart, and Moore (1992). More recently, see Strömberg (2000), Armour, Cheffins, and Skeel (2002), and Baird and Rasmussen (2002).

[2] In fact, each of the four European countries cited earlier have refurbished or added new reorganization codes within the last seven years (see Table 8.1).

(EU) now encourage member countries to adopt bankruptcy laws that have a reorganization code as one of their cornerstones.[3] Thus, from a public policy standpoint, U.S.-styled bankruptcy procedures appear to be quickly gaining the upper ground as the preferred mechanism for dealing with distressed companies.

Yet anecdotal evidence suggests that very few of these recent reorganization codes adopted by countries have been successful. For example, of all firms going bankrupt in Sweden over the 2000 to 2002 period, only 0.7 percent of the firms emerged under their new company reorganization code (*Företags-rekonstruktion*). Likewise, only 0.4 percent of bankrupt German firms filed for protection under the reorganization section of the new German Insolvency Act (*Insolvenzordnung*).

The goal of this chapter is to shed some light on these issues by suggesting a conceptual framework for thinking about bankruptcy law. As a starting point, we argue that the main role of corporate bankruptcy is to mitigate bargaining frictions in financial distress. We identify five roles for bankruptcy law in improving ex post bargaining efficiency: (1) verify assets and liabilities, (2) improve coordination among claimholders, (3) protect third-party claimants, (4) maintain asset value during bargaining, and (5) alleviate the impact of liquidity constraints among claimants and potential acquirers. In improving ex post efficiency, however, bankruptcy law also will affect the bargaining power of the claimants, which may have unintended consequences on ex ante efficiency.

We apply this framework to a comparison of the bankruptcy systems in six different countries: France, Germany, Japan, Sweden, the United Kingdom, and the United States. Virtually every bankruptcy system around the world can be described as a variant of one of these six systems; thus, our results are likely to be applicable generally. We find that, with the exception of the protection of third-party claimants, the U.S. Chapter 11 system seems to go the farthest in addressing ex post bargaining frictions. Although all the other countries have reorganization chapters of their own, which are similar to – and often modeled after – Chapter 11, the non-U.S. chapters lack important key features.

These weaknesses, in turn, appear to have discouraged the use of reorganization codes in these countries. We argue that when firms do reorganize in these countries, they do so under traditional "liquidation" (or cash auction) chapters. At the same time, the U.S. Chapter 11 bankruptcy

---

[3] For example, see World Bank Working Group on Rehabilitation (1999), and European Commission (2003).

procedures of today are geared toward the auctioning off of assets when it pays to do so. Hence, debtor-oriented reorganizations, sales of the assets as a going concern, or piecemeal liquidations can be obtained under either type of code. In fact, going-concern survival rates in countries dominated by a reorganization code can look very similar to the survival rates in countries that mostly use a liquidation code. The disadvantage from reorganizing under the liquidation code, however, is that these codes typically lack provisions for maintaining asset value and alleviating liquidity constraints during bankruptcy, potentially leading to a forced bankruptcy resolution and inefficient allocation of assets.

We then address the complicated issue of ex ante efficiency. Theoretically, an ex post inefficient bankruptcy code need not necessarily be inefficient ex ante. For example, a costly bankruptcy code may provide efficient incentives for firms to avoid financial distress in the first place. We argue that ex ante efficiency can be best understood by looking at the resolution of financial distress in a setting where private bargaining works well, such as venture capital (VC) financings. VC financings involve a small number of informed, sophisticated, and value-maximizing investors, and are therefore able to avoid many of the bargaining frictions that bankruptcy law are aimed at mitigating. Venture capitalist (VC) financial contracts share many of the characteristics of a typical debt contract. Yet VC contracts typically manage to opt out of bankruptcy law, relying instead on provisions in the ex ante contract to resolve financial distress. Although there are limitations to the VC financing analogy, the VC contract provisions offer guidance on the features that an optimal bankruptcy mechanism should incorporate.

We report preliminary evidence suggesting that venture capital reorganizations share many key features with reorganizations in U.S. Chapter 11, such as debtor-in-possession financing and deviations from absolute priority. One notable difference is that less power is given to equity-holders and other junior claimants in VC financings. However, because recent evidence suggests that the real impact of the equity-holder bias in Chapter 11 is small, we argue that it is unlikely that the U.S. system has significant ex ante inefficiencies. Moreover, the similarities between Chapter 11 and private contracting outcomes are hardly a coincidence, given that Chapter 11 evolved from the "equity receiverships" that were created during the 19th century as a market response to U.S. railroad failures.

We conclude by discussing some lessons and limitations of our results for designing bankruptcy law in developing countries. Our analysis suggests that a bankruptcy procedure should be oriented toward ensuring that asset values do not deteriorate during bargaining and to maximizing the liquidity of the auction process. We argue that these elements are equally applicable to developed and developing countries, and are suitable during times in which a country faces systemic financial distress.

The rest of the chapter proceeds as follows. Section 1 discusses the role of bankruptcy in a world of incomplete contracts. Section 2 applies this framework to an international comparison of bankruptcy laws. Section 3 addresses ex ante efficiency and argues that VC contracting can provide useful lessons about the construction of bankruptcy procedures. In Section 4, we draw policy implications from this characterization, and offer advice on how emerging market countries might best focus their energies on constructing bankruptcy systems.

1. THE ROLE OF BANKRUPTCY IN A WORLD OF INCOMPLETE CONTRACTING

1.1 Financial Distress and Incomplete Contracts

Financial distress occurs when a firm is not able to meet its debt obligations, or foresees that it will not be able to do so in the near future. If financial distress persists and leads to the firm defaulting on its obligations, a debt contract gives the lender certain control rights, such as seizing collateral, suing for repayment, or forcing the firm into bankruptcy. These rights need not necessarily be exercised, however, but serve as a starting point for a renegotiation between creditors and the owners of the firm (and possibly also including other stakeholders such as employees). Financial distress can be resolved outside of bankruptcy, through a private renegotiation between stakeholders. Only if one or more of the stakeholders exercise the right to put the firm in bankruptcy will distress be resolved under the rules dictated by bankruptcy law.

Thanks to modern financial contracting theory, economists now have a good understanding of the economic role of financial distress (see Hart 2001). A key to understanding financial distress and bankruptcy law is the insight that any financial contracts are by nature incomplete. In a world of complete, frictionless contracting, there is no need for financial distress and bankruptcy. Instead, when an entrepreneur or owner-manager seeks financing from investors, a complete contract will be written. This contract will specify, for all possible future states of the world, how the cash flows of the project will be split, in which instances the firm should be sold or liquidated, and more generally, what actions need to be taken in controlling the firm. Because the state-contingent contract specifies when the firm should be liquidated or sold, and how much investors will be paid back and in what order, the contract already encompasses a perfect mechanism to deal with "financial distress." Ex ante contracting will ensure that an economically optimal outcome will be achieved, and the only role for the legal system is to enforce the written contracts.

Obviously, such complete contracts are impossible to write and enforce in reality. Many relevant states of the world are impossible to foresee in advance. The possible state-space is too rich to be formulated in a written contract of finite length. Over the last 15 years, theorists have thought extensively about what optimal financial contracts might look like when contracts are incomplete (see Hart [1995, 2001] for overviews).

A key feature of the optimal incomplete contract is to allocate control rights between managers and investors in an efficient manner. Control rights are important because they determine which party has the right to decide on the actions of the firm, such as whether operations should be continued or shut down, or whether management should be replaced. One of the robust findings from the incomplete contracting literature is that the optimal contract often will call for control staying with the manager in the good states of the world, while in the bad state control rights will be transferred to investors (see Aghion and Bolton 1992; Dewatripont and Tirole 1994; and Hart and Moore 1998). In other words, this literature can explain why the optimal contract looks like a debt contract, where control of the firm's assets is transferred to creditors if the firm fails to meet its contracted payments. Such control transfer mechanisms are not only seen in debt contracts, however, but also in the preferred equity contracts used in venture capital financings (Kaplan and Strömberg 2003).

A second feature of these types of models is that the outcome of financial distress cannot be specified in contracts ex ante, but will be a result of renegotiation between the manager of the firm and its claimholders. The possible outcomes that can be attained are thus limited to the ones that are consistent with renegotiation. The incomplete contracting literature thus provides a meaningful framework to think about financial distress, namely, as the renegotiation between claimholders and managers (or the firm's original owners) that occurs once control has been transferred to the claimholders.

1.2 The Role of Bankruptcy in Improving on Free Contracting

The goal for an optimal financial distress resolution mechanism, and an optimal contract design more generally, is to get as close as possible to a socially efficient outcome. There are two separate, but related, notions of efficiency. *Ex post efficiency* refers to ensuring that the assets of a distressed firm are optimally allocated to their highest-valued use. An ex post efficient resolution of financial distress is one that ensures a value-maximizing decision with respect to whether a company should be reorganized, sold, or liquidated. *Ex ante efficiency*, by contrast, goes back to the point at which the firm was first started or financed. An ex ante efficient contract or mechanism is one that ensures that as many socially valuable projects as possible (and as few wasteful ones) get funded.

From an optimal contracting framework, it is not obvious why bankruptcy law is needed in the first place. For example, in the simple incomplete contracting settings of Aghion and Bolton (1992) and Hart and Moore (1998), there is no obvious place for bankruptcy law. In order to play an economic role, bankruptcy law has to improve on the outcome that would obtain by simply letting investors and entrepreneurs contract freely. As these chapters show, even in an incomplete contracting world, a carefully designed contract, in combination with efficient renegotiation in the case of subsequent contracting disputes, will go a long way toward achieving an ex ante optimal outcome. When evaluating bankruptcy law, we therefore need to identify the ways in which it makes contracting and renegotiation more efficient. Moreover, we need to identify the effects bankruptcy law will have both on ex post and on ex ante efficiency.

The policy discussion around bankruptcy law is typically preoccupied with ex post efficiency, and sees the aim of bankruptcy law to make sure that viable firms are not inefficiently liquidated. Theoretically, the Coase theorem shows that as long as property rights are well defined and there are no frictions to bargaining, private negotiations between the parties will ensure an ex post efficient outcome. For example, take a situation in which control has been transferred to creditors following a default, and the creditors have an incentive to liquidate the assets even though the firm is worth more as a going concern. In this case, the shareholders should be able to persuade the creditors to refrain from liquidation by offering them a side payment (or a fraction of the reorganized firm) equal to whatever the creditors would get in the liquidation, plus part of the going concern surplus. Similarly, in the case in which the debtor is still in

David Smith and Per Strömberg

control of the firm, and has an incentive to inefficiently continue a firm that should really be liquidated, the creditors should be able to make the managers shut down the operations by offering a large enough monetary incentive.[4]

In a less ideal world, however, bargaining may not be frictionless. Bankruptcy law can therefore improve on ex post efficiency by facilitating bargaining in a world with frictions. We will identify a number of bankruptcy mechanisms that could potentially achieve this purpose later.

Bankruptcy law also could have important implications for ex ante efficiency. Although often ignored in the policy debate, such implications are very important economically, as they affect the ability to set up and finance firms in the first place. Too much emphasis on improving ex post efficiency may even be harmful, since ex ante and ex post efficiency sometimes can conflict with each other. Although ex post efficiency is about maximizing the value of assets in financial distress, it is not affected by the way this value is split between claimants. This split of value between claimants, however, is central for the incentives of these claimants from the time the contracts are written, and can have important effects on ex ante efficiency. For example, one could argue that by writing down creditors' claims in favor of shareholders, bankruptcy increases ex post efficiency to the extent it allows viable firms to be reorganized.[5] But debt write-downs could make credit more expensive ex ante when the firm tries to obtain financing, leading to credit constraints and positive net present value projects not getting financed.[6]

It even may be optimal to sacrifice some of the ex post value in order to improve ex ante incentives. A general result in contract theory is that the ability to precommit to an ex post inefficient outcome will be at least weakly better for ex ante contracts. For example, in order to incentivize entrepreneurs to avoid financial distress, it may be beneficial to make financial distress costly for entrepreneurs by liquidating some viable firms in bankruptcy.

To summarize, in order to understand the effect of bankruptcy law on efficiency, we need to identify what the frictions are that prevent efficient

---

[4] In a similar fashion, Haugen and Senbet (1978) argue that bankruptcy costs cannot be important for capital structure choice if parties can negotiate out of court.

[5] Although, as we will emphasize later, we believe this view of reorganizations is rather too simplistic.

[6] Alternatively, Berkovitch, Israel, and Zender (1997) have argued that deviating from absolute priority in favor of managers (who are the sole equity holders in their model) is good for ex ante efficiency, because it encourages investment in firm-specific human capital.

bargaining from taking place, and to what extent the bargaining outcome can be distorted in order to improve ex ante incentives.

The Verification Role of Bankruptcy

One important impediment to bargaining is asymmetric and incomplete information (Ausubel, Cramton, and Deneckere 2002). If one of the parties is uninformed about the true value of the assets and the informed party cannot credibly convey this information, the bargaining outcome may be inefficient. Even worse, it may not be clear to the parties exactly what claims are outstanding on the firm.

Bankruptcy laws can play an important *verification role* by examining what assets belong to the bankruptcy estate and what claims are outstanding, thus reducing some of the informational asymmetries between the bargaining parties. In the costly state-verification models of Townsend (1979), Gale and Hellwig (1985), and others, bankruptcy is basically a policy for auditing the firm to figure out the value of its assets. Since auditing is costly, the optimal mechanism will try to economize on auditing as much as possible. As a result, such auditing happens when the firm fails to make its contracted payments, that is, bankruptcy only occurs in connection with a default. As we will show, most bankruptcy codes involve some aspects of auditing and verification of assets and liabilities.

The Role of Bankruptcy in Reducing Coordination Problems

Bargaining also will become more complex when there are more than two parties involved in negotiations, and *coordination problems* between claimants can impede an efficient outcome. Legal scholars, such as Jackson (1986), have argued that the main rationale for bankruptcy is to mitigate creditor coordination problems. A typical firm will have claims outstanding to several creditors, each of whom may have their claim secured by specific collateral. In the absence of bankruptcy law, such a situation may lead to a creditor "run" on the distressed firm to be the first to seize available collateral, analogous to the bank-run behavior in Diamond and Dybvig (1983). It may be rational for any one creditor to try to seize available collateral early, thereby forcing a piecemeal liquidation, even though collectively creditors would have received a higher payoff had the company been preserved as a going concern.[7] Bankruptcy law can play

---

[7] See Von Thadden, Berglöf, and Roland (2003) for a theoretical model of creditor runs as a rationale for bankruptcy law. Their model also shows why the firm will choose to borrow from several creditors, despite the possibility for runs and coordination inefficiencies.

a role in to preventing such runs, for example, by imposing an automatic stay on the firm's assets once it has entered bankruptcy.

Another coordination problem that has been identified in the academic literature is the hold out problem. Take a situation in which the firm needs to write down the amount of debt in order to be reorganized but the debt is owed to a large number of individually small, dispersed, creditors. A typical example could be a firm with public debt outstanding to numerous different bondholders, or trade credit owed to a large number of small suppliers. Rather than forgiving some of its claim, each small creditor has an incentive to hold out in the hope that the other creditors write down their claim instead. This can lead to a Nash equilibrium in which no one forgives its debt. As Gertner and Scharfstein (1991) show, bankruptcy law can reduce hold-out problems in several ways, for example, through voting rules which do not require unanimity in order to approve a reorganization plan, or by giving the bankruptcy judge the ability to "cram down" a reorganization proposal on unwilling creditors.

The Role of Bankruptcy for Protecting Third-Party Stakeholders
Related to coordination failures is the problem of third-party, "involuntary" claimholders. A firm typically will have many stakeholders that do not hold explicit financial claims on the firm, such as current employees who depend on the firm for their salary, previous employees who may depend on the firm for their pensions, tax authorities who may have unpaid taxes owed to them, and society at large, which may be affected by the firm's actions through effects on the environment. A negative externality can be created by the fact that these nonfinancial stakeholders are not present at the bargaining table with the debtor and creditors. Bankruptcy policy makers, particularly in Europe, have identified protection of third-party stakeholders as an important task of bankruptcy law.[8] Bankruptcy law can include provisions to mitigate these externalities in different ways, for example, by assigning a court-appointed official to participate in the bargaining, by representing the rights of third parties, or through government guarantees of employee and pension claims.

The Role of Bankruptcy for Maintaining Asset Value during Bargaining
Another set of important bargaining frictions are the transaction costs associated with negotiations. Negotiations can take considerable time, and

[8] This is evident from the recent European Commission (2003) report on bankruptcy reform, "Bankruptcy and a Fresh Start: Stigma on Failure and Legal Consequences of Bankruptcy" (http://europa.eu.int/comm/enterprise/entrepreneurship/support_measures/failure_bankruptcy/index.htm)

many of the costs linked to negotiation increase with time, such as lawyers' fees, administrative expenses, and the opportunity costs of time and organizational resources that the parties could have put to an alternative use. Such costs often are referred to in the literature as *direct bankruptcy costs*.

More important than these direct costs are *indirect bankruptcy costs*, defined to be the losses that occur from running the operations when the firm is financially distressed. One reason that preserving asset value in financial distress is difficult is the unwillingness of investors to provide new financing to a firm with a large debt overhang, as first demonstrated by Myers (1977). The resulting liquidity constraints will lead to underinvestment in new projects and assets (Myers 1977); difficulties in preserving relationships with employees, suppliers, and customers (Titman 1984); and an inability to respond strategically to the actions of competitors (Bolton and Scharfstein 1996). Also, to the extent that control of important firm decisions are transferred from managers to creditors who do not have the same expertise in running the firm (or whose interference diverts management's attention), operations will be run inefficiently and value will be lost. By contrast, leaving too much control to incumbent management in financial distress may lead to the firm to "gamble for resurrection" by taking suboptimally risky actions or by continuing operations too long (Jensen and Meckling 1976).

Bankruptcy rules can potentially affect the size of both direct and indirect costs of financial distress. Direct costs can be lowered by forcing the parties to come to an agreement within a limited period of time. Bankruptcy law can reduce indirect costs from liquidity constraints by facilitating the ability of firms to raise new financing. Also, bankruptcy law can give the managers more or less discretion to run the firm without interference from creditors or courts.

The Effects of Liquidity Constraints on Bargaining
One reason why frictionless bargaining will result in ex post efficiency is that the parties can use side payments to induce the party in control to take the efficient action. For this reason, bargaining will not necessarily work efficiently if shareholders, creditors, or other interested parties face liquidity constraints.[9] To the extent that bankruptcy law can alleviate the negative effects of these constraints, ex post efficiency can be enhanced.

---

[9] For example, the driving force behind Aghion and Bolton's (1992) result of state-contingent control being optimal relies on the fact the entrepreneur is more liquidity constrained than the investor. To get ex post efficiency, you want to leave as much control as possible to the entrepreneur, as the investor can bribe the entrepreneur into taking the efficient action but not the other way around.

Shleifer and Vishny (1992) use a liquidity argument to propose that reorganizations can be superior to auctions for reorganizing distressed firms. In their model, financial distress is correlated between firms, because the distress is the result of an industry downturn or a macro shock. As a result, when a firm is in financial distress, the potential bidders for the firm's assets are likely to face financial difficulties themselves. As a result, auctioning off the assets in distress is not likely to realize a very high value, and assets may not end up going to the highest value user.

The bankruptcy code can alleviate liquidity problems in a couple of ways. First, a firm operating under bankruptcy protection for some time could be allowed to postpone asset sales until liquidity in the market has improved. Second, by permitting bidders for the firm's assets to offer financial claims rather than cash, and by making it easier for a bankrupt firm to issue public securities (e.g., with less stringent registration requirements), liquidity constraints can possibly be relaxed.[10]

2. A COMPARISON OF INTERNATIONAL BANKRUPTCY LAWS

Now that we have described the different roles that bankruptcy law can play in affecting the ex post efficiency of financial distress resolution, we turn to examining how these roles differ across the bankruptcy systems of the United States, the United Kingdom, Japan, Germany, France, and Sweden. We are not the first to perform a comparative analysis of bankruptcy mechanisms. Apart from an extensive literature on the U.S. Chapter 11, previous comparative analyses of bankruptcy law include White (1996), Rajan and Zingales (1995), Ravid and Sundgren (1998), Biais and Malecot (1996), Franks and Nyborg (1996), Franks, Nyborg, and Torous (1996), Kaiser (1996), Berkovitch and Israel (1999), Armour, Cheffins, and Skeel (2002), and Claessens and Klapper (2002). Our goal is not to provide an exhaustive review of each country's bankruptcy system. Rather, we aim to highlight those features, described earlier, that influence the cost of bargaining in financial distress.

2.1 Reorganization versus Liquidation Codes

In earlier literature, cross-country comparisons of bankruptcy law have typically focused on the difference between reorganization-oriented and

---

[10] The bankruptcy reform proposal of Aghion, Hart, and Moore (1992) emphasizes the need to allow noncash bids in bankruptcy auctions. Also, see Hart (1995) for an overview of these arguments.

liquidation-oriented bankruptcy codes. Reorganization codes are built around the idea of giving the distressed firm a second chance. That is, the procedure is oriented toward restructuring creditor claims to provide some relief to the debtor, formalized in a reorganization plan, and allowing the existing company to continue to operations. Because the reorganization may take some time, the court may stay creditor attempts to collect on their debts and approve additional financing for the operations. Liquidation codes are geared toward auctioning off the assets of the distressed firm – either together as a going concern or piecemeal – to a new set of owners and dispersing the proceeds from the sale to creditors in accordance their payoff priority. Chapters 11 and 7 of the U.S. Bankruptcy Code are examples of reorganization and liquidation procedures, respectively.

2.2 A Taxonomy of Bankruptcy Laws

We now turn to the cross-country comparison, summarized in Table 8.1. The bankruptcy laws in our six countries are together broadly representative of bankruptcy codes in virtually all countries around the world. Indeed, bankruptcy codes in most countries are copied from French, German, Scandinavian, U.K., or U.S. bankruptcy law, or from some combination of these laws.[11]

Table 8.1 creates a taxonomy of the different bankruptcy laws based on the roles of bankruptcy outlined in Section 1. As seen from the table, all six of the countries have codes that include both liquidation and reorganization chapters. Three of the six countries have undergone major bankruptcy reform in recent years, and there have been recent discussions in France of further reform.

Verification Mechanisms

All bankruptcy laws have some rules regarding information disclosure and collection. Most codes require the debtor to submit information to the court at the time of filing, including lists of estate assets and claims, and sometimes financial statements. Some codes, such as Sweden's liquidation chapter, also require the trustee to collect data on the bankruptcy estate, including a preliminary valuation of its assets. Beyond the initial disclosure of financial information, U.S. law also subjects the debtor to examination by the committee of creditors, including the appointment of

---

[11] We thank Simeon Djankov for pointing this out.

Table 8.1. *Taxonomy of Corporate Bankruptcy Codes*

	United States	United Kingdom	Japan	Germany	France	Sweden
Liquidation code:	Chapter 7	Member's voluntary Creditor's voluntary Compulsory Receivership Administrative receivership	Hasan (Bankruptcy) Tokubetsu-seisan (Special liquidation)	New Insolvenzordnung (Insolvency Act: Reorganization or asset sale) Old Konkursordnung (Bankruptcy Act)	Reglements Amiable (Reorganization for companies not yet in default) Redressements Judiciares (Reorganization and Judicial Liquidation)	Konkurs (Bankruptcy)
Reorganization code:	Chapter 11	Company Voluntary Arrangement Sec. 425 Scheme of arrangement Administration	Kaisha-kousei (Company reorganization) Kaisha-seiri (Company arrangement) Minji-saisei (Civil rehabilitation)	New Insolvenzordnung (Insolvency Act: Liquidation) Old Vergleichsordnung (Composition Act)	Redressements Judiciares (Reorganization and Judicial Liquidation)	Företags-rekonstruktion (Company re-organization) Ackord (Composition)
Year of last major change	1978	2000	2000	1999	1985	1996

Verification:					
On filing, debtor furnishes schedule of assets and liabilities, a list of all creditors, and statement of financial affairs. Debtor must submit to examination by creditors. Creditors have right to appoint a special examiner. All court filings are public record.	Company Voluntary Arrangement: If debtor initiates, must supply statement of financial affairs, incl. information on assets and liabilities. Administration: Debtor responsible for submitting information on assets, liabilities, identity of creditors and other claimholders, and identity of employees to administrator.	Debtor furnishes balance sheet. On commencement, court gives public notice. Creditors have fixed period to submit claims. Can adjudicate in court.	Post-1999: Trustee prepares "table of claims" and list of estate assets.	Reglement Amiables: Debtor presents financial statements, table of claimants and summary of liens, proposed corrective measures and proposed new payment schedule. Redressements Judiciaries: The above plus observation of firm by court for up to 18 months.	Bankruptcy: Trustee does inventory of assets (including valuations) and liabilities at the beginning of procedure. Reorganization: Administrator does inventory in connection with reorganization plan.

(continued)

Table 8.1 (*continued*)

	United States	United Kingdom	Japan	Germany	France	Sweden
Coordinating mechanisms:						
Automatic stay in reorganization?	Yes.	Yes, for administration. Subject to application for voluntary arrangements No, for 425 schemes.	Not automatic and subject to many exceptions.	Post 1999: <u>Unsecured</u>: Yes. <u>Secured</u>: Requires an injunction. Pre-1999: <u>Unsecured</u>: No. Requires injunction <u>Secured</u>: No.	<u>Reglement Amiables</u>: No. <u>Redressements Judiciares</u>: Court sets a date for cessation of payments, which can be 18 months in advance of procedure commencement.	Yes.
Automatic stay in liquidation?	Yes.	Yes, for compulsory liquidation. No, for voluntary liquidation, and (administrative) receivership.	Not automatic, does not covered secured creditors.	<u>Unsecured</u>: Yes. <u>Secured</u>: Requires an injunction.	?	Yes.

Voting rules in reorganization?	Only impaired classes vote. 50 percent in number, ⅔ in value of each impaired class.	425 Scheme: >75 percent of creditors within each class. Administration: >50 percent of unsecured creditors. Secured creditors do not participate.	Unsecured: Must be consented by ⅔ of aggregate unsecured amount. Secured: at least ¾ of secured creditors (corporate re-organization)	Post-1999: Impaired classes vote, 50 percent in number and value in each class must approve. Pre-1999: 75 percent of value of 50 percent of all creditors present at meeting.	Reglement Amiables: Agreement among principal creditors. Redressements Judiciares: No voting by creditors. Judge makes decision.	Unsecured: ⅜ approval if >50 percent recovery, ¾ approval if >25 percent recovery, unanimity if <25 percent recovery. Secured: unanimity.
Cram-down in reorganization?	Yes.	No. If no consensus, case moves to liquidation.	No. If no consensus, court dismisses case or liquidates.	Post-1999: Court must ratify decision of creditors. Pre-1999: Yes, on creditor dissents and absent creditors.	Reglement Amiables: Yes. Redressements Judiciares: Final reorganization plan entirely at discretion of judge.	?
Creditor committees?	Unsecured creditors, typically composed of reps seven largest unsecured creditors.	Consists of creditors present as preplanned meetings.	Consists of creditors with claims >20 percent of total debt.	Post-1999: Creditor's "assembly" votes at outset to reorganize, sell assets, or liquidate.	Reglement Amiables: Officer of court appointed to represent creditors. Redressements Judiciares: No.	Yes.

(continued)

Table 8.1 (continued)

	United States	United Kingdom	Japan	Germany	France	Sweden
Flexibility in defining voting classes in reorganization?	Yes.	No.	No.	?	No.	No.
Maintaining asset value:						
Possession of assets in liquidation?	Trustee.	Trustee/receiver.	Trustee.	Liquidator.	Liquidators.	Trustee.
Possession of assets in reorganization?	Debtor generally. Trustee appointed in extraordinary circumstances.	Administrator	Debtor or Trustee, but debtor monitored by court-order supervisor.	Post-1999: Trustee. Although debtor can apply for self-management. Pre-1999: Trustee.	Reglement Amiables: Debtor. Redressements Judiciares: Debtor and receiver.	Administrator.
Seniority of new financing in reorganization?	Generally senior to unsecured. Under special circumstances senior to secured.	Not generally. However, administrator can borrow and be repaid ahead of floating charge holder.	No. Any new financing can be blocked with an injunction.	No. Company will be shut down if cash is insufficient keep operations going.	Redressements Judiciares: Yes, for creditors entering during judicial arrangement period.	Senior to unsecured.
Time limits to reorganization?	No.	?	?	?	?	3 months; can be extended to 12 months.

	Col 1	Col 2	Col 3	Col 4	Col 5	Col 6
Time limits to liquidation?	No.	No.	No.	?	?	12 months.
Protection of third-party claimants:						
Wage guarantee?	No.	No.	No.	Yes.	?	Yes in liquidation. No in reorganization.
Procedure should aim toward preserving employment?	No.	No.	?	Yes. Employees can only be fired by trustee in reorganization or asset sale.	Yes.	Yes in liquidation and reorganization.
Priority of wages?	Junior to many unsecured wages.	Preferentials paid prior to unsecured.	Senior to unsecured.	?	?	Senior to unsecured.
Limits to renegotiation:						
Limits on debt write-downs in reorganization?	Have to offer liquidation payoff.	No.	Civil Rehabilitation: Have to offer secured 100 percent recovery.	Post-1999: No. Pre-1999: Must pay 35 percent of claims within 1 year, 40 percent or more after that.	Redressements Judiciares: Cannot write down secured debt. Cannot force writedown of unsecured debt.	Have to offer unsecured >25 percent recovery. Have to offer secured 100 percent recovery.

(continued)

Table 8.1 (continued)

	United States	United Kingdom	Japan	Germany	France	Sweden
Limits on asset transfers?	No.	No.	?	Most likely unable to transfer assets to previous management.	No.	?
First-mover advantages in bargaining: Debtor has advantage in filing?	Yes.	No. Receivership filing by creditor overrules other filings.	Yes.	Post-1999: No. Creditors decide whether company can enter reorganization. Pre-1999: Yes, subject to court approval.	Reglement Amiables: Yes. Legally required to seek help when nearing default. Redressements Judiciaires: No. Court decides whether to pursue reorganization or liquidity (although company legally required to file at default).	Yes. Debtor applications approved automatically.

Who submits reorganization plan?	Debtor has exclusivity for at least 120 days.	Administrator.	Debtor or trustee. No exclusivity guarantee.	Post-1999: Debtor or trustee. No exclusivity guarantee. Pre-1999: Debtor.	Reglement Amiables: Debtor. Redressements Judiciares: Receiver.	Administrator.

Disposal of assets:

Sales mechanism?	Governed by Section 363 of Code. Allows for sales in both Chapter 11 and Chapter 7.	Trustee discretion subject to rules of court. Available only under liquidation code.	Trustee discretion. Available only under liquidation code.	Trustee discretion. Available only under liquidation code.	Trustee discretion. Available only under liquidation code.	Trustee discretion. Sale to management has to be preceded by public solicitation of bids. Available only under liquidation code.
Auctioneer/ trustee incentive compatible?	Yes.	Yes.	?	?	?	No.

Source: Kaiser (1996); Franks, Nyborg, and Torous (1996); European Commission (2003) (http://europa.eu.int/comm/enterprise/entrepreneurship/support_measures/failure_bankruptcy/bankruptcy.htm); Title 11 U.S. Bankruptcy Code (http://www4.law.cornell.edu/uscode/11/index.html); The U.K. Insolvency Act of 1986 (http://www.insolvency.co.uk/legal/ia1986.htm); and the World Bank Global Insolvency Law Database (http://wbln0018.worldbank.org/legal/gild/entry.nsf/entry?readform).

a special examiner, if warranted, to examine the financial status of the debtor. Moreover, all court filings, including financial information of the debtor and specific detail on the identity of claimholders, are part of the public record and therefore open to inspection by anybody wishing to obtain information on the debtor, creditors, or the progress of bankruptcy case.

Mechanisms for Reducing Coordination Problems
Bankruptcy law can address coordination problems in different ways. First, as many scholars have emphasized, the imposition of an automatic stay, in which a debtor is protected from creditor collection actions, is considered to play an important role in preventing collateral runs. Despite this, the degree of automatic stay differs significantly across countries. For example, Japan has particularly weak rules on stays, with little protection against secured creditors seizing their collateral. Without an automatic stay, secured creditors can effectively kill off any attempt to reorganize or sell the firm as a going concern by seizing collateral.

Second, voting rules are crucial to implementing reorganization plans when a minority of creditors might strategically oppose a plan. The U.S. Chapter 11 code has a particularly clever system to prevent holdouts. First, only "impaired" classes – defined to be those claimants that would receive some payoff less than their face value but greater than zero in liquidation – get to vote. Those classes that would receive nothing or be fully paid back in the plan, are precluded from voting, and thus strategically holding out. But creditors have to be offered a plan that at least covers their estimated payoff in case of liquidation. This is important, because it prevents the backers of the plan from simply overruling some classes of creditors by offering them a zero payout and locking them out from the voting. Second, only a majority of creditors in each class (two thirds in terms of value) have to approve the plan, rather than all of them. Third, the law gives some freedom in defining classes, so that creditors that are particularly important (or have particularly high bargaining power) can be offered a better deal. Finally, the bankruptcy judge has the power to cram down a reorganization plan on a dissenting class, at least as long as this class is deemed to do better under the plan that in a liquidation.

None of the other five systems offers the same ability to prevent hold-out problems in reorganizations to the extent of the U.S. system. Under the French code, debt write-downs require unanimous approval among creditors, although the judge can unilaterally impose a rescheduling of debt payments and extend maturity without creditor approval. In Sweden and Japan, secured debt cannot be written down without unanimous approval from secured creditors. Moreover, in Sweden, unanimous consent is required from unsecured creditors if their recovery ratio is expected to be below 25 percent. Britain and Germany have rules that come very close to the ones in the United States, but with some notable exceptions. In Britain, the judge does not have the ability to cram down a plan. The new German reorganization code appears superficially to have more or less identical rules as the United States. However, before even starting the reorganization procedure creditors have to agree to continue operating the firm. If they do not agree, the firm immediately enters liquidation. Also, the German system has a strong bias against keeping existing management in charge of the firm, which limits the possible reorganization plans that can be proposed.

To summarize, none of the systems surveyed seem to have as strong protection against coordination failures in their reorganization plans as U.S. Chapter 11.

Protection of Third-Party Claimants, Such as Employees
All bankruptcy systems take some extra care in protecting employees, although the United States and Japan provide relatively weak protection by only offering some limited seniority. In the European countries, the government actually guarantees wage claims to the extent bankruptcy proceeds are not high enough to fully cover them (up to some maximum amount). Moreover, in Germany, France, and Sweden, the law explicitly states that the courts should take particular care to protect employment. France is the extreme case, where firm survival is stated as the primary goal of bankruptcy law.

Maintaining Asset Value during Bargaining
The U.S. Chapter 11 stands out regarding its provisions aiming to ease the management of the firm's operations during negotiations. First, it gives the most autonomy to debtor management to continue running the firm without interference by a court official. Second, it provides the most access to senior financing in bankruptcy. Germany and Japan lack debtor-in-possession financing provisions altogether, and only the U.S. code allows for the possibility of superpriority financing over secured creditors. Some countries, such as Sweden and France, also limit the time the company can operate in bankruptcy.

Rules Affecting Liquidity in the Disposal of Assets

An important role of reorganization procedures is to avoid inefficient asset sales when buyers are liquidity constrained. One way reorganization procedures do this is by postponing the sale of the firm until liquid buyers have emerged. For this reason, being able to run the firm's operations during reorganization without a major loss in asset value is important. As mentioned in the previous subsection, the U.S. Chapter 11 procedure seems to have the most flexibility in keeping the firm's operations alive in bankruptcy.

U.S. bankruptcy code facilitates the competitive sale of assets, even for firms that are protected under Chapter 11. Section 363 of the code allows the debtor in Chapter 11 to seek competitive bids for all or part of its assets as long as the sale does not impair the interests of the creditors. Oftentimes, the creditors themselves encourage the "363 sales." More recently, this provision of the U.S. bankruptcy code has created a vibrant and often competitive market in asset sales out of bankruptcy.

Another way in which reorganization can alleviate liquidity constraints is by allowing potential buyers of the firm's assets to offer securities rather than cash. In a reorganization, it is not only important to be able to write down debt claims, but also to be able to exchange these claims with new securities such as equity or warrants. U.S. Chapter 11 helps to facilitate noncash bids by, for example, including rules that allow stakeholders to bypass some of the normal SEC registration requirements when issuing new securities in Chapter 11. This aspect have been largely ignored in many of the new reorganization procedures outside of the United States.

The sales mechanism used in the bankruptcy procedures are also important in order to create a liquid market for distressed assets. A market-based sales procedure, which allocates the firm's assets to the highest bidder (to the extent that there is one), has the advantage of encouraging investors to participate in an auction in the first place. By contrast, a procedure that allocates assets through judicial discretion or via a trustee may discourage external investors from bidding for the assets, as a bidder's ability to be rewarded for being the highest value user of the assets may be limited.

With the exception of France, the reorganization codes all involve a voting procedure, where claimholders can decide on whether to accept a "bid" (i.e., a reorganization plan). In France, however, implementing a reorganization plan is up to the discretion of the judge, and creditors cannot in principle affect the asset allocation decision.

The liquidation procedures, or "cash auction" procedures, in the different chapters generally delegate the sales decision to a trustee or judge. As a consequence, claimholders have no direct say in the asset allocation decision (although they may, have a say indirectly, as we will return to later). The exception is the U.K. receivership and administrative receivership codes, in which a receiver, appointed by senior creditors, is responsible for disposing of the assets. The administrative receivership code also allows for reorganizations rather than just cash bids. In the other codes, in which a trustee or judge is responsible for selling the assets, trustees typically have a lot of discretion in disposing of the assets. Codes generally do not specify that a certain sales method (such as an auction) should be used, which may be troublesome if the trustee does not have clear, value-maximizing incentives. To make this matter worse, some liquidation codes, such as the Swedish code, have no element of incentive pay for the trustee, but will simply pay an hourly wage, independent of proceeds realized.

2.3 Evidence on the Use of Bankruptcy Laws

The previous analysis suggests that compared to Chapter 11, the non-U.S. reorganization codes generally have less power to coordinate creditors, less ability to manage assets in negotiations, include fewer provisions aimed at enhancing liquidity, and give higher employee protection and more power to senior creditors. Have these differences affected the actual use of reorganization codes relative to liquidation codes?

Bankruptcy filing rates throw some light on this question. The top row of Table 8.2 compares for the five countries the proportion of bankruptcy filings that start under the country's reorganization code relative to the total number of firms filing for either reorganization or liquidation. One caveat regarding these numbers is that they do not take account of differences in overall bankruptcy filing rates between countries.[12]

Table 8.2 shows that with the exception of France, reorganization filings are much rarer outside the United States. But the high French figures are misleading because under French law, *all* firms filing for bankruptcy have to file under the "Redressement Judiciaire" procedure; a debtor or creditor cannot directly file for liquidation. The only firms counted as filing for liquidation are those that are immediately liquidated by the judge at

---

[12] See Claessens and Klapper (2002) for an analysis of cross-country variation in aggregate bankruptcy rates.

Table 8.2. Reorganizations as a Proportion of Total Bankruptcies

	United States	United Kingdom	Japan	France	Germany	Sweden
Reorganizations as percentage of total filings	28.6	6.7	4.4	73.8[a]	0.4	Less than 1 percent[a]
Successful reorganizations as percentage of all exiting bankruptcies	4–20[a]	2.4[a]		8.7	0.3	0.4
Years Covered	2000–2002	1999		2000–2001	1998	2000–2002
Source	American Bankruptcy Institute	Society of Practitioners of Insolvency, and Kaiser (1996)	Teikoku Data Bank	European Commission (2003), and Kaiser (1996)	German Statistical Yearbook	Swedish Statistical Office

Notes: a) Estimated using ancillary data.

the beginning of the procedure, when the judge decides that there is no hope of reorganization.

The second row of Table 8.2 reports successful reorganization completion rates, defined as the percentage of total firms exiting bankruptcy (including firms that cease to exist after liquidation) that exit reorganization under current management. In general, these rates are difficult to calculate because good data are spotty or lacking for most countries. Therefore, most of the completion rates that we report are estimates, and should be treated with caution.

For the U.S. completion rate, we provide a range from 4 percent to 20 percent of total exits. The estimate of 4 percent is based on the study of U.S. Chapter 11 cases by Flynn (1986). Using data from the Administrative Office of the U.S. Courts over the period 1979 to 1986, Flynn finds that only 17 percent of firms filing for Chapter 11 emerge as a going-concern under the same management. But the Flynn averages may be comparatively low for two reasons. First, Flynn documents an upward trend in confirmation rates over his period. To the extent that this trend may have continued, confirmation rates could be expected to be higher today. Second, the Flynn sample, comprising all Chapter 11 filings, is dominated by small firms, and small firms arguably are less likely to be successfully reorganized than large firms.

The estimate for the upper end, 20 percent, is based on Lynn Lopucki's sample of large (assets of at least $100 million), publicly trade firms filing over the period 1990 to 2002.[13] Lopucki's sample implies that 77 percent of firms entering Chapter 11 during this period were confirmed as going concerns. But estimates based on the Lopucki sample are biased upward because the sample is so heavily weighted toward the largest firms in the U.S. economy. Moreover, even for large firms, the Lopucki estimates probably overstate the rate at which firms emerge as a going concern with current management. Baird and Rasmussen (2002, 2004) argue that many of the Chapter 11 cases coded as "confirmed" in the Lopucki sample were actually sold in Chapter 11, either as a going concern or in pieces.

France appears to have a relatively high completion rate. However, this statistic suffers from two empirical problems. First, this statistic likely excludes small firms, which, as mentioned earlier, have much lower completion rates. Second, given that French bankruptcy law has the explicit goal

---

[13] The Lopucki sample represents one of the most complete and detailed samples of Chapter 11 filings and has been used extensively, especially in the legal bankruptcy literature. See, for example, Lopucki and Whitford (1990) and Lopucki and Eisenberg (1999).

of maintaining a firm's survival for the benefit of third-party claimants, it is not clear whether the survival rate in France is indicative of the rate at which companies are successfully reorganized.

It may be that the statistics simply are too heterogenous and speculative to really allow meaningful analysis. Still, we think there are a few conclusions that can be drawn from the filing data. For instance, even though many non-U.S. reorganization codes are modeled after Chapter 11, all of them have important differences. These differences seem to be important deterrents to the use of the codes. Ignoring the French statistics, which are harder to interpret, the U.K. system comes closest to the U.S. system.

2.4 Reorganization, Liquidation, and Firm Survival

Despite data problems, the previous section suggests that firms are not frequently successfully reorganized in many non-U.S. reorganization codes. Is this finding economically important? Does it mean that firms are less likely to survive financial distress in Germany, Sweden, or the United Kingdom, resulting in excess liquidations and ex post efficiencies? The answer is no. So far we have only considered firms that survive in the form of corporate reorganizations. But this does not mean that the rest of the firms are liquidated, despite the fact that many of them end up filing for "liquidation bankruptcy."

Studies of liquidation codes outside of the United States show that going concern sales are common. Available estimates of the fraction of liquidations ending up as going concerns include 76 percent for Sweden (Strömberg and Thorburn 1996), 47 percent for the United Kingdom (Kaiser 1996; receivership and administrative receivership only), and 30 percent for Finland (Sundgren 1995), using somewhat different methodologies and sampling criteria. Informal discussions with German bankruptcy practitioners suggest that this is a common outcome in Germany as well.[14]

Moreover, successful Chapter 11-type outcomes can be implemented within a liquidation code. Strömberg (2000) studied bankruptcy resolution in the Swedish liquidation code using a sample of 205 bankruptcies of closely held corporations.[15] In his sample, about two thirds of the going-concern sales were actually made back to the previous owner-manager,

---

[14] Personal communication with Arne Wittig.
[15] See also Thorburn (2000) for a related study.

with the asset purchase typically financed by an existing senior creditor, the firm's old bank. In other words, a large number of liquidation bankruptcies really end up looking like reorganizations, in which current management is allowed to continue running the firm, and the senior creditor rolls over its debt into the new reorganized firm. The results also indicate that such sale-backs are more likely when the market for the firm's assets is less liquid. Hence, a formal reorganization code is not necessary to avoid inefficient liquidations when markets are illiquid. Again, such sale-backs to current managers are not unique for Sweden. Kaiser (1996) reports that 54 percent of administrative receiverships end up in whole or partial going-concern sales back to current management.[16]

Why do firms end up being reorganized under the liquidation chapter, despite the fact that these countries have formal reorganization codes? There are a few possible reasons for this. In a liquidation code, reorganizations can be arranged in a private negotiation between senior creditors and the debtor, without major interference from courts and other claimants. Although outside of the United Kingdom, the asset sale is undertaken by a court-appointed trustee rather than a creditor-appointed receiver, the trustees are typically not involved except in expediting the formalities of the sale. Unsecured creditors, such as trade creditors and tax authorities, can be left out of negotiations, and their debt being written down effectively. The resolution is also fast, with sale-backs on average occurring less than two months after filing (the median is about one month).

So, what is the advantage of having formal reorganization codes such as Chapter 11, if firms can equally well be reorganized in a liquidation procedure? One important drawback to liquidation codes is the lack of transparency in the system, in combination with a lack of mechanisms that

---

[16] One potential caveat in interpreting these numbers is that they ignore the reorganizations that take place "in the shadow of bankruptcy," that is, private workouts. Unfortunately, systematic data on private workouts are hard to come by, especially for private companies, and only a few studies are available. In the studies of 169 distressed U.S. publicly traded firms in Gilson, John, and Lang (1990), half of the companies restructure successfully outside of Chapter 11, and Asquith, Gertner, and Scharfstein (1994) get a similar estimate in their sample of 76 distressed U.S. junk bond issuers. In Franks and Sussman's (2003) study of small and medium-sized bank-financed U.K. companies in distress, private workout rates are around 65 percent (see Table 1 of their paper, excluding ongoing cases), and Brunner and Krahnen (2001) estimate workout rates just below 70 percent for their sample of medium-sized German firms in distress (again, excluding ongoing cases). Still, these estimates are hard to evaluate, given the fact that there is no unambiguous definition of financial distress, and different studies use different criteria. Given this, and the lack of data from the other economies in our sample, it is hard to draw any cross-country conclusions from this.

facilitate running the firm as a going concern in bankruptcy. Strömberg (2000) shows that secured creditors implement sale-backs too often at the expense of junior creditors. This problem results from the desire to avoid the potential loss of going-concern value from postponing the sale in order to find alternative bidders. Because this potential loss would fall disproportionately on senior creditors, they prefer a fast sale to existing management to prolonging the search for outside bidders. An additional and related factor is that banks may prefer rolling over their debt in a sale-back in order to avoid booking a credit loss on the loan. By financing a sale-back at a price at least equal to the existing bank loan, the bank is able to "evergreen" the loan and avoid a write-down.[17]

This discussion suggests two important differences between a formal reorganization code and manager sale-backs under liquidation codes. First, a formal reorganization code contains provisions such as debtor-in-possession financing, allowing the firm to keep operating longer in bankruptcy. This might decrease the costs of delaying the bankruptcy resolution, thereby facilitating the assembly of alternative bidders to participate in the auction. Hence, liquidity is enhanced, increasing ex post efficiency. Second, in a cash auction, the negotiations between the claimants take place outside of the realms of the bankruptcy law, which leaves some parties, such as the junior creditors, without much power to affect the bankruptcy outcome. In a formal reorganization code, the bargaining of junior claimants can be increased through formal voting power, which may have impact on ex ante efficiency, as we discuss later. The increased transparency from keeping negotiations in court could also decrease the likelihood of inefficient self-dealing and exploitation of unsecured creditors.

In the same way as firms can reorganize under a liquidation code, formal reorganization procedures can also act as effective liquidation (i.e., auction) mechanisms. As mentioned earlier, assets can be sold off in Chapter 11 by invoking section 363 of the U.S. bankruptcy code. Under current practices in U.S. Chapter 11 filings, debtors often first seek a "stalking-horse" bidder to commit to purchase firm assets as part of a reorganization plan. Often, the stalking-horse bidder is an existing claimant, or an investor who has recently purchased claims on the distressed firm. The stalking-horse bid, which can be arranged in advance of filing, sets a floor on bids that can be entertained under an auction eventually run by the bankruptcy judge. Often, these sales are prepared for in advance

---

[17] See Smith (2003) for evidence of the evergreening behavior of Japanese banks.

of the Chapter 11 filing through prepackaged arrangements (commonly referred to as "prepacks") between the debtor and creditors, or as part of debtor-in-possession (DIP) financing agreements (Lease, McConnell, and Tashjian 1996; Skeel 2003). For these cases, Chapter 11 becomes an explicit mechanism for facilitating the transfer of control of assets to a high-valued bidder. According to Baird and Rasmussen (2004), more than half of large, publicly-traded firms currently entering Chapter 11 involve assets sales under section 363 resulting in a transfer of control of the company.[18]

Auctions in Chapter 11 can provide another advantage not typically available in sales through a liquidation code by allowing bidders to bid with securities. That is, bidders can offer existing stakeholders claims in the reorganized firm or in their own firm, as well as cash. Offering securities provides at least two benefits. First, it allows bidders who are liquidity constrained to compete without seeking other sources of financing. Thus, it increases the flexibility of the bidding process. Second, providing certain classes of existing stakeholders (e.g., managers or other informed shareholders) with a claim in the future value of the ongoing concern can provide incentives for these stakeholders to contribute to improving the value of the reorganized firm.

3. BANKRUPTCY LAW AND EX ANTE EFFICIENCY

3.1 Bargaining Power and Ex Ante Efficiency

In the previous section, we analyzed how different bankruptcy systems affect the ex post efficiency of financial distress resolution. The specific bankruptcy rules primarily aimed at affecting the ex post asset allocation decision, however, will also have ex ante effects. In particular, these rules will change the bargaining power among claimants. For example, voting rules requiring unanimity or a weak automatic stay will tilt bargaining power in the direction of creditors. Leaving the debtor in possession of the assets will likely tilt bargaining power in the other direction. Hence, given the previous discussion, many codes, such as the ones in the United Kingdom, Sweden, and Japan, end up giving more bargaining power to secured creditors, compared to the U.S. code. In addition, U.S. Chapter 11

---

[18] U.S. Chapter 11 appears to be the home for even the more traditional "piecemeal" liquidations of companies with little or no going-concern value. For instance, the recent liquidations of Enron, Worldcom, and Global Crossing all occurred through Chapter 11, rather than Chapter 7 of the U.S. bankruptcy code.

is the only code giving managers an exclusivity period to propose a reorganization plan. France is a special case, as is recognized in earlier literature (see Biais and Malecot 1996). The French system gives considerable bargaining power to courts, presumably tilting power toward third parties such as the government and employees. Everything else equal, changing bargaining power leads to a higher payoff for the party with increased bargaining power at the expense of the party with decreased bargaining power.

It is difficult to say whether tilting bargaining power to debtors, creditors, or third parties is good from an ex ante perspective. Increasing the bargaining power of equity at the expense of creditors can increase the cost of capital ex ante. Increasing the expected payouts to equity and management may also have adverse ex ante incentive effects, in that the disciplining role of debt is weakened. By contrast, tilting the bargaining power toward the managers or original owners decreases their incentive to go for broke, and may be beneficial for management's incentive to invest in firm-specific human capital.[19]

More generally, allowing renegotiation may lead to deviations from absolute priority, which makes it harder to write enforceable contracts, and this can lead to increased financing and agency costs ex ante. By contrast, allowing for renegotiation and deviations from absolute priority may be necessary to ensure ex post efficient bargaining and avoid inefficient asset allocation. Given the theoretical ambiguity, data are needed to evaluate this trade-off.

We argue that ex ante efficiency can be best understood by looking at the resolution of financial distress in a setting where private bargaining works well. Presumably, if there are no impediments to efficient ex post bargaining, parties will be able to resolve financial distress without relying on bankruptcy law. The parties can do equally well, and possibly better, by designing and including a distress resolution mechanism in their ex ante contracts. If such a setting exists, then it is likely to be as close as we can hope to get to ex ante efficiency.[20] Hence, to maximize ex ante efficiency, a bankruptcy system should try to achieve outcomes that are as close as possible to the way financial distress would have been resolved in this private setting. The problem is to find such a setting empirically.

---

[19] See White (1989), Berkovich et al (1997), and, more recently, Bebchuk (2003).

[20] The one caveat to this argument is the extent to which bankruptcy law serves as a pre-commitment device for the contracting parties not to renegotiate contracts. Given the extent to which renegotiation occurs even in very "creditor-friendly" codes, we do not think that bankruptcy law is very effective in preventing renegotiations from occurring.

3.2 Bankruptcy Law and Private Workouts

One possibility is to investigate the features of credit contracts that facilitate private workouts. There is nothing that prevents a borrower and its creditors from resolving financial distress privately and private workouts are common in many countries. However, examining the distress-related features of debt contracts is problematic, because these contracts are constructed in the "shadow" of bankruptcy law. That is, even though debtors and creditors can try to restructure out-of-court rather than file for bankruptcy, the outcome will be heavily influenced by the ability to file for bankruptcy if the private negotiations break down. For instance, if a certain claimant expects to get a large payoff in court, and she has the ability to file and put the firm in bankruptcy, she would not accept a lower payoff out of court. In the United States, out-of-court restructurings tend not to look all that different from Chapter 11 reorganizations (Franks and Torous 1994). Moreover, it is increasingly common to combine out-of-court and in-court restructuring, through so prepacks in which the parties have already negotiated a reorganization plan by the time the firm enters Chapter 11. Hence, the efficiency of bankruptcy law also depends on the effect it has on out-of-court bargaining. This makes any empirical evaluation of the efficiency of bankruptcy law extremely difficult, as systematic data on out-of-court renegotiations are very hard to come by.[21]

To find a setting in which private contracting and bargaining works well without bankruptcy law, we will have to look further than private workouts in the shadow of bankruptcy. We believe venture capital financing is one such setting.

3.3 Distressed Renegotiations in Venture Capital

As Baird and Rasmussen (2001, 2002) point out, looking at venture capitalist (VC) financing of start-up firms can teach us something about what optimal bankruptcy law should look like. Venture capital is a setting where contracting parties have largely managed to opt out of bankruptcy law. Instead, the financial distress procedures used in default are a result of the ex ante contracts written when the firm was first financed. Despite the recent crash in technology stocks, the VC industry has been very successful over the last decades. VCs have strong incentives to maximize value, but,

---

[21] There are a few exceptions, such as Franks and Sussman (2003), Franks and Torous (1994), Brunner and Krahnen (2001), and Brown, Ciochetti, and Riddiough (2003).

at the same time, receive few or no private benefits of control. Hence, we would expect them to write contracts and formulate procedures in order to maximize ex ante efficiency.[22]

VCs hold preferred equity securities rather than debt securities, and as a result, a default or insolvency does not give the firm (or any of its claimants) the right to file for bankruptcy. Still, as Kaplan and Strömberg (2003) show, these contracts share many important features of debt contracts.[23] Through their preferred claim, VCs are senior in liquidation to common equity-holders (which typically consist of founders and managers). Although entrepreneurs keep control of the venture as long as performance is satisfactory, control switches to VCs on bad performance. An important difference from debt is that the trigger of a change in control is typically not the default on a contracted payment. Rather, contracts often state that control is transferred to VCs when there is failure to meet some performance milestone, be it a financial measure, such as a profit threshold, or a nonfinancial measure, such as obtaining a patent or winning approval of a product from a regulatory agency. Moreover, staged financing, in which the VC initially only provides limited financing so that a subsequent refinancing will be needed, gives the ability for VCs to effectively take control in the bad state of the world by threatening to deny further capital to the firm, or by demanding a majority of both cash flow and control rights after the new financing round (Gompers 1998). Such financings are frequently referred to as "down rounds."

So what are the characteristics of the VC financial distress mechanism? Although aggregate statistics are difficult to come by, down rounds, as well as VC liquidations and reorganizations, have been increasingly common in the last few years, following the crash in technology stocks of the early 2000s. The discussion here relies on new evidence gathered from these events by Kaplan and Strömberg (2003, 2004), Kaplan, Martel, and Strömberg (2003), as well as work-in-progress by Kaplan, Lerner, and Strömberg (2004).

First, not surprisingly, we observe some ventures being shut down and liquidated, others being acquired or merged, and many being restructured and recapitalized, sometimes replacing management in the process.

Second, VCs (i.e., "creditors") are in control of the process. The VCs typically have effective board and voting control, and have most of the

---

[22] See Kaplan and Strömberg (2001) for a more detailed argument.
[23] Also, see Sahlman (1990) and Gompers (1998) for empirical analyses of venture capital contracts. Kaplan, Martel, and Strömberg (2003) present evidence suggesting that the U.S.-styled VC contracts are optimal across different legal regimes.

bargaining power in negotiations. As mentioned earlier, managers cannot file for bankruptcy "protection"; they derive bargaining power only insofar as they have unique skills needed to run the business. Hence, if the creditors/VCs decide that it is in their best interest to sell or liquidate the firm rather than have it reorganized, it will be sold or liquidated.

Third, renegotiations of existing contracts are common in connection with new rounds. Often, existing VC investors waive some of their contractual rights, such as liquidation preference, anti-dilution rights, and performance ratchets, in order to persuade new VCs to invest in the venture (Kaplan and Strömberg 2003, and Henig 2002).

Fourth, reorganizations always involve deviations from absolute priority. There are two main types of absolute priority violation. One is that management typically receives a fraction of the equity of the reorganized company, although all of the value should have gone to the senior claimants (i.e., the VCs) had the assets been sold or liquidated. The reason for this is simply that if the firm is to continue operating, managers need to be incentivized to put in effort.[24] The other is that VCs who do not participate in the new financing get diluted in favor of VCs who choose to put in new money in the firm. This happens despite the fact that VC contracts have antidilution clauses, which in good states of the world insure existing VCs by providing them with free shares in the event of new capital injections. When a firm is financially distressed, existing VCs often waive their antidilution rights in order to persuade new VCs to invest. Moreover, it is not uncommon to see so-called pay-to-play provisions in VC contracts, which explicitly state that the investor loses her anti-dilution rights if she fails to participate with a pro rata share in a subsequent financing round. In the last few years, so-called wash-out rounds have become increasingly common, in which the dilution of existing investors and shareholders is extreme, and the company ends up being more or less wholly owned by those VCs putting in new funds along with existing management (Gove 1999).

Fifth, although VCs have substantial control during the procedure, they typically do not personally manage the day-to-day business during distress (Kaplan and Strömberg 2004). The management team (which can be the original founder, but often is new management that the VC has put in place) is given considerable autonomy over the daily operations.

Sixth, it is common that ventures obtain some limited financing during negotiations, in order to keep it in operations until the financial distress

---

[24] This incentive reason for deviating from absolute priority has been pointed out by Baird and Rasmussen (2001) and Ayotte (2002).

is resolved. This is typically done through so-called bridge loans, that are provided by one or more of the existing VC investors. These loans are structured in such a way that if the venture subsequently obtains new financing, the loan converts into preferred equity securities at the same terms as this new financing round. If instead the venture is unsuccessful in getting a new round of financing, the bridge loan has seniority over all other existing securities, effectively giving the bridge financiers "super-priority" on the venture's assets.

The analysis of VC contracts suggests that features such as management control of assets during bargaining, deviations from absolute priority, and superpriority financings are consistent with ex ante efficiency. To understand the limits of the VC analogy, however, we need to understand why it is that VCs are able to "privatize" bankruptcy. In an earlier section, we went through a number of reasons why private contracting may not be enough and bankruptcy law may be needed to enhance efficiency. It turns out that in the VC context, several of these reasons are not relevant:

- VCs are atypically well informed investors, with considerable industry knowledge; they put major effort into screening and monitoring their investments. VCs are likely to have as good information as the entrepreneur about whether a particular business is economically viable or not. Hence, problems of asymmetric information are likely to be much lower than in a typical debtor-creditor relationship, and there will be less need for the verification role of bankruptcy.
- Although VC investments are often syndicated, the claims structure is not very dispersed (at least in early-stage financings). Moreover, VCs within a syndicate hold very similar claims that do not differ significantly in their rights or seniority. VCs also tend to syndicate with the same investors, and syndication networks are stable. Finally, VC securities are never secured with specific collateral. All of these factors decrease coordination and hold-out problems significantly. Moreover, contractual features such as "pay-to-play" provisions are frequently included in VC contracts in order to increase coordination.
- Start-up firms are typically smaller, and most key employees are also shareholders in the firm, which decreases the need for third-party protection.
- Because VCs also share in the upside if the venture is successful, they have a large incentive to make sure that asset value is preserved during negotiations. Also, VCs have particular skills in overseeing and replacing management of start-up firms (Hellman and Puri 2002).

- Liquidity constraints may be less important in the VC setting, although this may not always be so given the booms and busts that the VC market has experienced.
- Finally, as mentioned earlier, given the visible success of VC start-up financing in the United States, it is likely that private contracting in this market has evolved to become largely efficient. Hence, it seems unlikely that imposing rules that would restrict the contracting environment, or change the bargaining power between claimants, could increase ex ante efficiency.

Still, the VC resolution of financial distress shares surprisingly many important features with a formal bankruptcy code such as the U.S. Chapter 11. Firms end up being both sold, liquidated, and restructured. Existing management often runs the firm during bargaining and will often receive a stake in the ongoing firm. Restructuring typically involves deviations from absolute priority. Firms receive senior debtor-in-possession financing in order to keep operating during negotiations. The major difference, however, is that the bargaining power is firmly in the hand of the creditors, and the debtor is given no extra protection, rights, or first-mover advantages beyond that accorded to him by his creditors.

3.4 19th-Century U.S. Equity Receiverships

The similarity between U.S. Chapter 11 and the private VC distress resolution may not be a coincidence but may reflect instead Chapter 11's origins in private contracting. In particular, U.S. bankruptcy law has its roots in the Equity Receiverships of the late 19th century.

Prior to 1898, the United States had no formal corporate bankruptcy law.[25] Defaulting borrowers were subject to debt collection laws, which allowed creditors to call for foreclosure on a mortgaged property or seek appointment of a receiver to manage a debtor's assets. But beyond the existing debt collection laws, debtors and creditors had to rely on out-of-court solutions for resolving corporate distress.

Private restructurings required a new level of ingenuity with the creation of the large railroad corporations of the 19th century. These corporations were financed through public bond issuances underwritten by

---

[25] Although bankruptcy laws were passed in 1800, 1841, and 1867, each of these laws were quickly repealed. See Skeel (2001), p. 27. Much of the analysis from this section comes from the excellent history of U.S. bankruptcy provided in Skeel (2001).

investment banks and secured with the assets of the railroad. Oftentimes a security interest consisted of segments of the track being laid.

Beginning in the mid-1850s, competition between railroad companies and overcapacity within the industry led to a series of railroad failures. At the outset of these failures, it became apparent that individual fore-closures on secured property would result in small recoveries; owners of one segment of track would be hard pressed to find a valuable use for their piece of track beyond its worth as scrap metal. At the same time, coordinated settlements required getting agreement from dispersed bondholders across potentially different classes of bonds.[26]

From this dilemma grew the idea of an "equity receivership." The equity receivership worked as follows. On a default, creditors would call on a court, acting in the common-law tradition of an "equitable authority," to appoint a receiver to oversee the continuation of the property. The receiver had the legal right to stay payments and prevent foreclosures, thus keeping any single creditor from interfering by trying to collect on his debt. Meanwhile, the investment banks that underwrote the bonds would form bondholders' committees for each class of bond outstanding. Shareholders could similarly form a shareholder committee. Investors turned their bonds (or shares) over to the committee members, giving the committee the authority to bargain on behalf of all claimants within a given class. During these proceedings, the railroad company would continue operations. To finance the company's operations, suppliers were given "receivership certificates" that guaranteed repayment priority over all other claimants. Once a restructuring plan had been agreed on, the assets of the company would be transferred to a shell corporation, at which time new securities or cash would be dispensed to the claimants. Junior claimants agreeing to provide the new company with fresh cash were guaranteed priority over claimants that kicked in nothing.

The 19th-century equity receiverships share features in common with the VC restructurings seen today. Like a VC workout, the capital structure of a firm exiting receivership favored those investors willing to invest new cash into the firm. And, like a VC workout, receiverships offered a mechanism for providing supersenior priority to those that financed the firm in the process of bargaining.

But receiverships were set up to deal with large corporations that had complex and dispersed capital structures. As a result – and in contrast to

---

[26] Bondholders were also dispersed across a wide set of countries, as much of the railroad lending came from foreign capital.

the VC restructurings – bondholders chose to delegate the decision making by giving their votes to investment banks. This mitigated information asymmetries because control of the process was delegated to those investors with the best information about the distressed firm. Coordination problems also were reduced because bargaining was left to a smaller group of investors. Coordination was further improved by the establishment of bondholder committees, in which representatives from each bank could address specific issues related to bargaining. Moreover, receiverships developed a tool for preventing lone creditors from holding out for more money. Courts set "upset prices" at which creditors would be compensated if they did not participate in a negotiated settlement. These prices were set low enough to discourage creditors from bowing out of the bargaining process.

Again, the fact that many of the central features of Chapter 11 were introduced as a result of private contracting between investors and firms speaks in favor of this system not being too far from ex ante optimality. As with VC renegotiations, however, one important difference between the equity receiverships and Chapter 11 is the absence of rules biasing bargaining power in favor of equityholders and management (for example, the exclusivity period accorded to debtor management for proposing a reorganization plan). As documented in Skeel (2001), such rules were subsequently introduced by bankruptcy lawmakers, often in response to lobbying from different interest groups.

3.5 Inefficiencies in U.S. Chapter 11

The previous analysis suggests that if market participants where to design their own bankruptcy law, it would probably look very similar to the U.S. Chapter 11 code. The important exception is the deference U.S. Chapter 11 gives to debtor-managers. Indeed, this is the feature of Chapter 11 most widely criticized by academics. A number of theoretical papers have shown that this bias can lead to inefficiencies, such as excessive deviations from absolute priority in favor of equity, excessive risk-taking, and too many firms being continued under current management (see, for example, Bergman and Callen 1991, White 1989, 1996, and Gertner and Scharfstein 1991). Although theoretically compelling, it is unclear how important these inefficiencies are in practice. Most empirical evidence on inefficiencies of this sort in Chapter 11 refers to individual cases, most infamously the bankruptcy of Eastern Airlines (Weiss and Wruck 1998). Other evidence pointing toward inefficiencies is harder to interpret. For example, although Hotchkiss (1995) finds that firms emerging from Chapter 11 underperform relative to their industry benchmark, it is still not clear that creditors would have been better off if the firm had been liquidated. In contrast, in a detailed analysis of highly leveraged firms entering financial distress, Andrade and Kaplan (1998) find no systematic evidence of overinvestment or related costs. Rather, they conclude that the highly leveraged transactions that preceded financial distress were overall value increasing even for firms that eventually ended up in bankruptcy. Moreover, the recent studies by Baird and Rasmussen (2004) and Skeel (2003) suggest that Chapter 11 today exhibits very little equity or management bias, and that creditors have learned to undo such biases through private contracting, for example, within the initial debtor-in-possession credit agreements. Hence, our opinion is that the theoretical arguments of a harmful management bias in Chapter 11 are not very important in practice.

Another important criticism of reorganization codes such as Chapter 11 has to do with its possible negative impact on industry competition. If a financially distressed firm is given the ability to continue to operate under bankruptcy protection with the aid of superpriority financing, this may give the distressed firm an unfair advantage over its industry competitors. For example, it has been claimed that airlines and telecom companies operating under Chapter 11 have used predatory pricing strategies to hurt competitors. The little empirical evidence that exists, such as Borenstein and Rose (1995), does not find much evidence of such behavior, however. Although more empirical work may be needed in this area, we believe that this is not a major source of concern.

4. RECOMMENDATIONS AND CONCLUSIONS

Based on the earlier analysis, we now summarize the features we believe contribute most to a well-functioning bankruptcy procedure. The features can be categorized into two groups, (1) those that ensure the going-concern value of the firm during the procedure and (2) those that maximize the potential for bidders to compete for the reorganization of the firm.

We then examine how our proposals might work in developing countries, or in countries facing systemic financial distress. Although a well-functioning bankruptcy system likely works best in countries with developed financial and judicial systems, our recommended features do not rely on the level of country development. Indeed, we argue that a bankruptcy procedure should be constructed so as to minimize frictions that are common in developing markets. Likewise, the procedures we highlight should be helpful during systemic distress events, in which liquidity in markets is of special concern.

4.1 Features of a Well-Functioning Bankruptcy Procedure

We view bankruptcy as a mechanism for facilitating the efficient renegotiation of contracts that are incomplete. The bargaining that takes place when a default occurs on a debt contract involves deciding who should manage the assets of the defaulted firm and how claims on future cash flows from these assets should be distributed. This bargaining should work to maximize the ex post value of the assets without greatly distorting their ex ante value.

As highlighted in our earlier discussions, a well-functioning bankruptcy procedure should ensure that the going-concern value of a distressed firm's assets be maintained during the bargaining process. Simply put, mechanisms should be put in place to minimize the direct and indirect costs of bankruptcy that erode asset value. In the past, academics have suggested that bankruptcy costs are best reduced by encouraging procedures that favor a speedy resolution to the process, as these costs can increase with time (Jensen 1991 and Thorburn 2000). Our belief is that speed can actually work against a well-functioning procedure if time is required to properly assess the value of the assets and claims, allow for negotiations, search for potential bidders, and generally increase the liquidity of the bidding process. Instead, actions can be taken to minimize bankruptcy costs while allowing for sufficient time in the process. Specifically, we recommend that:

- *Creditors be automatically stayed from collecting collateral or suing for payment during the process.* As noted by Jackson (1986), individual creditor-collection efforts endanger the going-concern value of the assets to the creditors as a whole. Therefore, as a general rule, all creditors (included secured creditors) should be stayed from pursuing repayment during the bankruptcy process.[27]
- *Supersenior financing be available to allow for continued financing of operations.* Mechanisms should be in place to allow existing or new creditors that provide financing for ongoing operations to obtain liens

---

[27] This does not preclude the possibility that creditors be able to appeal for relief from the stay. For example, creditors as a whole may want to grant relief to a trade creditor that supplies a product crucial to the ongoing value of the firm.

or guarantees that give them first priority on the firm's assets. Without such guarantees, it seems unlikely that a distressed firm requiring financing will be able to operate smoothly during negotiations.

- *Decisions regarding who should manage the firm during bargaining should be left to the creditors.* The distressed firm should be managed by those who can best maximize the value of the assets on an ongoing concern. Appointed trustees – such as lawyers, accountants, or "insolvency experts" – may have little expertise in running a given distressed business. Creditors as a group – through early voting or committee representation – can best decide how to run the firm. Current management should not be excluded from the creditors' choice set, nor should they be granted protection from dismissal if creditors find a better management team.

A well-functioning bankruptcy procedure also should seek to maximize the potential for bidders to compete for reorganizing the firm. This can be accomplished by creating an environment that attracts investors and provides maximum financial flexibility to potential bidders, including among the existing set of claimants. In this regard, the process should:

- *Implement a verification and disclosure process that is credible and open to potential bidders.* Strong reporting and audit standards of a firm's assets and liabilities should be encouraged. This could include examinations of the debtor by outside auditors appointed at the request of creditors. As a general rule, all audit results should be made publicly accessible.
- *Allow bidders to offer securities, cash or both.* For example, allow debt-for-equity exchanges and the use of securities as a medium of exchange. This provides added flexibility to high-valuing bidders that might be liquidity-constrained.
- *Allow for deviations from absolute priority to claimholders that are willing to place competitive bids for the firm.* As used in VC workouts and 19th-century equity receiverships, this provides additional incentives for current claimants to enter the bidding process. The system should provide safeguards, however, so that some classes of claimants are not exploited; for example, creditors should receive at least the payout they would have received under a piecemeal liquidation or other asset sale alternative (i.e., the "fairness" criterion in Chapter 11).
- *Encourage secondary-market trading of claims on distressed assets.* This provides a way for high-valuing bidders to gain a foothold in the bargaining process and enables existing claimants to liquefy their positions. Current U.S. bond and syndicated loan markets facilitate

such purchases by making available distressed securities for sale in secondary markets.

- *Ensure that the bankruptcy procedure can go on for a while.* This is tied to ensuring that asset value is maintained during the bankruptcy process. Potential bidders may need time to evaluate the assets of the firm and obtain financing to make an offer. Overall, allowing relatively more time in the process should increase the chance that competitive bidders will enter.
- *Maximize the ability for existing claimholders, including junior claimants to make bids.* Try to avoid instances where one creditor can preclude junior claimants from bidding, as is the case when floating lien holders initiate receivership proceedings in the United Kingdom.

4.2 Application to Developing and Distressed Economies

Although we draw on the bankruptcy systems of developed countries to conduct our analysis, there is little reason to believe that the steps here could not apply to developing countries as well. For instance, the suggested features do not require large or especially sophisticated legal procedures, nor do they require a large administrative unit or an organization of trustees or insolvency professionals. Many of the features need not even be adopted as a law or formally worked out in a court. Instead, the features can be used as guidelines or "norms" in private restructurings. For example, nearly all of the points related to maximizing the potential for bidders to compete involve removing restrictions or regulations, rather than adding them.

Undoubtedly, our suggestions would work best when backed by a strong legal system. For instance, instituting an automatic stay or granting new first-priority liens on assets might require codified exceptions to general creditor collection laws that normally forbid such behavior. The exceptions would have to be enforceable during the bankruptcy period to prevent creditor runs or to head off costly and long legal disagreements. Yet, it is also important that creditor-collection laws be duly enforced outside of bankruptcy in order to ensure, for example, that new liens be honored and that ex-ante incentives are properly aligned in the first place.[28]

---

[28] Enforcement of creditor-collection laws can be problematic even in countries with developed legal systems. For instance, banks in Japan are often reluctant to seize assets backing loans that have gone bad. The existence of multiple lien-holders, laws protecting debtors, and threats from organized crime syndicates all work to make seizure unlikely. For example, see Kunii and Oba (1996).

Because developing countries often lack good legal systems, these suggestions may seem impractical. But substitutes to a strong legal system do exist and could be utilized in countries with weaker legal systems. Stays on collecting payments and agreements for superpriority financing can come privately from the creditors involved in the proceeding. Indeed, the "London Approach" to private workouts advocates both a voluntary stay and the creation of superpriority for interim financiers. The London Approach has been applied in developing countries, with some success.[29] Indeed, all that might be required is an "equitable authority" that referees the bargaining process much like the judges of 19th-century America. Moreover, corporations headquartered in countries with weak legal systems but with operations in countries with stronger legal systems, can opt to file for bankruptcy under the strong systems' laws. For instance, Avianca, Colombia's national airline, filed for bankruptcy protection in the United States under Chapter 11 in March 2003. According to Avianca's bankruptcy counsel, the company filed in the United States because "there was a serious question whether Avianca would be able to get protection from their creditors by filing in Colombia." (Hobday 2003, p. 1). Thus, companies can use the shadow of a strong legal nation's bankruptcy system to propel negotiations forward.

Holding the quality of the legal system constant, our suggested features are well-suited for countries facing systemic financial distress. Experts argue that countries facing systemic financial problems are exposed to risks of capital flight, lack of liquidity, debt overhang, and sharp declines in asset prices or asset "fire sales."[30] These risks often stem from a perceived nervousness on the part of investors (often foreign) that they need to "get out" or "call their loan" before circumstances worsen. Our proposals are meant to work against these tendencies by inducing creditors to step back from moving too quickly against the firm, by making available interim financing to the firm to prevent disruptions during bargaining, and by

---

[29] The "London Approach" to private debt restructurings is a set of principles created in the 1970s by the Bank of England to encourage private workouts in the United Kingdom. More recently, the London Approach has been applied to workouts in East Asian countries following the financial crisis of 1997. Like our work, the London approach recommends a stay of creditor collections and the institution of superpriority financing. In addition, it provides guidance on creditor voting (suggesting agreements should be unanimous) and payoff priorities (suggesting pro-rata loss-sharing). The London Approach is geared to reorganizing a firm under existing management and therefore makes no recommendations on attracting bidders to the firm. For further insight into the London Approach and its success, see Kent (1997), Meyerman (2000), and Armour and Deakin (2001).

[30] See, for example, Kindleberger (1978) and, more recently, Stiglitz (2001).

maximizing the flexibility with which creditors can choose management, and ultimately by helping to create liquidity at a time when liquidity is at its tightest.[31]

ACKNOWLEDGMENTS

We would like to thank Ulf Axelson, Douglas Baird, Simeon Djankov, Luc Laeven, Steve Kaplan, Frederic Martel, David Skeel, Stefan Sundgren, and Arne Wittig for helpful discussions, and Guillermo Noguera for research assistance. We are grateful to Lynn Lopucki for providing us with his Chapter 11 data and to Leora Klapper for sharing her international bankruptcy statistics. The opinions expressed here do not necessarily reflect those of the Federal Reserve Board or its staff.

[31] Miller and Stiglitz (1999) argue for a different framework than ours for dealing with bankrupt firms in markets facing systemic financial problems. They propose what they term a "Super Chapter 11," whereby government authorities force creditors to write down debt claims on distressed firms en masse, conditional on some macroeconomic event occurring, such as a large devaluation. Beyond the fact that their proposal bears no relation to actual Chapter 11 proceedings, their suggestions suffer from several problems. First, such a proposal invites gaming by debtors that can – possibly through coordinated action – influence the macroeconomic "tripwires" in a way that transfers wealth from creditors to debtors. Even if no gaming occurs, debtors' incentives could be distorted by the knowledge of an upcoming write-down. Thus, the ex ante costs imposed by such a system could be large. Third, it is unclear how such a system would be implemented in open economies as, to our knowledge, no precedent exists for the forced repricing of private contracts by government decree.

NINE

Crisis Resolution and Credit Allocation

The Case of Japan

Joe Peek and Eric Rosengren

INTRODUCTION

An incompletely resolved financial crisis can damage economic performance for years. After the bursting of the bubbles in stock prices and real estate prices at the beginning of the 1990s, Japanese economic performance deteriorated markedly, and has yet to recover the vigor that it exhibited for most of the postwar era. Why the Japanese economy has continued to stagnate and been unable to escape its persistent malaise has been the subject of considerable controversy. Although many have argued that resolving the banking crisis and repairing the damaged financial system are critical to the Japanese economic recovery (Greenspan 1999), others have argued that the essential problem is a liquidity trap rather than problems in the banking sector (Krugman 1998).

Determining the nature of the underlying problems is essential, as the appropriate policy prescriptions for these two alternatives are quite different. If the problems center on the banking crisis, then government needs, for example, to recapitalize banks, encourage new entry by well-capitalized foreign banks, and restore liquidity to the real estate market (Chapter 2, this book). Presuming that the problem is primarily a liquidity trap, Krugman (1998) advocates that the Bank of Japan should credibly commit to pursue an inflationary policy for periods "of at least a decade." With such different solutions being proposed, it is essential to understand whether Japanese banks are a key factor in the prolonged economic malaise experienced in Japan.

We use a rich new panel data set to examine how Japanese banks reacted to the economic problems in the 1990s, focusing on how banks allocated credit to Japanese firms. By using Japanese firm-level data, we are able not only to link Japanese firms to their banks, but also to identify the magnitude of their borrowing from their main bank, as well as from alternative sources of financing. Linking individual banks to individual borrowers is critical for understanding how lending disruptions created by problems at financial institutions can be transmitted to the real economy. Such a link cannot be made clearly in many other countries, such as the United States, where bank-borrower relationships are considered private information.

Understanding how banking crises can impact the real economy has been the focus of substantial research over the past two decades. Much of the research in the United States has focused on financial problems exacerbating the Great Depression (Bernanke 1983) and the problems created by the credit crunch period during the early 1990s (Bernanke and Lown 1991; Peek and Rosengren 1995a, 1995b; Hancock and Wilcox 1998). Although these studies have documented that bank lending was restricted during these periods and that the restricted bank lending was coincident with declines in real activity, the absence of a clear micro-level matching of borrower and bank has been a major handicap to isolating the impact of bank lending disruptions.

Establishing the impact of bank lending disruptions on real economic activity is also an important linkage for recent research focused on the "lending view" of monetary policy (Kashyap and Stein 1994, 1995, 2000; Kashyap, Stein, and Wilcox 1993; Stein 1998). If relatively small changes in bank loan supply induced by changes in Federal Reserve policy can affect the real economy, then there should be an even larger impact on loan supply of the much larger shock created by a banking crisis. This is particularly true in Japan, where the entire banking system was close to insolvency. The effect on the economy of banking problems are exacerbated when borrowers have few alternatives to domestic bank credit, such as nonbanks, foreign banks, or direct access to national credit markets, especially when much of the industrial structure is centered on the main banking system (Hoshi, Kashyap, and Scharfstein 1990, 1991; Hoshi, Scharfstein, and Singleton 1993).

Even though bank lending did not decrease dramatically as it did in the United States, Japanese bank behavior may still be critical to understanding the poor performance of the Japanese economy during the 1990s. For example, Peek and Rosengren (2003) have examined the probability of obtaining increased loans from Japanese banks and found that poor firm performance increases the likelihood of a firm getting additional bank loans. This study provides further support for the hypothesis that Japanese banks have misallocated credit, which in turn has impeded the resolution of the crisis created by the end of the bubble economy in the early 1990s.

The first section of the chapter documents the patterns of individual Japanese bank lending and shows that the main banking system remained intact and that troubled banks continued to lend. The second section discusses the data and methods used in our analysis of the patterns of bank lending. The third section provides the empirical results, indicating that bank lending tended to be directed to many of the weakest firms, suggesting that the quality rather than the quantity of bank lending may have been an important impediment to achieving an economic recovery. Importantly, main bank and keiretsu affiliations increased the likelihood that loans would be directed to the weakest firms. The final section provides conclusions.

1. DID JAPAN EXPERIENCE A CAPITAL CRUNCH?

Following the sharp decline in the Japanese stock market beginning in 1990 and the peak in land prices a year later, Japan experienced slower growth in its economy for the subsequent decade, measured both relative to its trend and relative to the United States. A leading candidate for the underlying cause of the persistence of the stagnation of the world's second largest economy has been the impaired health of the banking system. One channel through which banking problems can be transmitted to the real economy is a reduction in credit to creditworthy firms by financially troubled banks. As Bernanke and Lown (1991) and Peek and Rosengren (1995b) have shown for the United States in the early 1990s, banks faced with binding capital constraints tend to shrink their assets in order to improve their capital-to-asset ratios. If the capital constraint is sufficiently binding, banks can be forced to sharply reduce credit to healthy as well as troubled firms. A sharp reduction in credit supply could impede the ability of otherwise healthy firms to obtain needed credit, a characterization some have attributed to the period of slow growth experienced in the United States in the early 1990s.

This "traditional" capital crunch story is potentially more complicated in Japan. In the United States, capital ratio requirements were stringently enforced by bank supervisors through the use of formal regulatory actions that frequently required banks to restore capital ratios above the statutory minimum requirements (Peek and Rosengren 1995a). In contrast, capital standards in Japan were loosely enforced until quite recently, and bank examiners were far less aggressive in forcing shrinkage, mergers or recapitalization of troubled banks.

A further complication for the traditional capital crunch story is created by the far stronger lending relationships in Japan, compared to the United States. Banks and borrowers in Japan frequently have interlocking directorates, cross shareholdings, and main bank affiliations. Thus, the bank and the borrower have a much closer and far more complicated relationship than the typical bank-borrower relationship in the United States.

Should a Japanese bank choose to shrink, it has several options. First, it can choose to shrink its foreign operations, which will typically affect foreign borrowers with less of a banking relationship than is typical of domestic borrowers. This was the initial choice of Japanese banks (Peek and Rosengren 1997). However, if the bank's problems are too severe to be solved by shrinking only international operations, the bank must choose the least costly method for shrinking its domestic loans. First, a bank can choose to terminate its main bank commitment to some firms.[1] This would not only allow the bank to reduce lending but also would enable the bank to unwind its portfolio of share cross-holdings by selling the stock of the former borrower, possibly at a capital gain.[2] A second method of shrinking domestic loans would be to leave the main bank relationships intact, but to reduce lending to firms for which it is the main bank. This makes bank credit less available to firms, possibly at the time of their greatest need, likely reducing the value for firms of bank lending relationships. At least for the biggest and healthiest firms, this would likely encourage firms to make greater use of domestic and international debt markets.[3] The third method of

---

[1] Gibson (1995) examines three ways to identify a firm's main bank: whether a bank employee is on the Board of Directors of the firm, whether the bank is the largest bank shareholder of the firm, or whether the bank is listed first as the reference bank in the Japan Company Handbook. He finds a 95 percent correlation between these three methods of identifying the main bank and chooses the Japan Company Handbook method, as it has the best coverage of firms. Following Gibson, we use the Japan Company Handbook to identify main banks.

[2] Selling cross-shareholdings for a capital gain would increase tier 1 capital. If the firm also sells shares of the bank, it can pay down loans or replace credit it is no longer able to obtain from the bank.

[3] Until the 1970s, firms had to receive approval for issuing debt from the Bond Issuance Committee. This and other impediments to the bond market have prevented debt issuance from being a viable option for most firms until fairly recently. See Hoshi and Kashyap (1999) for more details.

Table 9.1 *Percentage Change of Total, Main Bank, and Secondary Sources of Loans*

Year	Observations	Total Loans	Main Bank Loans	Loans from Secondary Sources
Panel A: Full Sample				
1993	1134	1.83	5.87	1.31
1994	1139	−0.35	2.74	−0.76
1995	1142	−0.96	−2.05	−0.81
1996	1147	−3.15	−1.67	−3.35
1997	1147	−1.05	5.35	−1.95
1998	1025	1.58	−0.13	1.84
Panel B: Same Keiretsu Sample				
1993	389	1.16	2.15	1.03
1994	387	−2.06	2.48	−2.65
1995	403	−2.98	−0.80	−3.25
1996	409	−4.93	−3.28	−5.16
1997	412	−3.01	1.44	−3.65
1998	374	2.51	−0.71	3.00
Panel C: Different or No Keiretsu Sample				
1993	745	2.63	10.07	1.67
1994	752	1.61	3.02	1.42
1995	739	1.40	−3.50	2.07
1996	738	−1.11	0.29	−1.30
1997	735	1.38	9.73	0.23
1998	651	0.65	0.46	0.67

shrinking would be to leave the main banking relationships unchanged but to reduce lending commitments to firms for which it is not the main bank. Thus, firms would find lending reduced from secondary banks, which might, for some firms, be offset by increased credit from their main bank.

Table 9.1 examines the changes in loans for all firms that were in the first section of the Japanese stock market as of 1992. To be included in the table for a particular year, a firm's loan data must be available at the beginning and end of that year, the firm must report the same main bank at the beginning and end of that year, and the firm must not be involved in a merger during that year. The loan data span the period from 1992 through 1998 and are based on the fiscal years of the individual firms. For dating purposes, a firm's observation is assigned to the year in which its fiscal year ends. For example, for a firm with a fiscal year that ends in March, the most common fiscal year in Japan, the March 1995 observation is considered to be the firm's 1995 observation. Because firms may fail, merge, change their fiscal year, have missing data, or be removed as a first section firm, the number of firms with useable observations changes somewhat from year to year.

Table 9.1 has three panels. Panel A contains the data for the full sample. The other two panels are produced by partitioning the full sample into those observations of firms whose main bank is in the same keiretsu as the firm (Panel B) and the observations for the remaining firms that either are in a keiretsu but have a main bank that is not a member of their keiretsu or are not in a keiretsu (Panel C).

For the period from 1992 through 1998, Panel A shows no dramatic decline in total loans occurs for the set of first section firms. Although the biggest decline is 3.15 percent in 1996, the declines are only about one third of 1 percent in 1994, and about 1 percent in both 1995 and 1997. Total loans actually increase in both 1993 and 1998. This is in sharp contrast to the experience in the United States, where loans in some regions of the country declined by as much as 20 percent in a single year during the early 1990s. In fact, given that real GDP growth in Japan was quite lethargic, growing less than 2 percent for each year except 1996, presumably stifling loan demand, it is striking that a sharper decline in loans did not occur in Japan during this period.

Similarly, no evidence of a dramatic decline in main bank loans to first section firms is apparent. In fact, in both 1993 and 1994, main bank loans to first section firms grew more quickly than the real economy, with loan growth of 5.87 and 2.74 percent, respectively. Main bank loans declined in both 1995 and 1996, but actually increased substantially in 1997, before resuming the decline in 1998. Thus, main bank loans increased in three of the six years covered in the table, even though this period was characterized by deteriorating bank financial health, slow economic growth, reductions in Japanese bank lending abroad (Peek and Rosengren 2000), and Japanese banks paying large premiums on interbank borrowing (Peek and Rosengren 2001).

Loan growth from sources other than the firm's main bank was weaker. These loans decreased in each year from 1994 through 1997, increasing only in 1993 and 1998. Because main bank loans account for less than 15 percent of the loans to first section firms, on average, changes in loans from alternative sources have a disproportionate effect on total loan growth. The table also suggests a pattern whereby actions by main banks were followed in the subsequent year by the secondary lenders. The decrease in loans from main banks in 1995 was followed by an acceleration in the decline in loans from secondary lenders in 1996. Similarly, the continuing decline, although at a slower rate, in main bank loans in 1996 was followed by a continuing decline, also at a slower rate, by loans from secondary lenders. Then, the increase in loans by main banks in 1997 was followed by an increase in secondary source loans in 1998. Such a pattern is consistent with main banks serving as the delegated monitor for other potential sources of credit for the firm. Having the most extensive, and likely the most timely, information about the firm, the main bank would take the lead, which would then be followed by the firm's other lenders. Nonetheless, the pattern from 1992 through 1998 is consistent with lending from non-main-bank sources being flat, on average, over this seven-year period.

Panels B and C show quite different patterns in loan growth and shrinkage across these years. In particular, total loan growth was consistently weaker in each year for the same keiretsu firms compared to those firms either not in a keiretsu or, if in a keiretsu, not in the same keiretsu as their main bank. Similarly, same keiretsu firms exhibited slower main bank loan growth in each year, with the exception of 1995 when the only reduction in loans from main banks to the different or no keiretsu firms occurred. For loans from secondary lenders, again loan growth for same keiretsu firms is slower in each year except 1998, and the differences are typically large. In fact, Panel B indicates a substantial pullback in lending by secondary sources to the same keiretsu firms from 1994 through 1997 that did not occur for the different or no keiretsu sample of firms shown in Panel C. Thus, although total loans outstanding to the set of first-section firms were quite similar in 1992 and 1998, the distribution of loans across these firms appears to have changed substantially, both in terms of total loans and in the composition of the sources of those loans.

Table 9.2 examines which banks decreased their main bank commitments to first-section firms during the 1992 to 1998 period. Of the 1,186 first-section firms in 1992, 1,099 had the same main bank in 1998 (93 percent). Most banks had slightly fewer first-section firms listing them as their main bank in 1998. The major exception is Bank of Tokyo-Mitsubishi (BOTM), which had a net increase of seven additional firms listing it as their main bank, with eight firms switching to BOTM and one firm lost because of a merger. The number of firms associated with Asahi, Bank of Yokohama, and Sumitomo Trust were unchanged. Only the weakest banks experienced large declines in the number of firms listing them as their main bank. The biggest declines occurred at Hokkaido Takushoku and Long Term Credit Bank (LTCB), the two weakest banks on the list, both of which subsequently failed. Although main bank switching

Table 9.2. *Did Banks Reduce the Number of Firms that had*
Main Bank Commitment?

Bank	Total 1992	Same Bank	Switched From	To	Merged Same	Different	Delisted	Total 1998
City Banks and Long-Term Credit Banks								
BOTM	133	132	0	8	1	0	0	140
Sanwa	114	108	4	5	0	0	2	113
Sumitomo	129	122	3	4	2	1	1	126
Fuji	142	136	4	5	0	0	2	141
DKB	146	138	6	4	1	1	0	142
IBJ	95	85	5	8	3	2	0	93
Asahi	42	42	0	0	0	0	0	42
Tokai	60	58	0	1	0	1	1	59
Sakura	139	127	7	9	1	0	4	136
LTCB	21	15	5	0	0	0	1	15
Daiwa	31	28	2	1	0	0	1	29
Hokkaido Takushoku	9	0	8	0	0	0	1	0
Regional Bank								
Bank of Yokahama	14	13	0	1	0	1	0	14
Trust Banks								
Mitsui Trust	18	16	2	1	0	0	0	17
Mitsubishi Trust	14	10	3	1	0	1	0	11
Sumitomo Trust	17	14	2	3	0	1	0	17
Other Banks	62	55	6	6	0	0	1	61
TOTALS	1,186	1,099	57	57	8	8	14	1,156

occurred, other than for the weakest and strongest banks, the number of firms that switched from a bank tended to be roughly offset by firms switching to the bank. Thus, for most banks, little net effect occurred through firms switching their main bank allegiance.

Table 9.3 examines the extent to which banks reduced loans to firms that they served as main bank, and if so, whether any reduction was related to the financial condition of the bank. Table 9.3 includes only firms that maintained the same main bank relationship over the entire 1992 through 1998 period. Banks that had at least 10 first-section firms listing them as their main bank are shown separately. Banks with fewer than 10 first-section firms listing them as their main bank are aggregated into an "Other Banks" category. The Other Banks category includes primarily regional banks.

Table 9.3. Percentage Change of Loans from Previous Year by Main Bank to First Section Firms

Bank	1994 Rating	April 1999 Rating	1993	1994	1995	1996	1997	1998	Percent Change 1992–1998
City Banks and Long-Term Credit Banks									
BOTM	Aa3	A2	-2.41	1.73	-2.69	-12.30	1.40	-6.35	-19.55
Sanwa	Aa3	A2	9.12	1.42	-0.39	2.38	-4.63	0.67	8.36
Sumitomo	A1	A3	1.61	0.85	-3.46	-0.42	-1.66	2.12	-1.08
Fuji	A1	Baa1	-1.65	-1.34	-0.96	-5.63	4.26	1.36	-4.17
DKB	A1	Baa1	4.67	5.15	1.32	0.78	1.33	-1.75	11.90
IBJ	A1	Baa1	1.42	0.92	-2.27	2.62	13.26	-1.54	14.48
Asahi	A2	Baa1	27.89	6.22	8.37	-24.24	16.46	14.83	49.15
Tokai	A2	Baa1	-2.88	21.05	3.32	-0.77	3.10	5.67	31.32
Sakura	A2	Baa1	-1.28	-0.88	0.77	-4.77	14.11	-5.27	1.52
LTCB	A3	Baa2	5.42	-0.32	0.52	-5.16	2.51	-0.54	2.14
Daiwa	A3	Baa3	-0.93	7.96	-2.63	12.94	-1.43	4.79	21.49
Regional Bank									
Bank of Yokohama	A3	Baa2	0.05	16.79	0.95	-4.78	-4.16	5.10	13.14
Trust Banks									
Mitsubishi Trust	Baa1	Baa1	15.96	-2.23	-4.33	31.26	6.39	22.03	84.83
Sumitomo Trust	Baa1	Baa2	-2.05	-7.89	4.26	0.24	-10.37	5.18	-11.11
Mitsui Trust	Baa2	Baa2	7.19	-0.82	-4.19	-5.85	-7.69	-11.08	-21.28
Other Banks			12.09	-1.65	0.98	11.12	9.16	15.63	56.12
Total All Banks			2.41	2.12	-0.65	-2.29	3.31	-0.66	4.19

Overall, lending to first-section firms by their main banks grew by 4.19 percent from 1992 through 1998. In half the years, loan growth from the main bank was positive and exceeded 2 percent. Main bank loans declined in three years (1995, 1996, and 1998), although the only decline in excess of 1 percent occurred in 1996.

The aggregate data provide no evidence that banks with weaker ratings by Moody's substantially reduced their lending. In fact, the opposite appears to be the case. Among the city banks and long-term credit banks, the largest shrinkage occurred at Bank of Tokyo-Mitsubishi, with a decline of over 19 percent. Although much of the decline occurred around the time of the merger of Bank of Tokyo with Mitsubishi Bank, even excluding the merger period, the change in loans would be negative. The other two banks with declining loans over this period were Sumitomo and Fuji, which have ratings lower than BOTM, but still much higher than those for the weakest banks. In contrast, Daiwa, Asahi, and Tokai, banks with relatively weaker ratings, increased lending by more than 20 percent over this seven-year period.

Among the other individually listed banks, Mitsui Trust and Sumitomo Trust substantially reduced loans to firms listing them as their main bank, whereas Mitsubishi Trust substantially increased its lending. Bank of Yokohama, the only regional bank with at least 10 first-section firms listing it as their main bank, exhibited loan growth of 13 percent to firms for which it served as the main bank over this period, despite its relatively weak condition. Loan growth for the Other Banks category was positive in all but one year, increasing 56 percent from 1992 through 1998. Apparently, the regional banks were quite willing to provide financing for the few first-section firms that relied on them as their main bank.

Table 9.4 shows changes in loans from main bank and secondary sources for two subsets of firms: those with increased main bank loans over the 1992 through 1998 period and those with decreased main bank loans. The purpose of this table is to investigate the extent to which either main bank loan increases offset withdrawn credit from secondary sources or secondary sources fill the void left when the main bank reduces loans to a firm. The table shows that firms that had increased loans from their main bank during this period generally also had increased loans from their secondary sources. The firms experiencing the largest increases, on average, had Fuji and Asahi as their main banks, and firms with these main banks also experienced large increases in loans from their secondary sources. Similarly, firms using trust banks or banks in the Other Banks category as their main banks also experienced large increases in

Table 9.4. *Changes in Loans from Main Banks and Secondary Sources, 1992–1998*

Bank	Firms with Increased Main Bank Lending		Percent Change		Firms with Decreased Main Bank Lending		Percent Change	
	Number	Total	Main Bank	Secondary	Number	Total	Main Bank	Secondary
City Banks and Long-Term Credit Banks								
BOTM	49	38.67	48.45	36.59	50	-12.53	-39.37	-7.86
Sanwa	41	-2.96	48.44	-8.99	36	-10.09	-34.55	-7.03
Sumitomo	47	15.91	55.00	10.61	32	-41.67	-45.46	-41.09
Fuji	60	63.41	107.98	56.12	30	-27.12	-42.19	-25.41
DKB	59	4.29	62.04	-2.97	45	-19.10	-31.02	-17.67
IBJ	38	20.29	36.70	18.03	33	-21.32	-29.28	-19.95
Asahi	15	83.91	165.80	67.66	14	-35.96	-21.21	-43.59
Tokai	22	14.55	80.98	7.74	15	-10.28	-51.26	1.33
Sakura	59	50.58	87.44	46.26	38	-23.10	-46.14	-21.46
LTCB	6	-11.35	29.05	-17.30	7	-17.32	-22.06	-11.60
Daiwa	14	17.72	47.37	12.44	7	-24.26	-46.28	-20.23
Regional Bank								
Bank of Yokahama	5	42.55	31.16	46.36	5	-16.58	-24.46	-13.94
Trust Banks								
Mitsui Trust	8	40.37	43.83	39.85	7	-8.61	-49.94	-2.77
Mitsubishi Trust	8	78.72	95.63	73.45	2	-31.98	-26.11	-32.76
Sumitomo Trust	8	46.52	66.38	43.18	4	-40.67	-27.59	-42.71
Other Banks	22	57.02	75.83	50.95	10	4.31	-25.92	13.52
Total All Banks	461	19.17	58.05	13.87	335	-20.93	-38.19	-18.63

secondary loans. Only firms associated with Sanwa, DKB, and LTCB had increases in main bank loans and declines in loans from secondary sources, with the largest decline occurring at one of the more troubled banks, LTCB.

Firms that had decreases in main bank loans generally experienced declines in loans from their secondary sources as well. Only firms that had decreased main bank loans from Tokai and banks in the Other Banks category had an increase in secondary source financing. In general, Table 9.4 does not indicate that secondary source financing and main bank financing served as substitutes. Firms with a reduced volume of loans from their main bank also tended to have a reduction in loans from their secondary lenders, whereas firms with increased loans from their main bank also had increased loans from their secondary sources.

The number of firms with increased main bank loans during this period is somewhat larger than the number with decreased main bank loans. Among the major banks, only BOTM and LTCB, the strongest and weakest of the main banks, had more firms with decreased main bank loans than increased main bank loans. Among those banks with more associated firms with increased main bank loans, the numbers were relatively evenly split between firms increasing and decreasing main bank loans. Only Sumitomo, Fuji, DKB, and Sakura had substantially more firms with increased main bank loans than with decreased main bank loans. Given the difficulties experienced in the Japanese economy between 1992 and 1998, it is somewhat surprising that so many firms experienced increases in their main bank loans. This is in sharp contrast to the U.S. experience, in which troubled banks tended to sharply decrease lending in order to raise their capital-to-asset ratios.

The first four tables indicate that a traditional capital crunch did not occur in Japan during the period from 1992 through 1998. Poorly capitalized banks did not disproportionately cut back on loans, and overall lending did not decline dramatically. Nonetheless, the tables do suggest that strong rather than weak banks were more inclined to reduce lending, and that many of the weaker banks and regional banks were the most likely to increase lending. The tables also suggest a surprisingly even split at many banks between the number of firms that had increased loans from their main bank compared to those obtaining less credit from their main bank. Furthermore, in aggregate, firms with decreased lending from their main bank also tended to borrow less from their secondary lenders. Similarly, firms with increased borrowing from their main bank tended to increase their borrowing from their secondary source lenders. However, to better understand the forces determining the allocation of loans across firms with differing characteristics, it is necessary to examine micro-firm-level data. These are discussed in the next section.

2. DATA AND METHODS

While the traditional capital crunch story does not appear to apply to Japan, it is possible that banking problems nonetheless impaired economic growth. This can occur if weakened bank health causes a misallocation of credit, whereby too little credit is provided to healthy firms, whereas a substantial volume of loans is provided to firms with few prospects for being economically viable. By examining the firm-level data, we can better understand how bank loans were allocated to firms. The empirical tests examine several motivations that may affect how Japanese banks allocated credit to firms.

The first is the forbearance hypothesis. Banks seeking to avoid writing off loans, which would reduce their capital, have a perverse incentive to make loans that likely have a negative net present value in order to provide sufficient financing to keep otherwise bankrupt firms afloat. For example, banks might provide funds to firms to make the interest payments on their outstanding loans from the bank so that the loans are not classified as nonperforming loans. Although this "evergreening" of loans benefits the firm, it also improves the bank's reported balance sheet data (in the short run). The firm avoids (or delays) declaring bankruptcy and the bank avoids (or delays) a further increase in its reported nonperforming loans (that includes loans to bankrupt firms and loans that are not current on interest payments) and any associated increase in its loan-loss reserves that would reduce its income and capital. The incentive for a bank to engage in forbearance is likely to be greatest for firms with strong main bank attachments that include equity holdings by the bank, and this incentive may be even stronger if the main bank also has keiretsu ties to the firm. If the firm declares bankruptcy, the bank loses both its equity and some portion of its debt stake. If these firms take more risks, the bank benefits as an equity holder, to the extent the strategy is successful. However, in the long run, such a strategy could result in far greater losses to the bank and scarce credit being allocated to firms with the least productive investment opportunities.

Forbearance was particularly easy for Japanese banks because financial statements were not transparent and there was no tradition of disclosing emerging problems. The most obvious example of the lack of transparency is that problem loans were not disclosed prior to March 1993. Without such disclosure, depositors and stockholders did not have sufficient information to evaluate the condition of the bank. This inhibited the ability of market discipline to provide an incentive for management to quickly resolve emerging problems. Even after 1993, the definition of problem loans evolved only gradually toward definitions similar to those used in the United States and many other countries, with a major breakthrough occurring when the Financial Supervisory Agency (FSA) released its estimates of problem loans, which were substantially larger than those that had been released by the banks, although still far below private sector estimates. Although the FSA appears to be forcing greater disclosure, from 1992 until 1998, government policy did not clearly discourage banks from limiting disclosure and pursuing a policy of forbearance on problem loans, especially as much of the focus prior to 1998 was to avoid a capital crunch, whereby problems at the banks would seriously reduce credit available to firms.

Empirically, forbearance would appear as continued lending to firms that were unprofitable or had bleak prospects, as viewed by market participants through declines in the firm's stock price, and to industries such as real estate that were disproportionately affected by the problems in the Japanese economy. It is also more likely to occur for the firm's main bank, especially if that main bank is also in the same keiretsu as the firm.

The second hypothesis is the market hypothesis. This hypothesis assumes that main banks have superior information because of their access to confidential firm information. Main banks are often equity holders, may have representation on the board of the firm, and can monitor the cash flow of the firm. With this superior information, the bank is able to make credit decisions based on the expected profitability of the firm. Thus, the bank efficiently allocates credit to those firms with the highest expected returns, based on information that is superior to that publicly disclosed in Japan. In this case, no misallocation of scarce credit occurs, as banks ration loans according to the prospects of the firm. If so, a misallocation of credit by banks would not be responsible for the continuing poor performance of the Japanese economy, with aggregate credit not being sharply reduced and, more important, being allocated to those firms with the best prospects.

To test these hypotheses, this study utilizes a new data set that combines individual firm balance sheet, income statement, and stock price data with data on the firm's loans from its main bank, as well as its total borrowing. In addition, the database includes measures of the health of the firm's main bank and the keiretsu affiliations of the firms and main banks. This provides a database that can much more clearly detail the effects of loan supply shocks than in the United States, where data linking specific firms to their primary banks is considered private information.

We collected information on all first-section listed firms with a fiscal year that ends in March.[4] The main bank is identified as the first bank listed in the reference section of the Japan Company Handbook (Shikiho). We then obtained total borrowing and main bank loans from the Directory of Corporate Affiliations (Kigyo Keiretsu Soran). The keiretsu affiliations of the firms and the main banks are obtained from *Industrial Groupings in Japan: The Anatomy of the Keiretsu* by Dodwell Marketing Consultants. These data are then linked to the PACAP database that includes the financial statements and stock returns for each firm. The data set spans the period from 1993 through 1998.

We test the two hypotheses using the following basic specification:

$$\Delta\text{LOAN}_{i,t} = \alpha_0 + \alpha_1\text{FIRM}_{i,t-1} + \alpha_2\text{BANK}_{i,t-1} + \alpha_4\text{TIME} + \varepsilon_{i,t} \quad (9.1)$$

The dependent variable, ΔLOAN, represents three alternative dependent variables: the change in total loans to the firm, the change in main bank loans to the firm, and the change in secondary financing to the firm, with each change calculated between period t and t − 1 and then scaled by the value of firm assets at t − 1. For each firm, the dating of the variables is based on the year in which their fiscal year ends. For example, a fiscal year ending in March 1995 would be taken as the 1995 observation.

The first vector of variables is a set of firm-specific variables at time t − 1. These variables are intended to capture the financial condition of the firm and the degree of bank dependence. FIRM includes the firm's capital-to-asset ratio, return on assets, and percent change in market value, as well as the logarithm of the real value of firm assets. We have also included the ownership concentration of the firm's shares by financial institutions, other nonfinancial corporations, and foreigners, whether the firm enters the bond market (the first time it has a positive value for bonds outstanding), is in the bond market (has a positive value for bonds outstanding, other than the year in which it first enters the bond market), or exits the bond market (no longer has bonds outstanding) to capture the ability of the firm to access credit from sources outside of domestic

---

[4] We restrict the sample to firms with a March fiscal year end for two reasons. First, it avoids serious timing problems across firms. Second, it lines up with the bank data, as banks report fiscal year results in March.

banks. We also have included a set of dummy variables that indicate the firm's industry (disaggregated into nine industries). We have omitted the dummy variable for the services sector, so all estimated coefficients on the industry dummy variables indicate effects measured relative to the services industry.

The second vector of variables is a set of bank-specific variables, measured at time $t - 1$, that measure the health of the main bank. This set includes the return on assets (ROA), risk-based capital ratio, and ratio of nonperforming loans to assets for the firm's main bank. Were this a "capital crunch" as was reported in the early 1990s in the United States (Peek and Rosengren 1995b), we would expect that lending would decline as the ROA and risk-based capital ratio of the main bank declined, and as the bank's nonperforming loan ratio increased. The third vector of variables is a set of annual time dummy variables intended to control for the general macroeconomic conditions in Japan.

3. EMPIRICAL RESULTS

We provide the results for estimating equation (9.1) using both ordinary least squares (Tables 9.5–9.7) and fixed-effects (Tables 9.8–9.13) estimation methods for the changes in total loans, main bank loans, and secondary source loans, in each case scaled by the firm's total assets. Each table presents results for the full sample as well as two alternative sample splits related to keiretsu relationships. The first sample partition is between firms in the same keiretsu as their main bank and firms either not in a keiretsu or in a different keiretsu than their main bank. The second sample partition is between firms in a keiretsu and firms not in a keiretsu. The estimation uses annual observations for 1994–1998. The beginning of the sample period is restricted to 1994 because bank nonperforming loan data has been reported only since 1993 and we use its lagged value as an explanatory variable. The Hausman test statistic strongly rejects ordinary least squares (OLS) specification in favor of the fixed-effects specification. Still, we present the OLS regression results as a benchmark and because the OLS specification allows one to examine differences in lending patterns across industries. The t-statistics reported in the tables are based on robust standard errors calculated by relaxing the assumption of independence of the observations for a given year.

Table 9.5 contains the ordinary least squares estimates for the change in total loans to firms, scaled by the firm's total assets. Only three of the FIRM variables have statistically significant effects, using standard

Table 9.5. *Total Loans*

Factors Affecting the Change in Bank Loans to First-Section Firms
Estimation Method: Ordinary Least Squares; 1994–1998

	Full Sample	Same Keiretsu	Different or No Keiretsu	In Keiretsu	Not in Keiretsu
Firm Variables					
Log (Assets)	−0.250**	−0.409**	−0.179*	−0.406**	−0.174
	(3.45)	(3.40)	(1.93)	(3.49)	(1.83)
Capital/Assets	0.000	−0.002	0.005	−0.005	0.010
	(0.05)	(0.28)	(0.83)	(0.69)	(1.76)
Return on Assets	−0.097**	−0.119**	−0.089**	−0.130**	−0.090**
	(4.24)	(2.80)	(3.31)	(3.17)	(3.35)
Percent Change in	−0.002	−0.010*	0.003	−0.009	0.004
Market Value	(0.76)	(1.99)	(0.85)	(1.85)	(0.98)
In Bond Market	0.203	−0.007	0.438	−0.080	0.613
	(0.60)	(0.01)	(0.90)	(0.17)	(1.23)
Enter Bond Market	−0.769	−0.678	−0.931	−0.810	−0.703
	(1.67)	(1.04)	(1.40)	(1.26)	(1.04)
Exit Bond Market	0.919**	1.050*	0.775	0.758	1.044*
	(2.89)	(2.23)	(1.78)	(1.65)	(2.35)
Financial Ownership	0.011	0.019	0.004	0.016	0.008
	(1.53)	(1.60)	(0.50)	(1.45)	(0.88)
Business Ownership	0.005	0.001	0.006	0.008	0.003
	(0.85)	(0.13)	(0.92)	(0.82)	(0.48)
Foreign Ownership	0.001	0.009	−0.003	0.010	−0.006
	(0.11)	(0.78)	(0.39)	(0.94)	(0.75)
Bank Variables					
Return on Assets	−0.249	−0.289	−0.270	−0.457	0.047
	(0.68)	(0.50)	(0.56)	(0.84)	(0.09)
Risk-Based	−0.138	0.252	−0.411	0.212	−0.558
Capital Ratio	(0.37)	(0.39)	(0.85)	(0.35)	(1.14)
Nonperforming Loan	0.868	0.411	1.469	0.603	0.953
Ratio	(0.62)	(0.17)	(0.84)	(0.26)	(0.54)
Agriculture/Mining	−0.447	4.775*	−2.749*	2.669	−2.750*
	(0.44)	(2.46)	(2.28)	(1.53)	(2.20)
Construction	0.333	2.046	−0.254	1.109	0.056
	(0.39)	(1.26)	(0.26)	(0.75)	(0.06)
Manufacturing	−0.327	1.494	−1.026	0.752	−1.044
	(0.40)	(0.94)	(1.09)	(0.52)	(1.08)
Wholesale/Retail	−0.884	0.800	−1.320	0.152	−1.301
	(1.04)	(0.49)	(1.33)	(0.10)	(1.27)
Finance/Insurance	−2.134	−1.285	−1.021	−2.397	−0.811
	(1.88)	(0.67)	(0.64)	(1.32)	(0.51)
Real Estate	0.159	2.093	−0.516	0.900	−0.125
	(0.15)	(1.10)	(0.39)	(0.50)	(0.09)
Transportation/	−1.103	0.100	−1.425	−1.394	−0.522
Communication	(1.27)	(0.06)	(1.40)	(0.92)	(0.49)
Electric Power	1.327	–	0.634	–	0.751
and Gas	(1.25)		(0.55)		(0.65)
Observations	3576	1453	2123	1691	1885
R²	0.027	0.054	0.024	0.051	0.027

Notes: Each regression also includes a set of year dummy variables. Absolute values of t-statistics are in parentheses. * denotes significance at the 5 percent level; ** denotes significance at the 10 percent level.

levels of significance: the firm's size, the firm's return on assets (ROA), and the dummy variable that indicates when the firm exited the bond market. The negative estimated coefficient on firm size indicates that larger firms tend to obtain smaller increases in total loans. The negative estimated coefficient on firm ROA indicates that loans tend to increase as firm performance worsens. This is consistent with banks evergreening loans, increasing credit to the weakest firms. Similarly, although not statistically significant, the negative estimated coefficient on the percent change in the firm's market value also is consistent with the evergreening hypothesis.

The estimated coefficients on the bond market entry and exit variables suggest that bank loans serve as a substitute for bond debt. In particular, the significant negative coefficient on the dummy variable for exiting the bond market is consistent with firms exiting the arms-length credit market where they are charged an appropriate risk premium and returning to relationship financing with their banks, which may be undercharging the firm for loans. In fact, Smith (2003) finds that Japanese banks charge Japanese firms lower interest rates than do foreign banks.

Although none of the bank health variables have significant coefficients, the negative estimated coefficients on bank ROA and the bank risk-based capital ratio, as well as the positive estimated coefficient on the bank nonperforming loan ratio, are each consistent with banks tending to increase loans the weaker is bank health, a result that contrasts sharply with the U.S. experience but is consistent with the evergreening hypothesis. None of the industry dummy variables has statistically significant estimated coefficients. However, of the three with positive estimated coefficients, two are for the construction and real estate industries, indicating that they received larger increases in total loans relative to the services industry, other things equal. Given the significant decline in real estate prices before, during, and after the regression sample, one would not have expected these two industries to be among those with the largest increases in loans if credit were being allocated prudentially.

The remaining four columns allow one to contrast the results with and without keiretsu affiliations. In each instance, the firm's ROA retains a significant negative estimated coefficient, with the Same Keiretsu and In Keiretsu columns exhibiting the larger (in absolute value) effects, suggesting that weaker firms with keiretsu affiliations with their main banks, or even just being a member of a keiretsu, obtained even larger increases in total loans, other things equal. Similarly, the same two columns have

Table 9.6. Main Bank Loans

Factors Affecting the Change in Bank Loans to First-Section Firms
Estimation Method: Ordinary Least Squares; 1994–1998

	Full Sample	Same Keiretsu	Different or No Keiretsu	In Keiretsu	Not in Keiretsu
Firm Variables					
Log (Assets)	−0.064**	−0.119**	−0.050*	−0.134**	−0.034
	(2.50)	(2.81)	(1.52)	(3.31)	(0.99)
Capital/Assets	−0.001	−0.001	−0.001	−0.002	0.001
	(0.75)	(0.36)	(0.39)	(0.84)	(0.39)
Return on Assets	−0.033**	−0.037*	−0.030**	−0.042**	−0.029**
	(4.13)	(2.47)	(3.20)	(2.92)	(3.05)
Percent Change in	−0.000	−0.003	0.001	−0.002	0.001
Market Value	(0.39)	(1.51)	(0.81)	(1.34)	(0.76)
In Bond Market	0.053	−0.029	0.155	−0.008	0.140
	(0.45)	(0.17)	(0.91)	(0.05)	(0.79)
Enter Bond Market	−0.155	−0.126	−0.165	−0.161	−0.097
	(0.95)	(0.55)	(0.71)	(0.72)	(0.40)
Exit Bond Market	0.222*	0.219	0.267	0.166	0.312*
	(1.98)	(1.31)	(1.75)	(1.05)	(1.96)
Financial Ownership	−0.000	0.003	−0.002	0.000	−0.001
	(0.05)	(0.63)	(0.77)	(0.08)	(0.24)
Business Ownership	−0.001	−0.003	−0.000	−0.002	−0.000
	(0.29)	(0.68)	(0.02)	(0.64)	(0.05)
Foreign Ownership	0.001	0.004	−0.000	0.005	−0.002
	(0.50)	(0.97)	(0.14)	(1.40)	(0.59)
Bank Variables					
Return on Assets	0.026	−0.068	0.043	−0.030	0.103
	(0.20)	(0.33)	(0.25)	(0.16)	(0.57)
Risk-Based	−0.039	0.026	−0.053	−0.032	−0.068
Capital Ratio	(0.29)	(0.11)	(0.31)	(0.15)	(0.39)
Nonperforming	0.821	0.764	0.995	0.900	0.939
Loan Ratio	(1.65)	(0.87)	(1.62)	(1.12)	(1.47)
Agriculture/Mining	−0.575	−0.418	−0.693	−0.901	−0.428
	(1.59)	(0.61)	(1.64)	(1.48)	(0.95)
Construction	−0.109	−0.122	−0.183	−0.296	−0.041
	(0.37)	(0.21)	(0.53)	(0.57)	(0.11)
Manufacturing	−0.319	−0.465	−0.297	−0.532	−0.263
	(1.12)	(0.83)	(0.90)	(1.06)	(0.76)
Wholesale/Retail	−0.404	−0.320	−0.494	−0.423	−0.437
	(1.35)	(0.55)	(1.41)	(0.82)	(1.19)
Finance/Insurance	−0.679	−0.243	−1.518**	−0.375	−1.440*
	(1.70)	(0.36)	(2.69)	(0.60)	(2.53)
Real Estate	0.038	0.253	−0.169	0.077	−0.034
	(0.10)	(0.38)	(0.36)	(0.12)	(0.07)
Transportation/	−0.481	−0.899	−0.271	−0.977	−0.151
Communication	(1.58)	(1.52)	(0.76)	(1.85)	(0.40)
Electric Power	−0.229	–	−0.253	–	−0.184
and Gas	(0.62)		(0.62)		(0.44)
Observations	3576	1453	2123	1691	1885
R^2	0.016	0.027	0.020	0.028	0.018

Notes: Each regression also includes a set of year dummy variables. Absolute values of t-statistics are in parentheses.*denotes significance at the 5 percent level;** denotes significance at the 10 percent level.

negative estimated coefficients on the percent change in the market value of the firm, being statistically significant for same keiretsu firms, whereas the estimated coefficients are positive in the absence of the keiretsu affiliations. Although not significant, the firm's capital-to-asset ratio has negative estimated coefficients for the two keiretsu samples and positive estimated coefficients for the non-keiretsu samples. Thus, overall these results are consistent with keiretsu affiliations providing an added incentive for banks to make additional credit available to the weakest firms. Finally, the only industry with a significant estimated coefficient is the agriculture/mining industry. The effect is positive for the keiretsu samples and negative for the non-keiretsu samples. Agriculture is a politically favored industry, and it is possible that, as a consequence, same keiretsu main banks feel a special obligation to aid such firms.

Table 9.6 repeats the specifications in Table 9.5 for the change in main bank loans, scaled by the firm's total assets. The results are much the same as for total loans, although it is interesting that the estimated coefficients on the Finance/Insurance industry dummy variable are negative and significant for the non-keiretsu columns. This suggests that firms in this industry exhibited slower loan growth than firms in other industries, other things equal, in the absence of keiretsu support. Finally, Table 9.7 repeats the specifications for the change in loans from secondary sources, scaled by the firm's total assets. The results are much the same as for total loans.

Tables 9.8, 9.9, and 9.10 report the same set of regressions as the three previous tables using a fixed-firm-effect specification. Based on the Hausman test statistics, this specification is preferred over the corresponding ordinary least squares specifications. Just as with the previous tables, each regression also contains a set of annual time dummy variables (not shown in order to conserve space in the tables). Now that the specification controls for the fixed firm effect, more estimated coefficients that are statistically significant are obtained. In Table 9.8, among the FIRM variables, larger firms tend to have smaller increases in loans and firms with higher capital-to-asset ratios tend to obtain larger increases in loans. Although the firms' ROA consistently has a negative estimated coefficient, it is significant only for the total sample and for each of the two non-keiretsu subsamples. Again, this indicates that the weaker is the firm's performance, the larger is the increase in loans. However, in contrast to the OLS results, the magnitude of the effect is now larger for the non-keiretsu samples. The estimated coefficients on the percent change in the market value of the firm are negative only for the keiretsu subsamples,

Table 9.7. *Secondary Lender Loans*

Factors Affecting the Change in Bank Loans to First-Section Firms
Estimation Method: Ordinary Least Squares; 1994–1998

	Full Sample	Same Keiretsu	Different or No Keiretsu	In Keiretsu	Not in Keiretsu
Firm Variables					
Log (Assets)	−0.186**	−0.290**	−0.129	−0.272**	−0.140
	(3.27)	(3.06)	(1.77)	(2.97)	(1.88)
Capital/Assets	0.001	−0.001	0.005	−0.003	0.009*
	(0.40)	(0.19)	(1.23)	(0.51)	(2.06)
Return on Assets	−0.064**	−0.082*	−0.059**	−0.088**	−0.061**
	(3.54)	(2.45)	(2.78)	(2.74)	(2.88)
Percent Change in	−0.002	−0.007	0.002	−0.007	0.003
Market Value	(0.79)	(1.85)	(0.72)	(1.76)	(0.90)
In Bond Market	0.150	0.023	0.283	−0.071	0.472
	(0.56)	(0.06)	(0.74)	(0.19)	(1.21)
Enter Bond Market	−0.614	−0.551	−0.766	−0.650	−0.606
	(1.69)	(1.07)	(1.47)	(1.29)	(1.14)
Exit Bond Market	0.698**	0.831*	0.508	0.591	0.732*
	(2.78)	(2.24)	(1.49)	(1.64)	(2.09)
Financial Ownership	0.011*	0.016	0.007	0.016	0.009
	(1.96)	(1.75)	(0.98)	(1.81)	(1.23)
Business Ownership	0.006	0.004	0.007	0.011	0.004
	(1.20)	(0.48)	(1.18)	(1.33)	(0.64)
Foreign Ownership	−0.000	0.005	−0.003	0.005	−0.004
	(0.09)	(0.55)	(0.43)	(0.57)	(0.69)
Bank Variables					
Return on Assets	−0.275	−0.221	−0.313	−0.427	−0.057
	(0.96)	(0.48)	(0.83)	(1.00)	(0.14)
Risk-Based	−0.099	0.226	−0.358	0.244	−0.489
Capital Ratio	(0.33)	(0.44)	(0.95)	(0.52)	(1.27)
Nonperforming	0.047	−0.353	0.474	−0.296	0.013
Loan Ratio	(0.04)	(0.18)	(0.35)	(0.16)	(0.10)
Agriculture/Mining	0.128	5.194**	−2.056*	3.570**	−2.323*
	(0.16)	(3.39)	(2.18)	(2.60)	(2.36)
Construction	0.442	2.168	−0.071	1.405	0.098
	(0.66)	(1.69)	(0.09)	(1.21)	(0.12)
Manufacturing	−0.007	1.959	−0.729	1.283	−0.781
	(0.01)	(1.56)	(0.99)	(1.13)	(1.03)
Wholesale/Retail	−0.480	1.120	−0.826	0.575	−0.864
	(0.72)	(0.87)	(1.06)	(0.49)	(1.07)
Finance/Insurance	−1.456	−1.042	0.497	−2.022	0.629
	(1.63)	(0.69)	(0.39)	(1.42)	(0.50)
Real Estate	0.120	1.839	−0.348	0.823	−0.090
	(0.14)	(1.23)	(0.33)	(0.58)	(0.09)
Transportation/	−0.621	1.000	−1.154	−0.417	−0.371
Communication	(0.91)	(0.76)	(1.44)	(0.35)	(0.44)
Electric Power	1.556	−	0.888	−	0.935
and Gas	(1.87)		(0.98)		(1.02)
Observations	3576	1453	2123	1691	1885
R^2	0.027	0.062	0.024	0.056	0.028

Notes: Each regression also includes a set of year dummy variables. Absolute values of t-statistics are in parentheses. * denotes significance at the 5 percent level; ** denotes significance at the 10 percent level.

Table 9.8. *Total Loans*

Factors Affecting the Change in Bank Loans to First-Section Firms
Estimation Method: Fixed-Effects Specification; 1994–1998

	Full Sample	Same Keiretsu	Different or No Keiretsu	In Keiretsu	Not in Keiretsu
Firm Variables					
Log (Assets)	−2.849**	−6.060**	−0.802	−7.575**	0.580
	(2.94)	(3.34)	(0.69)	(4.45)	(0.49)
Capital/Assets	0.172**	0.180**	0.168**	0.141**	0.179**
	(7.39)	(3.76)	(6.26)	(3.27)	(6.49)
Return on Assets	−0.122**	−0.062	−0.188**	−0.031	−0.206**
	(2.95)	(0.83)	(3.61)	(0.45)	(3.99)
Percent Change in	0.003	−0.005	0.008	−0.004	0.011*
Market Value	(0.94)	(0.84)	(1.79)	(0.81)	(2.22)
In Bond Market	0.940	1.394	0.872	1.114	0.989
	(1.83)	(1.80)	(1.21)	(1.52)	(1.31)
Enter Bond Market	−0.971	−1.425	−0.651	−1.428	−0.398
	(1.82)	(1.84)	(0.85)	(1.91)	(0.51)
Exit Bond Market	1.459**	1.932**	1.215*	1.577**	1.443*
	(3.60)	(3.13)	(2.18)	(2.66)	(2.53)
Financial Ownership	0.075*	0.091	0.023	0.099	0.008
	(2.04)	(1.40)	(0.51)	(1.64)	(0.18)
Business Ownership	0.016	0.023	0.016	0.021	0.016
	(1.79)	(1.40)	(1.48)	(1.42)	(1.39)
Foreign Ownership	−0.008	−0.015	−0.008	−0.005	−0.016
	(0.88)	(0.94)	(0.74)	(0.35)	(1.44)
Bank Variables					
Return on Assets	−0.224	−0.501	−0.163	−0.605	0.074
	(0.52)	(0.72)	(0.29)	(0.93)	(0.13)
Risk-Based	−0.260	0.461	−0.606	0.240	−0.582
Capital Ratio	(0.53)	(0.56)	(0.98)	(0.31)	(0.90)
Nonperforming	−0.263	−4.882	1.992	−5.270	3.138
Loan Ratio	(0.10)	(0.96)	(0.61)	(1.11)	(0.94)
Observations	3576	1453	2123	1691	1885
R^2	0.277	0.307	0.297	0.300	0.301

Notes: Each regression also includes a set of year dummy variables. Absolute values of t-statistics are in parentheses. * denotes significance at the 5 percent level; ** denotes significance at the 10 percent level.

indicating that weaker firm performance is associated with larger increases in loans. However, the only estimated coefficient that is statistically significant is that for the Not in Keiretsu subsample. Thus, it appears that in the absence of keiretsu affiliations, lenders tend to make credit more available the better is firm performance, other things equal. Finally,

Table 9.9. *Main Bank Loans*

Factors Affecting the Change in Bank Loans to First-Section Firms
Estimation Method: Fixed-Effects Specification; 1994–1998

	Full Sample	Same Keiretsu	Different or No Keiretsu	In Keiretsu	Not in Keiretsu
Firm Variables					
Log (Assets)	−0.332	−1.427*	0.319	−1.964**	0.706
	(0.94)	(2.14)	(0.75)	(3.19)	(1.58)
Capital/Assets	0.057**	0.067**	0.055**	0.051**	0.059**
	(6.67)	(3.83)	(5.61)	(3.24)	(5.66)
Return on Assets	−0.037*	−0.046	−0.042*	−0.029	−0.043*
Return on Assets	(2.42)	(1.71)	(2.22)	(1.18)	(2.21)
Percent Change in	0.002	0.001	0.003	0.001	0.003
Market Value	(1.62)	(0.45)	(1.76)	(0.49)	(1.93)
In Bond Market	0.224	0.272	0.259	0.249	0.172
	(1.19)	(0.95)	(0.97)	(0.94)	(0.60)
Enter Bond Market	−0.190	−0.292	−0.120	−0.301	−0.010
	(0.98)	(1.02)	(0.43)	(1.11)	(0.03)
Exit Bond Market	0.318*	0.326	0.345	0.296	0.347
	(2.15)	(1.43)	(1.69)	(1.38)	(1.61)
Financial Ownership	0.016	0.021	0.007	0.011	0.012
	(1.21)	(0.87)	(0.43)	(0.50)	(0.65)
Business Ownership	0.001	0.000	0.003	−0.002	0.004
	(0.39)	(0.00)	(0.67)	(0.33)	(0.92)
Foreign Ownership	−0.000	0.001	−0.002	0.004	−0.005
	(0.09)	(0.14)	(0.43)	(0.73)	(1.13)
Bank Variables					
Return on Assets	0.075	−0.174	0.185	−0.101	0.256
	(0.48)	(0.67)	(0.90)	(0.43)	(1.15)
Risk-Based	−0.087	0.101	−0.169	0.002	−0.171
Capital Ratio	(0.49)	(0.33)	(0.74)	(0.01)	(0.70)
Nonperforming	1.606	−1.235	3.014*	−0.292	3.212*
Loan Ratio	(1.64)	(0.66)	(2.52)	(0.17)	(2.55)
Observations	3576	1453	2123	1691	1885
R^2	0.213	0.226	0.227	0.226	0.220

Notes: Each regression also includes a set of year dummy variables. Absolute values of t-statistics are in parentheses. * denotes significance at the 5 percent level; ** denotes significance at the 10 percent level.

greater ownership of the firm by financial institutions is associated with larger increases in loans, other things equal, with the estimated effect being statistically significant for the full sample. Thus, to the extent that lenders have an equity stake in the firm, they are more likely to increase lending to that firm, other things equal.

Table 9.10. *Secondary Lender Loans*

Factors Affecting the Change in Bank Loans to First-Section Firms
Estimation Method: Fixed-Effects Specification; 1994–1998

	Full Sample	Same Keiretsu	Different or No Keiretsu	In Keiretsu	Not in Keiretsu
Firm Variables					
Log (Assets)	−2.517**	−4.633**	−1.121	−5.612**	−0.126
	(3.33)	(3.26)	(1.25)	(4.22)	(0.14)
Capital/Assets	0.115**	0.112**	0.112**	0.091**	0.120**
	(6.36)	(3.01)	(5.42)	(2.69)	(5.63)
Return on Assets	−0.086**	−0.015	−0.145**	−0.002	−0.163**
	(2.65)	(0.26)	(3.61)	(0.03)	(4.08)
Percent Change in	0.001	−0.006	0.005	−0.005	0.007
Market Value	(0.45)	(1.28)	(1.47)	(1.27)	(1.93)
In Bond Market	0.716	1.122	0.614	0.866	0.817
	(1.78)	(1.84)	(1.09)	(1.52)	(1.39)
Enter Bond Market	−0.780	−1.133	−0.531	−1.127	−0.388
	(1.87)	(1.87)	(0.90)	(1.93)	(0.64)
Exit Bond Market	1.141**	1.606**	0.870*	1.280**	1.096*
	(3.60)	(3.32)	(2.02)	(2.76)	(2.48)
Financial Ownership	0.059*	0.070	0.016	0.088	−0.003
	(2.05)	(1.38)	(0.45)	(1.86)	(0.09)
Business Ownership	0.015*	0.023	0.014	0.023*	0.012
	(2.12)	(1.79)	(1.59)	(1.97)	(1.35)
Foreign Ownership	−0.008	−0.016	−0.006	−0.009	−0.012
	(1.09)	(1.26)	(0.75)	(0.79)	(1.31)
Bank Variables					
Return on Assets	−0.300	−0.328	−0.348	−0.504	−0.183
	(0.89)	(0.60)	(0.81)	(0.99)	(0.40)
Risk-Based	−0.173	0.360	−0.437	0.238	−0.411
Capital Ratio	(0.45)	(0.56)	(0.91)	(0.39)	(0.82)
Nonperforming	−1.869	−3.647	−1.022	−4.978	−0.074
Loan Ratio	(0.89)	(0.92)	(0.41)	(1.34)	(0.03)
Observations	3576	1453	2123	1691	1885
R^2	0.290	0.319	0.315	0.313	0.323

Notes: Each regression also includes a set of year dummy variables. Absolute values of t-statistics are in parentheses. * denotes significance at the 5 percent level; ** denotes significance at the 10 percent level.

With respect to the bank health variables, none has a significant effect. In four of the five specifications, the bank ROA has a negative estimated coefficient, indicating that the weaker is bank health, the more likely the bank will increase loans to firms. Similarly, for the full sample and for the two non-keiretsu subsamples, the estimated coefficient on the bank risk-based capital variable is negative, again indicating that weaker bank health is associated with larger changes in loans. Finally, for the non-keiretsu subsamples, the estimated coefficients on the bank nonperforming loan ratio are positive, indicating the more severe are reported problems with the main bank's loan portfolio, the more likely the bank will make larger loans to firms. The results for the non-keiretsu lenders are consistent with banks evergreening loans, insofar as the lower is the bank's ROA and capital ratio, and the larger is the bank's nonperforming loan ratio, the stronger is the bank's incentive to keep firms in a position to continue to make interest payments to keep their loans current or delay or avoid declaring bankruptcy.

Tables 9.11, 9.12, and 9.13 repeat the specifications contained in Tables 9.8, 9.9, and 9.10 with the variable measuring the percent change in the market value of the firm replaced by a set of $(1, 0)$ dummy variables indicating the quartile in which the percent change in the firm's market value fell in each year. The regressions include variables for the first three quartiles, so that their estimated coefficients indicate effects relative to that of the highest quartile effect. The estimated coefficients on the other variables are little affected.

In Table 9.11 for the change in total loans, a clear contrast exists between the estimated effects for the keiretsu and non-keiretsu subsamples. For both the Same Keiretsu and In Keiretsu subsamples, the estimated coefficients on the quartile dummy variables are always positive. For the lowest quartile of percent changes in firm market value (the weakest performing firms), the effect is statistically significant for the Same Keiretsu subsample, and just misses standard levels of significance for the In Keiretsu subsample. Similarly, for Quartile 2, the estimated effect is significant for the In Keiretsu subsample, and significant at the 10 percent level for the Same Keiretsu subsample. In contrast, the estimated effects for the non-keiretsu subsamples are negative, except in one instance in which the point estimate is essentially zero. Thus, it appears that banks tend to lend more to the weakest firms that have a keiretsu affiliation, other things equal. In contrast, for those firms in the non-keiretsu subsamples, such a perverse relationship between firm performance and lending is not apparent.

For the change in main bank loans shown in Table 9.12, a similar contrast appears. The keiretsu subsamples have positive estimated coefficients on the quartile dummy variables, whereas the non-keiretsu subsamples have negative estimated coefficients. However, in this case, it is the negative estimated coefficients for the non-keiretsu subsamples that

Table 9.11. *Total Loans*

Factors Affecting the Change in Bank Loans to First-Section Firms
Estimation Method: Fixed-Effects Specification; 1994–1998

	Full Sample	Same Keiretsu	Different or No Keiretsu	In Keiretsu	Not in Keiretsu
Firm Variables					
Log (Assets)	−2.894**	−6.240**	−0.839	−7.780**	0.504
	(2.99)	(3.44)	(0.73)	(4.58)	(0.42)
Capital/Assets	0.171**	0.177**	0.169**	0.139**	0.179**
	(7.36)	(3.71)	(6.29)	(3.23)	(6.50)
Return on Assets	−0.110**	−0.042	−0.180**	−0.010	−0.199**
	(2.65)	(0.57)	(3.47)	(0.15)	(3.84)
Percent Change in	0.052	0.817*	−0.431	0.692	−0.467
Market Value:	(0.23)	(2.18)	(1.51)	(1.95)	(1.59)
Quartile1					
Percent Change in	0.258	0.643	0.001	0.898*	−0.232
Market Value:	(1.15)	(1.73)	(0.00)	(2.56)	(0.78)
Quartile2					
Percent Change in	−0.135	0.461	−0.516	0.337	−0.419
Market Value:	(0.60)	(1.25)	(1.83)	(0.97)	(1.44)
Quartile3					
In Bond Market	0.953	1.372	0.813	1.180	0.951
	(1.85)	(1.76)	(1.12)	(1.61)	(1.25)
Enter Bond Market	−0.990	−1.428	−0.661	−1.476*	−0.407
	(1.85)	(1.84)	(0.87)	(1.97)	(0.52)
Exit Bond Market	1.453**	1.880**	1.145*	1.586**	1.409*
	(3.58)	(3.04)	(2.06)	(2.67)	(2.46)
Financial Ownership	0.066	0.076	0.016	0.083	0.003
	(1.80)	(1.17)	(0.35)	(1.37)	(0.05)
Business Ownership	0.017	0.023	0.017	0.022	0.017
	(1.87)	(1.38)	(1.57)	(1.46)	(1.47)
Foreign Ownership	−0.009	−0.016	−0.009	−0.007	−0.017
	(1.02)	(1.00)	(0.84)	(0.51)	(1.49)
Bank Variables					
Return on Assets	−0.217	−0.535	−0.128	−0.652	0.097
	(0.50)	(0.76)	(0.23)	(1.00)	(0.16)
Risk-Based	−0.255	0.485	−0.622	0.263	−0.612
Capital Ratio	(0.52)	(0.59)	(1.00)	(0.34)	(0.95)
Nonperforming	−0.375	−5.444	1.950	−5.882	3.152
Loan Ratio	(0.14)	(1.07)	(0.60)	(1.24)	(0.94)
Observations	3576	1453	2123	1691	1885
R^2	0.277	0.310	0.298	0.304	0.300

Notes: Each regression also includes a set of year dummy variables. Absolute values of t-statistics are in parentheses. * denotes significance at the 5 percent level; ** denotes significance at the 10 percent level.

Joe Peek and Eric Rosengren

Table 9.12. *Main Bank Loans*

Factors Affecting the Change in Bank Loans to First-Section Firms
Estimation Method: Fixed-Effects Specification; 1994–1998

	Full Sample	Same Keiretsu	Different or No Keiretsu	In Keiretsu	Not in Keiretsu
Firm Variables					
Log (Assets)	−0.349	−1.461*	0.306	−2.001**	0.680
	(0.99)	(2.18)	(0.72)	(3.25)	(1.52)
Capital/Assets	0.057**	0.067**	0.056**	0.050**	0.060**
	(6.69)	(3.80)	(5.68)	(3.22)	(5.72)
Return on Assets	−0.035*	−0.040	−0.043*	−0.023	−0.043*
	(2.29)	(1.49)	(2.24)	(0.94)	(2.23)
Percent Change in	−0.099	0.105	−0.229*	0.081	−0.253*
Market Value:	(1.20)	(0.76)	(2.18)	(0.63)	(2.28)
Quartile1					
Percent Change in	−0.023	0.028	−0.058	0.090	−0.096
Market Value:	(0.29)	(0.21)	(0.55)	(0.71)	(0.86)
Quartile2					
Percent Change in	−0.109	0.019	−0.188	0.020	−0.189
Market Value:	(1.34)	(0.14)	(1.81)	(0.16)	(1.73)
Quartile3					
In Bond Market	0.226	0.265	0.237	0.256	0.146
	(1.20)	(0.92)	(0.89)	(0.96)	(0.51)
Enter Bond Market	−0.191	−0.285	−0.117	−0.301	−0.002
	(0.98)	(1.00)	(0.42)	(1.11)	(0.01)
Exit Bond Market	0.318*	0.318	0.324	0.298	0.333
	(2.15)	(1.39)	(1.58)	(1.39)	(1.55)
Financial Ownership	0.015	0.018	0.007	0.008	0.012
	(1.12)	(0.74)	(0.39)	(0.36)	(0.65)
Business Ownership	0.002	−0.000	0.003	−0.002	0.004
	(0.47)	(0.00)	(0.73)	(0.28)	(0.98)
Foreign Ownership	−0.001	0.001	−0.002	0.003	−0.005
	(0.17)	(0.11)	(0.47)	(0.64)	(1.12)
Bank Variables					
Return on Assets	0.080	−0.176	0.195	−0.107	0.264
	(0.51)	(0.68)	(0.95)	(0.46)	(1.18)
Risk-Based	−0.088	0.112	−0.174	0.016	−0.181
Capital Ratio	(0.49)	(0.37)	(0.76)	(0.06)	(0.74)
Nonperforming	1.600	−1.287	3.016*	−0.372	3.228*
Loan Ratio	(1.63)	(0.69)	(2.53)	(0.22)	(2.56)
Observations	3576	1453	2123	1691	1885
R^2	0.213	0.226	0.229	0.226	0.221

Notes: Each regression also includes a set of year dummy variables. Absolute values of t-statistics are in parentheses. * denotes significance at the 5 percent level; ** denotes significance at the 10 percent level.

Table 9.13. *Secondary Lender Loans*

Factors Affecting the Change in Bank Loans to First-Section Firms
Estimation Method: Fixed-Effects Specification; 1994–1998

	Full Sample	Same Keiretsu	Different or No Keiretsu	In Keiretsu	Not in Keiretsu
Firm Variables					
Log (Assets)	−2.545**	−4.779**	−1.145	−5.780**	−0.176
	(3.37)	(3.36)	(1.28)	(4.36)	(0.19)
Capital/Assets	0.114**	0.110**	0.113**	0.089**	0.120**
	(6.31)	(2.94)	(5.42)	(2.64)	(5.61)
Return on Assets	−0.075*	−0.001	−0.137**	0.013	−0.155**
	(2.32)	(0.02)	(3.41)	(0.24)	(3.87)
Percent Change in	0.151	0.713*	−0.202	0.610*	−0.214
Market Value:	(0.86)	(2.43)	(0.91)	(2.21)	(0.94)
Quartile1					
Percent Change in	0.282	0.615*	0.059	0.807**	−0.136
Market Value:	(1.60)	(2.11)	(0.27)	(2.96)	(0.59)
Quartile2					
Percent Change in	−0.025	0.442	−0.328	0.317	−0.229
Market Value:	(0.15)	(1.53)	(1.50)	(1.17)	(1.01)
Quartile3					
In Bond Market	0.726	1.107	0.576	0.925	0.804
	(1.81)	(1.82)	(1.03)	(1.62)	(1.37)
Enter Bond Market	−0.800	−1.143	−0.544	−1.175*	−0.405
	(1.92)	(1.88)	(0.92)	(2.01)	(0.66)
Exit Bond Market	1.134**	1.562**	0.822	1.288**	1.076*
	(3.58)	(3.22)	(1.90)	(2.78)	(2.43)
Financial Ownership	0.051	0.058	0.010	0.075	−0.009
	(1.78)	(1.14)	(0.27)	(1.59)	(0.25)
Business Ownership	0.016*	0.023	0.014	0.023*	0.013
	(2.18)	(1.77)	(1.68)	(2.00)	(1.42)
Foreign Ownership	−0.009	−0.016	−0.007	−0.011	−0.012
	(1.22)	(1.33)	(0.87)	(0.95)	(1.37)
Bank Variables					
Return on Assets	−0.297	−0.359	−0.323	−0.544	−0.167
	(0.89)	(0.66)	(0.75)	(1.07)	(0.36)
Risk-Based	−0.168	0.373	−0.448	0.247	−0.432
Capital Ratio	(0.44)	(0.58)	(0.93)	(0.41)	(0.86)
Nonperforming	−1.975	−4.157	−1.066	−5.510	−0.076
Loan Ratio	(0.94)	(1.05)	(0.42)	(1.49)	(0.03)
Observations	3576	1453	2123	1691	1885
R^2	0.291	0.323	0.316	0.318	0.322

Notes: Each regression also includes a set of year dummy variables. Absolute values of t-statistics are in parentheses. * denotes significance at the 5 percent level; ** denotes significance at the 10 percent level.

have statistically significant coefficients for the lowest quartile for the percent change in the firm's market value. The results for the change in secondary source loans in Table 9.13 are more similar to those for total loans. The negative estimated coefficients for the quartile dummy variables for the keiretsu subsamples tend to be statistically significant, rather than the negative estimated coefficients for the non-keiretsu subsamples.

Thus, the overall evidence indicates that the largest increases in loans were to firms most severely impacted by the collapse of the bubble economy, with suggestive evidence that weaker banks had a tendency to expand lending more aggressively than stronger banks. This is in sharp contrast to the experience in the United States in the 1990s, when lending declined dramatically at troubled banks and to troubled firms. Although Japan has ameliorated the potential impact of a bank-induced credit crunch, it has done so at the expense of continuing to allocate credit to troubled firms that are least likely to have productive uses for the credit.

4. CONCLUSIONS

From 1992 through 1998, Japan did not experience a "capital crunch" similar to the one experienced in the United States in the early 1990s, despite having more widespread and more severe problems in its banking sector. Unlike the United States, where troubled banks aggressively shed assets to improve their capital ratios, many of the most troubled Japanese banks did not aggressively restructure or shrink domestic lending. We find little evidence that main bank relationships were breaking down, with more than one half of the first-section firms having increases in loans from their main banks over this six year period, despite the very weak performance of the overall Japanese economy. However, for those firms that did experience a reduction in main bank loans, loans from secondary lenders also declined.

The evidence is consistent with the Japanese borrower-lender relationships continuing to be quite different than in the United States. Main banks generally continued to support affiliated firms, despite problems at the bank and in the overall economy. Similarly, keiretsu affiliations tended to mitigate any declines in loans that might have otherwise occurred as firm health deteriorated. In fact, Peek and Rosengren (1997, 2000) have shown that Japanese banks aggressively shed international assets during the 1990s as they continued to insulate their domestic borrowers from a reduction in credit availability. Had bank loans been allocated to the healthiest firms, such a strategy should have insulated many healthy Japanese firms from the problems occurring at their bank. However, it appears that many of the weakest firms may have been the primary beneficiaries of additional bank lending.

Although many Japanese firms have been insulated by their strong bank-borrower relationships, this is not necessarily good news for the Japanese economy. If scarce credit is allocated to uncompetitive and troubled firms, the natural cleansing that would result from an economic downturn will not occur. If a disproportionate flow of funds is directed to zombie firms, then longer-run economic growth may be reduced. Thus, economic growth is not stifled from too little overall credit but, rather, from too much credit going to unproductive sectors of the economy, whereas too little is allocated to the most productive firms. In fact, this is what we do find. This misallocation of credit to deeply troubled firms, rather than the decline in aggregate lending, is why Japanese bank problems have stifled economic growth.

Banking Crisis Database

Compiled by Gerard Caprio, Daniela Klingebiel, Luc Laeven, and Guillermo Noguera

This table presents data on episodes of bank insolvency that have occurred since the late 1970s. This database updates the work by Caprio
and Klingebiel (1996, 1999) using various sources. It includes all countries that experienced banking crises for which information was available.
There likely are countries not shown that had smaller crises since the late
1970s. As noted in Caprio and Klingebiel (1996), some judgment has gone
into the compilation of this list, in particular in timing the episode of bank
insolvency. The second column presents the crisis dates. The third column
presents the lowest annual real GDP growth rate within the five-year period of the start of the crisis period, and the year that real GDP growth
takes its minimum value. Column 4 presents the share of nonperforming
loans at the peak of the crisis, and column 5 presents the share of insolvent
banks in total banking assets at the peak of the crisis, when available. Column 6 presents estimates of the fiscal costs of the crisis, when available.
These figures are mainly drawn from Honohan and Klingebiel (2003) and
are consensus numbers. Column 7 presents output losses, when available.
Estimates of the output losses of banking crises are sensitive to several
assumptions, not least of which are the problem of dating crises and the
difficulty in constructing a counterfactual for the growth path had there
been no crisis. For more discussion of these problems, see Hoggarth, Reis,
and Saporta (2002), and Honohan (2002). Notwithstanding the difficulties, output loss estimates have become so commonly used that we include the most widespread estimates using the "IMF methodology" (see
IMF, 1998). We use the World Economic Outlook database published
in September 2003 to calculate the output loss variable for all episodes
except for the ones where the values corresponding to the growth trend

overlap with other ongoing crises. As with the fiscal cost estimates, which also are subject to a number of assumptions, the estimates here are consensus numbers. Output loss is constructed by comparing, in real terms, the precrisis GDP growth rate of a certain country with the GDP growth rate during the following years until the precrisis rate is reached. This approach considers precrisis GDP growth rates to be the trend growth rate. The precrisis GDP growth is calculated as the average of GDP growth rates from year $t - 3$ to $t - 1$, where year t is the start of the crisis. Output loss is defined as the sum of the difference between the actual and the trend growth rate over all the years until the trend growth is reached again. Specific comments on the banking crisis are presented in column 8. The final column denotes whether the crisis was systemic or not. We follow the definition in Caprio and Klingebiel (1996) to identify systemic crises. An electronic copy of the database is available upon request from the authors.

Country	Timeframe	Lowest Real GDP Growth Rate %	Year	NPLs (Percentage of Total)	Insolvent Bank Assets (Percentage of Total)	Fiscal Cost (Percentage of GDP)	Output Loss (Percentage of GDP)	Comments	Systemic Crisis? (Yes/No)
Albania	1992–1996	−27.5	1991	31				0.0	After the July 1992 cleanup, 31 percent of "new" banking system loans were nonperforming. Some banks faced liquidity problems because of a logjam of interbank liabilities.	Yes
Algeria	1990–1992	−2.1	1993	50				0.0		Yes
Angola	1991–	−24.7	1993					36.5	Two state-owned commercial banks have experienced solvency problems.	No
Argentina	1980–1982	−5.7	1981	9	16	55.1		17.0	More than 70 institutions – accounting for 16 percent of commercial bank assets and 35 percent of finance company assets – were liquidated or subjected to central bank intervention.	Yes
Argentina	1989–1990	−7.5	1989	27	40			13.4		Yes
Argentina	1995	−4.2	1995			2		12.2	Eight banks suspended and three banks collapsed. Through the end of 1997, 63 of 205 banking institutions were closed or merged.	Yes

(continued)

Country	Timeframe	Lowest Real GDP Growth Rate		NPLs (Percentage of Total)	Insolvent Bank Assets (Percentage of Total)	Fiscal Cost (Percentage of GDP)	Output Loss (Percentage of GDP)	Comments	Systemic Crisis? (Yes/No)
		%	Year						
Argentina	2001–	−10.9	2002	20.1			15.0	In March 2001, a bank run started because of increasing doubts about the sustainability of the currency board, strong opposition from the public to the new fiscal austerity package sent to Congress, the resignation of president of the Central Bank, and the amendment to the convertibility law. On December 3, 2001, as several banks were at the verge of collapsing, partial withdrawal restrictions (corralito) were imposed to transactional accounts while fixed-term deposits (CDs) were reprogrammed (corralon) in order to stop outflows from banks. On February 4, 2002, bank assets were asymmetrically pesified adversely affecting the solvency of the banking system. In 2002, two voluntary swaps of deposits for government bonds were offered but received little interest by the public. In December 2002, the corralito was lifted. By August 2003, one bank has	Yes

310

Country	Period		Year					Description	Systemic
Armenia	1994–1996	−41.8	1992	50			0.0	been closed, three banks nationalized, and many other have reduced their staff and branches. Starting in August 1994, the Central Bank closed half of active banks.	Yes
Australia	1989–1992	−0.1	1990	6		2	0.0	Large banks continued to suffer from high nonperforming loans. The savings bank was financially weak. Two large banks received capital from the government to cover losses. Nonperforming loans rose to 6 percent of assets in 1991–1992.	No
Azerbaijan	1995–1996	−19.7	1994				0.0	Rescuing state-owned banks was estimated to cost 2 percent of GDP. Twelve private banks closed; three large state-owned banks deemed insolvent; one large state-owned bank faced serious liquidity problems.	Yes
Bangladesh	Late 1980s–96	2.2	1988	95	20		0.0	In 1987 four banks accounting for 70 percent of credit had nonperforming loans of 20 percent. From the late 1980s the entire private and public banking system was technically insolvent.	Yes
Belarus	1995–	−11.7	1994				0.5	Many banks undercapitalized; forced mergers burdened some banks with poor loan portfolios.	No
Benin	1988–1990	−2.9	1989	80	80	17	0.0	All three commercial banks collapsed.	Yes

(continued)

Country	Timeframe	Lowest Real GDP Growth Rate %	Year	NPLs (Percentage of Total)	Insolvent Bank Assets (Percentage of Total)	Fiscal Cost (Percentage of GDP)	Output Loss (Percentage of GDP)	Comments	Systemic Crisis? (Yes/No)
Bolivia	1986–1988	−2.6	1986				0.0	Five banks were liquidated. Banking system nonperforming loans reached 30 percent in 1987; in mid-1988 reported arrears stood at 92 percent of commercial banks' net worth.	Yes
Bolivia	1994–	1.6	1992		30		0.0	Two banks with 11 percent of banking system assets were closed in 1994. In 1995, 4 of 15 domestic banks, accounting for 30 percent of banking system assets, experienced liquidity problems and suffered high nonperforming loans.	Yes
Bosnia and Herzegovina	1992–							Banking system suffers from high nonperforming loans because of the breakup of the former Yugoslavia and the civil war.	Yes
Botswana	1994–1995	1.9	1993			0.6	0.6	One problem bank was merged in 1994, a small bank was liquidated in 1995, and the state-owned National Development Bank was recapitalized. Recapitalizing the National Development Bank cost 0.6 percent of GDP.	No

Country								Notes	
Brazil	1990	−4.3	1990	15	15.4	13.2	10.8	Deposits were converted to bonds.	Yes
Brazil	1994–1999	0.1	1998				0.0	In 1996 the negative net worth of selected state and federal banks was 5–10 percent of GDP. By the end of 1997 bank recapitalizations had cost $3 billion for Banco Economico, $3 billion for Bamerindus, $8 billion for Banco do Brazil, and $5 billion for Unibanco. By the end of 1997 the Central Bank had intervened in or put under temporary administration 43 financial institutions. Private banks returned to profitability in 1998, but public banks did not begin to recover until the following year.	Yes
Brunei	Mid-1980s	−2.7	1986	9				Several financial firms failed. The second largest bank failed in 1986.	No
Bulgaria	1996–1997	−9.4	1996	75	33		8.0	By early 1996 the sector had a negative net worth equal to 13 percent of GDP. The banking system experienced a run in early 1996. The government then stopped providing bailouts, prompting the closure of 19 banks accounting for one third of sector assets. Surviving banks were recapitalized by 1997.	Yes
Burkina Faso	1988–1994	−1.4	1987	34			0.0		Yes
Burundi	1994–	−8.4	1996	25			20.5	In 1995 one bank was liquidated.	Yes

(*continued*)

Country	Timeframe	Lowest Real GDP Growth Rate %	Lowest Real GDP Growth Rate Year	NPLs (Percentage of Total)	Insolvent Bank Assets (Percentage of Total)	Fiscal Cost (Percentage of GDP)	Output Loss (Percentage of GDP)	Comments	Systemic Crisis? (Yes/No)
Cameroon	1987–1993	−7.8	1988	65			111.4	Five commercial banks were closed and three banks were restructured.	Yes
Cameroon	1995–1998	−2.5	1994	30				Three banks were restructured and two were closed.	Yes
Canada	1983–1985	−2.9	1982				0.0	Fifteen members of the Canadian Deposit Insurance Corporation, including two banks, failed.	No
Cape Verde	1993–	3.3	1992	30					Yes
Central African Rep.	1976–1992	−8.1	1983				0.0	Four banks were liquidated.	Yes
Central African Rep.	1995–1999	−4.0	1996	40	90			The two largest banks, accounting for 90 percent of assets, were restructured.	Yes
Chad	1980s	−21.4	1979					Banking sector experienced solvency problems.	Yes
Chad	1992	−15.7	1993	35			10.1		Yes
Chile	1976	−11.4	1975					Entire mortgage system insolvent.	Yes
Chile	1981–1983	−10.3	1982	19	45	42	46.0		Yes
China	1990s–	3.8	1990	50	68	47		At the end of 1998, China's four large state-owned commercial banks, accounting for 68 percent of banking system assets, were deemed insolvent. Banking system nonperforming loans were	Yes

Colombia	1982–1987	0.9	1982	25		7.0	estimated at 50 percent at peak, 31 percent in 2001, 26 percent in 2002, and 22.6 percent in 2003. Net losses estimated to reach $428 billion, or 47 percent of GDP in 1999. The costs of a potential clean up of the banking system are estimated to reach RMB4800 billion or 47 percent of 2002 GDP.	Yes
Congo, Dem. Rep. of	1980s	−0.5	1982	5			The Central Bank intervened in six banks accounting for 25 percent of banking system assets.	Yes
Congo, Dem. Rep. of	1991–1992	−6.6	1990			26.4	Banking sector experienced solvency problems. Four state-owned banks were insolvent; a fifth bank was to be recapitalized with private participation.	Yes
Congo, Dem. Rep. of	1994–1996	−13.9	1993		75		Two state-owned banks have been liquidated and two other state banks privatized. In 1997, 12 banks were having serious financial difficulties.	Yes
Congo, Rep. of	1992–	−5.5	1994			61.4	Between 2001 and 2002, two large banks were restructured and privatized. The remaining insolvent bank is in the process of being liquidated. Situation aggravated by the civil war.	Yes

(continued)

Country	Timeframe	Lowest Real GDP Growth Rate		NPLs (Percentage of Total)	Insolvent Bank Assets (Percentage of Total)	Fiscal Cost (Percentage of GDP)	Output Loss (Percentage of GDP)	Comments	Systemic Crisis? (Yes/No)
		%	Year						
Costa Rica	1994–1996	0.9	1996	32	90		9.3	One large state-owned commercial bank was closed in December 1994. The ratio of overdue loans (net of provisions) to net worth in state commercial banks exceeded 100 percent in June 1995. Implied losses of at least twice the capital plus reserves.	Yes
Côte d'Ivoire	1988–1991	–0.3	1987		90	25	1.0	Four large banks affected, accounting for 90 percent of banking system loans; three definitely and one possibly insolvent. Six government banks closed.	Yes
Croatia	1996	–8.0	1993		50		0.0	Five banks accounting for about half of banking system loans were deemed insolvent and taken over by the Bank Rehabilitation Agency.	Yes
Czech Republic	1989–1991			38			0.0	Several banks have closed since 1993.	Yes
Denmark	1987–1992	0.0	1987			12	24.3	Cumulative loan-losses over 1990–1992 were 9 percent of loans; 40 of the 60 problem banks were merged.	No
Djibouti	1991–1993	–1.9	1992				31.8	Two of six commercial banks ceased operations in 1991–1992; other banks experienced difficulties.	Yes

Country	Period							Systemic
Dominican Republic	2003–					15	Collapse of Banco International SA, the country's second-largest bank, with liabilities exceeding assets by US$ 2.2 billion, as a result of fraud.	Yes
Ecuador	Early 1980s	–2.8	1983				Program exchanging domestic for foreign debt implemented to bail out banking system.	Yes
Ecuador	1996–1997	1.7	1995	65		0.4	The authorities intervened in several small financial institutions in late 1995. By the end of 1995, 30 financial societies (sociedades financieras) and 7 banks were receiving extensive liquidity support. In early 1996, the fifth largest commercial bank was intervened.	Yes
Ecuador	1998–2001	–6.3	1999		20	12.0	Seven financial institutions, accounting for 25–30 percent of commercial banking assets, were closed in 1998–1999. In March 1999 bank deposits were frozen for 6 months. By January 2000, 16 financial institutions accounting for 65 percent of the assets had either been closed (12) or taken over (4) by the government. All deposits were unfrozen by March 2000. In 2001 the blanket guarantee was lifted.	Yes
Egypt	Early 1980s	3.8	1991				The government closed several large investment companies.	Yes

(continued)

Country	Timeframe	Lowest Real GDP Growth Rate %	Year	NPLs (Percentage of Total)	Insolvent Bank Assets (Percentage of Total)	Fiscal Cost (Percentage of GDP)	Output Loss (Percentage of GDP)	Comments	Systemic Crisis? (Yes/No)
Egypt	1991–1995	1.1	1991				8.6	Four public banks were given capital assistance.	No
El Salvador	1989	1.0	1989	37			0.8	Nine state-owned commercial banks had nonperforming loans averaging 37 percent.	Yes
Equatorial Guinea	1983–85						0.0	Two of the country's largest banks were liquidated.	Yes
Eritrea	1993							Most of the banking system was insolvent.	Yes
Estonia	1992–1995	−21.2	1992		41	1.4		The Social Bank, which controlled 10 percent of financial system assets, failed. Five banks' licenses were revoked, and two major banks were merged and nationalized. Two other large banks were merged and converted to a loan recovery agency.	Yes
Estonia	1998	−0.6	1999				8.0	Three banks failed in 1998: Maapank (Agricultural Bank), which accounted for 3 percent of banking system assets, and two smaller banks: EVEA and ERA. Maapank's losses reached $500 million.	No

Country									
Ethiopia	1994–95	−5.1	1992	13			0.0	A government-owned bank was restructured, and its nonperforming loans were taken over by the government.	No
Finland	1991–94	−6.3	1991		31	11.2	21.0	Savings banks badly affected; government took control of three banks that together accounted for 31 percent of system deposits.	Yes
France	1994–95	−0.9	1993	8.9		0.7	0.0	Credit Lyonnais experienced serious solvency problems. According to unofficial estimates, losses totaled about $10 billion, making it the largest bank failure up to that time.	No
Gabon	1995–?	3.4	1994				0.0	One bank was closed temporarily in 1995.	No
Gambia, The	1985–1992	−0.8	1985				97.5	In 1992 a government bank was restructured and privatized.	No
Georgia	1991–1996	−44.9	1992	33				Largest banks virtually insolvent. So-called Giro-institutions faced problems.	Yes
Germany	Late 1970s	−1.3	1975						No
Ghana	1982–89	−6.9	1982		63	6	7.0	Seven of eleven audited banks insolvent; rural banking sector affected.	Yes
Ghana	1997–	4.6	1996	27	38		0.0		No
Greece	1991–1995	−1.6	1993				0.0	Localized problems required significant injections of public funds into specialized lending institutions.	No

(*continued*)

319

Country	Timeframe	Lowest Real GDP Growth Rate %	Year	NPLs (Percentage of Total)	Insolvent Bank Assets (Percentage of Total)	Fiscal Cost (Percentage of GDP)	Output Loss (Percentage of GDP)	Comments	Systemic Crisis? (Yes/No)
Guatemala	1990s	3.1	1990					Two small state-owned banks had high nonperforming assets; these banks discontinued operations in the early 1990s.	No
Guinea	1985	na	na		99	3	0.0	Six banks – accounting for 99 percent of system deposits – deemed insolvent. Repayment of deposits amounted to 3 percent of 1986 GDP.	Yes
Guinea	1993–1994	2.9	1992	45			0.0	Two banks deemed insolvent; one other bank had serious financial difficulties.	Yes
Guinea-Bissau	1995–1996	3.2	1994	45			0.0		Yes
Hong Kong, China	1982–1983	2.7	1982				10.6	Nine deposit-taking companies failed.	No
Hong Kong, China	1983–1986	0.2	1985					Seven banks or deposit-taking institutions were liquidated or taken over.	No
Hong Kong, China	1998	-5.0	1998				10.5	One large investment bank failed.	No
Hungary	1991–1995	-11.9	1991	23	25	10	14.0	In the second half of 1993 eight banks – accounting for 25 percent of financial system assets – were deemed insolvent.	Yes

Country									
Iceland	1985–1986	3.3	1985				0.0	One of three state-owned banks became insolvent and was eventually privatized in a merger with three private banks.	No
Iceland	1993	–3.3	1992				0.0	The government was forced to inject capital into one of the largest state-owned commercial bank after it suffered serious loan-losses.	No
India	1993–	4.9	1993	20			0.0		No
Indonesia	1994	7.5	1994	14		2	0.3	Nonperforming assets equal to more than 14 percent of banking system assets, with more than 70 percent in state banks. Recapitalization costs for five state banks amounted to nearly 2 percent of GDP.	No
Indonesia	1997–2002	–13.1	1998	70	35	55	39.0	Through May 2002, Bank Indonesia had closed 70 banks and nationalized 13, of a total of 237. Nonperforming loans for the banking system were estimated at 65–75 percent of total loans at the peak of crisis and fell to about 12 percent in February 2002.	Yes
Israel	1977–1983	0.0	1977		30			Almost the entire banking sector was affected, representing 60 percent of stock market capitalization. The stock exchange closed for 18 days, and bank share prices fell more than 40 percent.	Yes

(continued)

Country	Timeframe	Lowest Real GDP Growth Rate %	Year	NPLs (Percentage of Total)	Insolvent Bank Assets (Percentage of Total)	Fiscal Cost (Percentage of GDP)	Output Loss (Percentage of GDP)	Comments	Systemic Crisis? (Yes/No)
Italy	1990–1995	-0.9	1993		11		22.4	During 1990–1994, 58 banks (accounting for 11 percent of lending) were merged with other institutions.	No
Jamaica	1994	0.9	1994				11.5	In 1994 a merchant banking group was closed.	No
Jamaica	1996–2000	-1.1	1996			43.9	7.0	FINSAC, a government resolution agency, provided assistance to five banks, five life insurance companies, two building societies, and nine merchant banks. Government recapitalized 21 troubled institutions via nontradeable government guaranteed bonds. By June 30, 2,000 outstanding recap bonds estimated to account for 44 percent of GDP.	Yes
Japan	1992–	0.9	1992	35		24	48.0	Banks suffered from sharp decline in stock market and real estate prices. In 1995 the official estimate of nonperforming loans was ¥40 trillion ($469 billion, or 10 percent of GDP). An unofficial estimate put nonperforming loans at $1 trillion, equivalent to 25 percent of GDP. Banks made provisions for	Yes

							some bad loans. At the end of 1998 banking system nonperforming loans were estimated at ¥88 trillion ($725 billion, or 18 percent of GDP). In 1999 Hakkaido Takushodu bank was closed, the Long Term Credit Bank was nationalized, Yatsuda Trust was merged with Fuji Bank, and Mitsui Trust was merged with Chuo Trust. In 2002 nonperforming loans were 35 percent of total loans; with a total of 7 banks nationalized, 61 financial institutions closed and 28 institutions merged. In 1996 rescue costs were estimated at more than $100 billion. In 1998 the government announced the Obuchi Plan, which provided ¥60 trillion ($500 billion, or 12 percent of GDP) in public funds for loan-losses, bank recapitalizations, and depositor protection. By 2002, fiscal cost estimates rose to 24 percent of GDP.
Jordan	1989–1990	−13.5	1989	10	16.9	No	The third largest bank failed in August 1989. The central bank provided overdrafts equivalent to 10 percent of GDP to meet a run on deposits and allowed banks to settle foreign obligations.

(continued)

Country	Timeframe	Lowest Real GDP Growth Rate %	Year	NPLs (Percentage of Total)	Insolvent Bank Assets (Percentage of Total)	Fiscal Cost (Percentage of GDP)	Output Loss (Percentage of GDP)	Comments	Systemic Crisis? (Yes/No)
Kenya	1985–1989	1.8	1984		15		0.0	Four banks and twenty-four nonbank financial institutions – accounting for 15 percent of financial system liabilities – faced liquidity and solvency problems.	Yes
Kenya	1992	–0.8	1992				7.8	Intervention in two local banks.	Yes
Kenya	1993–1995	–0.8	1992		30		1.2		Yes
Kenya	1996–	4.1	1996	19					No
Korea, Rep. of	1997–2002	–6.7	1998	35		28	17.0	Through May 2002, 5 banks were forced to exit the market through a "purchase and assumption formula" and 303 financial institutions shutdown (215 were credit unions). Four banks were nationalized.	Yes
Kuwait	1980s	–20.6	1980	40					Yes
Kyrgyz Republic	1990s	–20.1	1994	85				Four small commercial banks closed in 1995.	Yes
Lao People's Democratic Republic	Early 1990s	4.1	1991			1.5		Some banks experienced problems. Recapitalization of state-owned commercial banks amounted to 1.5 percent of GDP.	No
Latvia	1995–1996	–34.9	1992		30	3	0.0	Between 1994 and 1999, 35 banks saw their license revoked, were closed, or ceased operations. In 1995 the negative net worth of the banking	Yes

system was estimated at $320 million, or 7 percent of 1995 GDP. Aggregate banking system losses in 1998 estimated at 100 million lats ($172 million), about 3 percent of GDP.

Country	Period		Year					
Lebanon	1988–1990	−42.5	1989	118.0			Four banks became insolvent. Eleven had to resort to Central Bank lending.	Yes
Lesotho	1988–	3.5	1987	0.0			One of four commercial banks suffered from large nonperforming loans.	No
Liberia	1991–95	−51.0	1990		64		Seven of eleven banks not operational; in mid-1995 their assets accounted for 64 percent of bank assets.	Yes
Lithuania	1995–1996	−9.8	1994	0.0	29		In 1995, of 25 banks, 12 small banks were liquidated, 3 private banks (accounting for 29 percent of banking system deposits) failed, and 3 state-owned banks were deemed insolvent.	Yes
Macedonia	1993–1994	−7.5	1993	0.7	32	70	The government took over banks' foreign debt and closed the second largest bank. Costs of banking system rehabilitation, obligations from assumption of external debt, liabilities regarding frozen foreign exchange, and contingent liabilities in banks together estimated at 32 percent of GDP.	Yes

(continued)

325

Country	Timeframe	Lowest Real GDP Growth Rate		NPLs (Percentage of Total)	Insolvent Bank Assets (Percentage of Total)	Fiscal Cost (Percentage of GDP)	Output Loss (Percentage of GDP)	Comments	Systemic Crisis? (Yes/No)
		%	Year						
Madagascar	1988	1.2	1987				0.0		Yes
Malaysia	1985–1988	–1.1	1985	25	7	5	14.3	Insolvent institutions accounted for 3 percent of financial system deposits; marginally capitalized and possibly insolvent institutions accounted for another 4 percent.	No
Malaysia	1997–2001	–7.4	1998	30	14	16.4	33.0	Finance company sector was restructured, and number of finance was reduced from 39 to 10 through mergers. Two finance companies were taken over by the Central Bank, including the largest independent finance company. Two banks deemed insolvent – accounting for 14 percent of financial system assets – were merged with other banks.	Yes
Mali	1987–1989	–0.5	1987	75			3.4		Yes
Mauritania	1984–1993	–3.2	1984	70		15	0.0	Five major banks had significant nonperforming assets.	Yes
Mauritius	1996	4.1	1995		17		0.0	The Central Bank closed 2 of 12 commercial banks for fraud and other irregularities.	No
Mexico	1981–1991	–4.2	1983					Government took over troubled banking system.	Yes

Mexico	1994–2000	−6.2	1995	18.9	19	19.3	10.0	Of 34 commercial banks in 1994, 9 were intervened in and 11 participated in the loan/purchase recapitalization program. The 9 intervened banks accounted for 19 percent of financial system assets and were deemed insolvent. In 1994 one percent of bank assets were owned by foreigner and by 2000, 50 percent of bank assets were held by foreign banks.	Yes
Morocco	Early 1980s	−2.8	1981				0.0	Banking sector experienced solvency problems.	Yes
Mozambique	1987–?	−11.4	1988					Main commercial bank experienced solvency problems that became apparent after 1992.	Yes
Myanmar	1996–	6.4	1996				2.0	The largest state-owned commercial bank reported to have large nonperforming loans.	No
Nepal	1988	1.7	1987				2.2	One large state-owned bank accounting for one quarter of banking assets experienced serious solvency problems because of high nonperforming loans. The bank required a capital injection equal to 1 percent of GDP.	Yes
New Zealand	1987–1990	−0.1	1988	29	25	1	0.0		No

(continued)

Country	Timeframe	Lowest Real GDP Growth Rate %	Year	NPLs (Percentage of Total)	Insolvent Bank Assets (Percentage of Total)	Fiscal Cost (Percentage of GDP)	Output Loss (Percentage of GDP)	Comments	Systemic Crisis? (Yes/No)
Nicaragua	Late 1980s–	−12.4	1988	50				Banking system nonperforming loans reached 50 percent of GDP in 1996.	Yes
Niger	1983–1996	−16.8	1984	50			25.3	In the mid-1980s banking system nonperforming loans reached 50 percent. Four banks were liquidated and three restructured in the late 1980s. In 2002, a new round of bank restructuring was launched. Four banks were experiencing serious difficulties. Two of them were restructured and the other two liquidated.	Yes
Nigeria	1991–1995	0.1	1994	77	50		68.4	In 1995 almost half the banks reported being in financial distress.	Yes
Nigeria	1997	2.7	1997		4				No
Norway	1990–1993	0.9	1989		85	8	0.0	The Central Bank provided special loans to six banks suffering from the recession of 1985–1986 and from problem real estate loans. The state took control of the three largest banks (with 85 percent of banking system assets, whose loan-losses had wiped out capital), partly through a Government Bank Investment Fund (five billion kroner), and the	Yes

							state-backed Bank Insurance Fund had to increase capital to 11 billion kroner. Recapitalization costs totaled 8 percent of GDP.	Yes
Panama	1988–1989	−13.4	1988			16.3	In 1988 Panama's banking system experienced a nine-week banking holiday. The financial position of most state-owned and private commercial banks was weak. As a result, 15 banks ceased operations.	
Papua New Guinea	1989–	−3.0	1990			11.9	Some 85 percent of savings and loan associations have ceased operations.	No
Paraguay	1995–2000	3.1	1994	10	13	0.0	The Government Superintendency intervened in two connected commercial banks, two other banks, and six related finance houses accounting for 10 percent of financial system deposits. By 1998, the government had intervened in six other financial institutions, including the country's largest public bank and the largest savings and loan institution. By the end of 1998, the government had intervened in most remaining domestic private and public banks and a number of finance companies. By end 1999 banks in Paraguay had become predominantly foreign owned, with over 80 percent of bank	Yes

(*continued*)

Country	Timeframe	Lowest Real GDP Growth Rate %	Year	NPLs (Percentage of Total)	Insolvent Bank Assets (Percentage of Total)	Fiscal Cost (Percentage of GDP)	Output Loss (Percentage of GDP)	Comments	Systemic Crisis? (Yes/No)
Paraguay	2001–	−0.3	2000					One bank was closed in 2001 and another one became insolvent in 2002. Banks in the system continue to experience rising NPLs against the background of an economic recession and a depreciation of the currency by around 50 percent from January 2002 to January 2003.	No
Peru	1983–1990	−11.8	1983				15.2	Two large banks failed. The rest of the system suffered from high nonperforming loans and financial disintermediation following the nationalization of the banking system in 1987.	Yes
Philippines	1983–1987	−7.3	1984	19	62	3	26.0	Problems in two public banks accounting for 50 percent of banking system assets, six private banks accounting for 12 percent of banking system assets, 32 thrifts accounting for 53 percent of thrift banking assets, and 128 rural banks.	Yes

The cell continuing from a prior page reads: assets in foreign hands. All banks were deemed sound by the Government Superintendency by the end of 2000.

Philippines	1998–	−0.6	1998	20		13.2	10.1	Since January 1998 one commercial bank, 7 of 88 thrifts, and 40 of 750 rural banks have been placed under receivership. Banking system nonperforming loans reached 20 percent in 1999.	Yes
Poland	1992–1995	−7.0	1991	24	90	3.5	0.0	In 1991, seven of nine treasury-owned commercial banks – accounting for 90 percent of credit – the Bank for Food Economy, and the cooperative banking sector experienced solvency problems.	Yes
Romania	1990–1996	−12.9	1991	30		0.6	21.8	In 1998, nonperforming loans reached 25–30 percent in the six main state-owned banks. The Agricultural Bank was recapitalized on a flow basis. In 1998 the Central Bank injected $210 million in Bancorex (0.6 percent of GDP), the largest state bank, and in 1999 another $60 million.	Yes
Russia	1995	−12.6	1994	40			0.0	In August 1995 the interbank loan market stopped working because of concerns about connected lending in many new banks.	Yes
Russia	1998–1999	−4.9	1998	40	50		3.0	Nearly 720 banks, or half of those operating, were deemed insolvent. These banks accounted for 4 percent of sector assets and 32 percent of retail deposits.	Yes

(continued)

331

Country	Timeframe	Lowest Real GDP Growth Rate %	Year	NPLs (Percentage of Total)	Insolvent Bank Assets (Percentage of Total)	Fiscal Cost (Percentage of GDP)	Output Loss (Percentage of GDP)	Comments	Systemic Crisis? (Yes/No)
								According to the Central Bank, 18 banks holding 40 percent of sector assets and 41 percent of household deposits are in serious difficulties and will require rescue by the state.	
Rwanda	1991–	–2.5	1991				2.6	One bank, with a well-established network, closed.	No
São Tomé and Príncipe	1980s and 1990s			90				At end-1992, 90 percent of the monobank's loans were nonperforming. In 1993, the commercial department of the former monobank was liquidated, as was the only financial institution. At the same time, two new banks were licensed that took over many of the assets of their predecessors. The credit operations of one new bank have been suspended since late 1994.	Yes
Senegal	1988–1991	–1.4	1989	50	25	17	0.0	In 1988, 50 percent of banking system loans were nonperforming. Six commercial banks and one development bank closed, accounting for 20–30 percent of financial system assets.	Yes

Country	Period		Year				Description	
Sierra Leone	1990–1996	−19.0	1992	45		28.6	One bank's license was suspended in 1994. Bank recapitalization and restructuring are ongoing.	Yes
Singapore	1982	7.1	1982	0.6		1.5		No
Slovakia	1991–1995	−14.6	1991			32.9	In 1997 unrecoverable loans were estimated at 101 billion crowns, or about 31 percent of loans and 15 percent of GDP.	Yes
Slovenia	1992–1994	−8.9	1991	67	14.6	0.0	Three banks – accounting for two thirds of banking system assets – were restructured.	Yes
South Africa	1977	−2.8	1977				Trust Bank experienced problems.	No
South Africa	1989–	2.4	1989			0.0	Some banks are experiencing problems.	No
Spain	1977–1985	2.8	1977	20	5.6	0.0	In 1978–83, 24 institutions were rescued, 4 were liquidated, 4 were merged, and 20 small and medium-size banks were nationalized. These 52 banks (of 110), representing 20 percent of banking system deposits, were experiencing solvency problems.	Yes
Sri Lanka	1989–1993	2.3	1989	35	5	1.0	State-owned banks comprising 70 percent of banking system estimated to have nonperforming loans of about 35 percent.	Yes

(continued)

Country	Timeframe	Lowest Real GDP Growth Rate %	Year	NPLs (Percentage of Total)	Insolvent Bank Assets (Percentage of Total)	Fiscal Cost (Percentage of GDP)	Output Loss (Percentage of GDP)	Comments	Systemic Crisis? (Yes/No)
Swaziland	1995–?	3.8	1995				0.0	Meridien BIAO Swaziland was taken over by the Central Bank. The Central Bank also took over the Swaziland Development and Savings Bank, which faced severe portfolio problems.	Yes
Sweden	1991–1994	–1.1	1991	13	22	4	11.0	Nordbanken and Gota Bank, accounting for 22 percent of banking system assets, were insolvent. Sparbanken Foresta, accounting for 24 percent of banking system assets, intervened. Overall, five of the six largest banks, accounting for more than 70 percent of banking system assets, experienced difficulties.	Yes
Taiwan, China	1983–1984	3.6	1982				0.0	Four trust companies and eleven cooperatives failed.	No
Taiwan, China	1995	6.4	1995				21.2	Failure of credit cooperative Changua Fourth in late July sparked runs on other credit unions in central and southern Taiwan.	No
Taiwan, China	1997–98	6.1	1996	26		11.5		In 1999 net losses estimated at $26.7 billion, or 11.5 percent of GDP.	Yes
Tajikistan	1996–	–16.7	1996				0.0	One of the largest banks is insolvent, one small bank has been closed, and another (out of 17) is in the process of liquidation.	No

Country	Years							
Tanzania	Late 1980s; 1990s			70	95	10	In 1987 the main financial institutions had arrears amounting to half their portfolios. In 1995 it was determined that the National Bank of Commerce, which accounted for 95 percent of banking system assets, has been insolvent since at least 1990.	Yes
Thailand	1983–1987	5.6	1983	33	25	0.7	0.1	Authorities intervened in 50 finance and security firms and 5 commercial banks, or about 25 percent of financial system assets; 3 commercial banks deemed insolvent (accounting for 14 percent of commercial bank assets). Government cost for 50 finance companies estimated at 0.5 percent of GNP; government cost for subsidized loans amounted to about 0.2 percent of GDP a year.	Yes
Thailand	1997–2002	−10.5	1998	33	34.8	40.0	By May 2002 the Bank of Thailand had closed 59 (of 91) financial companies that in total accounted for 13 percent of financial system assets and 72 percent of finance company assets. It closed one (of 15) domestic banks and nationalized four banks. A publicly owned assets management company held 29.7 percent of financial system assets as of March 2002.	Yes

(continued)

Country	Timeframe	Lowest Real GDP Growth Rate %	Year	NPLs (Percentage of Total)	Insolvent Bank Assets (Percentage of Total)	Fiscal Cost (Percentage of GDP)	Output Loss (Percentage of GDP)	Comments	Systemic Crisis? (Yes/No)
Togo	1993–1995	−15.1	1993				15.3	Nonperforming loans peaked at 33 percent of total loans and were reduced to 10.3 percent of total loans in February 2002. Banking sector experienced solvency problems.	Yes
Trinidad and Tobago	1982–1993	−5.2	1983				5.4	In the early 1980s several financial institutions experienced solvency problems, resulting in the merging of three government-owned banks in 1993.	No
Tunisia	1991–1995	3.9	1991			3	0.0	In 1991, most commercial banks were undercapitalized. During 1991–1994, the banking system raised equity equivalent to 1.5 percent of GDP and made provisions equivalent to another 1.5 percent. Thus, recapitalization through 1994 required at least 3 percent of GDP.	No
Turkey	1982–85	3.6	1982			2.5	0.0	Three banks were merged with the state-owned Agriculture Bank and then liquidated; two large banks were restructured.	Yes
Turkey	1994	−5.5	1994			1	10.0	Three banks failed in April 1994.	No

336

Turkey	2000–	−4.7	1999			30.5	0.0	Two banks closed and 19 banks have been taken over by the Savings Deposit Insurance Fund.	Yes
Uganda	1994–1996	8.3	1993		50		0.0	Between 1994 and 1998, half of the banking system faced solvency problems. In 1998, two banks were closed and one recapitalized and privatized. In 1999, another two banks were closed. In 2002, one small bank was intervened and two other banks were experiencing difficulties.	Yes
Ukraine	1997–1998	−10.0	1996	65			0.0	By 1997, 32 of 195 banks were being liquidated, while 25 others were undergoing financial rehabilitation. Bad loans accounted for 50–65 percent of assets even in some leading banks. In 1998 banks were further hit by the government's decision to restructure government debt.	Yes
United Kingdom	1974–1976	−1.6	1974					"Secondary Banking Crisis."	No
United Kingdom	1980s and 1990s							Notable bank failures included Johnson Matthey (1984), Bank of Credit and Commerce International (1991), and Barings (1995).	No

(continued)

Country	Timeframe	Lowest Real GDP Growth Rate		NPLs (Percentage of Total)	Insolvent Bank Assets (Percentage of Total)	Fiscal Cost (Percentage of GDP)	Output Loss (Percentage of GDP)	Comments	Systemic Crisis? (Yes/No)
		%	Year						
United States	1988–1991	4.2	1988	4.1		3.2	0.0	More than 1,400 savings and loan institutions and 1,300 banks failed. Cleaning up savings and loan institutions cost $180 billion, or 3 percent of GDP.	No
Uruguay	1981–1984	–10.3	1983		30	31.2	41.0	Affected institutions accounted for 30 percent of financial system assets; insolvent banks accounted for 20 percent of financial system deposits.	Yes
Uruguay	2002–	–10.8	20.02	25			8.3	The government-owned mortgage bank was recapitalized in December 2001. The banking system experienced a large outflow of deposits (33 percent during the first seven months of 2002). In 2002, four banks were closed (representing 33 percent of total bank assets). Fixed-term deposits (CDs) in public banks were restructured and their maturity extended. The cost of the recapitalizing the government-owned mortgage bank was estimated at $650 million, or 3 percent of GDP.	Yes

Country	Period						Notes	
Venezuela	Late 1970s and 1980s			35			Notable bank failures included Banco Nacional de Descuento (1978), BANDAGRO (1981), Banco de los Trabajadores de Venezuela (1982), Banco de Comercio (1985), BHCU (1985), BHCO (1985), and Banco Lara (1986).	No
Venezuela	1994–1995	−2.3	1994	35	22	14.0	Insolvent banks accounted for 35 percent of financial system deposits. In 1994 the authorities intervened in 17 of 47 banks that held 50 percent of deposits and nationalized nine banks and closed seven others. The government intervened in five additional banks in 1995.	Yes
Vietnam	1997–	8.1	1997	18	51	23.0	Two of four large state-owned commercial banks – accounting for 51 percent of banking system loans – deemed insolvent; the other two experienced significant solvency problems. Several joint stocks banks were in severe financial distress. Banking system nonperforming loans reached 18 percent in late 1998.	Yes

(continued)

Country	Timeframe	Lowest Real GDP Growth Rate		NPLs (Percentage of Total)	Insolvent Bank Assets (Percentage of Total)	Fiscal Cost (Percentage of GDP)	Output Loss (Percentage of GDP)	Comments	Systemic Crisis? (Yes/No)
		%	Year						
Yemen	1996–?	10.9	1995				18.9	Banks suffered from extensive nonperforming loans and heavy foreign currency exposure.	Yes
Zambia	1995–?	–8.7	1994		13	1.4	0.0	Meridien Bank, which accounted for 13 percent of commercial bank assets, became insolvent.	Yes
Zimbabwe	1995–1996	0.2	1995				0.0	Two of five commercial banks have high nonperforming loans.	Yes

References

Aghion, Philippe, and Patrick Bolton. 1992. "An Incomplete Contracts Approach to Financial Contracting." *Review of Economic Studies* 77: 338–401.

Aghion, Philippe, Oliver Hart, and John H. Moore. 1992. "The Economics of Bankruptcy Reform." *Journal of Law and Economics* 8: 523–46.

Alexander, William E., Jeffrey M. Davis, Liam P. Ebrill, and Carl-Johan Lindgren. 1997. *Systemic Bank Restructuring and Macroeconomic Policy*. Washington, DC: International Monetary Fund.

Allen, Franklin, and Douglas Gale. 2000. *Comparing Financial Systems*. Cambridge, MA: MIT Press.

Alonso, Irasema. 1996. "On Avoiding Bank Runs." *Journal of Monetary Economics* 37: 73–87.

Anari, Ali, James Kolari, and Joseph R. Mason. 2002. "Bank Asset Liquidation and the Propagation of the Great Depression." Wharton Financial Institutions Center Working Paper No. 02–35. Philadelphia: Wharton School.

Andrade, Gregor, and Steven N. Kaplan. 1998. "How Costly is Financial (Not Economic) Distress? Evidence from Highly Leveraged Transactions that Became Distressed." *Journal of Finance* 53: 1443–1532.

Andrews, Michael. 2003. "Issuing Government Bonds to Finance Bank Recapitalization and Restructuring: Design Factors That Affect Banks' Financial Performance." *IMF Policy Discussion Paper* 03/04.

Andrews, Michael, and Mats Josefsson. 2003. "What Happens After Supervisory Intervention? Considering Bank Closure Options." IMF Working Paper 03/17. Washington, DC: International Monetary Fund.

Armour, John, Brian Cheffin, and David A. Skeel, Jr. 2002. "Corporate Ownership Structure and the Evolution of Bankruptcy Law: Lessons from the United Kingdom." *Vanderbilt Law Review* 55: 1699–1785.

Armour, John and Simon Deakin. 2001. "Norms in Private Insolvency: the "London Approach" to the Resolution of Financial Distress." *Journal of Corporate Law Studies* 1: 21–51.

Asquith, Paul, Robert Gertner, and David Scharfstein. 1994. "Anatomy of Financial Distress: An Examination of Junk Bond Issuers." *Quarterly Journal of Economics* 109(3): 625–658.

Asser, Tobias M.C. 2001. *Legal Aspects of Regulatory Treatment of Banks in Distress.* Washington, DC: International Monetary Fund.

Ausubel, Lawrence, Peter Cramton, and Raymond Deneckere. 2002. "Bargaining with Incomplete Information." In Robert Aumann and Sergiu Hart (Eds.), *Handbook of Game Theory* Vol. 3, Amsterdam: Elsevier Science B.V.

Ayotte, Kenneth. 2002. "Bankruptcy and Entrepreneurship: The Value of a Fresh Start." Working Paper. Columbia University.

Baer, Herbert and Daniela Klingebiel. 1995. "Systemic Risk when Depositors Bear Losses: Five Case Studies." *Research in Financial Services Private and Public Policy* 7: 195–302.

Bagehot, Walter. 1873. *Lombard Street. A Description of the Money Market.* London: H. S. King.

Baird, Douglas G. 1986. "The Uneasy Case for Corporate Reorganizations." *Journal of Legal Studies* 15: 127–147.

Baird, Douglas G., and Randal Picker. 1991. "A Simple Noncooperative Bargaining Model of Corporate Bankruptcy." *Journal of Legal Studies* 20: 311–349.

Baird, Douglas G., and Robert K. Rasmussen. 2001. "Control Rights, Priority Rights, and the Conceptual Foundations of Corporate Reorganizations." *Virginia Law Review* 87: 921–959.

Baird, Douglas G., and Robert K. Rasmussen. 2002. "The End of Bankruptcy." *Stanford Law Review* 55: 751–789.

Baird, Douglas G., and Robert K. Rasmussen. 2004. "Chapter 11 at Twilight." *Stanford Law Review* 56: 673–700.

Barajas, Adolfo, Roberto Steiner, and Natalia Salazar. 2000. "The Impact of Liberalization and Foreign Investment in Colombia's Financial Sector." *Journal of Development Economics* 63: 157–196.

Barro, Robert. 1991. "Economic Growth in a Cross Section of Countries." *Quarterly Journal of Economics* 106(2): 407–443.

Barth, James R., and Philip F. Bartholomew. 1992. "The Thrift Industry Crisis: Revealed Weaknesses in the Federal Deposit Insurance System." In J.R. Barth and R.D. Brumbaugh Jr. (Eds.), *The Reform of Federal Deposit Insurance.* New York: Harper Business, pp. 36–116.

Barth, James R., Gerard Caprio Jr., and Ross Levine. 2004. "Bank Regulation and Supervision: What Works Best?" *Journal of Financial Intermediation* 13(2): 205–248.

Bartlett, Joseph. 1995. *Equity Finance: Venture Capital, Buyouts, Restructurings and Reorganizations.* New York: John Wiley & Sons.

Basel Committee on Banking Supervision. 2002. *Supervisory Guidance on Dealing with Weak Banks, Report of the Task Force on Dealing with Weak Banks.* Basel: Bank for International Settlements.

Basel Committee on Banking Supervision. 2004. *International Convergence of Capital Measurement and Capital Standards: A Revised Framework.* Basel Committee Publications No. 107. Basel: Bank for International Settlements.

Bebchuk, Lucian. 1988. "A New Approach to Corporate Reorganizations." *Harvard Law Review* 101: 775–804.

Bebchuk, Lucian. 1998. "Chapter 11." In J. Eatwell, M. Milgate, and P. Newman (Eds.), *The New Palgrave Dictionary of Economics and the Law*. New York: Palgrave/St. Martin's Press.

Bebchuk, Lucian. 2003. "Ex Ante Costs of Violating Absolute Priority in Bankruptcy." Working Paper. Harvard Law School.

Beck, Thorsten, Asli Demirgüç-Kunt, and Ross Levine. 2003. "Bank Concentration and Crises." Policy Research Working Paper 3041. Washington, DC: World Bank.

Berger, Allen B., Leora F. Klapper and Gregory F. Udell. 2001. "The Ability of Banks to Lend to Informationally Opaque Small Businesses." *Journal of Banking And Finance* 25: 2127–2167.

Berger, Allen B., Nathan H. Miller, Mitchell A. Petersen, Raghuram G. Rajan, and Jeremy C. Stein. 2004. "Does Function Follow Organizational Form? Evidence from Lending Practices of Large and Small Banks." *Journal of Financial Economics*, Forthcoming.

Berggren, Arne. 1995. "Events Leading to the Need of General Measures in a Bank Crisis: The Swedish Experience." Mimeo.

Bergman, Yaacov, and Jeffrey Callen. 1991. "Opportunistic Underinvestment in Debt Renegotiation and Capital Structure." *Journal of Financial Economics* 29: 137–171.

Berkovitch, Elazar, and Ronen Israel. 1999. "Optimal Bankruptcy Laws across Different Economic Systems." *Review of Financial Studies* 12: 347–377.

Berkovitch, Elazar, Ronen Israel, and Jamie Zender. 1997. "Optimal Bankruptcy Laws and Firm Specific Investment." *European Economic Review* 41: 487–497.

Bernanke, Ben S.. 1983. "Nonmonetary Effects of the Financial Crisis in the Propagation of the Great Depression." *American Economic Review* 73(3): 257–276.

Bernanke, Ben S. and Cara Lown. 1991. "The Credit Crunch." *Brookings Papers on Economic Activity* 2: 205–248.

Bhaumik, Sumon K. and Jenifer Piesse. 2003. "Are Foreign Banks Bad For Development Even If They Are Efficient? Evidence From the Indian Banking Industry." William Davidson Institute Working Paper 619. Ann Arbor, MI: University of Michigan.

Biais, Bruno, and Jean-Francois Malecot. 1996. "Incentives and Efficiency in the Bankruptcy Process: The Case of France." Working Paper. Private Sector Development Department. Washington, DC: World Bank.

Bolton, Patrick, and David Scharfstein. 1990. "A Theory of Predation Based on Agency Problems in Financial Contracting." *American Economic Review* 80: 94–106.

Bolton, Patrick and David Scharfstein. 1996. "Optimal Debt Structure and the Number of Creditors." *Journal of Political Economy* 104: 1–25.

Bonin, John P. and Paul Wachtel. 1999. "Towards Market-Oriented Banking in the Economies in Transition." In M. Blejer and M. Skreb (Eds.), *Financial Sector Transformation: Lessons from the Economies in Transition*, Cambridge: Cambridge University Press.

Bordo, Michael, Barry Eichengreen, Daniela Klingebiel, and Maria Soledad Martinez-Peria. 2001. "Is the Crisis Problem Growing More Severe?" *Economic Policy* 16(32): 51–82.

Borenstein, Severin and Nancy Rose. 1995. "Bankruptcy and Pricing Behavior in U.S. Airline Markets." *American Economic Review* 85: 397–402.

Breton, Albert and Ronald Wintrobe. 1978. "A Theory of "Moral" Suasion." *Canadian Journal of Economics* 11: 210–219.

Brewer, Elijah, III. 1995. "The Impact of the Current Deposit Insurance System on S&L Shareholders' Risk/Return Tradeoffs." *Journal of Financial Services Research* 9: 65–89.

Brickley, James A., James S. Linck and Clifford W. Smith, Jr. 2003. "Boundaries of the Firm: Evidence from the Banking Industry." *Journal of Financial Economics* 70: 351–383.

Brock, Philip L. 2000. "Financial Safety Nets: Lessons from Chile." *World Bank Research Observer* 15(1): 69–84.

Brown, David T., Brian A. Ciochetti, and Timothy J. Riddiough. 2003. "Theory and Evidence on the Resolution of Financial Distress." Working Paper. University of Florida.

Brunner, Antje, and Jan-Pieter Krahnen. 2001. "Corporate Debt Restructuring: Evidence on Lending Coordination in Financial Distress." CEPR Discussion Paper No. 3030. London: Center for Economic Policy Research.

Buch, Claudia M. 1997. "Opening Up For Foreign Banks: How Central And Eastern Europe Can Benefit." *Economics of Transition* 5(2): 339–366.

Bukharin, Nikolai. 1917. *Imperialism and World Economy*. New York: International Publishers (first published in English in 1929), Chapter 3.

Burns, Arthur F., and Wesley C. Mitchell. 1946. *Measuring Business Cycles*. New York: National Bureau of Economic Research.

Burnside, Craig, Martin Eichenbaum, and Sergio Rebelo. 1998. "Prospective Deficits and the Asian Currency Crisis." CEPR Discussion Paper No. 2015, Center for Economic Policy Research, London.

Calomiris, Charles W. 1989. "Deposit Insurance: Lessons from the Record." *Federal Reserve Bank of Chicago Economic Perspectives* 13: 10–30.

Calomiris, Charles W. 1993a. "Financial Factors and the Great Depression." *Journal of Economic Perspectives* 7: 61–85.

Calomiris, Charles W. 1993b. "Greenback Resumption and Silver Risk: The Economics and Politics of Monetary Regime Change in the United States, 1862–1900." In M. D. Bordo and F. Capie (Eds.), *Monetary Regimes in Transition*. Cambridge: Cambridge University Press, pp. 86–134.

Calomiris, Charles W. 1998. "Evolution of the Mexican Banking System." Columbia University, Unpublished manuscript.

Calomiris, Charles W. 1999. "Building an Incentive-Compatible Safety Net." *Journal of Banking and Finance* 23: 1499–1519.

Calomiris, Charles W., and Mark S. Carey. 1994. "Loan Market Competition Between Foreign and Domestic Banks: Some Facts About Loans and Borrowers." *Proceedings of the 30th Annual Conference on Bank Structure and Competition*. Chicago: Federal Reserve Bank of Chicago, pp. 331–351.

Calomiris, Charles W., and Gary Gorton. 1991. "The Origins of Banking Panics: Models, Facts, and Bank Regulation." In R. G. Hubbard (ed.), *Financial Markets and Financial Crisis*. Chicago: University of Chicago Press, pp. 109–173.

Calomiris, Charles W., and Charles M. Kahn. 1991. "The Role of Demandable Debt in Structuring Optimal Banking Arrangements." *American Economic Review* 81: 497–513.

Calomiris, Charles W., and Joseph R. Mason. 1997. "Contagion and Bank Failures During the Great Depression: The June 1932 Chicago Banking Panic." *American Economic Review* 87(5): 863–883.

Calomiris, Charles W., and Joseph R. Mason. 2003a. "How to Restructure Failed Banking Systems: Lessons from the U.S. in the 1930s and Japan in the 1990s." In Takatoshi Ito and Anne Krueger (Eds.), *Privatization, Corporate Governance and Transition Economies in East Asia*. Chicago: University of Chicago Press.

Calomiris, Charles W., and Joseph R. Mason. 2003b. "Fundamentals, Panics, and Bank Distress During the Depression." *American Economic Review* 93: 1615–1647.

Calomiris, Charles W., and Joseph R. Mason. 2003c. "Consequences of Bank Distress During the Great Depression." *American Economic Review* 93: 937–947.

Calomiris, Charles W., and Andrew Powell. 2001. "Can Emerging Market Bank Regulators Establish Credible Discipline? The Case of Argentina, 1992–1999." In F. S. Mishkin (Ed.), *Prudential Supervision*. Chicago: University of Chicago Press, pp. 147–196.

Calomiris, Charles W., and Berry Wilson. 2004. "Bank Capital and Portfolio Management: The 1930s Capital Crunch and Scramble to Shed Risk." *Journal of Business* 77: 421–456.

Caprio, Gerard and Daniela Klingebiel. 1996. "Bank Insolvencies, Cross-Country Experience." Policy Research Working Paper 1620. Washington, DC: World Bank.

Caprio, Gerard and Daniela Klingebiel, 1999. "Episodes of Systemic and Borderline Financial Crises." Mimeo. World Bank, January.

Chang, Roberto and Andres Velasco. 2001. "A Model of Financial Crises in Emerging Markets." *Quarterly Journal of Economics* 116: 489–517.

Claessens, Stijn, Asli Demirgüç-Kunt, and Harry Huizinga. 2001. "How Does Foreign Entry Affect Domestic Banking Markets?" *Journal of Banking and Finance* 25: 891–911.

Claessens, Stijn, Simeon Djankov, and Daniela Klingebiel. 1999. "Financial Restructuring in East Asia: Halfway There?" World Bank Financial Sector Discussion Paper No. 3, Washington, DC: World Bank.

Claessens, Stijn, Simeon Djankov, and Larry H.P. Lang. 1999. "Who Controls East Asian Corporations?" Policy Research Working Paper 2054. Washington, DC: World Bank.

Claessens, Stijn, Simeon Djankov, and Ashoka Mody. 2001. Eds., *Resolution of Financial Distress: An International Perspective on the Design of*

Bankruptcy Laws. World Bank Development Studies. Washington, DC: World Bank.

Claessens, Stijn, Simeon Djankov, and Leora Klapper. 2003. "Resolution of Financial Distress: Evidence from East Asia's Financial Crisis." *Journal of Empirical Finance* 10(1–2): 199–216.

Claessens, Stijn, and Leora Klapper. 2002. "Bankruptcy around the World: Explanations of its Relative Use." Policy Research Working Paper 2865. Washington, DC: World Bank.

Claessens, Stijn, Daniela Klingebiel, and Luc Laeven. 2001. "Financial Restructuring in Banking and Corporate Sector Crises: What Policies to Pursue?" NBER Working Paper No. 8386.

Claessens, Stijn, Daniela Klingebiel, and Luc Laeven. 2003. "Financial Restructuring in Systemic Crises: What Policies to Pursue?" In Michael Dooley and Jeffrey Frankel (Eds.), *Managing Currency Crises in Emerging Markets*. Chicago: University of Chicago Press, 2003.

Claessens, Stijn and Jong-Kun Lee. 2003. "Foreign Banks in Low-Income Countries: Recent Developments and Impacts." In J.A. Hanson, P. Honohan, and G. Majnoni (Eds.), *Globalization and National Financial Systems*. New York: Oxford University Press.

Clarke, George R.G., Juan M. Crivelli and Robert Cull. 2003. "The Impact of Bank Privatization and Foreign Entry on Access to Credit in Argentina's Provinces." *Journal of Banking and Finance*, Forthcoming.

Clarke, George R.G., and Robert Cull. 2002. "Political and Economic Determinants of the Likelihood of Privatizing Argentine Public Banks." *Journal of Law and Economics* 45: 165–197.

Clarke, George R.G., Robert Cull, and M. Soledad Martinez Peria. 2001. "Does Foreign Bank Penetration Reduce Access to Credit in Developing Countries? Evidence from Asking Borrowers." Policy Research Working Paper 2716. Washington, DC: World Bank.

Corrigan, E. Gerald. 1991. "The Risk of a Financial Crisis." In: Martin Feldstein (Ed.), *The Risk of Economic Crisis*. Chicago: University of Chicago Press, pp. 44–53.

Cull, Robert. 1998. "Structural Change: Internationalization, Consolidation, and Privatization in Argentina's Banking Sector." Mimeo. World Bank.

Cull, Robert, Lemma W. Senbet, and Marco Sorge. 2000. "Deposit Insurance and Financial Development." World Bank, mimeo, forthcoming, *Journal of Money, Credit and Banking*.

D'Amato, Laura, Elena Grubisic and Andrew Powell. 1997. "Contagion, Bank Fundamentals or Macroeconomic Shock: An Empirical Analysis of the Argentine 1995 Banking Problems." Central Bank of Argentina Working Paper No. 2.

Dages, B. Gerard, Linda Goldberg, and Daniel Kinney. 2000. "Foreign and Domestic Bank Participation in Emerging Markets: Lessons from Mexico and Argentina." Federal Reserve Bank of New York Economic Policy Review: 17–36.

De Juan, Aristobulo. 1999. "Clearing the Decks: Experiences in Banking Crisis Resolution." In Shahid J. Burki and Guillermo E. Perry (Eds.), *Banks and*

Capital Markets: Sound Financial Systems for the 21st Century. Washington, DC: World Bank.

De la Torre, Augusto. 2000. "Resolving Bank Failures in Argentina: Recent Developments and Issues." Policy Research Working Paper 2295. Washington, DC: World Bank.

De Luna Martinez, Jose. 2000. "Management and Resolution of Banking Crises: Lessons from the Republic of Korea and Mexico." World Bank Discussion Paper 413. Washington, DC: World Bank.

Delaney, John A. 1954. "Field Administration in the Reconstruction Finance Corporation." Ph.D. dissertation, George Washington University.

Demirgüç-Kunt, Asli, and Enrica Detragiache. 2002. "Does Deposit Insurance Increase Banking System Stability?" *Journal of Monetary Economics* 49(7): 1373–1406.

Demirgüç-Kunt, Asli, and Harry Huizinga. 1999. "Determinants of Commercial Bank Interest Margins and Profitability: Some International Evidence." *World Bank Economic Review* 13(2): 379–408.

Demirgüç-Kunt, Asli, and Harry Huizinga. 2004. "Market Discipline and Deposit Insurance." *Journal of Monetary Economics* 51: 375–399.

Demirgüç-Kunt, Asli, and Edward J. Kane. 2002. "Deposit Insurance Around the Globe: Where Does It Work?" *Journal of Economic Perspectives* 16: 175–195.

Demirgüç-Kunt, Asli, Ross Levine, and Hong-Ghi Min. 1998. "Opening to Foreign Banks: Issues of Stability, Efficiency, and Growth." In Seongtae Lee (Ed.), *The Implications of Globalization of World Financial Markets*, Seoul: Bank of Korea.

DeNicoló, Gianni, Patrick Honohan and Alain Ize. 2003. "Dollarization of the Banking System: Good or Bad?" Policy Research Working Paper 3116. Washington, DC: World Bank.

Dewatripont, Matthias, and Jean Tirole. 1994. "A Theory of Debt and Equity: Diversity of Securities and Manager-Shareholder Congruence." *Quarterly Journal of Economics* 109: 1027–1054.

Diamond, Douglas W., and Philip H. Dybvig. 1983. "Bank Runs, Deposit Insurance, and Liquidity." *Journal of Political Economy* 91: 401–419.

Diamond, Douglas, and Raghuram Rajan. 2001. "Liquidity Risk, Liquidity Creation and Financial Fragility: A Theory of Banking." *Journal of Political Economy* 109(2): 287–327.

Dinç, I. Serdar. 2002. "Politicians and Banks: Political Influences on Government-Owned Banks in Emerging Countries." *Journal of Financial Economics*, Forthcoming.

Djankov, Simeon, Oliver Hart, Tatiana Nenova, and Andrei Shleifer. 2003. "Efficiency in Bankruptcy." mimeo, Department of Economics, Harvard University, July.

Dooley, Michael, and Jeffrey Frankel, eds. 2003. *Managing Currency Crises.* Chicago: University of Chicago Press.

Dooley, Michael and Sujata Verma. 2003. "Rescue Packages and Output Losses Following Crises." In Michael Dooley and Jeffrey Frankel (Eds.), *Managing Currency Crises in Emerging Markets.* Chicago: The University of Chicago Press.

Dopico, Luis G., and James A. Wilcox. 2002. "Openness, Profit Opportunities and Foreign Banking." *Journal of Financial Markets, Institutions, and Money* 12(4–5): 299–320.

Drees, Burkhard, and Ceyla Pazarbasioglu. 1998. "The Nordic Banking Crisis: Pitfalls in Financial Liberalization." Occasional Paper No. 161. Washington, DC: International Monetary Fund.

Du, Julan. 2003. "Why Do Multinational Enterprises Borrow from Local Banks?" *Economics Letters* 78: 287–291.

Dziobek, Claudia. 1998. "Market-Based Policy Instruments for Systemic Bank Restructuring." IMF Working Paper 98/113. Washington, DC: International Monetary Fund.

Dziobek, Claudia and Ceyla Pazarbasioglu. 1998. "Lessons from Systemic Bank Restructuring." Economic Issues Paper 14. Washington, DC: International Monetary Fund.

Easterly, William. 2003. "IMF and World Bank Structural Adjustment Programs and Poverty." In Michael Dooley and Jeffrey Frankel (Eds.), *Managing Currency Crises in Emerging Markets*. Chicago: University of Chicago Press.

Eichengreen, Barry. 1992. *Golden Fetters: The Gold Standard and the Great Depression,1919–1939*. Oxford: Oxford University Press.

Eichengreen, Barry and Andrew Rose. 2003. "Does It Pay Back to Defend against a Speculative Attack?" In Michael Dooley and Jeffrey Frankel (Eds.), *Managing Currency Crises in Emerging Markets*. Chicago: University of Chicago Press.

Englund, Peter. 1999. "The Swedish Banking Crisis: Roots and Consequences." *Oxford Review of Economic Policy* 15(3): 80–97.

Engwall, Lars, Rolf Marquardt, Torben Pedersen, and Adrian E. Tschoegl. 2001. "Foreign Bank Penetration of Newly Opened Markets in the Nordic Countries." *Journal of International Financial Markets, Institutions, and Money* 11(1): 53–63.

Enoch, Charles, Gillian Garcia, and V. Sundararajan. 1999. "Recapitalizing Banks with Public Funds: Selected Issues." IMF Working Paper 99/139. Washington, DC: International Monetary Fund.

European Commission. 2003. "Best Project on Restructuring, Bankruptcy, and a Fresh Start." Mimeo. Brussels: European Commission.

Federal Deposit Insurance Corporation. 1998. *Resolutions Handbook: Methods for Resolving Trouble Financial Institutions in the United States*. Washington, DC: Federal Deposit Insurance Corporation.

Fisher, Irving. 1933. "The Debt Deflation Theory of Great Depressions." *Econometrica* 1: 337–357.

Friedman, Milton, and Anna J. Schwartz. 1963. *A Monetary History of the United States*. Princeton, NJ: Princeton University Press.

Folkerts-Landau, David, and Carl-Johan Lindgren. 1998. *Towards a Framework for Financial Stability*. Washington, DC: International Monetary Fund.

Franks, Julian, and Kjell Nyborg. 1996. "Control Rights and the Loss of Private Benefits: The Case of the U.K. Insolvency Code." *Review of Financial Studies* 9: 1165–1210.

Franks, Julian, Kjell Nyborg, and Walter Torous. 1996. "A Comparison of US, UK, and German Insolvency Codes." *Financial Management* 25(3): 86–101.

Franks, Julian R., and Oren Sussman. 2003. "Financial Distress and Bank Restructuring of Small- to Medium-size UK Companies." CEPR Discussion Paper No. 3915. London: Center for Economic Policy Research.

Franks, Julian R., and Walter Torous. 1994. "A Comparison of Financial Recontracting in Distressed Exchanges and Chapter 11 Reorganizations." *Journal of Finance* 35: 349–370.

Gale, Douglas and Martin Hellwig. 1985. "Incentive-Compatible Debt Contracts: The One-Period Problem." *Review of Economic Studies* 52: 647–663.

Garber, Peter. 1998. "Derivatives in International Capital Flows." NBER Working Paper No. 6623.

Gertner, Robert, and David Scharfstein. 1991. "A Theory of Workouts and the Effects of Reorganization Law." *Journal of Finance* 46: 1189–1222.

Gibson, Michael S. 1995. "Can Bank Health Affect Investment? Evidence from Japan." *Journal of Business* 68: 281–308.

Gilson, Stuart C., Kose John, and Larry H.P. Lang. 1990. "Troubled Debt Restructurings: An Empirical study of Private Reorganization of Firms in Default." *Journal of Financial Economics* 27: 315–353.

Goldberg, Linda, B. Gerard Dages, and Daniel Kinney. 2000. "Foreign and Domestic Participation in Emerging Markets: Lessons from Mexico and Argentina." NBER Working Paper No. 7714, Cambridge, MA: National Bureau of Economic Research.

Goldsmith, Raymond W. 1969. *Financial Structure and Development*. New Haven, CT: Yale University Press.

Goldstein, Morris, Graciela L. Kaminsky, and Carmen M. Reinhart. 2000. *Assessing Financial Vulnerability: An Early Warning System for Emerging Markets*. Washington, DC: Institute for International Economics.

Gompers, Paul. 1998. "An Examination of Convertible Securities in Venture Capital Investments." Working Paper. Harvard Business School.

Goodhart, Charles, and Gerhard Illing. 2002. *Financial Crises, Contagion, and the Lender of Last Resort*. Oxford: Oxford University Press. Gove, Alex. 1999. "Washouts Take a Bath: A Recent Court Case Raises Some Difficult Questions for Venture Capitalists and Struggling Start-Ups." *Red Herring*, December 1999.

Greenspan, Alan. 1999. "Lessons from the Global Crises." Remarks before the World Bank-IMF, Program of Seminars, Washington, D.C., September 27, http://www.federalreserve.gov/boarddocs/speeches/1999/199909272.htm.

Gropp, Reint, and Jukka Vesala. 2004. "Deposit Insurance, Moral Hazard and Bank Monitoring." ECB Working Paper No. 302. Frankfurt: European Central Bank.

Gros, Daniel. 2003. "Who Needs Foreign Banks?" CESifo Working Paper 998, Munich: Society for the Protection of Economic Research.

Guillén, Mauro and Adrian E. Tschoegl. 2000. "The Internationalization of Retail Banking: The Case of the Spanish Banks in Latin America." *Transnational Corporations* 9(3): 63–97.

Hammond, Bray. 1970. *Sovereignty and an Empty Purse: Banks and Politics in the Civil War*. Princeton, NJ: Princeton University Press.

Hancock, Diana and Jim Wilcox. 1998. "The Credit Crunch and the Availability of Credit to Small Business." *Journal of Banking and Finance* 22: 983–1014.

Harrington, Denis G. and Tom C. Lawton. 2003. "The Internationalization of Allied Irish Banks." ECCH Case 303–015–1.

Hart, Oliver. 1995. *Firms, Contracts, and Financial Structure*. Oxford: Oxford University Press.

Hart, Oliver. 2001. "Financial Contracting." *Journal of Economic Literature* 39(4): 1079–1100.

Hart, Oliver, Rafael La Porta Drago, Florencio Lopez-de-Silanes and John Moore. 1997. "A New Bankruptcy Procedure that Uses Multiple Auctions." *European Economic Review* 41: 461–73.

Hart, Oliver, and John Moore. 1998. "Default and Renegotiation: A Dynamic Model of Debt." *Quarterly Journal of Economics* 113: 1–41.

Hasan, Iftekhar and Katherin Marton. 2003. "Development and Efficiency of the Banking Sector in a Transitional Economy: Hungarian Experience." *Journal of Banking and Finance* 27: 2249–2271.

Haugen, Robert, and Lemma Senbet. 1978. "The Insignificance of Bankruptcy Costs to the Theory of Optimal Capital Structure." *Journal of Finance* 33(2): 383–393.

Heinkel, Robert L., and Maurice D. Levi. 1992. "The Structure of International Banking." *Journal of International Money and Finance* 16: 251–72.

Hellman, Thomas F., Kevin C. Murdock and Joseph E. Stiglitz. 2000. "Liberalization, Moral Hazard in Banking, and Prudential Regulation: Are Capital Requirements Enough?" *American Economic Review* 90(1): 147–165.

Hellman, Thomas and Manju Puri. 2002. "Venture Capital and the Professionalization of Start-up Firms: Empirical Evidence." *Journal of Finance* 57(1): 169–197.

Henig, Peter. 2002. "Fair Game: Extortion-Style Funding Dies an Early (and Timely) Death." *Red Herring*, September 6, 2002.

Hewison, Kevin. 2001. "Pathways To Recovery: Bankers, Business and Nationalism in Thailand." Southeast Asia Research Centre Working Paper No. 1. Hong Kong (China): City University of Hong Kong.

Hobday, Nicola. 2003. "Coming to America." *The Deal.com* (June 26, 2003).

Hoelscher, David S., and Marc Quintyn. 2003. "Managing Systemic Banking Crises." IMF Occasional Paper 224. Washington, DC: International Monetary Fund.

Hoggarth, Glenn, Ricardo Reis, and Victoria Saporta. 2002. "Costs of Banking System Instability: Some Empirical Evidence." *Journal of Banking and Finance* 26(5): 825–855.

Honohan, Patrick. 1996. "Does It Matter How Seigniorage is Measured?" *Applied Financial Economics* 6(3): 293–300.

Honohan, Patrick. 1997. "Banking System Failures in Developing and Transition Countries: Diagnosis and Prediction." BIS Working Paper 39, January. Shortened and revised version in *Economic Notes* 29(1): 83–109 (2000).

Honohan, Patrick. 2002. "Discussion" of Hoggarth, Glenn, Ricardo Reis and Victoria Saporta, "Cost of Banking System Instability: Some Empirical Evidence." *Journal of Banking and Finance* 26(5): 857–860.

Honohan, Patrick. 2003. "Recapitalizing Banking Systems." Policy Research Working Paper 2540. Washington, DC: World Bank.

Honohan, Patrick and Jane Kelly. 1997. "The Insurance Corporation Collapse: Resolving Ireland's Worst Financial Crash." *Administration* 45(3): 67–77.

Honohan, Patrick and Daniela Klingebiel. 2003. "The Fiscal Cost Implications of an Accommodating Approach to Banking Crises." *Journal of Banking and Finance* 27(8): 1539–1560.

Hoshi, Takeo and Anil Kashyap. 1999. "The Japanese Banking Crisis: Where Did It Come From and How Will It End?" *NBER Macroeconomics Annual* 14, 129–212.

Hoshi, Takeo, Anil Kashyap, and David Scharfstein. 1990. "The Role of Banks in Reducing the Costs of Financial Distress in Japan." *Journal of Financial Economics* 27(1): 67–88.

Hoshi, Takeo, Anil Kashyap, and David Scharfstein. 1991. "Corporate Structure, Liquidity, and Investment: Evidence from Japanese Industrial Groups." *Quarterly Journal of Economics* 106(1): 33–60.

Hoshi, Takeo, David Scharfstein, and Kenneth J. Singleton. 1993. "Japanese Corporate Investment and Bank of Japan Guidance of Commercial Bank Lending." In Kenneth J. Singleton (Ed.), *Japanese Monetary Policy*. Chicago: University of Chicago Press.

Hotchkiss, Edith. 1995. "Postbankruptcy Performance and Management Turnover." *Journal of Finance* 50(1): 3–21.

Hotchkiss, Edith, and Robert Mooradian. 1997. "Vulture Investors and the Market for Control of Distressed Firms." *Journal of Financial Economics* 43: 401–432.

Hotchkiss, Edith, and Robert Mooradian. 1998. "Acquisitions as a Means of Restructuring Firms in Chapter 11." *Journal of Financial Intermediation* 7: 240–262.

Hovakimian, Armen, Edward J. Kane, and Luc Laeven. 2003. "How Country and Safety-Net Characteristics Affect Bank Risk-Shifting." *Journal of Financial Services Research* 23: 177–204.

Huang, Yasheng, and Wenhua Di. 2003. "A Tale of Two Provinces: The Institutional Environment and Foreign Ownership in China." MIT, Unpublished Paper.

Hutchinson, Michael. 2003. "A Cure Worse Than the Disease? Currency Crises and the Output Costs of IMF-Supported Stabilization Programs." In Michael Dooley and Jeffrey Frankel (Eds.), *Managing Currency Crises in Emerging Markets*. Chicago: University of Chicago Press.

Hymer, Stephen H. 1976. *The International Operation of National Firms: A Study of Direct Investment*. Cambridge, MA: MIT Press.

Ignatiev, Petar. 1997. "Development of the Bulgarian Banking System between 1992 and 1996." *Monthly Bulletin*, July, Sofia: Bulgarian National Bank, pp. 27–31.

International Monetary Fund. 1998. "Financial Crises: Characteristics and Indicators of Vulnerability." *World Economic Outlook*, Chapter 4. Washington, DC: International Monetary Fund.

International Monetary Fund. 1998. "World Economic Report: Financial Turbulence and the World Economy." Washington, DC: International Monetary Fund. October.

International Monetary Fund. 2001. "Mexico: Financial System Stability Assessment." IMF Country Report No. 01/192. Washington, DC: International Monetary Fund. October.

International Monetary Fund. 2003. "A Framework for Managing Systemic Banking Crises." Mimeo. Washington, DC: International Monetary Fund.

Jacklin, Charles J., and Sudipto Bhattacharya. 1988. "Distinguishing Panics and Informationally-Based Bank Runs: Welfare and Policy Implications." *Journal of Political Economy* 96: 568–592.

Jackson, Thomas H. 1986. *The Logic and Limits of Bankruptcy Law*. Cambridge, MA: Harvard University Press.

James, Cyril F. 1938. *The Growth of Chicago Banks*. New York: Harper & Bros.

Jensen, Michael. 1989. "Active Investors, LBOs, and the Privatization of Bankruptcy." *Journal of Applied Corporate Finance* 2: 235–244.

Jensen, Michael. 1991. "Corporate Control and the Politics of Finance." *Journal of Applied Corporate Finance* 4: 13–33.

Jensen, Michael, and William Meckling. 1976. "Theory of the Firm: Managerial Behavior, Agency Costs and Ownership Structure." *Journal of Financial Economics* 3: 305–360.

Kaiser, Kevin. 1995. "Prospects for Reorganization within European Bankruptcy Laws." INSEAD Working Paper. Paris: Institut Européen d'Administration des Affaires.

Kaiser, Kevin. 1996. "European Bankruptcy Laws: Implications for Corporations Facing Financial Distress." *Financial Management* 25(3): 67–85.

Kahn, Charles M., and Joao A. C. Santos. 2001. "Allocating Bank Regulatory Powers: Lender of Last Resort, Deposit Insurance and Supervision." BIS Working Paper 102. Basel: Bank for International Settlements.

Kane, Edward J. 1989. *The S&L Insurance Mess: How Did It Happen?* Cambridge, MA: MIT Press.

Kane, Edward and Daniela Klingebiel. 2002. "Alternatives to Blanket Guarantees for Containing a Systemic Crisis." Mimeo. Washington, DC: World Bank.

Kaplan, Steven and Per Strömberg. 2001. "Venture Capitalists As Principals: Contracting, Screening, and Monitoring." *American Economic Review Papers and Proceedings* 91(2): 426–430.

Kaplan, Steven, and Per Strömberg. 2003. "Financial Contracting Theory Meets the Real World: Evidence from Venture Capital Contracts." *Review of Economic Studies* 70: 281–315.

Kaplan, Steven, and Per Strömberg. 2004. "Characteristics, Contracts, and Actions: Evidence from Venture Capitalist Analyses." *Journal of Finance*, forthcoming.

Kaplan, Steven, Josh Lerner, and Per Strömberg. 2004. "Renegotiations of Venture Capital Contracts." Mimeo, Harvard Business School and University of Chicago.

Kaplan, Steven, Frederic Martel, and Per Strömberg. 2003. "How Do Legal Institutions and Learning Affect Financial Contracts?" NBER Working Paper 10097. Cambridge MA: National Bureau of Economic Research.

Kashyap, Anil K., and Jeremy C. Stein. 1994. "Monetary Policy and Bank Lending." In N. Gregory Mankiw (Ed.), *Monetary Policy*. Chicago: University of Chicago Press.

Kashyap, Anil K., and Jeremy C. Stein. 1995. "The Impact of Monetary Policy on Bank Balance Sheets." *Carnegie-Rochester Conference Series on Public Policy* 42: 151–195.

Kashyap, Anil K., and Jeremy C. Stein. 2000. "What Do A Million Observations on Banks Say about the Transmission of Monetary Policy?" *American Economic Review* 90(3): 407–428.

Kashyap, Anil K., Jeremy C. Stein and David W. Wilcox. 1993. "Monetary Policy and Credit Conditions: Evidence from the Composition of External Finance." *American Economic Review* 83(1): 78–98.

Kaufmann, Daniel, Aart Kraay, and Pablo Zoido-Lobatón. 1999. "Governance Matters," Policy Research Working Paper 2196. Washington, DC: World Bank.

Kent, Pen. 1997. "Corporate Workouts: A U.K. Perspective." Working Paper. London: Bank of England.

Keynes, John M. 1931. "The Consequences to Banks of the Collapse of Money Values." Republished in *Essays in Persuasion*. New York: W. W. Norton, 1963, pp. 168–180.

Kindleberger, Charles P. 1969. *American Business Abroad.* New Haven, CT: Yale University Press.

Kindleberger, Charles P. 1978. *Manias, Panics, and Crashes: A History of Financial Crises.* New York: John Wiley and Sons.

Kirkpatrick, Colin and David Tennant. 2002. "Responding to Financial Crisis: The Case of Jamaica." *World Development* 30(11): 1933–1950.

Klingebiel, Daniela. 2000. "The Use of Asset Management Companies in the Resolution of Banking Crises: Cross-Country Experience." Policy Research Working Paper 2284. Washington, DC: World Bank.

Klingebiel, Daniela and Luc Laeven. Eds. 2002. *Managing the Real and Fiscal Effects of Banking Crises.* World Bank Discussion Paper No. 428. Washington, DC: World Bank.

Klingebiel, Daniela, Randall Kroszner, and Luc Laeven. 2002. Financial Crises, Financial Dependence, and Industry Growth." Policy Research Working Paper 2855. Washington, DC: World Bank.

Koford, Kenneth. 2000. "Citizen Restraints on "Leviathan" Government: Transition Politics in Bulgaria." *European Journal of Political Economy* 16: 307–338.

Koford, Kenneth and Adrian E. Tschoegl. 2002. "Foreign Banks in Bulgaria, 1875–2002." William Davidson Institute, Working Paper 537. Ann Arbor: University of Michigan.

Kroszner, Randall. 1998. "On the Political Economy of Banking and Financial Regulatory Reform in Emerging Markets." *Research in Financial Services* 10: 33–51.

Kroszner, Randall. 1999. "Is It Better to Forgive than to Receive? Repudiation of the Gold Indexation Clause in Long-Term Debt During the Great Depression." Mimeo. Chicago: University of Chicago.

Krugman, Paul R. 1998. "It's Back: Japan's Slump and the Return of the Liquidity Trap." *Brookings Papers on Economic Activity* 2: 137–205.

Kunii, Irene M., and Satsuki Oba. 1996. "A Yakuza Boss Defends his Gang's Business Ethics." *Time International* 147, p. 8.

La Porta, Rafael, Florencio Lopez-de-Silanes, and Andrei Shleifer. 2002. "Government Ownership of Banks." *Journal of Finance* 57: 265–301.

References

La Porta, Rafael, Florencio Lopes-de-Silanes, Andrei Shleifer, and Robert Vishny. 1998. "Law and Finance." *The Journal of Political Economy* 106(6): 1113–1155.

La Porta, Rafael, Florencio Lopez-de-Silanes, and Guillermo Zamarripa. 2003. "Related Lending." *Quarterly Journal of Economics* 118(1): 231–268.

Laderman, Elizabeth S. 1999. "The Shrinking of Japanese Branch Business Lending in California." *FRBSF Economic Letter* No. 99–14.

Laeven, Luc. 1999. "Risk And Efficiency In East Asian Banks." Policy Research Working Paper 2255. Washington, DC: World Bank.

Laeven, Luc. 2001. "Insider Lending and Bank Ownership: The Case of Russia." *Journal of Comparative Economics* 29(2): 207–229.

Laeven, Luc, Daniela Klingebiel, and Randall Kroszner. 2002. "Financial Crises, Financial Dependence, and Industry Growth." Policy Research Working Paper No. 2855. Washington, DC: World Bank.

Lease, Ronald, John McConnell, and Elizabeth Tashjian. 1996. "Prepacks: An Empirical Analysis of Prepackaged Bankruptcies." *Journal of Financial Economics* 40: 135–162.

Lee, Jong-Wha and Yung Chul Park. 2003. "Recovery and Sustainability in East Asia." In Michael Dooley and Jeffrey Frankel (Eds.), *Managing Currency Crises in Emerging Markets*. Chicago: University of Chicago Press.

Lensink, Robert and Niels Hermes. 2004. "The Short-Term Effects of Foreign Bank Entry on Domestic Bank Behavior: Does Economic Development Matter?" *Journal of Banking and Finance* 28(3): 553–568.

Levine, Ross. 2002. "Denying Foreign Bank Entry: Implications for Bank Interest Margins." University of Minnesota, Unpublished Paper.

Levine, Ross. 2004. "Finance and Growth: Theory, Evidence, and Mechanisms." in: Phillipe Aghion and Steven Durlauf, eds. *Handbook of Economic Growth*. Amsterdam: North-Holland Elsevier Publishers, forthcoming.

Lindgren, Carl-Johan, J.T. Balino, Charles Enoch, Anne-Marie Gulde, Marc Quintyn and Leslie Teo. 1999. *Financial Sector Crisis and Restructuring: Lessons from Asia*. IMF Occasional Paper 188. Washington, DC: International Monetary Fund.

Lindgren, Carl-Johan, Gillian Garcia, and Matthew I. Saal. 1996. *Bank Soundness and Macroeconomic Policy*. Washington, DC: International Monetary Fund.

Lopucki, Lynn, and Theodore Eisenberg. 1999. "Shopping for Judges: An Empirical Analysis of Venue Choice in the Bankruptcy Reorganization of Large, Publicly Held Companies." *Cornell Law Review* 84: 967–1003.

Lopucki, Lynn, and William C. Whitford. 1990. "Bargaining Over Equity's Share in the Bankruptcy Reorganization of Large, Publicly Held Companies." *University of Pennsylvania Law Review* 132: 125–196.

Lwiza, Daudi R.B. and Sonny Nwankwo. 2002. "Market-Driven Transformation of the Banking Sector in Tanzania." *International Journal of Bank Marketing* 20(1): 38–49.

Macaulay, Frederick. 1938. *Some Theoretical Problems Suggested by the Movements of Interest Rates, Bond Yields, and Stock Prices in the United States Since 1856*. New York: National Bureau of Economic Research.

Mackey, Michael W. 1999. Report on the Comprehensive Evaluation of the Operations and Functions of the Fund for the Protection of Bank Savings "FOBAPROA" and Quality of Supervision of the FOBAPROA Program 1995–1998. Report submitted to the Congress of Mexico.

Majnoni, Giovanni, Rashmi Shankar, and Eva Varhegyi. 2003. "The Dynamics of Foreign Bank Ownership: Evidence from Hungary." Policy Research Working Paper 3114. Washington, DC: World Bank.

Marichal, Carlos. 1997. "Nation Building and the Origins of Banking in Latin America, 1850–1930." In A. Teichova, G. Kurgan-Van Hentenryk, and D. Ziegler (Eds.), *Banking, Trade And Industry: Europe, America and Asia from the Thirteenth to the Twentieth Century*. Cambridge: Cambridge University Press.

Martinez Peria, M. Soledad. 2000. "The Impact of Banking Crises on Money Demand and Price Stability." Policy Research Working Paper 2305. Washington, DC: World Bank.

Martinez Peria, M. Soledad, and Sergio L. Schmukler. 2001. "Do Depositors Punish Banks for Bad Behavior? Market Discipline, Deposit Insurance, and Banking Crises." *Journal of Finance* 56: 1029–1051.

Mason, Joseph R. 1996. "The Determinants and Effects of Reconstruction Finance Corporation Assistance to Banks During the Great Depression." Ph.D. Dissertation, University of Illinois.

Mason, Joseph R. 2001. "Do Lender of Last Resort Policies Matter? The Effects of Reconstruction Finance Corporation Assistance to Banks During the Great Depression." *Journal of Financial Services Research* 20: 77–95.

McQuerry, Elizabeth. 1999. "The Banking Sector Rescue in Mexico." Federal Reserve Bank of Atlanta *Economic Review*, Third Quarter: 14–29.

Merton, Robert. 1977. "An Analytical Derivation of the Cost of Deposit Insurance Loan Guarantees: An Application of Modern Option Pricing Theory." *Journal of Banking and Finance* 1: 3–11.

Meyerman, Gerald E. 2000. "The London Approach and Corporate Debt Restructuring in East Asia." In C. Adams, R. E. Litan, and M. Pomerleano (Eds.), *Managing Financial and Corporate Distress: Lessons from Asia*. Washington, DC: Brookings Institution Press, pp. 299–322.

Miller, Jeffrey B. and Stefan Petranov. 1996. *Banking in the Bulgarian Economy*. Sofia: Bulgarian National Bank.

Miller, Jeffrey B. and Stefan Petranov. 2001. *The Financial System in the Bulgarian Economy*. Sofia: Bulgarian National Bank.

Miller, Marcus and Joseph Stiglitz. 1999. "Bankruptcy Protection Against Macroeconomic Shocks: The Case for a 'Super Chapter 11'." Presented at a Conference on Capital Flows, Financial Crisis and Policies at the World Bank, Washington, DC, April 15/16, 1999. Mimeo.

Mitchell, Wesley C. 1903. *A History of the Greenbacks*. Chicago: University of Chicago Press.

Moffett, Michael H., Arthur Stonehill, and Morten Balling. 1989. "Multinational Bank Strategy in Theory and Practice: Towards the EC Internal Market and 1992." Oregon State University, Unpublished Paper.

Mulás, Alberto. 2001. "Corporate Debt Restructuring in a Systemic Financial Crisis: Mexico's Experience, 1996–1998." In Claessens S., S. Djankov, and A. Mody (Eds.), *Resolution of Financial Distress: An International Perspective on the Design of Bankruptcy Laws*. WBI Development Studies. Washington, DC: World Bank, pp. 149–166.

Myers, Stewart. 1977. "Determinants of Corporate Borrowing." *Journal of Financial Economics* 5: 147–175.

Nyberg, Peter. 1997. "Authorities' Roles and Organizational Issues in Systemic Bank Restructuring." IMF Working Paper 97/92. Washington, DC: International Monetary Fund.

Olson, James S. 1972. "The End of Voluntarism: Herbert Hoover and the National Credit Corporation." *Annals of Iowa* 41: 1104–1113.

Olson, James S. 1977. *Herbert Hoover and the Reconstruction Finance Corporation, 1931–1933*. Ames: Iowa State University Press.

Olson, James S. 1988. *Saving Capitalism*. Princeton, NJ: Princeton University Press.

Packer, Frank. 2000. "The Disposal of Bad Loans in Japan: The Case of the CCPC." In Takeo Hoshi and Hugh Patrick (Eds.), *Crisis and Change in the Japanese Financial System*. Boston: Kluwer Academic Publishers.

Packer, Frank, and Marc Ryser. 1992. "The Governance of Failure: An Anatomy of Corporate Bankruptcy in Japan." Center on Japanese Economy and Business Working Paper No. 62, Columbia University.

Peek, Joe and Eric S. Rosengren. 1995a. "Bank Regulation and the Credit Crunch." *Journal of Banking and Finance* 19(1): 679–692.

Peek, Joe and Eric S. Rosengren. 1995b. "The Capital Crunch: Neither a Borrower nor a Lender Be." *Journal of Money, Credit, and Banking* 27(3): 625–638.

Peek, Joe and Eric S. Rosengren. 1997. "The International Transmission of Financial Shocks: The Case of Japan." *American Economic Review* 87(4): 495–505.

Peek, Joe and Eric S. Rosengren. 2000. "Collateral Damage: Effects of the Japanese Bank Crisis on Real Activity in the United States." *American Economic Review* 90(1): 30–45.

Peek, Joe and Eric S. Rosengren. 2001. "Determinants of the Japan Premium: Actions Speak Louder than Words." *Journal of International Economics* 53(2): 283–305.

Peek, Joe, and Eric S. Rosengren. 2002. "Corporate Affiliations and the (Mis)Allocation of Credit." Working Paper. University of Kentucky.

Peek, Joe and Eric S. Rosengren. 2003. "Unnatural Selection: Perverse Incentives and the Misallocation of Credit in Japan." NBER Working Paper 9643, April 2003.

Phylaktis, Kate. 1988. "Banking in a British Colony: Cyprus, 1878–1959." *Business History* 30(4), 416–431.

Prat, Andrea. 2003. "The Wrong Kind of Transparency." CEPR Discussion Paper No. 3859.

Rajan, Raghuram, and Luigi Zingales. 1995. "What Do We Know about Capital Structure? Some Evidence from International Data." *Journal of Finance* 50: 1421–1460.

Rajan, Raghuram and Luigi Zingales. 1998. "Financial Dependence and Growth." *American Economic Review* 88(3): 559–596.

Ravid, Abraham, and Stefan Sundgren. 1998. "The Comparative Efficiency of Small-Firm Bankruptcies: A Study of the US and Finnish Bankruptcy Codes." *Financial Management* 27(4): 28–40.

Repullo, Rafael. 2000. "Who Should Act as Lender of Last Resort? An Incomplete Contracts Model." *Journal of Money, Credit, and Banking* 32: 580–605.

Repullo, Rafael. 2004. "Liquidity, Risk-Taking, and the Lender of Last Resort." CEMFI Working Paper. Madrid: Centro de Estudios Monetariosy Financieros.

Reynoso, Alejandro. 2002. "Can Subsidiaries of Foreign Banks Contribute to the Stability of The Forex Market in Emerging Economies? A Look at Some Evidence from the Mexican Financial System." NBER Working Paper 8864. Cambridge, MA: National Bureau of Economic Research.

Roe, Mark J. 1983. "Bankruptcy and Debt: A New Model for Corporate Reorganization." *Columbia Law Review* 83: 527–602.

Rojas-Suarez, Liliana, and Steven R. Weisbrod. 1995. *Financial Fragilities in Latin America: The 1980s and* 1990s. International Monetary Fund Occasional Paper 132. Washington, DC: International Monetary Fund.

Roulier, Richard. 1995. *Bank Governance Contracts: Establishing Goals and Accountability in Bank Restructuring*. World Bank Discussion Paper 308. Washington, DC: World Bank.

Sahlman, William. 1990. "The Structure and Governance of Venture Capital Organizations." *Journal of Financial Economics* 27: 473–521.

Sarkar, Jayati, Subrata Sarkar, and Sumon K. Bhaumik. 1998. "Does Ownership Matter? – Evidence from the Indian Banking Industry." *Journal of Comparative Economics* 26: 262–281.

Šević, Željko. 2000. "Banking Reform in South East European Transitional Economies: An Overview." *MOCT-MOST* 3–4: 271–283.

Šević, Željko. 2001. "Politico-Administrative Relationships in Small States." *Bank of Valetta Review* 23: 63–76.

Sheard, Paul. 1989. "The Main Banking System and Corporate Monitoring and Control in Japan." *Journal of Economic Behavior and Organization* 11: 399–422.

Sheng, Andrew, ed. 1996. *Bank Restructuring: Lessons from the 1980s*. Washington, DC: World Bank.

Shleifer, Andrei, and Robert W. Vishny. 1992. "Liquidation Values and Debt Capacity: A Market Equilibrium Approach." *Journal of Finance* 47: 1343–66.

Skeel, David A., Jr. 2003. "Creditor's Ball: The "New" New Corporate Governance in Chapter 11." *University of Pennsylvania Law Review*, forthcoming.

Skeel, David A., Jr. 2001. *Debt's Dominion: A History of Bankruptcy Law in America*. Princeton, NJ: Princeton University Press.

Smith, David, C. 2003. "Loans to Japanese Borrowers." *Journal of the Japanese and International Economies* 17: 283–304.

Squire, Lyn. 1989. "Project Evaluation in Theory and Practice." In H. B. Chenery and T. N. Srinivasan (Eds.), *Handbook of Development Economics*, Vol. II. Amsterdam: North Holland.

358 References

Stein, Jeremy C. 1998. "An Adverse Selection Model of Bank Asset and Liability Management with Implications for the Transmission of Monetary Policy." *RAND Journal of Economics* 29: 466–486.

Stiglitz, Joseph E. 2001. "Bankruptcy Laws: Some Basic Economic Principles." In Stijn Claessens, Simeon Djankov, and Ashoka Mody (Eds.), *Resolution of Financial Distress*. Washington, DC: World Bank Institute.

Stiglitz, Joseph E., and Andrew Weiss. 1981. "Credit Rationing in Markets with Imperfect Information." *American Economic Review* 71: 393–410.

Strömberg, Per. 2000. "Conflicts of Interest and Market Illiquidity in Bankruptcy Auctions: Theory and Tests." *Journal of Finance* 55: 2641–2691.

Strömberg, Per, and Karin Thorburn. 1996. "An Empirical Investigation of Swedish Corporations in Liquidation Bankruptcy." EFI Research Report, Stockholm School of Economics.

Sundgren, Stefan. 1995. *Bankruptcy Costs and the Bankruptcy Code*. Doctoral dissertation, Swedish School of Economics and Business Administration, Helsinki.

Tan, Ruth S.K., Pheng L. Chng and Tee W. Tan. 2001. "CEO Ownership and Firm Value." *Asia Pacific Journal of Management* 18(3), 355–371.

Temin, Peter. 1989. *Lessons from the Great Depression*. Cambridge, MA: MIT Press.

Thorburn, Karin. 2000. "Bankruptcy Auctions: Costs, Debt Recovery, and Firm Survival." *Journal of Financial Economics* 58(3): 337–368.

Titman, Sheridan. 1984. "The Effect of Capital Structure on a Firm's Liquidation Decision." *Journal of Financial Economics* 13: 137–151.

Townsend, Robert M. 1979. "Optimal Contracts and Competitive Markets with Costly State Verification." *Journal of Economic Theory* 21(2): 265–293.

Triner, Gail D. 1996. "The Formation of Modern Brazilian Banking, 1906–1930: Opportunities and Constraints Presented by the Public and Private Sectors." *Journal of Latin American Studies* 28(1): 49–74.

Triner, Gail D. 2002. "British Banking in Brazil during the First Republic." Mimeo. Rutgers University.

Tschoegl, Adrian E. 1981. *The Regulation of Foreign Banks: Policy Formation in Countries Outside the United States*. Salomon Brothers Center for the Study of Financial Institutions, Monograph Series in Finance and Economics, Monograph No. 1981–2.

Tschoegl, Adrian E. 1988. "Foreign Banks in Japan." Bank of Japan, Institute for Monetary and Economic Studies, *Monetary and Economic Studies* 6(1): 93–118.

Tschoegl, Adrian E. 2001. "Foreign Banks in the United States since World War II: A Useful Fringe." In Geoffrey Jones and Lina Gálvez-Muñoz (Eds.), *Managing Foreign Business in the US*. London: Routledge, pp. 149–168.

Tschoegl, Adrian E. 2002a. "Entry and Survival: The Case of Foreign Banks in Norway." *Scandinavian Journal of Management* 18(2): 131–153.

Tschoegl, Adrian E. 2002b. "FDI and Internationalization: Evidence from US Subsidiaries of Foreign Banks." *Journal of International Business Studies* 33(4): 805–815.

Tschoegl, Adrian E. 2002c. "Foreign Banks in Saudi Arabia: A Brief History." *Transnational Corporations* 11(3): 123–154.

Tschoegl, Adrian E. 2003. "The World's Local Bank: HSBC's Expansion in the US, Canada and Mexico." Wharton School, Unpublished Paper.

Tschoegl, Adrain E. 2004. "Who Owns the Major US Subsidiaries of Foreign Banks? A Note." *Journal of International Financial Markets, Institutions & Money*, Forthcoming.

Unite, Angelo A. and Michael J. Sullivan. 2002. "The Effect of Foreign Entry and Ownership Structure on the Philippine Domestic Banking Market." *Journal of Banking and Finance* 27: 2249–2271.

Von Thadden, Ernst-Ludwig, Erik Berglöf, and Gerard Roland. 2003. "Optimal Debt Design and the Role of Bankruptcy," Working Paper. University of Lausanne.

Weill, Laurent. 2003. "Banking Efficiency in Transition Economies: The Role of Foreign Ownership." *Economics of Transition* 11(3): 569–592.

Weiss, Lawrence, and Karen Wruck. 1998. "Information Problems, Conflicts of Interest, and Asset Stripping: Chapter 11's Failure in the Case of Eastern Airlines." *Journal of Financial Economics* 48: 55–97.

White, Michelle. 1989. "The Corporate Bankruptcy Decision." *Journal of Economic Perspectives* 3: 129–152.

White, Michelle. 1996. "The Costs of Corporate Bankruptcy: A U.S.-European Comparison." In J. Bhandari and L. Weiss (eds.): *Corporate Bankruptcy: Economic and Legal Perspectives*. Cambridge: Cambridge University Press.

Wicker, Elmus. 1996. *The Banking Panics of the Great Depression*. Cambridge: Cambridge University Press.

Williams, Barry. 1996. "Determinants of the Performance of Japanese Financial Institutions in Australia 1987–1992." *Applied Economics* 28(9): 1153–1165.

Wiwattanakantang, Yupana, Raja Kali, and Chutatong Charumilind. 2002. "Crony Lending: Thailand before the Financial Crisis." Center for Economic Institutions, Institute of Economic Research, Working Paper. Tokyo: Hitotsubashi University.

World Bank. 1998. "Argentina: Financial Sector Review." Report No. 17864-AR. Washington, DC: World Bank.

World Bank. 2000. "Thailand: Social and Structural Review. Beyond the Crisis: Structural Reform for Stable Growth." Report No. 19732-TH. Washington, DC: World Bank.

World Bank. 2001. "Mexico: Report on Proposed Second Bank Restructuring Facility Adjustment Loan." Report P7452-ME. Washington, DC: World Bank.

World Bank Working Group on Rehabilitation. 1999. "Rehabilitation." in: *Building Effective Insolvency Systems*. Washington, DC: World Bank.

Index

361

Siam Commercial Bank, 224
Sierra Leone, 333
sight deposits, Serfin versus Banamex, 60
signals, 141, 142, 149
silent run, 94
simplicity of debt forgiveness, 47
Singapore
  Allied Irish Bank (AIB) in, 200
  in the banking crisis database, 333
  family control of corporations, 222
  size, liability of, 228
SKB Banka (Slovenia), 202
skill transfer by a foreign bank, 229
SLIPS (Stapled Limited Interest Preferred
  Securities), 70
Slovakia, 333
Slovenia, 333
small firms, 228
SMEs (small and medium-sized
  enterprises)
  restarting lending to, 38
  strengths of Punto Final mainly confined
    to, 41
social cost of public funds, 147
socialization of costs, 6
Société Générale (France), 201, 202
soft information, small banks as better at
  processing, 228
solvency
  policy approaches to restoring, 31–72
  regulations for UK insurance companies,
    8
  supervision of branches abroad, 211
  support, 129
  triggers, 88
Somaia group (Mauritius), 211
South Africa, 333
Spain, 333
speed of recovery, 185
Sri Lanka
  in the banking crisis database, 333
  terms of capital claims, 122
stability versus cost in containment, 10
stabilization package, backing up a blanket
  guarantee, 96
staff, required for closures and resolutions,
  106
stalking-horse bidder, 260
Standard Chartered Bank (U.K.), 223
Stapled Limited Interest Preferred
  Securities (SLIPS), 70

start-up firms
  as typically smaller, 266
  VC financing of, 263
stop-loss guarantees, 119, 124
strategic investors, 199
strict approach to crisis resolution, 176
strike price of abandoning a subsidiary, 210
structural reforms, 17–21, 172
subordinated debt as Tier 2 capital, 93
subordinated liabilities as "capital", 120
subsidiaries
  benefiting from a flight to quality, 209
  foreign banks operating as, 206, 207, 212
  less flexibility in tax management, 209
  merged by multi-bank holding
    companies, 208
  not as affected by local crises, 214
  solvency supervision of, 211
subsidization of delinquent borrowers, 115
substantial liquidity support, 176
succession process, 230
Sumitomo, 283, 284, 285, 286, 287
Sumitomo Bank, 204
Sumitomo Trust, 282, 283, 284, 285, 286
Super Chapter 11, 275
super-senior financing, 271
supervisors, 105, 145, 177
  in the bank runs model, 141
  closures delayed by, 76
  corrective measures employed by, 89
  and debt forgiveness, 48
  equilibrium expected cost for, 145
  observing a signal on the return of a
    risky asset, 148
  policies implemented in the bank runs
    model, 139
  protecting under the law, 103
supervisory forbearance. *See* forbearance
support buying, 222
Swaziland, 334
Sweden
  AMCs in, 48–50
  in the banking crisis database, 334
  bankruptcy in, 242, 258
  corporate bankruptcy code of, 244
  financial sector regulation, 48
  liquidations ending up as going concerns,
    258
  no element of incentive pay for the
    trustee, 255
  recession, 48